Microsoft®Press

Microsoft® Introducing Windows® 2000 Professional

Jerry Honeycutt

PUBLISHED BY
Microsoft Press
A Division of Microsoft Corporation
One Microsoft Way
Redmond, Washington 98052-6399

Library of Congress Cataloging-in-Publication Data
Honeycutt, Jerry.
    Introducing Microsoft Windows 2000 Professional / Jerry Honeycutt.
        p. cm.
    Includes index.
    ISBN 0-7356-0662-5
    1. Microsoft Windows (Computer file)   2. Operating systems
(Computers)   I. Title.
    QA76.76.O63H663   1999
    005.4'469--dc21   99-10773
                                                             CIP

Printed and bound in the United States of America.

1 2 3 4 5 6 7 8 9   QMQM   4 3 2 1 0 9

Distributed in Canada by Penguin Books Canada Limited.

A CIP catalogue record for this book is available from the British Library.

Microsoft Press books are available through booksellers and distributors worldwide. For further information about international editions, contact your local Microsoft Corporation office or contact Microsoft Press International directly at fax (425) 936-7329. Visit our Web site at mspress.microsoft.com.

Macintosh, QuickTime, and TrueType fonts are registered trademarks of Apple Computer, Inc. Intel is a registered trademark of Intel Corporation. Active Desktop, Active Directory, ActiveX, BackOffice, Direct3D, DirectAnimation, DirectDraw, DirectInput, DirectMusic, DirectPlay, DirectShow, DirectSound, DirectX, DoubleSpace, DriveSpace, Hotmail, IntelliMirror, Microsoft, Microsoft Press, MS-DOS, NetMeeting, NetShow, OpenType, Outlook, Visual Basic, Visual C++, Visual InterDev, Visual Studio, Win32, Windows, and Windows NT are either registered trademarks or trademarks of Microsoft Corporation in the United States and/or other countries. MD5 is a trademark of RSA Data Security. Other product and company names mentioned herein may be the trademarks of their respective owners.

The example companies, organizations, products, people, and events depicted herein are fictitious. No association with any real company, organization, product, person, or event is intended or should be inferred.

Acquisitions Editor: Juliana Aldous
Project Editor: Maureen Williams Zimmerman
Technical Editor: Steve Perry

For my dad, Gerald P. Honeycutt—I love you.

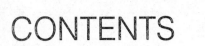

CONTENTS

PART I: AN OVERVIEW OF WINDOWS 2000 PROFESSIONAL

CHAPTER ONE

What's New in Windows 2000 Professional   3

CHAPTER SIX

Better Mobile Computing Support **123**

CHAPTER SEVEN

Superior Multilingual Support **147**

CHAPTER EIGHT

More Imaging and Printing Capabilities **167**

PART III: FAST, SAFE, AND SECURE

CHAPTER NINE

Best Performance **187**

CHAPTER TEN

Most Reliable and Stable **211**

CHAPTER ELEVEN

Strongest Local and Network Security **221**

CHAPTER TWENTY

Lower Total Cost of Ownership with Microsoft Windows 2000 Server **363**

FOREWORD

In September 1996, we embarked on a mission to develop the next major client release of the Windows operating system, which is now called Microsoft Windows 2000 Professional. We always knew that Windows 95 and Windows 98 were good steps forward in making computers easier to use—yet we recognized that businesses really required additional reliability, security, and manageability beyond what those systems provided. These features were in Windows NT 4.0, but this system compromised in other areas where Windows 95 and Windows 98 excelled, such as the simplicity of Plug and Play devices, great mobile capabilities, and power management. So we set out to design an operating system that would meet the ever-changing needs of today's businesses and give users the best of both worlds.

The mission of the Windows 2000 Professional development team was to create a mainstream client operating system that goes beyond Windows 98 in simplicity; that goes beyond Windows NT 4.0 Workstation in terms of reliability, security, and power; and that reduces the costs associated with managing networks. Windows 2000 Professional is the result of this effort, and we believe it will be a compelling upgrade for organizations of all types and sizes.

To make Windows 2000 Professional even easier to use, we included intelligence in areas such as a Start menu that automatically reduces its size and complexity, a new interface for creating and managing different types of network connections, wizards that assist in the completion of common tasks, and many new advancements designed to simplify the process of browsing the Internet. We have also included in Windows 2000 Professional the best business features of Windows 95 and Windows 98, such as Plug and Play, Advanced Power Management, and support for new hardware standards (such as USB, IEEE 1394, AGP, and IR) and hardware devices (such as digital cameras, scanners, and DVD).

Because Windows 2000 Professional was built on Windows NT technology, it has inherited many of the traditional strengths of Windows NT, including mandatory logon, object permissions, a secure file system (NTFS), and the performance of a completely multithreaded, microkernel-based operating system. In many instances, we have extended Windows NT's core strengths. For example, we have improved reliability in a number of ways (e.g., removing reboots required for most configuration changes), we have added new transparent security features such as file-level encryption and support for Smart Cards, and—in many cases—we have improved performance.

And, finally, we have integrated technology that will reduce the overall cost of managing Windows, including support for disk duplication as a means of deploying the operating system; a new application installation service that helps manage the installation, repair, upgrade, and removal of applications; support for multiple languages; and, of course, Y2K support and support for the euro.

When this book is released, the development team will be hard at work putting the finishing touches on Windows 2000 Professional. This book will give you early insight into that operating system.

I hope you enjoy the book and, ultimately, the product.

—Jim Allchin
Senior Vice President

ACKNOWLEDGMENTS

I consider myself fortunate to have had the opportunity to write *Introducing Microsoft Windows 2000 Professional*—I thank Juliana Aldous and Anne Hamilton for that. They know their business incredibly well, and it's a pleasure working with them.

I wish that I could take credit for this entire book, but my contributions pale in comparison to the editors, artists, and reviewers who worked on it. The editors, who must surely be mind readers, made sure that what you see on the pages of this book is what I meant to write. Maureen Zimmerman ran the show, editing and coordinating the entire book. When you think of her, imagine a juggler with twenty different balls in the air, some of which are actually hot coals (thanks for everything). Jocelyn Markey manuscript-edited the entire book, a job that requires incredible attention to detail. To this day, I'm still amazed with the edits she made, and I envy her capabilities. Steve Perry had another of those detail-oriented jobs. He edited the book to ensure each fact was accurate. Not only did he test the book against Windows 2000 Professional Beta 3, but he also made sure that I used terminology correctly and consistently throughout the book. If you think this book flows well, thank him. Joel Panchot and Rob Nance took my chicken-scratched hand drawings and turned them into the artwork you see in this book. They did a terrific job, considering what it takes to read my handwriting. Last, but certainly not least, Patricia Masserman and Linda Robinson proofread the book. The editors and I had looked at these manuscripts one too many times, so fresh sets of eyes were essential to catching last-minute problems.

One last group of individuals deserves a special nod. A variety of Microsoft Windows 2000 Professional developers and managers took time out of their busy schedules to review this book. Russ Madlener provided the original vision for this book and spearheaded the entire review process, while the following folks reviewed one or more chapters: Andrew Mackles, BJ Whalen, Dave Fester, Eugene Lin, Kartik Raghavan, Keith White, Leighton Smith, Michael Aldridge, Michael Cherry, Patrick Franklin, Peter Houston, and Simon Earnshaw. If I've inadvertently left anyone out of this list, please accept my sincerest apologies.

PART I

AN OVERVIEW OF WINDOWS 2000 PROFESSIONAL

CHAPTER ONE

What's New in Windows 2000 Professional

Microsoft has traditionally positioned Windows NT Workstation 4.0, the predecessor of Microsoft Windows 2000 Professional, as its premier desktop operating system. Windows NT 4.0 has incredible strengths: rock-solid stability, great performance, and the strongest security ever implemented in Microsoft Windows. For those reasons and many more, I abandoned all other operating systems long ago, favoring Windows NT Workstation's constancy. As good as it is, though, Windows NT 4.0 does not share the popularity of its low-end counterparts, Windows 95 and Windows 98—even in corporate circles. Windows NT 4.0 isn't as flexible as Windows 98. It doesn't support the wide variety of hardware and software that Windows 98 supports. It isn't as easy to use, either. Developers use Windows NT Workstation—average desktop users do not.

All of that changes with Windows 2000 Professional. This latest incarnation of Microsoft's premier desktop operating system is easier to use than any previous member of the Windows family. It expands on the traditional strengths of Windows NT—stability, reliability, and security—and it includes numerous innovative features, as well as the best of Windows 98 (such as hardware flexibility and easy device configuration). Windows 2000 Professional also costs less to own than its predecessors and is far easier to manage.

This chapter provides an overview of many of the new features and improvements in Windows 2000 Professional. Note that the organization of this chapter closely follows the organization of the book, and each section refers you to other chapters in the book where you can get more detailed information.

Easier to Use

Windows 2000 Professional is the easiest version of Windows yet. The user interface is simpler, with fewer items on the desktop, making it easier to find files and folders. This new operating system makes configuring the computer much easier by providing tools such as the Network Connection Wizard, the Add/Remove Hardware Wizard, and many more. Windows 2000 Professional also includes advanced support for mobile users that enables them to be more productive, such as allowing them to pack up important files and take them anywhere they go. And finally, this operating system includes better multilingual support and more printing capabilities than ever before.

Simpler User Interface

Personalized menus and customizable toolbars remove obstacles from the user's path. The operating system continuously monitors items on the Start menu, displaying frequently used commands at the top of each menu while hiding less frequently used commands. The user uncovers hidden commands by clicking the double-arrow at the bottom of the menu. In addition, users can customize their environments when working with Windows Explorer; they can add or remove buttons and change the order of buttons on the Windows Explorer toolbar.

Files are simpler to work with in Windows 2000 Professional. In particular, the following list describes new features that make locating a document quicker and more intuitive:

- **Improved Open With menu** Users right-click a document icon in Windows Explorer and then choose the Open With command from the pop-up menu to display a menu of applications that are known to work with that type of document. If users don't see the application they want to use, they can choose the Any Program command from the pop-up menu to browse the computer for a different application and, after opening the document, Windows 2000 Professional will add the application to the Open With menu for use the next time around.

- **Open and Save As dialog boxes** The Open and Save As dialog boxes have new options that make locating files easier. Clicking the Recent icon displays recently visited local and network folders. The remaining icons are self-explanatory: My Documents, Desktop, Favorites, and My Network Places.

■ **Most Frequently Used lists**   Windows 2000 Professional makes more pervasive use of Most Frequently Used lists. In places such as the Open, Save As, Find Files, and Map Network Drive dialog boxes, Windows 2000 Professional automatically provides a list of the most frequently used files from which the user can choose.

■ **AutoComplete**   Most dialog boxes that accept paths and filenames automatically complete words as the user types them. This helps increase the user's accuracy in places such as the Open and Save As dialog boxes, as well as in the Run dialog box and in Windows Explorer.

Not only does Windows 2000 Professional help users locate files, it also helps them organize files on their local file systems. No longer do users have to wonder where they saved important documents. All of this is achieved by a combination of features, including these:

■ **My Documents folder**   Windows 2000 Professional greatly expands the use of the My Documents folder so users don't have to look in every nook and cranny of their computers for documents. The operating system directs applications to the My Documents folder by default.

■ **My Pictures folder**   This new folder provides a central place to store images on the user's computer. It allows the user to preview full-sized images within Windows Explorer. Not only that, but the user can zoom, pan, and print images from within Windows Explorer without actually opening the image in a viewer. Note that the user can customize any folder on their computer or on the network to display images just like the My Pictures folder does.

■ **My Network Places folder**   The new My Network Places folder replaces the Network Neighborhood folder. It makes locating network resources quicker by providing a number of alternative views, such as Recently Visited Places and Computers Near Me. Users can add network shortcuts to the My Network Places folder.

■ **Enhanced searching**   Windows Explorer's new integrated search feature makes finding files easier. It includes a variety of new options that allow the user to search the local computer, the network, or even the Internet. Windows 2000 Professional indexes the local computer's content—a capability it borrows from Internet Information Services (IIS)—allowing the user to find documents faster.

The final user interface improvement discussed here is possibly the most underrated. Error messages, presented in dialog boxes, are easier to understand in Windows 2000 Professional. Microsoft has rewritten them using simpler language, and they provide more direction for solving problems. In cases where the user doesn't respond to an error message within a certain period of time, the dialog box can automatically use a default response.

See Chapter 4 to learn more about the following topics:

- Personalized menus
- Customizable toolbars
- Open With menu
- Open and Save As dialog boxes
- Most Frequently Used lists
- AutoComplete
- My Documents folder
- My Pictures folder
- My Network Places folder
- Integrated searching
- Error messages and handling

Easier Setup and Configuration

The Computer Management console consolidates a number of management tools that were previously separate. Thus, users have one place to go in order to configure most of their computers' settings, and administrators can perform most of their duties via the Computer Management console—locally or remotely. You'll find the Local Users And Groups, Event Viewer, Group Policy, and Services tools here, all of which provide the same capabilities as they did in Windows NT Workstation 4.0. You'll also find the new Device Manager—which looks very similar to Windows 98's Device Manager—and other tools such as System Information, Shared Folders, and Storage.

One of the most lauded improvements you'll find in Windows 2000 Professional is the ease with which users can add hardware to their computers and then configure the operating system to work with the new hardware. The Add/ Remove Hardware Wizard automatically detects and configures Plug and Play devices that the user installs on the computer. It also installs the appropriate device drivers. The wizard also has the capability to help the user diagnose devices that aren't working correctly. Other hardware innovations that make the operating system easier to use include power management schemes, which you'll learn about in "Broad Hardware Support" later in this chapter, and the Add Printer Wizard, which you'll learn about in "More Imaging and Printing Capabilities" later in this chapter.

The Add/Remove Programs dialog box is greatly enhanced in Windows 2000 Professional to provide the user with more information and more capabilities. The dialog box makes installing applications from the network straightforward. It also provides the user with details such as size, frequency of use, and last date used for each installed application. The new Add/Remove Programs dialog box is optimized for use with Windows 2000 Professional's new Windows Installer Service, making it easier to install, repair, remove, update, and track applications on the user's computer. You'll learn more about the Windows Installer Service in "More Reliable and Stable" later in this chapter.

One of the problems many people have with Windows NT Workstation 4.0 is the effort it takes to keep their configurations current. In Windows 2000 Professional, Microsoft remedies this situation somewhat by providing the Windows Update Web site. The Windows Update Web site can automatically update the user's configuration with the latest device drivers and enhancements from the Internet, matching its search criteria to the user's current configuration. As described in "Lower Total Cost of Ownership" later in this chapter, administrators have control over what kinds of updates the users are allowed to download and can optionally disable this feature. In addition, Microsoft has identified more than 75 configuration changes that cause Windows NT Workstation 4.0 to reboot and—by shutting down and restarting individual services—has reduced that number to seven. Thus, users won't have to reboot the computer after each configuration change.

See Chapter 5 to learn more about the following topics:

- Computer Management console
- Add/Remove Hardware Wizard
- Power management schemes
- Add Printer Wizard
- Add/Remove Programs dialog box
- Windows Update Web site
- Fewer reboots

The topic of fewer reboots is also covered in Chapter 10.

Better Mobile Computing Support

Several hardware innovations make Windows 2000 Professional an ideal platform for mobile computing. With the operating system's new power management features, users have greater control over the computer's power consumption and can extend battery life considerably. The operating system's support for the PC Card specification and new network features, such as those described in the following list, also make it an ideal operating system for mobile users:

- **Network Connection Wizard** In Windows 2000 Professional, users have one location in which to configure all their network connections. The Network Connection Wizard is a new tool that can create dial-up connections; virtual private networks (VPNs); and direct infrared, parallel, or serial connections. Users can also configure their computers as dial-in servers, allowing their computers to accept incoming calls from other computers.

- **Virtual private networks** Windows 2000 Professional provides the Point-to-Point Tunneling Protocol (PPTP); the Layer 2 Tunneling Protocol (L2TP), a more secure version of PPTP; and Internet Protocol security (IPSec). These protocols allow users to create secure connections to corporate networks through the Internet. You'll learn more about these protocols in "Stronger Local and Network Security" later in this chapter.

Mobile users aren't hobbled when they roam away from the network anymore, either. Three key features that enable mobile users to be fully productive when not connected to the network are offline file and folder access, offline Web page access, and the Synchronization Manager. The Synchronization Manager ties the whole thing together. Users can take a network file or folder offline by simply choosing the Make Available Offline command from the file's or folder's pop-up menu. When a user works with offline files and folders, those files and folders look as though the user is still connected to the network. Users can work with Web pages offline just as easily as they can work with files and folders offline. Likewise, when a user views an offline Web page, the page looks as though the user is still connected to the Internet. The Synchronization Manager provides a central location for users to manage all their offline content, including documents, folders, and Web pages. The user can set preferences that determine when synchronization occurs: when the user logs off, when the user connects to or disconnects from the network, while the computer is idle, or at a scheduled time. Applications can extend the Synchronization Manager's capabilities to do sub–file-level as well as file-level synchronization.

See Chapter 6 to learn more about the following topics:

- Power management
- PC Card support
- My Network Places folder
- Network Connection Wizard
- Virtual private networks (VPNs)
- Offline files and folders
- Synchronization Manager

See Chapter 16 to learn more about Offline Web pages.

Superior Multiple Language Support

Windows 2000 Professional is based on Unicode 2.0 and contains all the files necessary to input and output any language that the operating system supports.

Users can view information in any language supported by Windows 2000 Professional because they can install all the components, fonts, and symbols necessary to support multilingual documents in the languages they prefer. For example, users can view a document created in the German edition of Microsoft Word using the English edition of the same program. (However, this assumes an ability to read German on the user's part!) Finally, Windows 2000 Professional provides code page support for the new euro.

See Chapter 7 to learn more about the following topics:

- Unicode 2.0 support
- Multilingual documents
- Support for the euro

More Imaging and Printing Capabilities

Windows 2000 Professional includes numerous improvements to existing printing capabilities as well as a number of new features. The Add Printer Wizard is greatly enhanced. Users can locate a printer by searching the network using attributes such as paper size, double-sided printing, resolution, and color. Installing a network printer is as simple as choosing Install from the printer's pop-up menu—the operating system copies the driver files directly from the network. Local printers are almost as easy to install but require device drivers.

Windows Professional 2000 extends users' reach beyond printers attached to the network. Users can now send jobs over the Internet to a printer connected to a computer running Windows 2000 Server. This feature is based on the new standards-based Internet Printing Protocol (IPP). Printing over the Internet is a great alternative to fax, e-mail, or postal mail. Imagine printing a reservation on a hotel's Internet-connected printer rather than faxing them the same information. Capabilities of Internet printing include printing to a URL, viewing a print queue within any Web browser, and installing a printer driver over the Internet.

Other imaging and printing innovations you'll find in Windows 2000 Professional include the following:

- **Scanners and digital cameras** In "Broad Hardware Support" later in this chapter, you'll learn about Windows 2000 Professional's support for the latest hardware standards. Among the new device classes that the operating system supports are scanners and digital cameras.

- **Image Color Management (ICM) 2.0** Windows 2000 Professional's support for ICM 2.0 means that users don't have to worry about the problem of colors being printed and displayed differently on different devices. ICM 2.0 ensures that colors are always faithfully reproduced on any display or any printer—even if the image is transferred from one application to another.

- **OpenType fonts** In addition to TrueType fonts, Windows 2000 Professional includes a new universal font format called OpenType. OpenType combines the prevailing font technologies such as TrueType and Type 1. OpenType fonts are reliably supported across all platforms and are ideal for the Internet and the World Wide Web since they're built for quick downloading and can be used as dynamic fonts on a Web page.

See Chapter 8 to learn more about the following topics:

- Add Printer Wizard
- Internet-based printers
- Scanners and digital cameras
- Image Color Management (ICM) 2.0
- OpenType fonts

Fast, Safe, and Secure

Windows 2000 Professional builds on the traditional strengths of Windows NT technology: performance, stability, and security. Consequently, Windows 2000 Professional has advantages over Windows 98 in several key areas.

Better Performance

Windows 2000 Professional provides a more responsive computing environment, which includes smoother multitasking as well as scalable memory and processor support. The bottom line is that users gain access to information faster.

However, to find the biggest performance gains in Windows 2000 Professional, you must look at the file systems. The operating system maintains support for the File Allocation Table (FAT) system, as always, but it also contains support for the FAT32 file system popularized by Windows 98. FAT32 offers more efficient use of disk space, potentially freeing hundreds of megabytes and supporting disks larger than 2 gigabytes. The operating system also contains version 5.0 of the NTFS file system, which is enhanced to provide file security, content indexing, property sets, and better volume management. Users can enable many of these features using the Advanced Attributes dialog box, which can be activated by clicking the Advanced button in a file's or folder's Properties dialog box. File security comes from the new Encrypting File System (EFS) and allows users to encrypt individual files or entire folders. Content indexing is technology borrowed from Internet Information Services (IIS) that makes locating documents quicker because it indexes the keywords found in documents on the computer.

One sorely missed utility in Windows NT Workstation 4.0 was a disk optimization tool. Windows 2000 Professional includes such a tool that has the capability to optimize disk usage by defragmenting the disk. It does so by organizing each file's clusters so that they reside contiguously on the disk, rather than spread out across the disk. Optimizing the disk can improve the computer's performance considerably. The disk optimization utility works with the FAT, FAT32, and NTFS file systems.

See Chapter 9 to learn more about the following topics:

- Architectural changes
- FAT16, FAT32, and NTFS 5.0
- Encrypting File System (EFS)
- Content indexing
- Disk optimization

More Reliable and Stable

Device driver signing and the new Windows Installer Service make Windows 2000 Professional more reliable than its predecessors. Using existing cryptographic technologies, Microsoft digitally signs drivers that have passed the Windows Hardware Quality Lab (WHQL) tests. By using signed drivers, users are getting the highest-quality drivers available.

The new Windows Installer Service defines a new method for installing, repairing, removing, updating, and tracking applications. It also tracks dependencies among groups of files, registry entries, shortcuts, and other portions of the operating system that must be managed together. The benefits of the Windows Installer Service are many: more reliable applications, self-repairing applications, undo capabilities, component updates, applications that are removable, and easily customized applications.

See Chapter 10 to learn more about the following topics:

■ Device driver signing

■ Windows Installer Service

Stronger Local and Network Security

Windows 2000 Professional contains more extensive support for security over public networks. For example, public key security allows users to be sure of the identity of e-mail messages, drivers, applications, and remote computers. It also allows for secure Internet connections and secure transactions. PPTP was available in Windows NT Workstation 4.0; Windows 2000 Professional goes further by introducing more secure methods for creating VPNs over public networks, including L2TP, a more secure version of PPTP. Windows 2000 Professional also introduces Internet Protocol security (IPSec), a standards-based protocol that allows everything above the networking layer to be encrypted.

Windows 2000 Professional also contains innovations for local security. You've already read about the new Encrypting File System. EFS allows users to encrypt individual files or entire folders, and the whole process is transparent to the user. Two other innovations secure the computer and the network by making it harder for unauthorized users to gain access to resources:

■ **Kerberos authentication** Kerberos, an industry-standard network authentication protocol, makes it possible for the user to log on once. Users can log on to a Microsoft network or even a mixed network by providing their credentials once. Windows 2000 Professional's implementation of Kerberos is based on RFC 1510 and supports Novell NetWare, UNIX, HP-UX, LINUX, SGI IRIX, and Sun Solaris.

■ **Smart Card authentication** Windows 2000 Professional extends Kerberos authentication to support other security infrastructures and devices such as Smart Cards. Rather than relying on a single factor to authenticate the user's credentials, multifactor authentication relies on a combination of credentials such as a username/password combination and a Smart Card.

See Chapter 11 to learn more about the following topics:

■ Public key security

■ Virtual private networks (VPNs)

■ Encrypting File System (EFS)

■ Kerberos authentication

■ Smart Card authentication

Best of Windows 98

Windows 2000 Professional borrows the best of Windows 98. Most of the borrowed features allow Windows 2000 Professional to support a wide variety of hardware, software, and network services.

Easy Device Installation

Windows 2000 Professional is a more realistic option for desktop users now that it supports Plug and Play. Through the Advanced Configuration and Power Interface (ACPI) and the Win32 driver model (WDM), Windows 2000 Professional supports dynamic hardware configuration and resource allocation. Windows 2000 Professional's implementation of Plug and Play automatically loads the appropriate drivers for each device and allows each driver to interact with the Plug and Play interface. In most cases, the operating system automatically recognizes new hardware after the user installs it. However, the user can also use the new Add/Remove Hardware Wizard to install support for a particular device or to troubleshoot devices that aren't working correctly. As a note, Windows 2000 Professional provides enhanced support for removable devices such as CD-ROMs, digital versatile disks (DVDs), batteries, PC Cards, and many more.

Perhaps you've grown accustomed to the Windows 98 boot menu, which allows you to boot to safe mode or to the command prompt. It's an invaluable tool that you can use to get the computer running when it won't start otherwise. For example, if you install a device driver and the machine no longer starts, you can almost always boot to safe mode in order to fix the problem. Windows 2000 Professional provides a similar boot menu. While the operating system is starting, you can press F8 or an arrow key to display the boot menu. From there, you can choose one of the following boot options: Safe Mode, Safe Mode With Networking, Safe Mode With Command Prompt, or Last Known Good Configuration.

See Chapter 12 to learn more about the following topics:

- Plug and Play
- Advanced Configuration and Power Interface (ACPI)
- Win32 driver model (WDM)
- Diagnostic booting options

Broad Hardware Support

Windows 2000 Professional provides more support for legacy hardware than its predecessors did. To make sure of this, Microsoft directed testing efforts toward thousands of devices, including a variety of legacy printers, scanners, and digital cameras.

Windows 2000 Professional includes support for a number of new hardware standards, among which you'll find universal serial bus (USB) and IEEE 1394 (Fire Wire). USB allows for the hot insertion and removal of up to 127 devices on a single computer. Although most USB-enabled computers provide only two USB ports, you can add USB hubs or daisy chain USB devices. When a user plugs in a USB device, which has a throughput 10 times greater than a standard serial device, the operating system automatically installs and configures the appropriate drivers. IEEE 1394 is another new hardware standard built into the operating system that supports high-speed serial communications. With 100-, 200-, and 400-megabytes-per-second transfer rates, IEEE 1394 is well suited to streaming I/O, which is used for applications such as digital video and desktop teleconferencing.

Windows 2000 Professional includes support for a host of removable storage devices such as DVD players and Zip drives. The Microsoft DVD Player application supports movie playback.

Windows 2000 Professional has support for the ACPI. The ACPI enables Windows 2000 Professional to integrate power management throughout the operating system, including support for legacy devices. On computers that support the ACPI, the operating system takes power management over from Advanced Power Management (APM). The ACPI allows the operating system to have direct control over how power is consumed on the computer. It can control when the computer enters and leaves sleep states. It also allows the operating system to put individual devices, including the CPU, in low-power states based upon usage. In either case, power schemes determine battery-management policy. These schemes allow users to set the low-battery and battery-warning points and calculate the remaining battery life and capacity. Schemes also allow the user to define the point at which the system, the monitor, and the disk drive enter a sleep state for different configurations such as Home/Office Desk, Portable/Laptop, Presentations, etc. On systems that do not support the ACPI, Windows 2000 Professional supports a compatibility mode, which allows users to take advantage of basic power management functionality.

See Chapter 13 to learn more about the following topics:

- USB and IEEE 1394
- Removable storage support
- Power management schemes
- Advanced Power Management (APM)

Awesome Multimedia and Graphics

Like Windows 98, Windows 2000 Professional supports multiple monitors, which can be set to different resolutions, display schemes, and refresh rates. This feature gives the user more screen real estate, a valuable commodity for Web designers and other developers.

Microsoft DirectX, the multimedia driver architecture for the Windows family of products, provides compatibility with countless multimedia applications. While Windows 2000 Professional does require a set of drivers that are different from those for Windows 98, most software vendors will not hesitate to write them. The operating system's DirectX implementation includes DirectDraw, Direct3D, DirectSound, DirectInput, DirectMusic, DirectPlay, DirectShow, and DirectAnimation.

Windows 2000 Professional supports the new OpenGL 1.2 specification, an open standard for 3D graphics programming used in professional computer-aided design (CAD) and scientific visualization applications.

See Chapter 14 to learn more about the following topics:

- Multiple display support
- DirectX
- OpenGL 1.2

Advanced Networking Capabilities

Windows 2000 Professional includes numerous improvements to the Transfer Control Protocol/Internet Protocol (TCP/IP). Among the many improvements that Windows 2000 Professional makes to the TCP/IP stack are support for larger windows, the ability to have more data packets in transit, selective acknowledgments, better round-trip estimation time, and better allocation for media traffic. Other, more general improvements include those in the following list:

- **Internet network naming** Windows 2000 Professional is making the move away from NetBIOS-based names such as "Computer" to Internet-based names such as jerry@ntw50dsk01.honeycutt.com. Combined with Windows 2000 Server and the new Dynamic Domain Naming System (DDNS), Internet-based names provide for faster authentication and better support for mixed networking environments.

- **Automatic IP addressing for workgroups** Frequently, small workgroup networks don't have a dynamic host configuration protocol (DHCP) server available. If Windows 2000 Professional doesn't find a DHCP server on the network, it assigns itself an IP address, checking first to make sure that the address is unique on the network.

- **Internet Protocol security (IPSec)** IPSec allows everything above the networking layer to be encrypted, enabling secure network connections such as VPNs.

Other enhancements and protocols that ship with Windows 2000 Professional include the following:

- **Quality of Service (QoS)** Quality of Service allows applications to prioritize individual network packages. An example would be NetShow, which uses QoS to guarantee enough bandwidth to produce high-quality streaming video.

- **Bandwidth Allocation Control Protocol (BACP)** Windows 2000 Professional supports BACP to allow client/server negotiation and dynamic control of the Multilink Point-to-Point Protocol (MPPP). For example, Multilink is used to negotiate Integrated Services Digital Network (ISDN) channels.

- **Extensible Authentication Protocol (EAP)** Support for EAP makes VPNs more secure, because it protects the computer against brute-force attacks and password guessing. EAP supports the use of token cards, one-time passwords, and other custom authentication packages.

■ **Remote Authentication Dial-In User Service (RADIUS)** RADIUS is a standards-based authentication protocol that's commonly used by Internet service providers. Windows 2000 Professional supports RADIUS accounting, which is useful for third-party accounting and auditing packages.

■ **Telephony Application Programming Interface (TAPI)** Windows 2000 Professional includes more advanced TAPI support—TAPI 3.0—which unifies voice, video, and data into a single protocol that's based on the IP protocol. TAPI 3.0 allows developers to create enhanced applications for telecommuting, real-time document collaboration, video conferencing, and much more.

Asynchronous Transfer Mode (ATM), an emerging technology that's commonly used in cable modems, is the next generation of LAN switching technology. ATM can transfer data, voice, and video, enabling a whole new generation of real-time and video applications. While Ethernet is a connectionless network service, simply taking a packet and sending it along, ATM is a connection-oriented network service. This means that ATM allows an application on one machine to establish a connection to another application on a remote machine. Windows 2000 Professional includes support for ATM technology.

NOTE: Windows 2000 Professional plays well in UNIX environments. The add-on product called Windows NT Services for UNIX v.1 adds these capabilities to the operating system: Network File System (NFS) client and server, Telnet client and server, UNIX scripting commands, and one-way password authentication.

See Chapter 15 to learn more about the following topics:

■ TCP/IP stack improvements

■ Automatic IP addressing for workgroups

■ Internet Protocol security (IPSec)

■ Quality of Service (QoS)

■ Bandwidth Allocation Control Protocol (BACP)

■ Extensible Authentication Protocol (EAP)

■ Asynchronous Transfer Mode (ATM)

■ UNIX interoperability

Integrated Web and Desktop

Microsoft Internet Explorer 5, included with Windows 2000 Professional, provides the user with a terrific browsing experience by implementing numerous enhancements that make it perform better than Internet Explorer 4. Web pages—particularly those that include Dynamic HTML (Hypertext Markup Language) and data binding—render faster on the screen. Internet Explorer 5 also provides vastly improved error messages that give the user directions for correcting a problem. A little-noticed Internet feature that's now built into Windows 2000 Professional is FTP. Explorer allows users to browse FTP (File Transfer Protocol) sites as though they were extensions of their own computers.

See Chapter 16 to learn more about the following topics:

- Dynamic HTML improvements
- Faster page rendering
- Improved error messages

Wide Application Support

In an effort to ensure compatibility with legacy applications, Microsoft has tested more MS-DOS–based and Win16-based applications. These include applications that shipped prior to Windows 95.

See Chapter 17 to learn more about the following topics:

- MS-DOS–based and Win16-based applications
- Win32-based applications

Lower Total Cost of Ownership

Total cost of ownership (TCO) is a growing concern in corporate communities. Each computer sitting on a desktop has a direct impact on an organization's bottom line. Windows 2000 Professional addresses those concerns by being easier to deploy and easier to manage. When you combine Windows 2000 Professional with Windows 2000 Server and its IntelliMirror technology, the cost of each desktop is reduced dramatically.

Easier Deployment

Windows 2000 Professional provides a migration path for most earlier versions of Windows, including Windows 95 and Windows 98. The Setup Manager, disk image preparation (Sysprep), and the Remote Windows Installation tool are additional capabilities that make the operating system easier to deploy:

- **Setup Manager**   New to Windows 2000 Professional is the Setup Manager, which is a wizard that walks you through creating unattended-setup files and distribution shares. You can configure the amount of user interaction; set up computer names; set display and network settings; supply drivers not found on the source media; and launch commands before, during, and after the installation process.

- **Disk image preparation**   Sysprep allows you to duplicate the entire disk of a computer running Windows 2000 Professional onto another computer with identically configured hardware. Sysprep automatically regenerates SIDs (security identifiers) to eliminate duplicates, writes values to the registry that indicate the machine is a duplicate, and launches the Mini-Setup Wizard.

- **Remote windows installation**   The Remote Windows Installation tool requires Windows 2000 Server. It gives you the ability to put the Windows 2000 Professional source files and other components in a central location; then, DHCP-based remote boot-enabled clients can remotely install a local copy of the operating system from the remote installation server. Remote boot-enabled clients include Net PCs that support one of the PXE (pre-boot execution environment) DHCP-based boot ROMs.

See Chapter 18 to learn more about the following topics:

- Setup Manager
- Disk image preparation
- Remote windows installation

Better Management Tools

Computer management is achieved through the Microsoft Management Console (MMC) program. By itself, MMC doesn't provide any management capabilities; it serves as an environment for snap-ins instead, which Microsoft and third-party independent software vendors (ISVs) provide. Snap-ins are ActiveX controls, so you can add virtually any type of tool to an MMC console. The

Computer Management console is a tool that consolidates management components such as the Event Manager and the User Manager, which were previously separate tools. An administrator can use the Computer Management console to administer any network computer that's running Windows 2000 Professional. The Computer Management console includes the following three components:

- **System Tools**   These tools include Local Users And Groups Manager, System Information, Services, Group Policy, Shared Folders, Event Viewer, Device Manager, and Certificate Manager.

- **Storage**   This component includes all the tools used for managing local disks and offline storage.

- **Server Applications And Services**   Tools in this component, some of which are only shipped with Windows 2000 Server, are those that are optionally installed on the system. Here, you'll find services such as DNS, DHCP, Windows Internet Naming Service (WINS), and BackOffice applications.

Whereas the Computer Management console allows for hands-on management of local and remote computers, the ability to automate repetitive tasks or write scripts that perform routine maintenance on remote computers will save you a great deal of time. Windows 2000 Professional includes the Windows Scripting Host (WSH), a language-independent script interpreter that provides that capability. By default, the operating system includes scripting engines for Microsoft Visual Basic, Scripting Edition, and JavaScript. You can, of course, install other scripting engines into the WSH. Examples of engines that you're likely to encounter include Perl, Tool Command Language (TCL), REXX, and Python.

The Windows Update Web site also makes your job easier, by providing an online extension that keeps the organization's computers healthy. It automatically updates networked computers with new device drivers, service packs, and new features that are specifically designed to work with those computers. Users choose to have Windows Update look for updates that apply to their particular configurations. Windows 2000 Professional does allow the administrator to control the types of updates that users are allowed to download, even to the point that the Windows Update feature is disabled altogether.

Another of Windows 2000 Professional's management features is less tangible than the others, but equally important.

Windows Management Instrumentation (WMI) is Microsoft's implementation of the Desktop Management Task Force's Web-Based Enterprise Management (WBEM) standard. WMI publishes information, configures device settings, and supplies event notifications from device drivers. WMI is an integral part of the WDM. For example, the System Information component of the Computer Management console uses WMI to collect the information that it displays.

See Chapter 19 to learn more about the following topics:

- Microsoft Management Console (MMC)

- The Computer Management console

- Windows Scripting Host (WSH)

- Windows Update Web site

- Windows Management Instrumentation (WMI)

Lower Total Cost of Ownership with Microsoft Windows 2000 Server

IntelliMirror is an exciting technology that brings with it a host of new opportunities to lower the total cost of ownership. However, IntelliMirror's capabilities are only available when you combine Windows 2000 Professional and Windows 2000 Server. Those capabilities include the following:

- **Replaceable workstation**   The Remote Windows Installation tool, when combined with IntelliMirror, brings you a bit closer to the reality of a replaceable machine. The user's entire environment—including the operating system, applications, documents, and desktop settings—can be totally replicated on another machine by providing nothing more than the user's credentials.

- **Document management**   Through IntelliMirror, Windows 2000 Professional ensures the availability of a predefined set of folders, documents, and data. The specified documents are always mirrored on the client and server computers. Windows 2000 Professional opens both the client and server copies of a document and, as the user makes changes, the operating system mirrors the user's changes to both versions of the document. Even if the network copy of a document isn't immediately available, the user can still edit the local copy and allow the operating system to synchronize changes as soon as the network copy is available. Documents are stored as part of the user's profile, so the user can log on to any workstation and still access them.

- **Software installation and maintenance**   IntelliMirror improves application availability and reliability. It makes applications easier to install and upgrade. It eliminates those ubiquitous "Unknown file type" messages when opening a file. Finally, applications are stored as part of the user's profile, allowing the user to log on to different workstations and still access them. To ensure that this capability doesn't bog down the network, Windows 2000 Professional installs applications from the network when the user tries to launch them for the first time. Prior to installing the application, however, its shortcut still appears on the user's Start menu.

■ **User settings management**   As with other facets of IntelliMirror, users' settings are stored as part of their profiles. Thus, the Start menu, Favorites folder, and other desktop items follow users to any workstations they use. Note that this capability includes policies that the administrator sets to control what the user can do as well as where, when, and how.

See Chapter 20 to learn more about the following topics:

■ IntelliMirror

■ Remote windows installation

CHAPTER TWO

Meet the Windows Family

This chapter describes the Microsoft Windows product family, including its history, and takes a brief look at those versions that Microsoft no longer recommends for deployment (Windows 3.1 and Windows 95 are examples).

This chapter compares Microsoft Windows 98, Microsoft's most recent consumer operating system, to Microsoft Windows 2000 Professional, Microsoft's most recent business desktop operating system. Aside from comparing the two operating systems' setup requirements, this chapter compares hardware compatibility, software compatibility, networking support, and administrative support. The results show that Microsoft has taken Windows 2000 Professional well beyond the capabilities and performance levels of Windows 95 and Windows 98.

Since you're reading this book in advance of Windows 2000 Professional's delivery, you're likely to be evaluating the software for deployment. To speed you along, this chapter makes recommendations that will help make the deployment process as simple as possible. In particular, note that the best migration path to Windows 2000 Professional is through Microsoft Windows NT Workstation 4.0, even though Windows 2000 Professional does provide a migration path from Windows 95 or Windows 98. Thus, I recommend you only purchase new computers that have Windows NT Workstation 4.0 preinstalled. When the time comes, you'll be ready for Windows 2000 Professional.

Family History

Microsoft was primarily a programming language company throughout the seventies, shipping languages such as BASIC, FORTRAN, and COBOL-80. To this day, Microsoft continues a strong tradition in language development by publishing ubiquitous products such as Visual Basic and, more recently, Visual Studio. The pace picked up for Microsoft when it introduced MS-DOS for the IBM PC in 1981. After a time, Microsoft had licensed versions of MS-DOS for virtually every PC-compatible computer on the market. Microsoft's entry into operating systems was a huge success, and it laid down the foundation for the first versions of Windows. Figure 2-1 shows the history of the various Windows operating systems.

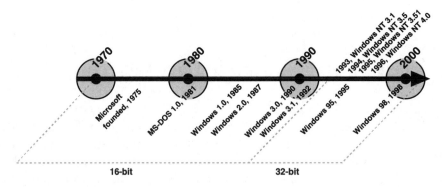

Figure 2-1
History of Microsoft Windows operating systems.

The first time anyone heard the name *Microsoft Windows* was in 1983, when Microsoft announced Windows 1.0. Windows 1.0 was a graphically oriented extension to MS-DOS that allowed users to view multiple applications at the same time and share data among applications using a clipboard metaphor. The user interface was a bit clunky, however, and Windows 1.0 wasn't very popular since there were but a handful of applications to run on it. Windows 1.0 actually shipped in 1985, and it did so to a less-than-receptive market. Realizing the awesome power of which Windows was capable, Microsoft did not give up, and eventually followed Windows 1.0 with other 16-bit versions, as shown in Figure 2-1, including these:

- **Windows 2.0** Microsoft announced plans for Windows 2.0 in 1987. Designed to take advantage of Intel's new 80286 processors, it had an appearance that was similar to the OS/2 Presentation Manager (the graphical user interface to IBM's OS/2 operating system). It supported overlapping and tiled windows, provided better performance, and included support for expanded memory hardware. However, even with these improvements, Windows 2.0 was still cumbersome and not widely adopted.

- **Windows 3.0 and Windows 3.1** Microsoft announced Windows 3.0 at the City Center Theatre in New York. Windows 3.0 and its follow-on versions were the first versions of Windows to gain worldwide acceptance. Windows 3.0 offered enhanced performance—partially due to its support for the Intel 80386 processor—and was easier to use than any of its predecessors. Microsoft sold over 100,000 copies of Windows 3.0 in the first two weeks after it shipped in 1990. Windows 3.1 followed in 1992, with over 1000 enhancements and 1 million advance orders. It seemed that the world was finally ready for a graphical user interface, as Windows was one of Microsoft's hottest product offerings.

■ **Windows for Workgroups 3.1** Windows for Workgroups 3.1 was Microsoft's first desktop operating system to contain built-in support for networking—including clients, protocols, and network interface card (NIC) drivers. The ease with which you could add a computer running Windows for Workgroups to an existing network made it an incredibly popular business solution. It didn't hurt that the operating system made building workgroup networks—networks without a central server—easy. Microsoft shipped over 300,000 copies of Windows for Workgroups in the first few months after its release in 1993. Microsoft followed version 3.1 of Windows for Workgroups with version 3.11.

Windows 3.1 and Windows for Workgroups 3.11 were the end of the line for the code that started out as Windows 1.0. Yes, you can be certain that Microsoft reused some of the 16-bit code from these products in Windows 95. You can be equally certain that the Windows NT developers borrowed bits of code from both operating systems. For all intents and purposes, however, Windows 95 and Windows NT represent new branches on the product family tree.

Windows 95 and Windows 98

Microsoft announced Windows 95 in 1994 and shipped the product in August of 1995. It represented the first fully 32-bit operating system designed to replace the various 16-bit versions such as Windows 3.1. Within the first four days, consumers purchased over 1 million copies of Windows 95, and they purchased 6 million more copies by October. Windows 95 was easily one of the most popular software products ever published. Even though Windows 95 is a consumer-oriented operating system, many businesses chose to deploy it over Windows NT Workstation, since Workstation did not support the hardware and software used in those organizations. Thus, Windows 95 had more business support than most industry analysts expected it to have.

Windows 98 is Windows 95's successor. Shipped in June of 1998, Windows 98 is a significant upgrade from Windows 95 that adds support for a whole new generation of hardware, makes the operating system much easier to support, and provides a richer Internet experience than its predecessor. Although Windows 98 is a consumer-oriented product that's positioned toward game playing and Internet browsing, it improves on Windows 95 for business use, as the following list indicates:

- **Ease of support** Windows 98 contains a variety of new support tools that make deploying and maintaining the operating system easier than with Windows 95. These include the System Information tool, Registry Checker, Version Conflict Manager, Maintenance Wizard, and several troubleshooters.

- **Support for new hardware** Windows 98 includes support for new hardware standards, including USB (universal serial bus) and IEEE 1394. In addition, it includes support for the latest generation of Plug and Play and power management devices. Keep in mind that Windows 98 provides support for the latest hardware innovations while maintaining support for the legacy devices you still use.

- **Better Internet experience** Microsoft improved the operating system's Internet support by integrating the browser, Microsoft Internet Explorer 4, right into Windows 98. Not only does this make browsing the Internet a better experience for the user, it also makes the operating system itself easier to use, since browsing the local computer is similar to browsing a Web page.

Windows NT

Microsoft recruited David Cutler from Digital Equipment Corporation in 1988. His charge was to build a whole new operating system for personal computers that satisfied stringent business requirements such as reliability and security. In other words, Cutler and a team of engineers, testers, and managers were to build an operating system that would run mission-critical applications on personal computers—a product that was unprecedented at the time. The many design goals for this new operating system—Windows NT—included the following:

- **Extensibility** Employ a modular architecture that allows the operating system to expand and grow as the market's business requirements change.

- **Portability** Allow the operating system to take advantage of new generations of hardware by being portable, enabling it to work with various processors and architectures.

- **Reliability**   Proactively protect itself and applications from internal errors and outside attempts to damage it. More importantly, the operating system should always respond predictably to any sort of error.

- **Compatibility**   Ensure that the API (application programming interface) and user interface are compatible with current Microsoft applications and file systems, as well as with future developments.

- **Scalable performance**   Support multiprocessing, allowing the operating system to scale its performance on single-processor and multiprocessor computers.

Windows NT 3.1 was first demonstrated in 1991, publicly announced in 1992, and shipped the following year. Two versions were available: Workstation and Server. Workstation was for the desktop and Server was for the network. Version 3.5 followed in 1994, and version 3.51 followed in 1995. The development team met their marketing goals as well as their design goals, which included a range of features from POSIX (Portable Operating System Interface for UNIX) compliance to C2 security.

Microsoft shipped Windows NT Workstation 4.0 in 1996. This was a major update to Windows NT Workstation that contained numerous improvements, including the next-generation user interface (already available in Windows 95), which helped make the operating system much easier to use. The primary focus for this version of Windows NT was fourfold: better manageability, faster performance, increased reliability, and better security. The development team succeeded in meeting these and other goals.

The successor to Windows NT Workstation 4.0 is Windows 2000 Professional. Formerly known as Windows NT Workstation 5.0, Windows 2000 Professional is part of the natural evolution of Windows NT technology.

Windows NT 4.0, Terminal Server Edition

Microsoft Windows NT 4.0, Terminal Server Edition (TSE) delivers the Windows experience to diverse types of desktop hardware. TSE runs 32-bit applications on a server, sending an application's output to new Windows-based terminal devices and machines running Microsoft Windows. If you have computers that aren't capable of running Windows 2000 Professional, TSE will allow the machines to remain productive until the company can replace them. Visit Microsoft's Web site at *http://www.microsoft.com/ntserver* to learn more about TSE.

Let's Talk About Names

On the 27th of October, 1998, Microsoft announced that a change was in order. Instead of calling the next product built on Windows NT technology *Windows NT 5.0,* they are now calling it *Windows 2000.* To avoid confusion, each Windows 2000 product carries the tagline, "Built on NT Technology." Although the names have changed, the features of the various products have not. The features that were planned for Windows NT Workstation 5.0 are being implemented in Windows 2000 Professional, and this book describes most of them. Table 2-1 summarizes the new product names. The following list describes the differences between the products and introduces you to a new kid on the block, Windows 2000 Datacenter Server.

■ **Windows 2000 Professional**   Windows 2000 Professional is the best operating system for any size business. It builds on the traditional strengths of Windows NT, providing the highest level of security, reliability, and performance. And it's the easiest version of Windows yet for working with your computer, setting up and configuring your system, working offline, and browsing the Web. For administrators, Windows 2000 Professional provides a desktop that is easy to deploy, manage, and support—the result is lower costs.

■ **Windows 2000 Server**   Windows 2000 Server is the next version of Microsoft's traditional server product, which includes support for two-way symmetric multiprocessing (SMP). It's good for small-sized to medium-sized application deployment, Web servers, workgroups, branch offices, and the like. Microsoft expects Windows 2000 Server to be its most popular server product.

■ **Windows 2000 Advanced Server**   A more advanced departmental and applications server, Windows 2000 Advanced Server supports four-way SMP and more physical memory, as well as clustering and load-balancing services. This server product is ideal for large, database-intensive applications.

■ **Windows 2000 Datacenter Server**   This is the most powerful server operating system ever offered by Microsoft. It offers 16-way SMP and can utilize up to 64 gigabytes of physical memory—and clustering and load-balancing services are built into the operating system. This server product is targeted at large data warehouses, econometric analysis, large-scale simulations in science and engineering, online transaction processing (OLTP), and server consolidation projects.

This Product	Has This New Name
Windows NT Workstation 5.0	Windows 2000 Professional
Windows NT Server 5.0	Windows 2000 Server
Windows NT Server 5.0 Enterprise Edition	Windows 2000 Advanced Server
N/A	Windows 2000 Datacenter Server

Table 2-1
Old and new names for products built on Windows NT technology.

There are plenty of reasons for the name change. First of all, the "2000" designation is consistent with Microsoft's other product names, including Microsoft Office 2000. The 2000 designation also communicates a vision that takes companies into the new millenium. Beyond that, however, Windows 2000 represents a major milestone—so much so that companies who had never considered deploying Windows NT are now considering Windows 2000 for key roles in their organizations, and the press is making comments about Windows 2000 that suggest that the operating system has finally "arrived." For instance, Ziff-Davis' NT 5.0 Preview Web site contains the comment, "Any way you slice it, Microsoft [Windows 2000 Professional] looks as if it finally will embody all the qualities corporate America wants in an operating system." And last, changing the name is just good horse sense. The term *workstation* continues to confuse people, leading them to believe that the product is for high-powered computers running CAD and image processing software. The new name clearly describes what the product is—the mainstream desktop operating system for businesses of all sizes.

Desktop Operating System Comparison

The goal of Microsoft as I see it is to put the best possible operating system on each computer. What qualifies as "the best" is the operating system that most reduces the total cost of ownership (TCO) and most tightly secures your company's valuable resources. There is little doubt that Windows 2000 Professional—with the traditional strengths of Windows NT—is a far better business operating system than Windows 98, but you probably won't be able to install Windows 2000 Professional on every desktop. Thus, consider the following questions before choosing Windows 98 or Windows 2000 Professional as the operating system for an individual computer:

- Does the computer meet the minimum hardware requirements?
- Does the operating system support the devices installed in the computer?
- Does the operating system provide support for the required applications?
- Does the operating system offer connectivity to the organization's network?
- Does the operating system perform satisfactorily?

The sections that follow—"Setup Requirements," "Hardware Compatibility," "Software Compatibility," "Networking Support," and "Administrative Support"—compare Windows 98 to Windows 2000 Professional so that you can answer these questions.

If you find that a desktop computer isn't ready for Windows 2000 Professional, take a look at "Getting Ready for Windows 2000 Professional" later in this chapter for suggestions on how to make it so. This task might involve replacing the entire computer, upgrading memory, or replacing specific devices. It might also necessitate updating the software running on the computer. Keep in mind that virtually all Intel-compatible computers sold in recent years are capable of running Windows 2000 Professional well, and most popular 32-bit Windows-based applications are compatible with the operating system. Problems should only develop with legacy computers that haven't been updated in quite some time.

Setup Requirements

Table 2-2 describes Windows 98's recommended setup requirements versus those of Windows 2000 Professional. Note that Windows 2000 Professional supports Compaq Computer Corporation's Alpha EV4 processor in addition to Pentium-class processors in a single-processor or multiprocessor configuration. Both operating systems require certain equipment, including a CD-ROM drive, a VGA display adapter, and a mouse or similar pointing device. Note also that the chosen file system, cluster size, free memory, and setup options impact the amount of actual disk space required to install either operating system. The performance of both operating systems increases dramatically as you add more resources to the computer.

Requirement	Windows 98	Windows 2000 Professional
Minimum recommended RAM	32 MB	64 MB
Minimum recommended free disk space	500 MB	1 GB
Minimum recommended processor	Pentium	Pentium 233 MHz

Table 2-2
Recommended hardware requirements for satisfactory performance.

Hardware Compatibility

Table 2-3 on the following page describes the hardware features that Windows 98 and Windows 2000 Professional support. The table leads you to believe that Windows 2000 Professional can do anything Windows 98 can do. For the most part, that's true. However, even though Microsoft has tested Windows 2000 Professional with more devices than any previous version of Windows NT, Windows 2000 Professional is still compatible with fewer devices than Windows 98. To determine whether Microsoft has tested a particular device with Windows 2000 Professional, examine the hardware compatibility list (HCL). You can find the HCL on the Windows 2000 Professional CD-ROM in the Support folder, and on Microsoft's Web site at *http://www.microsoft.com/ hwtest/hcl*. Both versions are long but searchable. Keep in mind that just because a device is missing from the list doesn't mean it won't work. Here are some additional tips for determining whether a device works with Windows 2000 Professional:

- Look up the device in Windows 2000 Professional's Add/Remove Hardware Wizard. Many times, you'll find devices listed here that are not listed in the HCL. If you don't see a device listed in the Hardware Wizard, look in the driver library, which you can find in the Drvlib folder on the CD-ROM.
- Consult the device's manufacturer. Usually, a quick trip to the company's Web site will yield a list of drivers for Windows 2000 Professional. Note that you can't use many device drivers designed for Windows NT 4.0 in Windows 2000 Professional.
- Test the device in Windows 2000 Professional. Many times, the operating system detects the device and installs compatible drivers for it even though the operating system doesn't officially support the device. Examples include mice, SoundBlaster-compatible sound cards, and display adapters based on the S3 chip set.

■ Look for device drivers at a Web site that indexes them. One such example is Frank Condron's World O'Windows site at *http://worldowindows.com*. This site indexes thousands of device drivers from over 830 manufacturers.

Feature	Windows 98	Windows 2000 Professional
Plug and Play	Yes	Yes
Universal serial bus (USB), IEEE 1394, Accelerated Graphics Port (AGP)	Yes	Yes
Driver Signing	Yes	Yes
Win32 Driver Model (WDM)	Yes	Yes
Multiprocessor	No	Yes
Compaq Alpha EV4 processor	No	Yes
FAT file system	Yes	Yes
FAT32 file system	Yes	Yes
NTFS file system	No	Yes

Table 2-3
Hardware features supported by Windows 98 and Windows 2000 Professional.

Software Compatibility

Regardless of which operating system you choose to deploy on a given computer—Windows 98 or Windows 2000 Professional—always purchase and use 32-bit applications. They're the easiest to use and they offer the best performance, stability, security, and cost.

Table 2-4 describes some of the characteristics of Windows 98 and Windows 2000 Professional that affect software compatibility. Windows 98 is compatible with most 32-bit Windows-based applications. Microsoft has tested Windows 2000 Professional with hundreds of commercial business applications. If in doubt, consult the manufacturer of the software in question to learn about compatibility with Windows 2000 Professional. As a personal note, I've installed and used products from Adobe, Micrografx, Microsoft, Netscape, Visio, and a host of others without a single hiccup. Determining whether an application will run well in Windows 2000 Professional is straightforward:

- Consult the "Application Notes" section of the Windows 2000 Professional release notes, which you can find in the root folder of the CD-ROM. This section describes known issues regarding particular applications and often includes workarounds for those issues.

- Check out Microsoft's Compatibility Web site at *http:// www.microsoft.com/windows/compatible.*

- Listen to other users. DejaNews (*http://www.dejanews.com*) maintains a searchable database of UseNet postings. Search this database using the name of the software product combined with *Windows 2000 Professional,* and read the resulting messages for information on whether the application is compatible with Windows 2000 Professional.

- Consult the software vendor regarding support for Windows 2000 Professional. Even though an application might run correctly with the previous operating system, you might need an upgrade pack (upgrade packs contain migration DLLs) to ensure that it works properly when you upgrade to Windows 2000 Professional.

If you're tied to 16-bit legacy hardware and software, your choices are much clearer. If you must use a 16-bit MS-DOS or Windows-based device driver in order to support a legacy device, you'll need to install Windows 98 instead of Windows 2000 Professional. However, many MS-DOS and 16-bit Windows applications will run on Windows 2000 Professional.

Feature	Windows 98	Windows 2000 Professional
Limit on resources used	Expanded since Windows 3.1	None
16-bit preemptive multitasking	No	Yes
32-bit preemptive multitasking	Yes	Yes
32-bit Windows application programming interface (Win32 API)	Subset	Yes
Support for MS-DOS applications	Yes	Most
Support for MS-DOS device drivers	Yes	No
Support for 16-bit Windows-based applications	Yes	Yes

Table 2-4   *(continued)*
Features related to software compatibility.

Table 2-4. *continued*

Feature	Windows 98	Windows 2000 Professional
Support for 16-bit Windows-based device drivers	Yes	No
Portable Operating System Interface for UNIX (POSIX)	No	Yes
Multimedia APIs (DirectX)	Yes	Yes

Networking Support

Most important, if you're still using real mode networking components, it's time to upgrade to protected mode components. The administrative features of Windows 98 and Windows 2000 Professional don't work on top of real mode networking components.

As shown in Table 2-5, both Windows 98 and Windows 2000 Professional provide similar networking support where it counts. They both provide built-in support for the most popular clients, protocols, and adapters. They both have an open networking architecture that allows you to easily add third-party clients, protocols, and adapters to the operating system. The differences are in the power and usability of the two operating systems' networking tools. Windows 2000 Professional takes networking support much further and also makes networking tools easier to use. Windows 98 doesn't provide the Network Connection Wizard, for example. Windows 98 also doesn't take full advantage of Windows 2000 Server. The partnership between Windows 2000 Professional and Windows 2000 Server enables the use of technology such as Microsoft IntelliMirror, which you will learn about in Chapter 20, "Lower Total Cost of Ownership with Microsoft Windows 2000 Server."

Feature	Windows 98	Windows 2000 Professional
Built-in support for popular clients, protocols, and adapters	Yes	Yes
Open networking architecture	Yes	Yes
Support for mobile users	Yes	Yes
Internet connectivity	Yes	Yes
Works with Windows 2000 Server	Limited	Fully

Table 2-5
Networking support.

Administrative Support

Table 2-6 describes the administrative features that Windows 98 and Windows 2000 Professional provide. Both operating systems have virtually the same capabilities, though Windows 2000 Professional takes each capability much further than its counterpart. Both operating systems provide setup and deployment tools, for example, but only Windows 2000 Professional, when combined with Windows 2000 Server, supports the Remote Windows Installation tool. Both operating systems support multiple users via user profiles, but only Windows 2000 Professional—when used with Windows 2000 Server—provides the capability to mirror the user's local documents on a network. Windows 2000 Professional introduces the concept of a replaceable desktop; Windows 98 does not.

The administrative features of the two operating systems are therefore not the primary criteria when determining which system to install. Total cost of ownership, and other considerations such as hardware and software support, will be more likely to influence your choice of operating system for a particular computer.

Feature	Windows 98	Windows 2000 Professional
Setup and deployment tools	Yes	Yes
Remote administration tools	Yes	Yes
Support for multiple users (user profiles)	Yes	Yes
Support for restrictions (system policies)	Yes	Yes
Performance monitoring	Yes	Yes
Advanced scripting (Windows Scripting Host)	Yes	Yes
Windows Management Instrumentation (WMI)	Yes	Yes
IntelliMirror	No	Yes
Year 2000–ready	Yes	Yes

Table 2-6
Administrative support.

Getting Ready for Windows 2000 Professional

Instead of letting Windows 2000 Professional sneak up on you, get ready for it now. If your company is purchasing new computers, insist on the following specifications taken from Microsoft's Windows 2000 Ready PC requirements:

- Pentium II–class processor (233 MHz or faster) with 64 megabytes of RAM
- Universal serial bus (USB) built into the motherboard
- Accelerated Graphics Port (AGP) slot and adapter
- Advanced Configuration and Power Interface (ACPI)–ready
- Year 2000–ready
- Windows NT Workstation 4.0 preinstalled

Figure 2-2 provides an overview of what you can do to start preparing existing computers for Windows 2000 Professional today, and what it's going to take later to make the actual change. The following sections provide a bit more detail. To summarize, ensure that all new machines come with Windows NT Workstation 4.0, which provides the best migration path to Windows 2000 Professional. Upgrade machines that are not capable of running Windows 2000 Professional to Windows 98—then start considering their replacement. Last, consider using Microsoft TSE and installing the Terminal Server Client on computers that aren't capable of running either operating system and start considering their replacement with modern hardware.

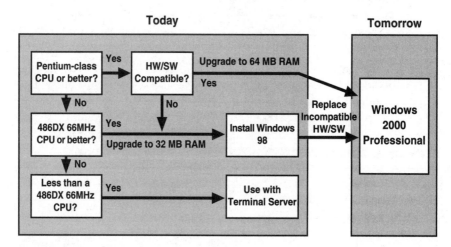

Figure 2-2
Preparing for Windows 2000 Professional.

Windows NT Workstation 4.0

The reason Windows NT Workstation 4.0 is recommended for a Windows 2000 Ready PC is that it provides the best migration path to Windows 2000 Professional. That is, upgrading to Windows 2000 Professional is easier from Windows NT Workstation 4.0 than from Windows 95 or Windows 98. Both operating systems—Windows NT 4.0 and Windows 2000 Professional—share the same registry organization, ensuring that users' settings migrate when upgrading, and both have a common architecture.

Upgrade existing Pentium-class (233 MHz or faster) computers to at least 64 MB of RAM. These computers will be ready for Windows 2000 Professional when it becomes available. You will inevitably lose some application settings when you upgrade from Windows 95 or Windows 98 to Windows 2000 Professional, but you can restore most of them by reinstalling the applications in question.

Windows 98

Windows 98 is not the best migration path to Windows 2000 Professional, but it's relatively painless nonetheless—particularly if upgrade packs are available for the applications on the computer. If you don't have an upgrade pack for an application, you'll lose some of its settings due to differences in the registry. Some applications won't work correctly in Windows 2000 Professional until you get a version designed for that operating system. Windows 2000 Professional will redetect the hardware installed on the computer—Plug and Play as well as legacy devices—restoring the hardware settings lost during the upgrade process.

Computers that can't benefit from Windows 2000 Professional can definitely benefit from Windows 98. Windows 98 is easy to maintain and deploy, and it provides support for a large variety of new and old hardware. It doesn't reap the advantages of features such as IntelliMirror, however, which require the cooperation between Windows 2000 Professional and Windows 2000 Server. Windows 98 also doesn't provide many of Windows NT's traditional strengths, such as an extra measure of stability and industrial-strength security. If a computer doesn't have a Pentium-class processor, but has at least a 66-megahertz 486DX, upgrade the computer to 32 megabytes of RAM and install Windows 98. The following list helps you identify additional scenarios in which you must install Windows 98 rather than Windows 2000 Professional:

- The hardware isn't compatible with Windows 2000 Professional.

- Processing power and memory are insufficient for Windows 2000 Professional.

- Required 16-bit legacy applications don't work in Windows 2000 Professional.

Microsoft Terminal Server Edition and Terminal Services

Computers that aren't capable of running Windows 98 or Windows 2000 Professional—those with less than a 66-megahertz 486DX processor or incompatible hardware—can still provide the user with access to 32-bit applications. This is accomplished by using one of two possible server products: Windows NT Server 4.0, Terminal Server Edition, or Windows 2000 Server. Windows 2000 Server comes with the Terminal Services component, which provides this capability. There are two circumstances in which you should consider using this type of arrangement:

■ As support for legacy computers when they're unable to upgrade to Windows 2000 Professional or Windows 98. Use until you can replace the legacy computers.

■ As a server for dedicated, Windows-based terminals. At a cost of less than $500, Windows-based terminals give single-task workers access to the power and flexibility of 32-bit Windows-based applications.

2000 and Beyond: Looking Forward

Start preparing to upgrade your hardware to meet the demands of Windows NT technology. First, make sure new computers have the best technology available, including the fastest processor available and an appropriate amount of RAM. Also make sure that new computers purchased prior to the release of Windows 2000 Professional have Windows NT Workstation 4.0 preinstalled. And last, use Windows 98 in situations where you can't deploy Windows 2000 Professional. Windows 98 doesn't require extensive changes to your Windows 95 deployment plan, yet the operating system is easier to support, and it offers better performance and integration than its predecessor does.

CHAPTER THREE

Setup Guide

Installing Microsoft Windows 2000 Professional is no more difficult than installing its predecessor, Microsoft Windows NT Workstation 4.0. You'll find, in fact, that installing the latest incarnation of Windows NT technology is easier thanks to a variety of improvements in the setup program as well as enhancements to the operating system's capabilities. For example, Windows 2000 Professional automatically detects and configures most popular devices, minimizes the number of questions that you must answer, and provides an upgrade path from versions of Windows other than Windows NT, including Windows 98, Windows 95, and Windows 3.1. The setup program's command line is substantially simpler, too.

The early steps of Windows 2000 Professional's setup process are not very different from those of Windows NT Workstation 4.0. Intentional or not, this helps you install the operating system faster—if you're already familiar with how to start the setup program and the information required during the first several steps. The blue MS-DOS setup screens would be familiar, for example, as would be the partition selection and file copying processes. All in all, if you have experience installing Windows NT Workstation 4.0, you'll have no problems installing Windows 2000 Professional. The later steps have changed a bit because Windows 2000 Professional offers an upgrade path from Windows 98, requiring the setup program to make provisions such as an upgrade report that details any compatibility problems it finds.

This chapter describes the entire setup process. It starts by showing you how to meet the requirements of the setup program. Then it describes a handful of advanced setup procedures, including how to install Windows 2000 Professional along with another operating system. Last it shows you how to run the setup program, either to upgrade from another version of Windows, or to install a clean copy of the operating system.

Setup Preparation

Before taking the Windows 2000 Professional CD-ROM out of its jewel case and before running the setup program, make sure you've prepared the computer for the setup process. The following sections tell you more about this preparation:

- "Know the Hardware Requirements" describes the recommended hardware requirements for installing and running Windows 2000 Professional.

- "Create a Computer Account on the Server" tells you how to create a computer account on the server and how an administrator can provide a user with credentials for creating such an account.

- "Record the Computer's Configuration" lists a variety of settings that you should record and files that you should back up before trying to install Windows 2000 Professional.

- "Get the Computer Ready for Setup" describes preparations that you must physically make on the computer, such as disabling virus scanners.

The Windows 2000 Professional CD-ROM provides a number of documents in the Support folder that will help you prepare for installing the operating system. These documents supplement the material you will read in this chapter. Make sure you consult all of them before performing a serious deployment and, at the very least—if you are installing Windows 2000 on a single machine only—consult the Read1st.txt file. Here's a list of those documents that will prove to be most useful:

Setup.txt	Basic information about installing the operating system
Read1st.txt	Critical last-minute information that didn't find its way into the documentation or into any other TXT file on the CD-ROM
AdvSetup.txt	Advanced information about installing the operating system, including information about upgrading and information about creating a dual-boot combination
RelNotes.htm	Comprehensive information about the operating system's new features and compatibility with other hardware and software

Know the Hardware Requirements

The hardware requirements for running Windows 2000 Professional on an Intel-based (or compatible) computer have escalated a bit since Windows NT Work-station 4.0. First, the computer must have a Pentium-class processor. It also must have a VGA or better resolution display adapter, along with a keyboard and a pointing device such as a mouse. The computer must have 32 MB of RAM, but 64 MB is more appropriate.

The setup program has additional hardware requirements. Table 3-1 sum-marizes these requirements as well as the requirements for running Windows 2000 Professional once it is set up. An Intel-based computer must have at least 300 MB of free disk space before you even start the setup program. Remember, though, that cluster size, RAM size, and choice of file system affect how much space is actually required. The setup program will notify you if it doesn't find enough space. The computer must also have a CD-ROM drive if you're installing from a disc or, if you're installing from a network, it must have a network adapter and access to the appropriate network file share.

	Recommended to Install	Recommended to Run
Intel-based	1 GB free disk space	Pentium-class processor
	CD-ROM drive to install from the CD-ROM	64 MB of RAM
		VGA display adapter
	Network adapter and file share for network install	Keyboard and mouse
Compaq Alpha	500 MB free disk space	Compaq Alpha EV4 200 MHz or better processor
	CD-ROM drive to install from the CD-ROM	96 MB of RAM
	Network adapter and file share for network install	VGA display adapter
		Keyboard and mouse

Table 3-1
Recommended hardware requirements for installing and running Windows 2000 Professional.

Compaq Alpha computers have similar requirements to Intel-based computers. The computer must have a 200-megahertz Compaq Alpha EV4 or better processor and at least 48 MB of RAM (96 MB recommended). It must have a VGA or higher resolution monitor, a keyboard, and a pointing device such as a mouse. To start the setup program, the computer must have 400 MB (500 MB recommended) of disk space available. Installing Windows 2000 Professional from a CD-ROM requires that the computer have a CD-ROM drive. A network installation requires a network adapter with access to the appropriate network file share.

Windows 2000 Professional requires that a Compaq Alpha computer have a recent version of the firmware. The specific version required depends on the type of Alpha system. Older Alpha computers use Advanced RISC Computing (ARC) firmware, while newer Alpha systems use AlphaBIOS (Basic Input/ Output System). If the computer already has the correct firmware for running Windows NT Workstation 4.0, you don't necessarily need to upgrade. However, Compaq Computer Corporation recommends that you upgrade to the latest version to get the latest enhancements and bug fixes. You can find more information about updating your firmware at *http://www.windows.digital.com/ support*. Alternatively, call the Compaq Computer Corporation support line at (800) 354-9000.

> NOTE: The ultimate guide for determining whether a computer's hardware is compatible with Windows 2000 Professional is the hardware compatibility list (HCL). You can find the HCL on the Windows 2000 Professional CD-ROM in the Support folder and on Microsoft's Web site at *http://www.microsoft.com/hwtest/hcl*. Both versions are long but searchable. Just because a device is missing from the list doesn't mean it won't work. If in doubt, test the device in a safe environment.

Create a Computer Account on the Server

A *computer account* provides an operating system access to the resources on a Microsoft network. It identifies a computer on the network. If the user configures a computer to be able to boot either of two different operating systems (dual-boot), the computer might need two different computer accounts—one for each operating system. A computer account is different from a user account in that a user account provides credentials and permissions for an individual user, rather than for an individual computer. Note that Windows 98 doesn't require a computer account in order to access a Microsoft network. Only members of the Windows NT and Windows 2000 family require computer accounts.

If you're upgrading to Windows 2000 Professional from Windows NT Workstation, you don't have to create a new computer account on the server. Windows 2000 Professional uses the current computer account. However, if you're upgrading to Windows 2000 Professional from MS-DOS, Windows 3.1, Windows 95, or Windows 98, you must create a computer account on the server. In addition, if you're installing Windows 2000 Professional in a dual-boot combination with Windows NT Workstation, you must create a separate computer account for the new operating system. There are two ways you can handle creating computer accounts:

- **Create a computer account before running the setup program**   A domain administrator uses the Server Manager to create a computer account prior to the user running the setup program. This solution requires domain administrators to create each computer account in advance of the user installing Windows 2000 Professional. One advantage to this method is that domain administrators can control the names given to specific computers in the organization.

- **Create a computer account during setup**   The setup program allows the user to create a computer account towards the end of the installation process. However, the user must have administrator credentials on the domain, or must at least be able to provide a user name and a password that have administrative-level privileges. This is often the easiest solution, freeing the domain administrator from having to manually create accounts for each computer connecting to the server; however, this solution prevents the domain administrator from maintaining any sort of control over the names given to the computers by the users. Rather than distribute administrator credentials to all users, the domain administrator might create temporary administrator accounts that give just enough permission for users to create their own computer accounts on the server.

Record the Computer's Configuration

One of the biggest mistakes I've made recently is formatting a computer's hard drive in preparation for installing Windows 2000 Professional without first recording the computer's hardware configuration. Even though Windows 2000 Professional is a Plug and Play operating system and should detect most popular devices, situations frequently arise in which you have to manually configure a bit of hardware. Nothing is more frustrating than having to create and format an MS-DOS partition just so you can start some antiquated hardware configuration program that will help you recall what you should have written down in the first place—the interrupt request (IRQ) used by a legacy network adapter.

What Are Computer Accounts?

Network administrators manage computers in logical groups called *domains.* A computer running Windows 2000 Server (or another member of the Windows NT Server family), called a domain controller, provides a common collection of user accounts and a security database for the entire domain, enabling each user to have a single account that's recognized by all computers in the domain. A computer participates in a particular domain if it uses the domain's security database to validate users' credentials when they log on to the computer. Keep in mind that a domain does not imply the location of a computer or even how the computer is connected to the network. Computers in a domain can be scattered all over the world and use many different types of physical connections.

In order for Windows 2000 Professional to use a domain to authenticate users, the machine running Windows 2000 Professional must have a computer account on the domain. This is in contrast to Windows 98, which does not require a computer account. A domain administrator can create computer accounts before users install Windows 2000 Professional, or users can create computer accounts during the installation process. Windows 2000 Professional uses the computer account to identify itself to the domain controller and set up a security communications channel between itself and the server. So what does Windows 2000 Professional get out of being a domain member? The operating system can use accounts and global groups from the domain, as opposed to being limited to accounts and groups stored on the local computer. Also, the computer running Windows 2000 Professional can be managed remotely by domain administrators.

The most reliable method for recording most of this information is to print it. In Windows 95 or Windows 98, you can print the computer's configuration from the Device Manager. In Windows NT Workstation, you can print similar information from Windows NT Diagnostics. Both provide the IRQ, the direct memory access (DMA), and the port settings for each device in the computer. Certain other information must be recorded manually—the most important of which is the network configuration, including the computer account, the workgroup or domain name, the WINS (Windows Internet Naming Service) and DNS (Domain Name System) server IP addresses, the network adapter configuration, and any other settings required to connect the computer to the network.

Still more information is required if you want to get Windows 2000 Professional running quickly. Most of this additional information is actually in files that you can copy to a floppy disk and then restore after installing Windows 2000 Professional:

- Important batch files and scripts that you want to keep

- Scheduled jobs in the Task Scheduler or the AT command

- Any folders in the user profile that you want to keep: Favorites, Send To, and so on

- Registry customizations that you want to repeat (Export to an REG file)

- Other configuration files that you will require in Windows 2000 Professional

Get the Computer Ready for Setup

To eliminate nasty surprises, prepare the computer before starting the Windows 2000 Professional setup program. The most important task is to back up any important data on the computer. This includes configuration files and data files. Don't forget items such as batch files, scripts, and Internet shortcuts. The surest way to back up these files is to use the backup program that the operating system provides. In Windows 95, Windows 98, and Windows NT Workstation 4.0, you can install the backup program from the Add/Remove Programs dialog box.

To Accomplish This	Do This
Back up files in Windows 95 or Windows 98	Choose Programs from the Start menu. Then choose Accessories, System Tools, Backup from the submenus.
Back up files in Windows NT 4.0	Choose Programs from the Start menu. Then choose Administrative Tools (Common), Backup from the submenus.

After backing up your files, shut down those programs that cause problems for the setup program. Specifically, shut down all virus scanners as well as third-party network clients and services before starting the setup program. These programs can prevent the setup program from operating normally or from configuring Windows 2000 Professional correctly. For example, virus scanners prevent the setup program from modifying the boot sector. What's more, most virus scanners designed for Windows 98 and Windows NT Workstation 4.0 don't work properly with Windows 2000 Professional. Check with the software vendor, because they are likely to have an update or a new version that's designed for Windows 2000. An *upgrade pack*—which updates a program so that it works properly in Windows 2000 Professional—provided by the vendor would be enough to make a virus scanner compatible with Windows 2000. Examples of virus scanners that are known to cause problems include InocuLAN, which you can learn about at Computer Associates' Web site, *http://www.cai.com,* and McAfee AntiVirus, which you can learn about at McAfee's Web site, *http://www.mcafee.com.*

Microsoft recommends that you disable a few other things before running Windows 2000 Professional's setup program. In particular, break any disk mirrors and disconnect any uninterruptible power supply (UPS) devices. Both items interfere with the proper configuration of the operating system when upgrading.

If you're installing Windows 2000 Professional from MS-DOS, which you'll do if you're reformatting your hard disk to accept a clean install of the operating system, Microsoft recommends that you install Smartdrv. Smartdrv is a disk caching device driver that greatly improves the performance of the setup program. MS-DOS comes with Smartdrv as do Windows 95 and Windows 98. Look in the DOS or Windows folder on the CD-ROM for Smartdrv.exe and copy it to the target computer's boot disk. To start Smartdrv, add the command *smartdrv.exe* to the autoexec.bat file. I compared the setup program's performance with and without Smartdrv and found a ten-fold improvement with Smartdrv (from several hours to about 45 minutes).

Windows 2000 Professional's setup program can generate a compatibility report that alerts you to possible incompatibilities. To generate a compatibility report without installing the operating system, run Winnt32.exe with the /checkupgradeonly command line option. In Windows 98, the setup program saves the compatibility report to a file called Upgrade.txt in the Windows folder. In Windows NT Workstation 4.0, the setup program saves the report to a file called Winnt32.log. If the report doesn't indicate any problems that prevent you from using the operating system, proceed with the installation.

The following list summarizes the steps necessary to prepare a computer for Windows 2000 Professional:

1. Back up the computer's files.

2. Disable any service that might interfere with the setup program's ability to properly install and configure Windows 2000. Here are some examples:

   ❑ Virus scanners

   ❑ Disk mirrors

   ❑ Third-party network clients and services

   ❑ Uninterruptible power supplies

3. If you're starting the setup program from MS-DOS, install Smartdrv.

4. If you're upgrading from a previous version of Windows, generate a compatibility report by entering *Winnt32.exe /checkupgradeonly* in the command line.

NOTE: Before upgrading to Windows 2000 Professional, make sure the computer is working properly. That is, make sure that all the settings are correct, that each device works properly, and that the computer can connect to the network. As a result, the setup program will be able to retain the previous operating system's settings, making the setup process go smoothly. If the setup program finds a working network configuration during an upgrade, for example, it won't have to prompt the user for that information when installing Windows 2000 Professional.

Advanced Setup Options

A basic setup is the result of accepting the default responses to the setup program's prompts. I recommend a basic setup for most users. In some cases, however, the user must deviate from a basic setup in order to accomplish things such as a dual-boot configuration with another operating system, or a conversion between a FAT file system and the NTFS file system. The following sections describe the three most common advanced options:

- "Partitioning the Hard Disk" describes why you might need to repartition the computer's hard disk before installing Windows 2000 Professional.

- "Choosing Between NTFS and FAT" helps you make the critical decision of whether you should use the NTFS file system or one of the FAT file systems.

- "Dual-Boot Combinations with Other Systems" describes how to create a dual-boot combination with Windows 2000 Professional and another operating system.

Partitioning the Hard Disk

If you have ever installed Windows NT Workstation 4.0, recall how frustrating it was to cleanly install the operating system on a partition larger than 2 GB. A clean install in such a situation requires that you format the partition with the FAT16 file system first, and then convert the partition to the NTFS file system during the setup process. Since FAT16 is limited to 2-GB partitions, you couldn't install the operating system on anything larger unless you used a third-party utility to expand the partition after installing the operating system. As a result, many computers are sitting around with extremely large hard disks and system partitions of only 2 GB. Some users who had their wits about them used the Disk Manager to format the remaining unused space and use it for extra storage, but most didn't. Still fewer users knew that there was a third-party product that could expand the system partition to reclaim unused space.

With the Windows 2000 Professional setup program, users can easily create a clean install on partitions larger than 2 GB. The setup program can install the operating system on a FAT32 partition and then convert the partition to NTFS. This allows for system partitions of up to 2 terabytes, theoretically, or up to 32 GB, practically. To do this, use Fdisk (an MS-DOS command) to enable large disk support, and remove each partition on the hard disk. Then create a system partition that uses the entire hard disk or whatever portion of it that's appropriate. After partitioning the hard disk, format it. The result is a FAT32 partition that's potentially larger than 2 GB. The setup program will successfully install Windows 2000 Professional on the FAT32 partition, and then convert the partition to NTFS as one of the later steps in the process.

> **NOTE :** One terabyte (TB) is about 10^{12} bytes. One exabyte (EB) is about 10^{18} bytes.

Partitioning a disk on a Compaq Alpha computer is a bit more straightforward. The last partition on the disk is the system partition and it must be 6 MB. The first partition occupies the remaining space on the disk and is usually configured with NTFS. If the computer has the AlphaBIOS firmware, use the AlphaBIOS setup program to automatically create both partitions. Otherwise, use the Arcinst program to create them. To learn more about partitioning the hard disk on a Compaq Alpha computer, see the hardware documentation or visit *http://www.windows.digital.com/support.*

> **CAUTION :** Microsoft does not support upgrading to the final Windows 2000 Professional release from an earlier beta version of the same product. The results are unpredictable and could result in instability, data loss, or worse. Always reformat a partition and reinstall Windows 2000 Professional if you've previously installed a beta version of the product on that partition.

Choosing Between NTFS and FAT

The setup program uses the computer's current file system as the default. However, it gives you the opportunity to override the default and choose FAT16, FAT32, or NTFS. Choosing a file system is easy if Windows 2000 Professional is going to be the only operating system on the computer. In that case, NTFS is the best choice as it offers better performance, security, and efficiency. If you have a dual-boot combination with an operating system that doesn't support NTFS—Windows 98, Windows 95, or Windows 3.1—you must use FAT16 or possibly FAT32. Table 3-2 on the following page helps you choose among the file systems by comparing the operating system support, the minimum and maximum disk size, and the maximum file size for each.

If you choose to use NTFS, you must make one other decision: convert the existing file system or replace it. That is, you can convert an existing FAT partition to NTFS, keeping all the existing files, or you can reformat a partition with NTFS, losing all existing files. If you don't want the hassle of replacing important files on the file system, converting to NTFS is the best choice. If you want a fresh start or if you want to recover a large amount of space that's wasted on useless files, reformatting the partition with NTFS is the best choice. In general, I prefer to back up important files, reformat with NTFS, and restore the important files after installing Windows 2000 Professional. You might not be able to afford this luxury, however, since it requires you to spend considerable time customizing the operating system and reinstalling each application.

	FAT16	FAT32	NTFS
Minimum partition size	N/A	512 MB	20 MB
Maximum partition size	2 GB (4 GB with Windows NT 3.51 or 4.0)	2 TB	15 EB
Maximum file size	2 GB	4 GB	N/A
Operating systems	MS-DOS Windows 3.1 Windows 95 Windows 98 Windows NT 3.1 Windows NT 3.5 Windows NT 3.51 Windows NT 4.0 Windows 2000	Windows 98 Windows 95 OSR2 Windows 2000	Windows NT 4.0 Windows 2000

Table 3-2
Comparison of FAT16, FAT32, and NTFS.

If Windows 2000 Professional is sharing a partition with an operating system that doesn't support NTFS, such as Windows 98, Windows 95, or Windows 3.1, you must use one of the FAT file systems. Use FAT32 if the other operating system is Windows 98 or Windows 95 OSR2 (the second release of Windows 95). Otherwise, if the other operating system is MS-DOS, Windows 3.1, or Windows 95 OSR1 (the original release of Windows 95), you must use FAT16. What's the difference? FAT16 is less efficient than FAT32 (on disks larger than 2 GB), but it supports disks much smaller than what FAT32 supports. FAT16 is limited to disks up to 2 GB in size (4 GB with Windows NT 3.51 and Windows NT 4.0) and files up to 2 GB in size. FAT32 works with disks from 512 MB to 2 TB in size, and the maximum file size for FAT32 is 4 GB. Windows 2000 Professional will recognize an existing FAT32 partition of any size, but it will only format 32 GB of a FAT32 partition. Microsoft recommends FAT32 for disks that are larger than 2 GB, but it recommends FAT16 for disks that are smaller than 2 GB. FAT32 is not efficient on small disks.

NTFS 5, the latest version of NTFS, is the recommended file system for Windows 2000 Professional. It has advanced features that beat all the others. It does everything FAT does—and it provides industrial-strength security, space-saving compression, and scalability to utilize disks of sizes that don't even exist yet. The minimum partition size is 20 MB, so you can't use NTFS on floppy disks, and the theoretical maximum partition size is 16 EB. However, the practical maximum partition size is 2 TB. The one drawback is that the only two desktop operating systems that can use NTFS 5 are Windows NT Workstation 4.0 and Windows 2000 Professional—which means that you can't use NTFS 5 if you have a dual-boot combination with any other operating system on the same partition.

Windows NT Workstation 4.0 requires Service Pack 3 or Service Pack 4 in order to read an NTFS 5 partition—although Service Pack 3 requires a replacement Ntfs.sys file that is automatically provided by the Windows 2000 setup program. With either of these service packs installed, Windows NT Workstation 4.0 will operate as described in Table 3-3.

Only Windows 2000 Professional can use certain features of NTFS 5, so Windows NT Workstation 4.0 can't take advantage of them. Again, Table 3-3 describes those features. Highlights include data encryption, disk quotas, Distributed Link Tracking, mount points (also known as reparse points or junction points), and native structured storage (NSS) files. Even with Service Pack 4, Windows NT Workstation 4.0 can't take advantage of these features. When trying to access these features from within Windows NT Workstation 4.0, the operating system will display an error message such as "access denied."

NTFS 5.0 Feature	Windows NT 4.0	Windows 2000 Professional
Folder and file security settings	Yes	Yes
Recovery log that helps restore a partition in the event of failure	Yes	Yes
Flexible formatting options for space efficiency	Yes	Yes
File compression for saving disk space	Yes	Yes
Partition extension to use unallocated disk space	Yes	Yes

Table 3-3 *(continued)*

Comparison of NTFS support in Windows NT 4.0 and Windows 2000 Professional.

Table 3-3. *continued*

NTFS 5.0 Feature	Windows NT 4.0	Windows 2000 Professional
Striped partitions for high-speed data access	Yes	Yes
Data encryption to protect individual files	No	Yes
Partition extensions without restarting the computer	No	Yes
Disk quotas to monitor and control disk usage	No	Yes
Distributed Link Tracking to preserve shortcuts when files are moved	No	Yes
Mount points to graft another volume onto an NFTS folder	No	Yes
Full text and property indexing to allow fast retrieval of documents	No	Yes

NOTE: Any operating system, including Mac OS, MS-DOS, Windows 3.1, Windows 95, and Windows 98, can read files off an NTFS 5 partition over a network, since the network redirector makes the file system irrelevant. Thus, don't let your network schema determine which file system you choose.

Dual-Boot Combinations with Other Systems

A dual-boot combination is a configuration in which two operating systems are installed on a single computer. As the computer starts, you can choose the operating system you want to use for that session. Windows 2000 Professional can be installed in a dual-boot combination with a variety of operating systems, including MS-DOS, Windows 95, and Windows 98. You can even create a dual-boot combination with Windows 2000 Professional and Windows NT Workstation 4.0. If you're a bit uneasy about whether must-have applications will run well in Windows 2000 Professional, create a dual-boot combination with the previous operating system so that you can make sure those applications will be available. Keep Windows 98, for example, until you have successfully installed and tested all of your applications in Windows 2000 Professional.

Installing Windows 2000 Professional in the same folder as the previous operating system is considered to be upgrading. You won't be able to choose between Windows 2000 Professional and the previous operating system at startup, since the setup program replaces or removes many of the previous operating system's files.

Installing Windows 2000 Professional in a different folder than the previous operating system creates a dual-boot combination. Since the previous operating system is left intact, you can choose between the operating systems as the computer starts. You can install Windows 2000 Professional on the same partition as—but in a different folder than—the previous operating system. However, I recommend that you install Windows 2000 Professional on a different partition than the previous operating system. That way you won't have to worry about file system compatibility as much and, more important, you won't have to worry about Windows 2000 Professional replacing important files that the previous operating system requires in order to start.

To create a dual-boot configuration, choose the Clean Install option during the setup process and select an unused partition that will contain Windows 2000 Professional's system files.

Creating a dual-boot combination has some caveats that you should be aware of, especially if you're creating a dual-boot combination with Windows NT Workstation 4.0:

- The order in which you install Windows 98 and Windows 2000 Professional doesn't matter. The boot drive must be formatted using any version of the FAT file system—preferably FAT32.

- To create a dual-boot combination with Windows 2000 Professional and MS-DOS, install MS-DOS first; otherwise, MS-DOS overwrites the boot sector required to start Windows 2000 Professional. The boot drive must be formatted using FAT16.

- To create a dual-boot combination with Windows 2000 Professional and Windows 95, install Windows 95 first so that Windows 95 doesn't overwrite the startup files required to start Windows 2000 Professional. The boot drive must be formatted using FAT16, if you're using OSR1, or either version of FAT, if you're using OSR2.

- You can't install Windows 2000 Professional on a compressed partition, unless the partition is compressed using NTFS. In other words, Windows 2000 doesn't support the DriveSpace or DoubleSpace compression technologies found in MS-DOS, Windows 95, and Windows 98.

- On a computer that is already configured in a dual-boot combination with OS/2 and MS-DOS, the Windows 2000 Professional setup program will configure the computer in a dual-boot combination with Windows 2000 and the operating system most recently used before starting the setup program. For example, if you start the setup program from MS-DOS, the computer will be configured in a dual-boot combination with MS-DOS and Windows 2000 Professional.

- Windows 95, Windows 98, and Windows 2000 Professional are all Plug and Play operating systems. Any of these operating systems might try to reconfigure the computer's hardware when it starts, preventing one or more devices from working properly as you switch back and forth between operating systems.

- If Windows 2000 Professional is in a dual-boot combination with another member of the Windows NT family, such as Windows NT Workstation 4.0, each operating system must have a unique computer account on the network domain.

- You can't reinstall Windows NT Workstation 4.0 on a partition after installing Windows 2000 Professional on the same partition.

- You have to reinstall any applications that you were using in the previous operating system if you want to use them in Windows 2000 Professional.

- Windows NT Workstation 4.0's Chkdsk and Defrag don't work on an NTFS 5 volume. You must use the Windows 2000 Professional versions of these tools.

- You can't use Windows NT Workstation 4.0's Emergency Repair Disk utility after installing Windows 2000 Professional.

- Files created or saved in Windows 2000 Professional might not be accessible in Windows NT Workstation 4.0. For example, files encrypted using Windows 2000 Professional are not accessible using Windows NT Workstation 4.0.

- Removable disks that are formatted with NTFS 4 are automatically converted to NTFS 5 when they're first mounted. To access NTFS 5 volumes from Windows NT Workstation 4.0, you must have Service Pack 4 installed (or Service Pack 3 with the replacement Ntfs.sys file from the Windows 2000 Professional CD-ROM).

- You can't create a dual-boot combination with Windows 2000 Professional and Windows NT 3.51.

Running the Setup Program

You can install Windows 2000 Professional from MS-DOS as well as from any version of Windows, including Windows 95, Windows 98, and Windows NT Workstation 4.0. The CD-ROM comes with two different setup programs, Winnt.exe and Winnt32.exe, each of which is described here:

- **Winnt.exe** is the 16-bit MS-DOS setup program. It's only appropriate when performing a clean install or when upgrading from a 16-bit version of Windows.

- **Winnt32.exe** is the 32-bit Windows setup program. It's only appropriate when installing Windows 2000 Professional from Windows 95, Windows 98, or Windows NT Workstation. This setup program can upgrade an existing operating system or perform a clean install. The user chooses between these options early in the setup process, as shown in Figure 3-1.

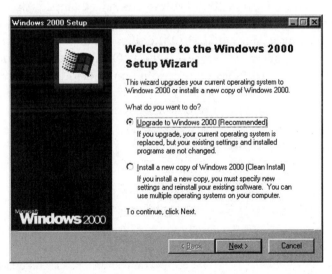

Figure 3-1
Choose whether to upgrade the existing operating system or to perform a clean install.

To install Windows 2000 Professional from MS-DOS or any 16-bit version of Windows such as Windows 3.1, type *winnt.exe,* followed by the appropriate command line options at the MS-DOS command prompt, and press Enter. For more information about the command line options available, see "Winnt.exe

Command Line," later in this chapter. Windows 95, Windows 98, and Windows NT Workstation 4.0 start Winnt32.exe automatically when a user inserts the CD-ROM disc. A user can click the Yes button to continue installing the operating system, or click the No button and then launch Winnt32.exe manually. To launch Winnt32.exe from Windows 95, Windows 98, or Windows NT Workstation, choose Run from the Start menu, and then type *d:\i386\winnt32.exe* (where *d* is the CD-ROM's drive letter) and click the OK button. "Winnt32.exe Command Line," later in this chapter, describes a handful of command line options that users can specify for Winnt32.exe.

If the computer has a bootable CD-ROM—otherwise known as a CD-ROM drive implementing the El Torito Specification—users can start the computer using the Windows 2000 Professional CD-ROM disc. This is only useful if the hard disk doesn't have an operating system already installed or if the user wants to perform a clean install using Winnt.exe. To start Winnt.exe using a bootable CD-ROM drive, insert the disc in the drive, power down the computer, and then wait several seconds before restarting it. If the CD-ROM is indeed bootable, Winnt.exe will start automatically.

Installing Windows 2000 Professional on a Compaq Alpha computer is a bit different than it is on an Intel-based computer. Start the setup program from the BIOS by inserting the CD-ROM disc in the drive and restarting the computer. The computer will start with the BIOS and you can choose the Install Windows From CD-ROM command if you're using the AlphaBIOS, or the Supplementary Menu command followed by the Install Windows NT From CD-ROM command if you're not using the AlphaBIOS.

Winnt.exe Command Line

The following describes the command line for Winnt.exe:

```
Winnt [/s[:]sourcepath] [/t[:]tempdrive] [/i[:]inffile]
[/u[:scriptfile]] [/r[x]:directory] [/e:command] [/a]
```

/a	Enables accessibility options.
/e	Specifies command to be executed at the end of graphical user interface setup.
/i[:]inffile	Specifies the filename (no path) of the setup information file. The default is Dosnet.inf.
/r[:]directory	Specifies optional directory to be installed.

/rx:*directory*	Specifies optional directory to be copied.
/s[:]*sourcepath*	Specifies the source location of Windows 2000 files. Must be a full path of the form *d:\[path]* or \\server\share[\path] where *d* is the letter of the drive. The default is the current directory.
/t[:]*tempdrive*	Specifies a drive to contain temporary setup files. If not specified, Winnt.exe will attempt to locate a drive for you.
/u[:*scriptfile*]	Unattended operation and optional script file (requires /s).

NOTE: The command line for the Windows 2000 Professional setup program is simpler than for the Windows NT Workstation 4.0 setup program. Several command line options are conspicuously missing, including /b for floppy-less operation and /x to create the setup boot disks. In fact, you now install Windows 2000 Professional directly to the hard disk without using floppy disks at all.

Winnt32.exe Command Line

The following describes the command line for Winnt32.exe:

```
winnt32 [/s:sourcepath] [/tempdrive:drive_letter]
[/unattend[num][:answer_file]] [/copydir:folder_name]
[/copysource:folder_name] [/cmd:command_line]
[/debug[level][:filename]] [/udf:id[,UDF_file]]
[/syspart:drive_letter]
```

/checkupgradeonly	Creates a compatibility report and does not install Windows 2000. The setup program saves the report to a file called Upgrade.txt in Windows 98 or to a file called Winnt32.log in Windows NT Workstation 4.0.
/copydir:*folder_name*	Creates an additional folder within the folder where the Windows 2000 files are installed. For example, if the source folder contains a folder called Private_drivers that has modifications just for your site, you can type */copydir:Private_drivers* to have Winnt32.exe copy that folder to your installed Windows 2000 folder. You can use the /copydir option to create as many additional folders as you like.

/copysource:*folder_name*	Temporarily creates an additional folder within the folder where the Windows 2000 files are installed. For example, if the source folder contains a folder called Private_drivers that has modifications just for your site, you can type */copysource:Private_drivers* to have Winnt32.exe copy that folder to your installed Windows 2000 folder and use its files during the setup process. Unlike the folders created by the /copydir option, folders created using /copysource are deleted after the setup process completes.
/cmd:*command_line*	Instructs Winnt32.exe to carry out a specific command before the final phase of the setup process (that is, after your computer has restarted twice and after Winnt32.exe has collected the necessary configuration information, but before the setup process is complete).
/debug[*level*] [:*filename*]	Creates a debug log at the level specified. The default creates a log file (Winnt32.log) that has the level set to 2 (Warning).
/s:*sourcepath*	Specifies the location of the Windows 2000 files. To simultaneously copy files from multiple servers, specify multiple /s sources.
/syspart:*drive_letter*	Specifies that you can copy startup files to a hard drive, mark the drive as active, and then install the drive in another computer. When you start that computer, Winnt32.exe automatically starts with the next phase. You must always use the /tempdrive parameter with the /syspart parameter.
/tempdrive: *drive_letter*	Directs Winnt32.exe to place temporary files on the specified drive and to install Windows 2000 on that drive.
/unattend	Upgrades your previous version of Windows 2000 in Unattended mode. All user settings are taken from the previous installation, so no user intervention is required during the setup process.
/unattend[*num*]: [*answer_file*]	Performs a fresh install in Unattended mode. The answer file provides your custom specifications to Winnt32.exe. *Num* is the number of seconds between the time that Winnt32.exe finishes copying the files and when it restarts. You can use the *num* option only on a computer running Windows NT. *Answer_file* is the name of the answer file. For more information about answer files, see the Windows 2000 Deployment Guide.

`/udf:id[,UDF_file]`   Indicates an identifier (*id*) that Winnt32.exe uses to specify how a Uniqueness Database File (UDF) works with an answer file (see the /unattend entry). The UDF overrides values in the answer file, and the identifier determines which values in the UDF are used. For example, /udf:RAS_user, Our_company.udf uses the Our_Company.udf file to override settings specified for the identifier RAS_user. If no *UDF_file* is specified, Winnt32.exe prompts the user to insert a disk that contains the $Unique$.udf file.

Upgrading to Windows 2000 Professional

Recall the differences between installing a new operating system and upgrading an existing operating system. Installing Windows 2000 Professional into a folder other than the current operating system's folder is installing a new operating system. This creates a dual-boot configuration that allows the user to choose which operating system to use. Installing Windows 2000 Professional into the existing operating system's folder is upgrading. This replaces the existing operating system with Windows 2000 Professional and migrates as many of the previous operating system's settings as possible.

Most users will upgrade their desktops rather than installing a clean copy of Windows 2000 Professional. They can't afford the down time required to reinstall needed applications and reconfigure their computers. An exception is when users are concerned about whether all their applications will work properly with Windows 2000 Professional. In those cases, they should install the operating system in a new folder, or even on a separate partition, so that they can use either Windows 2000 or the previous operating system. Windows 2000 Professional provides an upgrade path from just about every recent member of the Windows product family as well as from MS-DOS. Upgrades from the following operating systems are supported:

- MS-DOS
- Windows 95 OSR1
- Windows 95 OSR2
- Windows 98
- Windows NT 3.51
- Windows NT 4.0

When you upgrade to Windows 2000 Professional, the setup program migrates as many settings, user preferences, and application installations as possible. It preserves almost all the user's application preferences, for example, and it does so with a large percentage of the user's operating system preferences. Given this fact, the user should make sure that the computer is working properly before trying to upgrade to Windows 2000 Professional. Doing so ensures that settings are properly migrated and the setup process goes as smoothly as possible. For example, getting a networking connection to work properly is much easier to do in Windows 98 than it is during the Windows 2000 Professional setup process.

Describing the exact steps required for upgrading to Windows 2000 Professional is impractical, as the steps are different for various circumstances. The following sections describe many of the different processes and screens that the user might see during the setup process. Most of these screens require responses from the user unless a domain administrator has created an answer file, allowing the user to install Windows 2000 Professional with little interaction. Alternatively, users can use Winnt32's */unattend* command line option, which causes it to copy responses from the current operating system rather than prompt the user for them.

The following steps provide an overview of the setup process used with Winnt32.exe, and the sections that follow this one describe the steps that require user interaction:

1. Start Winnt32.exe, and specify that you want to upgrade to Windows 2000 Professional, as shown earlier in Figure 3-1.

2. Read and accept the license agreement.

3. Specify any upgrade packs required to make your applications work properly with Windows 2000 Professional. See "Provide Upgrade Packs," later in this chapter.

4. Select the partition onto which you want to install Windows 2000 Professional. If installing the operating system onto an existing FAT partition, specify whether you want to convert it to NTFS. See "Upgrading to Windows NT File System (NTFS)," later in this chapter.

5. Review the upgrade report that Winnt32.exe generates. Continue the setup process only if the problems reported won't hamper the user's ability to work. See "Upgrade Report," later in this chapter.

6. Allow Winnt32.exe to copy the files required to install Windows 2000 Professional to the computer. Winnt32.exe restarts the computer a couple of times during this process. After copying the files to the computer, Winnt32.exe converts the partition to NTFS if you chose to do so.

7. Winnt32.exe detects the devices installed on the computer. When upgrading, Winnt32.exe uses the current operating system's configuration for hints regarding the configuration of each device.

8. Join a network domain. First specify whether the computer participates in a network domain, and if so, provide the domain name as well as the credentials required to add the computer to the domain if it's not already present. See "Domain Membership," later in this chapter.

9. Install necessary components such as Start menu items, application upgrades, and system settings. During this phase, Winnt32.exe registers each component, saves the operating system's settings to the registry, and removes the temporary files it created during the setup process.

10. Finish the setup process by logging on to the operating system for the first time. "Logging On for the First Time," later in this chapter, describes what users see the first time they log on to Windows 2000 Professional.

NOTE: When Winnt32.exe finishes, it gives you the opportunity to review any errors it encountered. In most cases, the errors it reports will not prevent the operating system from starting properly. You should make sure you take advantage of this opportunity, however, as this might be the only time the operating system reports these errors.

Provide Upgrade Packs

Upgrade packs contain migration DLLs (dynamic-link libraries) that update an application so that it works properly in Windows 2000 Professional. While you might find some upgrade packs on the final Windows 2000 Professional CD-ROM, you'll probably have to get upgrade packs directly from the software vendors; check the vendors' Web sites for more information.

You specify upgrade packs in Winnt32's Provide Upgrade Packs dialog box shown in Figure 3-2. Select the Yes, I Have Upgrade Packs To Provide option button if you have upgrade packs to install; then click the Add button for each upgrade pack you want to add to the Upgrade Pack List. If you don't have any upgrade packs to provide, select the No, I Don't Have Any Upgrade Packs option button.

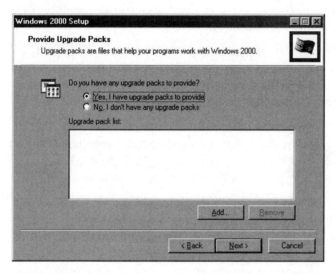

Figure 3-2
Specifying upgrade packs that the setup program will install at the end of the installation process.

Upgrading to Windows NT File System (NTFS)

"Choosing Between NTFS and FAT," earlier in this chapter, helps you choose among the FAT16, FAT32, and NTFS file systems. You should make this decision before starting Winnt32.exe.

The Upgrading To Windows NT File System dialog box allows you to choose the file system you want to use. It allows you to leave a FAT partition alone or convert a FAT partition to NTFS. However, it does not allow you to convert an NTFS partition to FAT. Select the Yes, Upgrade My Drive option button if you want to upgrade a FAT partition to NTFS; otherwise, select the No, Do Not Upgrade My Drive option button.

Upgrade Report

Midway through the setup process, before Winnt32.exe finalizes its settings, it generates an upgrade report, shown in Figure 3-3, that alerts the user to any compatibility problems Winnt32.exe finds. This portion of the setup process can be quite lengthy, so be patient. Winnt32.exe scans every application installed on the computer for known problems, recommending upgrade packs in certain situations. In most cases, you can continue the setup process even though the upgrade report shows a list of errors. These usually relate to using a specific application and you can resolve them after completing the setup process but before using the application. For instance, Winnt32.exe usually reports that the version of MAPI (Messaging Application Programming Interface) installed for the user's e-mail client is incompatible with Windows 2000 Professional. Continuing the setup process is safe, and the user can install the appropriate upgrade pack later.

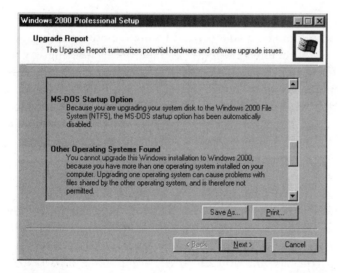

Figure 3-3
The upgrade report alerts the user to any software incompatibilities.

Networking Settings for an Upgrade

If you follow the advice given earlier in this chapter, you will configure your current operating system to connect to your network before you upgrade to Windows 2000 Professional. Doing so makes the setup process go a bit more smoothly.

If you didn't configure the previous operating system to connect to your network prior to starting the setup process, though, you can still connect to the network during the setup process. Winnt32.exe displays the Networking Settings dialog box, which allows you to create a typical network connection or a custom network connection. The typical network connection uses the Client For Microsoft Networks client, the File And Print Sharing For Microsoft Networks service, and the TCP/IP protocol. If your requirements differ, create a custom network connection and add the clients, services, and protocols necessary to connect the operating system to your network.

Creating a network connection during setup is certainly optional. Users can choose to install Windows 2000 Professional without a network connection, and can then add the required network components after the operating system is working properly.

Domain Membership

If you're not upgrading from Windows NT Workstation, and you want to participate in a network domain, you must add your computer to it. For example, Windows 98 does not require a computer account on the domain, so you must create a computer account when you upgrade it to Windows 2000 Professional. "Create a Computer Account on the Server," earlier in this chapter, describes the situations that require a computer account and whether these accounts should be created before the setup process or during it. If domain administrators want to remain in control of the names assigned to individual computers, they should create the computer accounts before the users upgrade; otherwise, they can allow the users to create computer accounts as they install the operating system.

Toward the end of the setup process, the setup program displays the Domain Membership dialog box. Select the No, This Computer Is Not On A Network, Or Is On A Network Without A Domain option button if the computer will not participate in a domain. If the computer will participate in a workgroup, type the workgroup's name in the Workgroup Name text box. Select the Yes, Make This Computer A Member Of The Following Domain option button if the computer will be a member of a domain. Type the name of the domain in the Computer Domain text box. If the setup program doesn't find an existing computer account for the computer, it displays the Join Computer To *Name* Domain dialog box. You must provide the credentials of a user with domain administrator permissions to create a computer account on the domain. If a domain administrator is installing Windows 2000 Professional, this is easy enough. But if individual users are installing the operating system, you don't want them to have domain administrator credentials. The solution is to create and distribute a temporary set of administrator credentials with just enough permission to add computers to the domain; then, when the deployment process is complete, remove the temporary administrator credentials.

Clean Install of Windows 2000 Professional

A *clean install* is when the user installs Windows 2000 Professional in a folder or a partition other than that of the current operating system. This allows the user to create a dual-boot combination with Windows 2000 Professional and the previous operating system. Notice that when performing a clean install, the setup program redetects each device on the computer and does not migrate any settings from the previous operating system. In addition, users must reinstall each application in Windows 2000 Professional.

Choosing an Upgrade or a Clean Install

Upgrading to Windows 2000 Professional has numerous benefits over a clean install. The upgrade process migrates many of the user's application and operating system settings. It migrates most of the computer's device configurations. Users can still use their favorite applications without having to reinstall them in Windows 2000 Professional. The only drawback to upgrading is that users can't create a dual-boot combination with the previous operating system, which is desirable if compatibility is at all a concern.

A clean install doesn't migrate the user's settings. The setup program initializes the operating system and redetects the computer's devices. The worst part about a clean install is that users have to reinstall any applications they want to use in the new operating system, since the previous operating system's settings are not migrated into Windows 2000 Professional. So why in the world would users want to do a clean install? Either to create a dual-boot combination with the previous operating system, ensuring that must-have applications are always available, or to get a fresh start, recovering mounds of wasted disk space.

All told, upgrading to Windows 2000 Professional is the least disruptive choice. In most cases, users are back to work in little over an hour. A clean install requires users to reinstall their applications and invites them to spend countless hours customizing their configurations so that they can pick up where they left off. A clean install is the only choice, however, if users want to keep the previous operating system around—just in case.

You can use Winnt.exe or Winnt32.exe to perform a clean install of Windows 2000 Professional. During the first half of the 16-bit (Winnt.exe) setup program's process, during which it copies files to the computer, you'll see MS-DOS–based character-oriented screens. The second half of the process, during which you configure the operating system, has a graphical user interface and occurs after Winnt.exe installs the operating system on the computer. The 32-bit (Winnt32.exe) setup program is predominantly graphical but has a brief interlude during which you see MS-DOS–based character-oriented screens.

The following sections describe many of the different processes, screens, and dialog boxes that the user might see during the setup process. Most of these screens and dialog boxes require responses from the user unless a domain administrator has created an answer file, allowing the user to install Windows 2000 Professional with little interaction. The clean install goes something like this:

1. Start the setup program—Winnt.exe from MS-DOS or Winnt32.exe from Windows 95, Windows 98, or Windows NT Workstation 4.0— and then, if running Winn32.exe, specify that you want to cleanly install Windows 2000 Professional.

2. Read and accept the license agreement.

3. If you're running Winnt32.exe, select any special options you want to use in the Select Special Options dialog box. See "Select Special Options," later in this chapter.

4. Select the partition onto which you want to install Windows 2000 Professional. If installing the operating system onto an existing FAT partition, specify whether you want to convert it to NTFS. See "Choosing the System Partition," later in this chapter.

5. Allow Winnt32.exe to copy the files required to install Windows 2000 Professional to the computer. The setup program restarts the computer a couple of times during this process. After copying the files to the computer, the setup program converts the system partition to NTFS if you chose to do so earlier in the setup process.

6. The setup program detects the devices installed on the computer.

7. Provide a name for the computer as well as a local administrator password. See "Computer Name and Administrator Password," later in this chapter.

8. Configure the computer's network connection. You can choose a typical connection, consisting of the components required to connect to a Microsoft network, or you can choose to create a custom

connection that's based on the typical connection. See "Networking Settings for an Upgrade," earlier in this chapter.

9. Join a domain. First specify whether the computer participates in a domain, and if so, provide the domain name as well as the credentials required to add the computer to the domain if it's not already present. See "Domain Membership," earlier in this chapter.

10. Install necessary components such as Start menu items, application upgrades, and system settings. During this phase, the setup program registers each component, saves the operating system's settings to the registry, and removes the temporary files it created during the process.

11. Finish the setup process by logging on to the operating system for the first time. As part of the first logon process, the operating system starts the Network Access Wizard to help create a user account. "Network Access Wizard," later in this chapter, describes this wizard. "Logging On for the First Time" describes what users see after completing the Network Access Wizard.

NOTE: When installing Windows 2000 Professional from MS-DOS, you might see a message that says, "Program is too large to fit into memory." Alternatively, the system might lock when you see "Building list of files to copy" on the screen. This indicates that the setup program doesn't have enough conventional memory—memory below 640 kilobytes (KB)—to operate properly. The solution is to make more conventional memory available by loading devices and drivers in upper memory. You can also load the setup program into upper memory by using the LOADHIGH command, as in the following command line: *lh winnt.exe*

Select Special Options

The setup program's Select Special Options dialog box allows you to perform three advanced tasks early in the installation. You only see this dialog box when using Winnt32.exe. Winnt.exe does allow you to change the installation path, but it doesn't allow you to change accessibility or language options.

Click the Language Options button to display the Language Options dialog box, which allows you to choose the primary language as well as any additional character sets you want to install. You can choose among Arabic, Armenian, Baltic, Central European, Cyrillic, Georgian, Greek, Hebrew, Indic, Japanese, Korean, Simplified Chinese, Thai, Traditional Chinese, Turkic, Vietnamese, and Western Europe and United States.

Click the Advanced Options button to display the Advanced Settings dialog box, shown in Figure 3-4, which allows you to specify the location of Windows 2000's source files—the default is the i386 folder on the CD-ROM—and the installation folder. If you specify the same folder as the existing operating system, the setup program upgrades it. If you specify a separate folder, the setup program creates a dual-boot configuration. If you check the Choose Installation Partition check box, the setup program allows you to choose a partition other than the system partition in which to install the operating system. If you check the Copy Files From CD-ROM To Hard Drive check box, the setup program copies installation files to the hard disk so that you no longer have to have the CD-ROM in the drive in order to install the operating system.

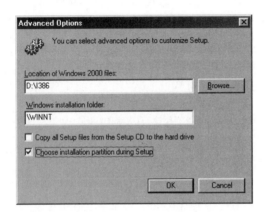

Figure 3-4
Check the Choose Installation Partition check box if you want the opportunity to install Windows 2000 Professional on a partition other than the default.

Click the Accessibility Options button to display the Accessibility Options dialog box, which allows you to specify whether you want to use the Microsoft Magnifier or the Microsoft Screen Reader during the setup process. The Microsoft Magnifier makes reading onscreen text easier by enlarging it in a separate window. The Microsoft Screen Reader reads the contents of the screen to the user, which is particularly useful for users who have impaired vision.

> T I P : If you're concerned about users who require the accessibility options in order to use the setup program, but can't get far enough in the process to enable those options in the Select Special Options dialog box, provide them with a batch file that launches the setup program using the /a command line option. This command line option only works with Winnt.exe, not Winnt32.exe.

Choosing the System Partition

Both Winnt.exe and Winnt32.exe restart the computer to finish copying files to the hard disk. Part of this process is to determine where to install Windows 2000 Professional. If you're installing the operating system on an existing FAT partition, you can leave the FAT file system alone or convert it to NTFS. If you're creating a new partition for the operating system, you can choose whether to format it with the FAT file system or with NTFS. Immediately after you accept the licensing agreement, the setup program displays a list of existing partitions and unused space. You can select any of the following options in this list:

To Accomplish This	Do This
Install Windows 2000 Professional on an existing partition	Select a partition shown in the list, and press Enter.
Create a new partition on which to install Windows 2000 Professional	Press C, and then follow the instructions you see on the screen.
Delete an existing partition	Select a partition shown in the list, press D, and follow the instructions you see on the screen.

After you choose the partition on which to install Windows 2000 Professional, the setup program allows you to choose how to format the partition. If you're installing the operating system on an existing FAT partition, and you want to convert that partition to NTFS, select Convert The Partition To NTFS and press Enter. On the following screen, press C to confirm that you want to convert the partition to NTFS, or press Esc to cancel and select a different partition.

Computer Name and Administrator Password

Windows 2000 Professional requires a computer name and a local administrator password. This administrator password is for the local administrator account. If you're replacing Windows NT Workstation 4.0 with a clean install of Windows 2000 Professional, you can reuse Windows NT Workstation 4.0's computer account. Whether or not you are reusing an existing account, you provide the name of the computer in the Computer Name And Administrator Password dialog box. Type the computer's name in the Computer Name text box (the setup program recommends a name); then type the local administrator password in the Administrator Password text box and confirm it in the Confirm Password text box.

Local and Global User Accounts

Windows 2000 Professional authenticates local accounts, while a Windows 2000 domain authenticates global accounts. You know which type of account you're using by checking the Log On To list in the Log On To Windows dialog box when you log on to the operating system. You choose to log on to the domain by choosing the domain's name from the list. Alternatively, you can choose to log on to the local computer by choosing the computer's name from the list. If the computer is a member of a domain, logging on to the domain is better than logging on to the local computer. Note also that, if you have a domain user account, you can go to any computer that's a member of the domain and log on to it.

The group to which a user account belongs determines what the user can do. For example, a user account that belongs to the local computer's Administrators group gives the user complete control over the computer, while a user account that belongs to the local computer's Users group provides basic rights to use the computer but no rights to administer it. Windows 2000 Professional defines several groups, including Administrators, Backup Operators, Guests, Power Users, and Users. A similar collection of groups (global groups) exists at the domain level. Windows 2000 Professional defines local groups, and the domain controller defines global groups.

When you install Windows 2000 Professional, it creates three different local user accounts: Administrator, Guest, and an account for the user. The Administrator account has complete control over the computer, allowing the administrator to install hardware and software. The Guest account can do very little on the computer. During the setup process, you tell Windows 2000 Professional to which group the initial local user belongs. By default, it adds the initial local user to the Power Users group, giving that user a moderate amount of control over the computer, but you can change the initial local user's group membership during the setup process or at any later time. Note that by not assigning the initial local user to the Administrators group, you protect the computer from viruses that require administrative access to the computer to do their harm and from user errors that occur when users have too much power and not enough knowledge.

Networking Settings for a Client Install

You configure the computer's network connection with the setup program's Networking Settings dialog box. This dialog box has two option buttons: Typical Settings and Custom Settings. The first creates a typical network connection without requiring much interaction. This type of connection uses the Client For Microsoft Networks client, the File And Print Sharing For Microsoft Networks service, and the TCP/IP protocol with automatic IP addressing.

The second option button, Custom Settings, allows the user to create a custom network connection. This option begins with the typical network connection, described in the previous paragraph, allowing users to customize their connections easily during setup rather than after the setup process is complete. For example, if the network still uses WINS for name resolution, the user can alter the computer's configuration to include the WINS server's IP address. After you select the Custom Settings option button and click the Next button, the setup program displays the Networking Components dialog box, which allows you to do the following:

To Accomplish This	Do This
Add a component to the networking configuration	Click the Install button. Then, in the Select Network Component Type dialog box, select the type of component to install, click the Add button, and follow the instructions on the screen.
Remove a component from the networking configuration	Select the component in the list, and then click the Uninstall button. Confirm that you want to remove the component by clicking the Yes button in the Uninstall dialog box.
Change a component's properties	Click the component in the list, and then click the Properties button. Edit the component's properties, and then click the OK button to save your changes.

The setup program automatically recognizes and configures most popular network adapters during installation. However, you might have to manually install some Peripheral Component Interconnect (PCI), PC Card, and Industry Standard Architecture (ISA) Plug and Play adapters after the setup program is finished. Also, some network adapters will no longer work after upgrading to

Windows 2000 Professional from Windows NT Workstation 4.0. This is primarily because of changes in the registry, including driver name changes and service dependency changes, or because of obsolete network drivers. In those cases, consult the driver vendors for updated drivers.

After configuring the computer's network connection, the setup program displays the Domain Membership dialog box. This is the same dialog box you learned about earlier in "Domain Membership." You can choose to participate in a workgroup, a domain, or none of the above. If you choose to add the computer to a domain, either a computer account must already exist, or the user must be able to provide credentials with enough permission to add a computer account to the domain.

Network Access Wizard

At the end of the setup process, before the user logs on to Windows 2000 Professional for the first time, the operating system starts the Network Access Wizard to help the user or the domain administrator create a user account. The idea here is that, for everyday use, the user will log on to the computer with an account other than the local administrator account. The Network Access Wizard's Set Permissions dialog box collects the user's new username and the domain to which the user belongs. In this dialog box, the user (acting as administrator on the local computer) or a domain administrator can specify the type of access that will be granted: standard, restricted, or custom.

To Accomplish This	Do This
Specify that the new user is a power user who can change computer settings and install programs	Select the Standard Access (Power Users Group) option button.
Specify that the user has restricted access to the computer	Select the Restricted Access (Users Group) option button.
Specify that the user is a member of a different group	Click the Custom button, and choose a group from the list.

Logging On for the First Time

After completing the installation process, the setup program displays the Welcome To Windows dialog box. Press Ctrl-Alt-Delete to display the Log On To Windows dialog box. Note that the reason users must press Ctrl-Alt-Delete before logging on to the operating system is to prevent Trojan horses from stealing passwords. In the Log On To Windows dialog box, type your username in the Username text box and your password in the Password text box. Click the OK button, and the operating system will verify your credentials with the network domain if logging on to the domain, or with the local computer's security database if logging on locally.

Windows 2000 Professional displays the Welcome To Windows 2000 window after you start the computer for the first time. The operating system will continue to display this window each time you log on to the computer unless you clear the Show This Screen At Startup check box before closing the window. Other actions you can perform from the Welcome to Windows 2000 window include the following:

To Accomplish This	Do This
Take a tour of Windows 2000 Professional's new features	Click the Discover Windows button.
Connect Windows 2000 Professional to the Internet	Click the Connect To The Internet button.
Schedule jobs in the Task Scheduler to keep the computer running at its best automatically	Click the Maintain Your Computer button.

P A R T   I I

EASIER TO USE

CHAPTER FOUR

Simpler User Interface

Microsoft Windows 2000 Professional's user interface enhancements are not the operating system's most impressive new features. Features such as the advanced mobile support have that honor. Still, the user interface enhancements are what most users will notice first. Since these are the most visible changes to the operating system, and since they make the best fodder for artwork, the user interface enhancements are what you'll read about most in some of the trade magazines as well. That said, you'll find plenty of artwork in this chapter that illustrates the following enhancements:

- Windows 2000 Professional lets users personalize elements on the desktop, including Windows Explorer toolbars, taskbars, and the Start menu.

- Windows 2000 Professional provides quicker access to files and folders by implementing features such as a new Open With menu, improved Open and Save As dialog boxes, pervasive use of Most Frequently Used lists, and AutoComplete.

- Windows 2000 Professional makes locating files and folders easier with the new My Network Places, My Documents, and My Pictures folders as well as vastly improved integrated searching.

- Windows 2000 Professional is more friendly toward users because it provides better error messages and improved online help. The result is users who are more self-sufficient and who call the help desk less frequently.

This chapter describes all of these new features. One caveat, though: some of the new features have already been introduced via Microsoft's Internet Explorer—Active Desktop and Web integration are examples—so I don't cover them in much detail here, reserving most of this chapter's space for newer features. In fact Internet Explorer 5 is fully integrated into Windows 2000 Professional and provides rich integration between the Web and the desktop.

A More Personal Desktop

Windows 2000 Professional refines the concept of an operating system that adapts to how users accomplish tasks on their computers. For example, the operating system continuously monitors how users launch programs, and then it makes adjustments that make launching those programs quicker. It does the same for the files and folders users access most, as well as the commands they execute in Windows Explorer.

Controlling the User Interface

Chapter 19, "Better Management Tools," describes how to use the Microsoft Management Console (MMC) program along with management snap-ins to edit *policies*. Policies allow network administrators to control the user's desktop to a very large degree. Network administrators can implement rather draconian policies that restrict users who are focused on a single task or who need to be prevented from tampering with configurations. Administrators can implement more lenient policies for users who require more freedom to configure their computers.

For example, just about every facet of the Start menu is under administrative control. Network administrators can remove almost any submenu from the Start menu and prevent users from using Drag And Drop to customize the menu. The desktop is equally under administrative control. Administrators can remove various icons from the desktop and prevent changes to it—or disable the Active Desktop altogether.

One of the user interface elements given the most administrative control is Windows Explorer. Network administrators can force users to use the classic shell. Administrators can remove the File menu. They can disable pop-up menus. They can specify the location of each shell folder. They can control what features are available in the common Open and Save As dialog boxes. They can configure offline access to files and folders. The list goes on and on.

If this type of control interests you, as an administrator, take a look at Chapter 19. It provides an overview of MMC.

The remainder of this section describes the new features in Windows 2000 Professional that automatically personalize the operating system and those that allow users to further personalize it. And don't forget the features that Windows 2000 Professional inherits because of the full integration of Internet Explorer, such as the following:

■ **Customizable Start menu** Microsoft Internet Explorer added Web features to the Start menu. For example, users can choose an Internet link from the Favorites submenu. Users can also drag items on the Start menu to change their order, or right-click an item to display its pop-up menu.

■ **Extensible taskbar** Internet Explorer adds the Quick Launch bar to the taskbar, making frequently used programs readily available. Other toolbars, such as the Address, Links, and Desktop bars, have also been added. Not only that, but users can create new toolbars based on the content of any folder.

■ **Web-enabled Windows Explorer** Internet Explorer adds features to Windows Explorer that enable it to work more like a Web browser. The new single-click interface makes launching documents more intuitive—though some argue differently—and users can view folders as they would view Web pages. Windows Explorer even allows users to customize the HTML (Hypertext Markup Language) that it uses to display a folder.

■ **Explorer bars** The most lauded improvement in Windows Explorer is the addition of *Explorer bars*. This nifty feature allows users to split Windows Explorer into two panes. The right pane contains a view of the current folder's contents. The left pane varies depending on which Explorer bar the user opens: Search, Favorites, History, or Folders. In Windows 2000 Professional, the Channels Explorer bar is integrated into Favorites rather than being displayed separately.

■ **Active Desktop** Active Desktop brings Web content to the user's desktop. Content is easy to add and, thanks to subscriptions, the operating system automatically updates that content on a regular schedule. Users can quickly toggle between Active Desktop and the classic desktop.

Personalized Start Menu

Windows 2000 Professional inherits several features because of the full integration of Internet Explorer 5, including enhancements to the Start menu. Those enhancements include the ability to sort the menu by dragging items, the ability to drag items from one submenu to another, and the ability to open an item's pop-up menu by right-clicking it.

Windows 2000 Professional expands on these capabilities, though, by making them a bit more intuitive and thus a bit easier to use. For instance, in previous versions of Windows, dragging items on the Start menu was not intuitive because the only thing users saw was an insertion point—nothing more than a horizontal line across the menu—as they moved the mouse pointer around looking for a place to drop the item. In Windows 2000 Professional, users actually drag the item's name around until they find a place to drop it. Moving an item is as simple as dragging its name from one submenu to another, pointing at each submenu along the way in order to open it.

Another big improvement, demonstrated in Figure 4-1, reduces screen clutter by continuously monitoring the items that users choose from the Start menu. It shows those items that they use frequently while hiding those that they use less frequently. However, users can quickly display hidden items by clicking the arrow at the bottom of the menu. Just in case this feature dazes some users, causing them to wonder where all the items went, Windows 2000 Professional displays a hint in a ScreenTip that tells them how to display the hidden items. This hint continues to appear until a user clicks the arrow the first time, demonstrating an understanding of the process. Later we'll describe how users can turn off this feature altogether if desired.

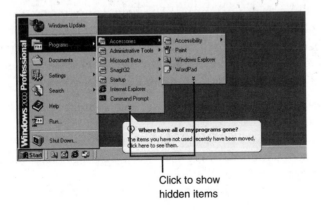

Click to show
hidden items

Figure 4-1
The Start menu with some items hidden.

Some of you may remember Tweak UI (an optional control panel tool for Windows 95). One of its best features was the ability to add the Control Panel folder or the Printers folder to the Start menu as a submenu. Users no longer need Tweak UI to do this. They can use the Start Menu Options tab in the Taskbar Properties dialog box to specify which folders Windows 2000 Professional adds to the Start menu. To add or remove submenus from the Start menu, right-click the taskbar and choose the Properties command to display the Taskbar Properties dialog box. Click the Start Menu Options tab, which you see in Figure 4-2 on the following page, and then check each of the following items that you want to enable:

- **Display Administrative Tools**   Checking this box adds the Administrative Tools submenu to the Programs submenu. This box is cleared by default. The Administrative Tools submenu includes the following items: Component Services, Computer Management, Data Sources, Event Viewer, and Performance.

- **Display Favorites**   Checking this box adds the Favorites submenu to the Start menu. This is the same menu that users see in Internet Explorer, and it contains the Internet links that have been stored in the Favorites folder as part of the user's profile.

- **Display Logoff**   Checking this box adds Log Off *Name* to the bottom of the Start menu, providing a quick method for logging off the computer. Users normally log off by pressing Ctrl-Alt-Delete to display the Microsoft Windows NT Security dialog box, and then clicking the Log Off button.

- **Expand Control Panel**   On the Start menu, users choose Settings, and then Control Panel to open a submenu that displays each Control Panel icon. Some of the icons lead to additional submenus. For instance, the Printers icon leads to a submenu that lists each printer installed on the computer. Users can double-click the Control Panel command to open the Control Panel folder in Windows Explorer.

- **Expand My Documents**   Users choose Documents from the Start menu to open a submenu displaying the most recently used documents. With the Expand My Documents box checked, users can choose My Documents at the top of the Documents submenu to open another submenu that displays all files and folders located in the user's My Documents folder. Each folder leads to an additional submenu so users can open any file in the My Documents folder from the Documents submenu.

- **Expand Network And Dial-Up Connections** On the Start menu, users choose Settings, and then Network And Dial-Up Connections to open a submenu that displays each network connection as well as the Make New Connection command and the Open Folder command. Users double-click Network And Dial-Up Connections to open the Network And Dial-Up Connections folder in Windows Explorer.

- **Expand Printers** On the Start menu, users choose Settings, and then Printers to open a submenu that displays each printer installed on the computer, as well as the Add Printer command and the Open Folder command. Users double-click Printers to open the Printers folder in Windows Explorer.

- **Scroll the Programs menu** Checking this box allows Windows 2000 Professional to scroll the Program menu's submenus if they don't fit in a single column on the screen. This is in lieu of truncating the submenu or attempting to display the submenu using multiple columns.

- **Use Personalized Menus** Checking this box enables the personalized menus, with hidden items, that you read about earlier in this section. With this check box cleared, Windows 2000 Professional will never hide items on the Start menu.

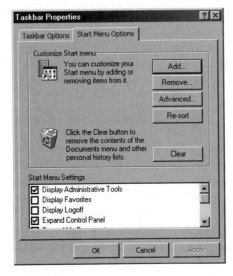

Figure 4-2
The Start Menu Options tab of the Taskbar Properties dialog box.

Customizable Toolbars

Whether browsing the hard disk, the local area network, the intranet, or the Internet, Windows 2000 Professional allows users to remain in a single window and easily customize their toolbars. By doing so, users can get tasks done quicker since they're likely to become more familiar with an environment that they customized themselves.

Right-click anywhere in a toolbar, and choose Customize to display the Customize Toolbar dialog box shown in Figure 4-3 on the following page. This dialog box is familiar to many users, as other Microsoft products use a similar one for performing the same task. Users can add any button in the Available Toolbar Buttons list or remove any of the current toolbar buttons. In addition, users can choose whether the toolbar buttons are small or large and whether all, some, or none of the buttons show text labels. The following table describes the variety of tasks that users can perform in the Customize Toolbar dialog box:

To Accomplish This	Do This
Add a button to the toolbar	In the Available Toolbar Buttons list, select a button; then click the Add button
Remove a button from the toolbar	In the Current Toolbar Buttons list, select a button; then click the Remove button
Move a button on the toolbar	In the Current Toolbar Buttons list, select a button; then do one of the following:
	Click the Move Up button to move the button up in the list, which is the same as moving the button left on the toolbar
	Click the Move Down button to move the button down in the list, which is the same as moving the button right on the toolbar
Select text options for a toolbar	In the Text Options list, select one of the following:
	Show text labels
	Selective text on right
	No text labels
Configure the size of the buttons on the toolbar	In the Icon Options list, select one of the following:
	Small icons
	Large icons

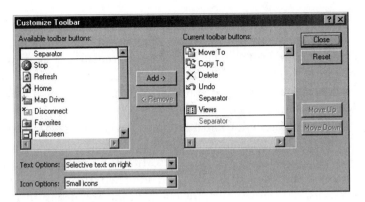

Figure 4-3
The Customize Toolbar dialog box.

Quick Launch Bars

Toolbars on the taskbar are not unique to Windows 2000 Professional. Internet Explorer 4 added them to Windows 95, Windows 98, and Windows NT Workstation 4.0. Since most folks never discovered these toolbars, and since they are becoming truly discoverable for the first time in Windows 2000 Professional, I'll cover them here so that you don't miss a beat.

Figure 4-4 shows a sample of each type of toolbar that users can add to Windows 2000 Professional's taskbar. To display a toolbar on the taskbar, right-click the taskbar and choose Toolbars; then choose one of the following:

- **Address** is the same Address bar that users see in Internet Explorer.

- **Links** is the same Links bar that users see in Internet Explorer.

- **Desktop** is a toolbar that contains a button for each item on the user's desktop. It provides quick access to the desktop when multiple open windows obscure the desktop from view.

- **Quick Launch** is a toolbar that provides buttons for the most commonly used programs in Windows 2000 Professional. This toolbar is enabled by default.

Users can create their own toolbars as well. Windows 2000 Professional gets the content of each toolbar from a folder. The operating system displays each item it finds in the folder as a button on the toolbar. Users can create toolbars that resemble the Start menu, for example, providing extremely fast access to their programs. Figure 4-4 shows an example of a custom toolbar, which contains the contents of the Start menu's Programs folder. To create a custom toolbar, users right-click the taskbar, choose Toolbars followed by New Toolbar, and then locate a folder from the list.

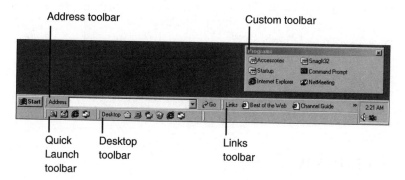

Figure 4-4
Toolbars on the Windows 2000 Professional taskbar.

Once one or more toolbars are on the taskbar, users can customize them in different ways. They can control whether they see a toolbar's title, for instance. They can choose between large and small buttons. They can also choose to display a toolbar in its own window on the desktop (*undocked*) rather than on the taskbar (*docked*), freeing up precious real estate on the taskbar. Working with an undocked toolbar is just like working with any other window—and that includes resizing and moving the window around on the desktop. One note about dragging and resizing toolbars, though: users must drag the toolbar's handle, which is the vertical line on the left side of a docked toolbar or the horizontal line on the top of an undocked toolbar. The following table describes a variety of common tasks that users might perform on a toolbar:

To Accomplish This	Do This
Toggle a toolbar's title on or off	Right-click the toolbar and choose Show Title
Toggle between large and small buttons	Right-click the toolbar, choose View, and then do one of the following:
	Choose Large to display large buttons
	Choose Small to display small buttons

(continued)

continued

To Accomplish This	Do This
Undock a toolbar	Drag the toolbar's handle onto the desktop
Dock an undocked toolbar	Drag the toolbar's title bar to the taskbar
Stack two or more toolbars in a single undocked window	Drag the first toolbar onto the desktop, then drag each additional toolbar from the taskbar to the first toolbar's window

Quicker Access to Files

Windows 2000 Professional combines a handful of new features to make accessing files quicker. The following sections describe these new features:

- "Open With Menu" describes the new Open With menu, which makes opening a file of unknown type easier.

- "Open and Save As Dialog Boxes" describes improvements to these common dialog boxes that help the user find the correct folder in which to locate or save a file.

- "Most Frequently Used Lists" describes the pervasive use of Most Frequently Used lists, which make opening a previously used file much quicker.

- "AutoComplete" describes the feature that automatically completes words as the user types them, resulting in fewer errors when locating a file.

Open With Menu

This feature doesn't introduce new functionality to Windows 2000 Professional, but it does make pre-existing functionality easier to use. In previous versions of Windows, users held down the Shift key as they right-clicked a file icon; then they chose Open With from the pop-up menu to display the Open With dialog box, which allowed them to choose the program in which to open the file. This was not an intuitive solution to the problem of opening unknown file types. It also did not provide a convenient way for a user to edit a file with a variety of programs. Windows 2000 Professional has a solution. The new Open With menu is always available when users right-click a file icon. They choose Open

With from the pop-up menu, and then they see a submenu that looks similar to Figure 4-5. They can then choose one of the applications that are known to open that type of file, or they can choose Any Program to display the traditional Open With dialog box. This dialog box displays each application's icon and friendly name. Users can choose an unregistered program by clicking the Other button. If the user selects Always Use This Program To Open These Files, Windows 2000 Professional makes that program the default program for opening that file and other files of the same type.

Figure 4-5
The new Open With menu.

The next time users activate the Open With pop-up menu, they see all the programs they have chosen in the Open With dialog box. This frees them from having to repeat those tedious steps every time they want to change the program used to open a file. This feature allows users to choose different programs with which to edit a file without requiring complex customizations that involve Windows Explorer's Folder Options dialog box or—gasp—the registry.

T I P : In Windows 2000 Professional, users can easily change the default program used to open a file. In earlier versions of Windows, this change required users to use the File Types tab of the Folder Options dialog box. Now users simply choose Properties from the file's pop-up menu, and then click Change.

Open and Save As Dialog Boxes

You have to see the new Open and Save As dialog boxes to appreciate them; thus, take a look at the Save As dialog box shown in Figure 4-6 on the following page. It is easier to use and it provides new options for locating those folders that tend to elude the user. The icons along the left of the dialog box are the most noticeable changes. As with the Outlook Bar in Microsoft Outlook, users click an icon to quickly open the folder associated with it. Microsoft anticipates that users will find most of their documents in a handful of standard places, each of which is represented by one of the following icons:

- History
- Desktop
- My Documents
- My Computer
- My Network Places

Figure 4-6
The new Save As dialog box.

Most Frequently Used Lists

Virtually any dialog box that prompts users for a filename keeps a list of their most recently used files. This means that, rather than typing a filename repeatedly, users can simply pick a frequently used filename from a list. Take another look at Figure 4-6 and notice that File Name is a drop-down list. Users click the arrow to open the Most Frequently Used list. Windows 2000 Professional constrains this list to those files that match the file type selected in the Save As Type or Files Of Type list; thus, users see different lists depending on the file type they select. The operating system continually updates the Most Frequently Used lists. Examples of locations where the user sees the Most Frequently Used lists include the New, Open, Save As, Find Files, and Map Network Drive dialog boxes.

AutoComplete

AutoComplete—it's such a small feature requiring so little space to discuss, but it makes locating files much quicker and it increases the user's accuracy. Here's how it works: as the user types a filename, Windows 2000 Professional displays a list of suggestions immediately below the text box. The user can continue typing the filename, or the user can pick a matching filename from the list of suggestions. The closest thing to compare this feature to would be an incremental search. And users familiar with Microsoft Excel or Microsoft Word have grown to love AutoComplete, as it's been around in those products for some time. AutoComplete is pervasive, appearing throughout the collection of dialog boxes that request a filename, including the Open, Save As, and Run dialog boxes.

The AutoComplete feature is also implemented as part of the integration of Internet Explorer 5 into Windows 2000 Professional. It remembers text that users type in each of a form's text boxes. To learn more about the AutoComplete feature in Internet Explorer 5, see Chapter 16, "Integrated Web and Desktop."

Easier-to-Find Files and Folders

The features that the previous sections describe help make accessing files quicker. They do so by anticipating what the user needs or by learning about the files the user accesses, and then offering suggestions from which the user can choose. In short, these features free the user from having to type a filename repeatedly.

The features that this section describes take a different approach. They help users organize their files better. They also provide advanced capabilities for searching the computer for files using a variety of criteria. You'll learn about these features in the following sections:

- "My Network Places" describes the new My Network Places folder, which replaces the Network Neighborhood folder.

- "My Documents and My Pictures" describes how Windows 2000 Professional implements the traditional My Documents folder and introduces the new My Pictures folder.

- "Integrated Searching" describes Windows 2000 Professional's new search capabilities, which make locating a file simple.

My Network Places

The My Network Places folder, which you see in Figure 4-7, replaces the Network Neighborhood folder. The new name is consistent with the names of other folders, such as My Documents and My Pictures, and the My Network Places folder is more powerful than its predecessor.

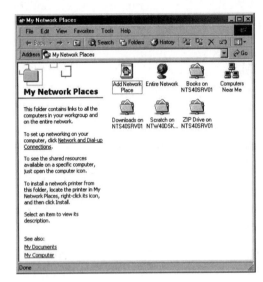

Figure 4-7
The My Network Places folder.

The My Network Places folder provides alternative views of the network. For example, users can choose to view recently visited places. When used in combination with Windows 2000 Server, the Active Directory on the server offers additional functionality, such as allowing users to locate and view other computers near their own computer. For more information about using Active Directory on Windows 2000 Server, read *Introducing Microsoft Windows 2000 Server*, Microsoft Press, 1999.

The My Network Places folder uses the traditional hierarchy formerly seen in the Network Neighborhood folder. One of the items listed in the My Network Places folder is Entire Network. The Entire Network folder contains a list of all of the network clients, and each network client contains a list of all of the domains and workgroups on that network. Each domain or workgroup contains a list of participating computers, and each computer contains a list of resources shared by that computer.

This organization might seem to make accessing network resources a bit tedious, since users have to click the mouse no less than four times in order to view a computer's resources. Windows 2000 Professional makes accessing network resources quicker by allowing the user to create shortcuts and put them in the top level of the My Network Places folder. Microsoft calls these shortcuts *network places.* Think of these as the user's favorite network connections, much like Internet Explorer's Favorites menu contains the user's favorite Internet links. The easiest way to add a shortcut to the My Network Places folder is to right-click a server icon, and then choose Create Shortcut from the pop-up menu. Users can also create shortcuts to computers using the Add Network Place Wizard, represented by the first icon in the My Network Places folder. Note that users can create shortcuts to an unlimited number of servers, and they can rename any connection in the My Network Places folder.

> **NOTE:** Network administrators can use policies to automatically put network connections in each user's My Network Places folder.

My Documents and My Pictures

Windows 2000 Professional supports the pervasive use of the My Documents folder. It makes this folder the default location for saving documents, providing users with a consistent place to store all of their work. Most programs that use the common Open and Save As dialog boxes will automatically take advantage of the My Documents folder. Some programs—particularly older programs that don't rely on these common dialog boxes—won't.

Windows Explorer displays the My Documents icon at the top of its hierarchy, immediately beneath the Desktop icon. However, this is a shortcut for the actual My Documents folder. The actual folder is in the user's profile in the folder Documents And Settings*username*\\My Documents. You can right-click the My Documents shortcut icon and choose Properties from the pop-up menu to change the actual location of the folder. (See Figure 4-8 on the following page.)

> **NOTE:** Network administrators can use policies to specify the target folder of the My Documents shortcut icon. They can locate the My Documents folder anywhere on the user's computer or even on the network. And with the Microsoft Distributed File System (Dfs), this redirection is transparent to the user, even if the administrator chooses to scatter the user's documents across different file systems or if the target location of the folder changes. In addition, administrators can cause Windows 2000 Professional to mirror the user's documents in real time, which means that the operating system keeps a local copy and a server copy of each document. If the server goes down, the user's documents are still available—the operating system updates the server copies as soon as the network becomes available. For more information about this feature, see the discussion of IntelliMirror

in Chapter 20, "Lower Total Cost of Ownership with Microsoft Windows 2000 Server."

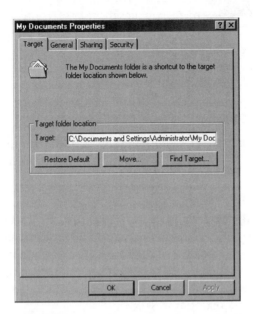

Figure 4-8
Changing the location of the My Documents folder.

The My Documents folder provides a consistent spot for storing documents, but it's not nearly as exciting as the My Pictures folder. The My Pictures folder does the same thing for images as the My Documents folder does for documents—it provides a consistent storage location. This folder is the default location for storing images from digital cameras, scanners, and other digital imaging devices, and it has unique features that make it ideal for images. Most notably, it allows users to preview images in Windows Explorer. It also allows the user to view thumbnails or full screen previews; to zoom in and out; to pan left, right, up, and down; or to print an image—all without ever opening a file in an image editor.

Figure 4-9 shows the My Pictures folder in Windows Explorer. The right pane contains a file list, which users can view in a number of different formats, including large icons or thumbnails. The left side of the right pane is the preview area, the bottom of which shows a preview of the selected image. The buttons along the top of the preview area allow the user to zoom, pan, view full screen, and print the image. As usual, double-clicking an image file opens it in the program associated with it.

Image information

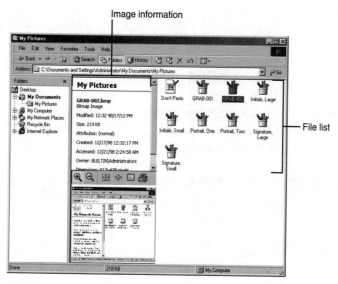

File list

Figure 4-9
The new My Pictures folder.

Integrated Searching

The Search tool is now integrated into Windows Explorer. It's actually an Explorer bar that users can open anytime by clicking the Search button on Windows Explorer's toolbar or by right-clicking My Computer and then choosing Search from the pop-up menu. Alternatively, users can choose Search from the Start menu, and then choose the type of search they want to perform: For Files Or Folders, On The Internet, or For People.

Figure 4-10 on the following page shows the newly integrated search feature in Windows Explorer. Since this is an Explorer bar, it temporarily replaces the Folders Explorer bar or whatever Explorer bar was previously active. Users provide the same types of information as they did in Windows 98's Find dialog box: a file specification, search text, and a starting folder. Users can choose advanced search options by checking any combination of the following check boxes:

- **Date** Users can specify whether they're searching for files modified, created, or last accessed within a certain period of time. They can specify a time frame in terms of a number of months, a date, or an interval between two dates.

- **Type** Users can select a specific file type for which they're searching. They can select one file type from a list of friendly file type names.

This list does not allow users to specify file extensions. To provide a specific file extension, users can type it in the Search For Files Named text box.

- **Size** Users can specify that a file must be at least or at most a certain size.

- **Advanced** Users can choose whether to search subfolders and can choose whether the search is case-sensitive, uses regular expressions, or looks for files over slow links.

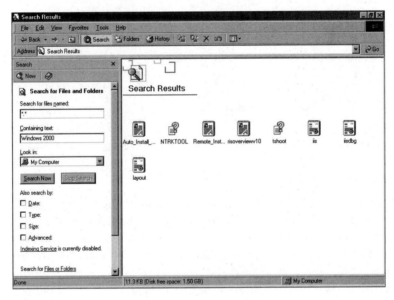

Figure 4-10
Windows Explorer's integrated search feature.

The most exciting aspect of Windows Explorer's integrated search feature is that it is all-encompassing. Users use the same Search bar to search for anything—this includes searching the Internet. At the bottom of the Search bar, users see links to other types of searches. They can search for computers and printers on the network. They can search for people in the organization. They can also search the Internet for Web pages, newsgroups, and more. Clicking these links changes the appearance of the Search bar so that it can collect the information required to perform that type of search. This is in lieu of opening a different window or dialog box in order to do the particular search.

Content indexing makes searching much faster. The Indexing Service creates a database that indexes the keywords found in each file. When users search the computer for files containing certain keywords, the operating system looks in the database and displays any matches it finds. Contrary to what you might have already read, this feature does not require Windows 2000 Server in order to use it on the computer's local disks, but Windows 2000 Professional does not enable it by default. To enable content indexing, click the Indexing Service link in the Search bar. For more information about content indexing, take a look at Chapter 9, "Best Performance."

> **NOTE:** Using content indexing on the network does require Windows 2000 Server. *Introducing Microsoft Windows 2000 Server* describes how to enable and administer this feature.

Better Guidance for Users

Windows 2000 Professional isn't just easier to use—it's friendlier, too. See the following sections:

- "Error Messages" describes Windows 2000 Professional's new error messages.
- "HTML Help" describes Windows 2000 Professional's new online help.

Error Messages

Windows 2000 Professional's error messages aren't quite as terse as the error messages in previous versions of Windows. They provide more information about the error and, more important, more information about how to solve the problem. The Windows 2000 Professional operating system improves all messages, including those seen on the screen, those seen in the event log, and those seen in Internet Explorer. These messages tend to use simpler language that's easier for the user to understand.

Figure 4-11 on the following page shows an example of an error message in Internet Explorer. The top portion of the error message describes the error. The bottom portion describes several possible corrections—different ways the user can correct the error. Notice the simple language that is used to describe the error and to suggest corrections.

In cases where the operating system expects a response from the user, such as when prompting the user to click Yes or No, the operating system defaults to an appropriate response if the user fails to answer the question within a certain amount of time. Friendlier error messages make it much easier for the user to understand what the operating system is doing, and the combination of these friendly messages with the execution of appropriate responses after a time-out period reduces the need for support calls.

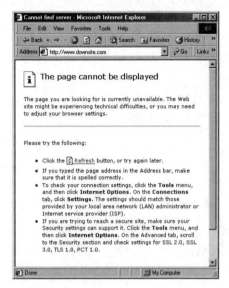

Figure 4-11
An Internet Explorer error message.

HTML Help

Windows 2000 Professional's online help is greatly improved over Windows NT Workstation 4.0's online help. It's similar to the help provided with Windows 98. That is, online help is task-based, describing the tasks users might need to perform. It also describes many of the concepts behind those tasks. For instance, the Hardware section contains additional sections that describe how to install and uninstall devices, unplug and eject devices, manage devices, and manage disks and partitions. These sections contain overviews of Plug and Play, hardware profiles, and various hardware types.

The most useful additions to Windows 2000 Professional's online help are the *troubleshooters.* Troubleshooters help users become self-sufficient by allowing them to solve their own problems. Troubleshooters guide the user through a series of questions that result in a diagnosis and a possible solution. To start a troubleshooter, choose Troubleshooting And Maintenance from Help's contents; then, choose Use The Interactive Troubleshooters. Online help provides troubleshooters for:

■ Client Service for NetWare
■ Displays

- Hardware

- Internet connections

- Modems

- MS-DOS programs

- Multimedia and games

- Networking and TCP/IP

- Printing

- Remote access to networks

- Sound

- System setup

- Windows 3.0 and Windows 3.1 programs

Some additional troubleshooters that are listed in online help are only available if you're also using Windows 2000 Server. Those include troubleshooters for Dynamic Host Configuration Protocol (DHCP), Directory Services, Domain Name System, Policies, Offline Files, Startup, Shutdown, Stop, Errors, Transmission Control Protocol/Internet Protocol (TCP/IP), and Windows Internet Naming Service (WINS). Any attempt to use these troubleshooters in Windows 2000 Professional without a connection to Windows 2000 Server yields a screen that says, "This information does not apply."

Online Help's user interface deserves a special nod. It's simpler to use than Windows NT Workstation 4.0's online help, behaving more like a Web browser. Indeed, Windows 2000 Professional's online help is based on Internet Explorer. If in doubt about this, right-click anywhere within a help topic, choose Properties from the pop-up menu, and you'll see Internet Explorer's friendly Properties dialog box, which contains information about the current page and allows users to analyze the page for errors. Figure 4-12 on page 99 shows what the new user interface looks like. The following list describes each of the tabs:

- **Contents**　This tab provides an outline that users can browse for help topics.

- **Index**　This tab provides a list of keywords that Microsoft compiled from the help content. In the Type In The Keyword To Find textbox, users type a keyword and online help displays the closest match in the list. Once users are satisfied with online help's find, they click the Display button to open the help topic in the right pane.

■ **Search** This tab allows users to quickly search online help for specific keywords. In the Type In The Word(s) To Search For textbox, users type one or more keywords that they're trying to find, and then click the List Topics button. Next, they select a topic in the Select Topic list and click the Display button to view it in the right pane.

■ **Favorites** This tab provides a bookmarking feature similar to Internet Explorer's Favorites menu. Upon finding a bookmark-worthy help topic, users click the Favorites tab and then click the

Other User Interface Improvements

Windows 2000 Professional is loaded with many other smaller but nevertheless significant user interface improvements. Taken by themselves, these improvements may seem trivial, but as a whole, they make the user's experience with Windows 2000 Professional much more positive than with earlier members of the Windows family of operating systems.

One feature that has benefited from some improvement is the Registry Editor—it was bare bones in earlier versions of Windows. Windows 2000 Professional's Registry Editor is improved with a new bookmarking feature that makes it much friendlier. Users can bookmark a frequently visited registry key, and then quickly return to that key by choosing it from the Favorites menu.

Notepad now has a more accessible search-and-replace feature. Earlier versions of Notepad required users to choose Find from the Search menu in order to search a text file. This was inconvenient, given that most other Windows programs allow the user to press Ctrl-F to search. Now Notepad also supports Ctrl-F.

The separate Channels bar in Internet Explorer has been integrated into Favorites, providing a less cluttered approach to accessing shortcuts to all your favorite places on the Internet.

The list goes on. Now users can find their folder options on Windows Explorer's Tools menu and their Internet options on Internet Explorer's Tools menu. Windows 2000 Professional stores user profiles in the Documents And Settings folder, instead of burying them in the Windows installation folder. The Control Panel is simpler, containing fewer icons and combining many of the traditional icons such as Sounds and Multimedia.

The best way to learn about all of these little enhancements is to sit down and discover them for yourself.

Add button to add that topic to a list of favorites. When they want to go back to that topic, they click the Favorites tab, select the topic in the Topics list, and then click the Display button.

Some additional features of the Help window are described in the table below:

To Accomplish This	Do This
Hide the left pane of the Help window	Click the Hide button
View previously visited help topics	Do one of the following:
	Click the Back button to view the previous topic in the history list
	Click the Forward button to view the next topic in the history list
Print the current help topic	Click the Options button and choose Print from the menu
Open Microsoft Support Online	Click the Web Help button, then follow the instructions you see on the screen

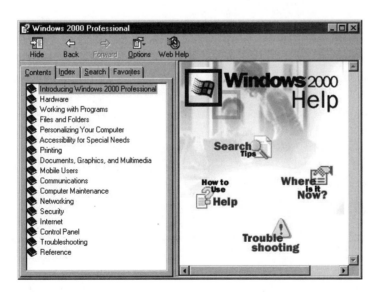

Figure 4-12
HTML Help.

CHAPTER FIVE

Easier Setup and Configuration

Microsoft Windows 2000 Professional makes that first configuration—the inevitable whirlwind tour through the Control Panel that most users take after installing the operating system—much easier. Aside from the fact that the setup program is more comprehensive, the operating system makes adding software and hardware much easier. Network connections, task schedules, and user accounts are also easier to configure due to a variety of new wizards.

One enhancement to Windows 2000 Professional is very subtle, but it has a huge impact on how easy the operating system is to configure. Whereas more than 50 configuration changes in Microsoft Windows NT Workstation 4.0 required the operating system to restart, only 7 configuration changes require Windows 2000 Professional to restart. This means that users don't have to restart the computer nearly as often, which makes the configuration process much more pleasant. For more information about the specific configuration changes that require the operating system to restart, see Chapter 10, "Most Reliable and Stable."

Most users make the same types of configuration changes immediately after installing an operating system such as Windows 2000 Professional. First, they change—or should change—the screen resolution and color depth to something that's a bit more usable than what the setup program specifies. Following that, they usually create the local area network (LAN) and dial-up networking connections they need. Then they install printers and other devices, along with a handful of programs. Finally, they schedule some routine maintenance. This chapter describes how Windows 2000 Professional facilitates this configuration process and, in particular, how this latest member of the Windows NT product family makes the process easier than Windows NT Workstation 4.0 did.

More Comprehensive Setup Program

The setup program is a bit more comprehensive in Windows 2000 Professional than it was in previous members of the Windows NT product family—the setup program now covers more of the computer's initial configuration. For example, network configuration is almost automatic for computers connecting to a typical Microsoft network. And the setup program automatically detects and configures most types of hardware, such as display adapters and network interface cards, before users log on to the computer for the first time. The setup program even helps users create a user account. For more information about the initial configuration that the setup program creates, see Chapter 3, "Setup Guide."

The variety of methods that network administrators can use to automatically install Windows 2000 Professional makes it easier to deploy in large organizations. Disk duplication helps administrators configure multiple computers. To do this, they use the SysPrep tool to prepare a master computer for duplication, and then duplicate the disk image using a third-party product such as Symantec's Norton Ghost. As a second option, administrators can arrange for unattended installations where the setup program automatically installs the operating system on each computer by following a setup script (sometimes called an answer file and often named Unattend.txt). The last option is remote installation, which allows a client computer to connect to a special server that installs Windows 2000 Professional. In all of these cases, a good portion of the initial configuration is done for users prior to the first time they log on to the operating system. For more information about these capabilities, take a look at Chapter 18, "Easier Deployment."

Quicker Display Configuration

The computer's display configuration is and should be one of the first things most users change. The setup program doesn't always leave users with the best display configuration, sometimes setting the display to 640 by 480 pixels with 16 colors. At a minimum, users should configure the display to 800 by 600 pixels with 16-bit (high-color) color. Assuming that the hardware is compatible with this configuration, it gives users a better experience than 640 by 480 pixels when viewing most Web pages or editing documents. In addition, users should make sure that Windows 2000 Professional has correctly configured the computer's monitor—at the very least with one of the standard monitor configurations such as Laptop Display Panel (800 by 600). Windows 2000 Professional will not correctly configure the monitor if the monitor is not Plug and Play or if the operating system doesn't recognize the monitor.

Windows 2000 Professional's display configuration is a bit different than the configuration for Windows NT Workstation 4.0. Double-click the Display icon in the Control Panel and click the Settings tab, which looks very similar to the same tab in Windows 98. In the Colors list, select the color depth you want to use. Move the Screen Area slider to the left to decrease screen resolution or to the right to increase screen resolution.

Click the Advanced button to open the display's Properties dialog box as shown in Figure 5-1 on the following page. This is where you configure the display adapter, the monitor, the color management settings, and so forth. You will see five tabs, as described below:

- **General** Changes the size of the fonts on the display and selects whether Windows 2000 Professional restarts the computer after changing the display settings.

- **Adapter** Configures the display adapter, including the driver and resources assigned to it, and lists all the modes available for the display adapter.

- **Monitor** Chooses the refresh frequency (scan rate) of the monitor and determines whether Windows 2000 Professional hides modes not supported by the monitor.

- **Troubleshooting** Troubleshoots the display adapter by changing the level of acceleration for the graphics hardware.

- **Color Management** Manages color profiles. For more information about color profiles, see Chapter 8, "More Imaging and Printing Capabilities."

Changes to the display resolution and color depth can be quick, since Windows 2000 Professional won't restart the computer if users configure the display correctly. In the General tab of the display's Properties dialog box, users can select Apply The New Display Settings Without Restarting, and the operating system will test the settings—asking the user for confirmation that the settings work properly—and apply those settings without restarting the computer. Some display adapters have utilities for quicker configuration settings; Diamond Multimedia is one such example.

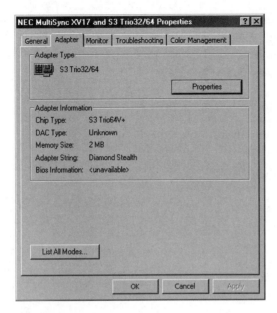

Figure 5.1
The Properties dialog box for a display.

Accessibility Options

Windows 2000 Professional provides accessibility options similar to those in Windows 98. Users access these features by choosing Programs from the Start menu, followed by Accessories and Accessibility:

- **Accessibility Wizard**   Similar to the Windows 98 Accessibility Wizard, Windows 2000 Professional's Accessibility Wizard helps users quickly and easily turn on a variety of accessibility features by asking users questions about their particular needs.

- **Magnifier**   The Magnifier utility is for users who need a bit of extra help reading the contents of the screen. It sets aside a small portion of the screen to magnify whatever users point to with the mouse. Users can configure how it behaves and the magnification level.

- **Narrator**   As additional help for folks who need help reading the screen, the Narrator utility reads the contents of the screen aloud. It also offers navigational queues for users by reading the contents of labels, buttons, and other controls in dialog boxes.

■ **On-Screen Keyboard** The On-Screen Keyboard utility provides an alternative to the regular keyboard. Users type by clicking the On-Screen Keyboard with the mouse.

Plug and Play Hardware Installation

Chapter 12, "Easy Device Installation," describes Windows 2000 Professional's implementation of Plug and Play as well as the plethora of devices that this operating system supports. I mention hardware installation in this chapter because it's one of the key ingredients that make the operating system so easy to configure. First of all, the setup program automatically recognizes and installs most popular hardware devices, making configuration that much easier for the user. Upgrading from Windows NT Workstation 4.0 is the best-case scenario for hardware detection, but my experience suggests that Windows 2000 Professional also correctly detects most devices when upgrading from Windows 98 and when performing a clean install on a freshly formatted hard disk.

If Windows 2000 Professional fails to recognize or properly configure a Plug and Play device or a legacy device, users can use the Add/Remove Hardware Wizard to install and configure the device. Users double-click the Add/Remove Hardware Wizard icon in the Control Panel to start the wizard. The wizard looks different from the Add/Remove Hardware Wizard in Windows 98, but it has similar features. It gives users the choice of adding a new device, uninstalling a device, or troubleshooting. When the Add/Remove Hardware Wizard detects a new device, it starts the Found New Hardware Wizard to install the device. This wizard can search for drivers on a floppy disk, on a CD-ROM, at the Windows Update Web site, or in another location specified by the user. And if the wizard doesn't find a device-specific driver, it frequently can use one of the standard drivers, which work in many cases.

If the Add/Remove Hardware Wizard fails to find a new device, it displays a list of the existing devices and asks you if you want to troubleshoot any of them (see Figure 5-2 on the following page). After you select a device from the list, the wizard displays the status of the device, indicating whether the device can't start or is not configured properly, and then it launches the Hardware Troubleshooter to help the user repair it.

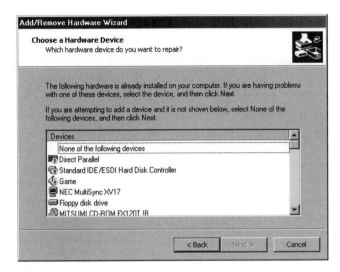

Figure 5.2
Choosing a device to troubleshoot.

Icons in the Control Panel

In the process of describing how to use Windows 2000 Professional, this chapter touches on a good number of the icons you see in the Control Panel. These include the Display, Printers, Scheduled Tasks, Users and Passwords, Network And Dial-Up Connections, Administrative Tools, Add/Remove Hardware Wizard, Add/Remove Programs, Phone And Modem Options, Power Options, and System icons.

This book covers some of the other Control Panel icons in other chapters. You'll learn about the Fonts icon in Chapter 8, "More Imaging and Printing Capabilities," the Internet Options icon in Chapter 16, "Integrated Web and Desktop," the Regional Options icon in Chapter 7, "Superior Multilingual Support," and the Scanners And Cameras icon in Chapter 8, "More Imaging and Printing Capabilities." This book does not cover the remaining Control Panel icons—Date/Time, Folder Options, Game Controllers, Keyboard, Mouse, and Sounds And Multimedia—since their capabilities haven't changed much since Windows NT Workstation 4.0 or Windows 98.

Aside from helping users install hardware on their computers, Windows 2000 Professional implements the Advanced Configuration and Power Interface (ACPI), an open standard for power management that helps the operating system manage the electrical power used by that hardware. Users configure the operating system's power management features by double-clicking the Power Options icon in the Control Panel to display the Power Options Properties dialog box. This dialog box allows them to choose from a variety of power schemes that reflect different ways they might use their computers. A user with a portable computer might choose the Portable/Laptop power scheme, for example, while a user with a desktop computer might choose the Home/Office Desk power scheme. If none of the available schemes suits a user's needs, the user can create new schemes. For more information about how the operating system implements power management, see Chapter 13, "Broader Hardware Support."

Much Easier Network Connections

As you've already read, users create their LAN connections during the setup process. In fact, the setup program automatically creates a typical network configuration (called a connection) for each network interface card—and users are free to customize the connections at this point. Each connection includes the following components:

- Client for Microsoft Networks

- File and Printer Sharing for Microsoft Networks

- Transmission Control Protocol/Internet Protocol (TCP/IP) with Dynamic Host Configuration Protocol (DHCP) enabled

If the typical network connection doesn't work properly or if users skip that portion of the setup program, they can always go back and configure the LAN connection in the Network And Dial-Up Connections folder, opened by double-clicking the Network And Dial-Up Connections icon in the Control Panel. When users first open this folder, they see one or more icons: Make New Connection, which starts the Network Connection Wizard, and one icon for each network interface card installed on the computer. Within this folder, users can open and close a connection, check the status of a connection, and change a connection's properties.

A variety of other settings are accessible from the Advanced menu of the Network And Dial-Up Connections folder. You can specify dialing preferences and network identification, and you can install optional networking components such as the Simple Network Management Protocol (SNMP) service or the TCP/IP Print Server. Choose Advanced Settings from the Advanced menu to change the components bound to each adapter or the order in which the computer accesses information on the network. Choose Network Identification from the Advanced menu to change the computer's name and domain membership—a process that's simpler than it was in Windows NT Workstation 4.0.

The Network And Dial-Up Connections folder also provides a considerable amount of feedback, which is a big improvement over previous versions of Windows. First, users can select any connection icon to display text that indicates the connection's type, device, owner, and status. Second, they can double-click a connection icon to open the connection's Status dialog box, as shown in Figure 5-3, which displays information concerning the connection's performance and the amount of data sent or received. Users can also display the status of any connection on the taskbar by checking the Show Icon In Taskbar When Connected checkbox in the connection's Properties dialog box (available from its pop-up menu). Pointing to the button on the taskbar displays the connection's status, also shown in Figure 5-3, and clicking the button opens the connection's Status dialog box.

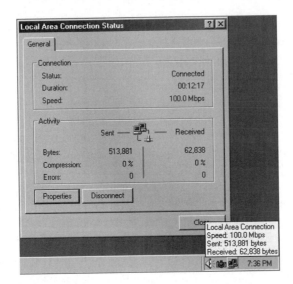

Figure 5-3
The Local Area Connection Status dialog box.

The Network Connection Wizard is a much easier way to configure network connections than anything provided by Windows NT Workstation 4.0. When the wizard starts, it asks the user what type of connection to create. The possibilities include the following:

- Dial-Up To Private Network
- Dial-Up To The Internet
- Connect To A Private Network Through The Internet
- Accept Incoming Connections
- Connect Directly To Another Computer

Dial-Up Connections

Most users will want to create their dial-up connections—private and Internet—as part of their initial configurations. The Network Connection Wizard makes short work of this process and is far and away easier than Windows NT Workstation 4.0's Dial-Up Networking. The biggest user-oriented advantage of the Network And Dial-Up Connections folder over Windows NT 4.0's Dial-Up Networking is that the former is part of Windows Explorer's hierarchy—making connections quicker to locate, configure, and dial—while the latter required users to open a separate window in which they dealt with connections.

The Network Connection Wizard asks users for a phone number, and that's about it. After completing the wizard, users see a new icon in the Network And Dial-Up Connections folder. Each connection is highly configurable. Users choose Properties from a connection's pop-up menu to open the connection's Properties dialog box, shown in Figure 5-4 on the following page. This dialog box has four tabs, as follows:

- **General**   Modem configuration, phone number, and dialing rules
- **Options**   Dialing options, such as whether Windows 2000 Professional prompts the user before dialing, and redialing options, such as the number of attempts
- **Security**   Password security (unsecured, secured, or Smart Card), dialing scripts, and advanced security settings such as password authentication protocols
- **Networking**   Server type—Point-to-Point Protocol (PPP) or Serial Line Internet Protocol (SLIP)—advanced settings such as multilink, and installed networking components bound to the connection

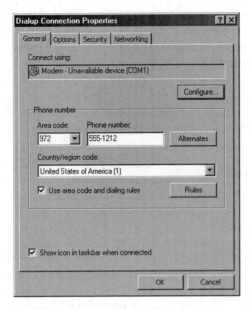

Figure 5-4
The Properties dialog box for a dial-up connection.

If Windows 2000 Professional doesn't find any dial locations when it's creating an Internet connection, it prompts the users for information about their current location. That information includes the country or region and the area code from which they're dialing. Then, the operating system displays the Phone & Modem Options dialog box so that users can further refine the dial location's configuration. Users can also open this dialog box by clicking the Phone And Modem Options icon in the Control Panel. Each dial location defines the country or region, the area code, and various dialing rules that determine how the operating system dials a telephone number from that location. With recent changes in area code rules across the country, these improvements are a boon to all users. For instance, in many U.S. cities, there are numerous area codes, and those area codes are not separated geographically. To make matters worse, some prefixes within the same area code require dialing a 1 while others don't. Windows 2000 Professional handles these situations by allowing users to specify which area codes and prefixes require dialing a 1, or the area code, or both.

Virtual Private Networks (VPNs)

Virtual private networks (VPNs) allow users to connect to a private network securely via a public network such as the Internet. Since users connect using local telephone numbers (possibly via a local Internet service provider) instead of expensive long-distance or 800 numbers, VPNs reduce the cost of reaching remote offices and users significantly.

A VPN connection creates a secure tunnel through the Internet and connects to a remote access server. One of two protocols—Point-to-Point Tunneling Protocol (PPTP) or Layer 2 Tunneling Protocol (L2TP)—maintains the tunnel. Both of these security protocols support the most common network protocols—including TCP/IP and Internetwork Packet Exchange/Sequenced Packet Exchange (IPX/SPX)—through the tunnel. The Internet connection itself can be through a LAN, a service such as asymmetric digital subscriber line (ADSL), or an Internet service provider. For more information about VPNs, including details about PPTP and L2TP, see Chapter 11, "Strongest Local and Network Security."

VPN connections aren't quite as daunting as they sound. The Network Connection Wizard is used to create such a connection. The wizard asks if users want the VPN connection to dial the Internet connection, and it also asks for the host name or IP address of the remote access server. That's all there is to creating a VPN connection. Connecting is simple, too: users double-click the connection's icon in the Network And Dial-Up Connections folder. Furthermore, VPN connections, like dial-up connections, are highly configurable. The General tab of a VPN connection's Properties dialog box contains the remote access server's host name or IP address. The remaining three tabs—Options, Security, and Networking—are the same as those in the Properties dialog box of an ordinary dial-up connection.

Incoming Connections

Windows 2000 Professional supports incoming connections of three different types: dial-up, VPN, and direct. This means that if you have administrator rights on your computer, you can configure your computer to be a remote access server. The operating system can accept up to three incoming calls, one on each type of connection. Thus, the operating system doesn't support two dial-up connections at one time, but it does support a dial-up, a VPN, and a direct connection all at once.

You can use the Network Connection Wizard to create and configure an incoming connection. First, use the wizard to specify the devices that will be allowed to accept incoming calls and whether the connection will accept VPN connections. Continue using the wizard to specify which users in the local user database will be allowed to connect and to set their passwords. At this point, you can also configure callback options. Once you have completed the wizard, you can further configure the connection by right-clicking its icon to display the Incoming Connections dialog box. You can add additional users via the Users tab. Use the Networking tab to specify the networking components that will be bound to the connection. By default, the operating system binds the currently installed components to the connection, but users can disable some components, or even install and enable additional components for the connection.

Direct Connections

More and more users rely on two computers—a desktop and a portable. Many of these users have no convenient method for transferring data between the two computers other than using a floppy disk. Windows 2000 Professional's direct connection feature provides a sort of "poor man's LAN" for those users, allowing them to connect two computers by using modems, ISDN devices, infrared ports, serial cables, or DirectParallel cables—including Parallel Technologies' Basic or Fast parallel cables. In essence, a direct connection can take the place of a network interface card.

The requirements for creating a direct connection are simple. The remote computer must have an incoming connection configured to accept connections via one of the devices or cables listed earlier. The client computer must have a direct connection configured for that same device or cable. The remote computer might be running Windows 2000 Professional, or it might be a remote access server running Windows NT Server 4.0.

Local Area Networks

Creating a LAN connection is not one of the options that the Network Connection Wizard presents because the setup program creates this connection automatically and users can't remove it from the Network And Dial-Up Connections folder. However, LAN connections are still configurable, and configuring LAN connections is simpler than doing so in Windows NT Workstation 4.0—due in large part to the simpler user interface. You don't install a Workstation service anymore—you install the Client For Microsoft Networks. You don't install a server service anymore—you install File And Printer Sharing For Microsoft Networks. Computer identification is now treated separately from the network configuration, and it is now accessed via the Network Identification command on the Advanced menu in the Network And Dial-Up Connections folder. Most of the esoteric services are configured separately, too. Figure 5-5 shows a LAN connection's Properties dialog box, which you may recognize as being somewhat similar to Windows 98's. The three items in the list are part of a typical network configuration and require very little if any change. If users must change a LAN connection, they can select any item in the list and then click Properties to customize its configuration.

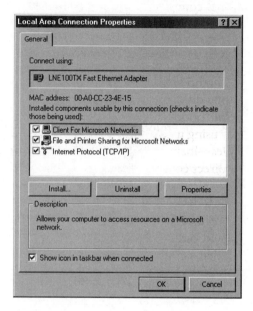

Figure 5-5
The Properties dialog box for a typical LAN connection.

Installing a new networking component is straightforward. Click Install in a connection's Properties dialog box to display the Select Network Component Type dialog box. Then, select a component type from the list and click Add. In the Select Network Component dialog box, select the component you want to install. As of this writing, Windows 2000 Professional provides the components that Table 5-1 describes, but you can be sure that more will be available as the operating system comes to market. The Client for Microsoft Networks supports connections to Microsoft networks such as Windows 2000 or Windows NT domains. The Client Service for NetWare supports connections to Novell NetWare 3 and 4 but doesn't support IP connections to NetWare 5. You'll learn more about all these components in Chapter 15, "Advanced Networking Capabilities."

Component Type	Components
Client	Client for Microsoft Networks
	Client Service for NetWare
Service	File and Printer Sharing for Microsoft Networks
	Quality of Service (QoS) Packet Scheduler
	Service Advertising Protocol (SAP) Agent
Protocol	AppleTalk Protocol
	Data Link Control (DLC) Protocol
	Transmission Control Protocol/Internet Protocol (TCP/IP)
	NetBIOS Enhanced User Interface (NetBEUI) Protocol
	Network Monitor Agent v2 Driver
	NWLink IPX/SPX/NetBIOS Compatible Transport Protocol
	Open Systems Interconnection/Local Area Network (OSI LAN) Protocol
	Streams Environment

Table 5-1
Available networking components.

Simpler Printer Installation

Another task that most users do immediately after completing the setup process is to install a local or network printer. Chapter 8, "More Imaging and Printing Capabilities," describes Windows 2000 Professional's printing enhancements. Here's a quick overview:

- **New Print dialog box** The Print dialog box makes choosing a printer easier and allows users to locate a printer by searching the network.

- **Improved Add Printer Wizard** The Add Printer Wizard makes installing a local or network printer a snap. Users can install a printer using its Uniform Naming Convention (UNC) path or Uniform Resource Locator (URL), or they can locate a printer by searching the network.

- **Point and Print printer installation** Installing network printers has never been easier. Users choose Install from a network printer's pop-up menu, and Windows 2000 Professional installs the printer, copying its driver files from the network.

■ **Internet printing**   Users can print on remote printers via the Internet.

Current System Configurations

Immediately after installing Windows 2000 Professional and configuring an Internet connection, users should check the Windows Update Web site for important software updates. Windows Update, first pioneered in Windows 98, allows users to make sure that their configurations are current. No longer do they have to wonder if they have the most recent drivers or the latest improvements. Users open Windows Update by choosing Windows Update from the Start menu. Alternatively, they can open *http://windowsupdate.microsoft.com* in Microsoft Internet Explorer. Figure 5-6 shows Windows Update. Features available at this time include:

■ **Product updates**   Windows Update can check the computer to see if it would benefit from new drivers, enhancements, or other downloads. Windows Update selects downloads that apply specifically to that computer's configuration, too.

■ **Support information**   Windows Update provides easy access to Microsoft's online support, which answers most questions that users and administrators have about using and supporting Windows 2000 Professional.

Figure 5-6
The Windows Update Web site.

NOTE: Administrators who are concerned about users' ability to download updates can use policies to limit the availability of Windows Update's features. Some administrators have legitimate concerns about controlling an organization's desktops. Imagine 500 users installing whatever updates they happen to find on Windows Update—gasp! Allowing users to download new drivers, enhancements, and improvements in a willy-nilly fashion adds risk to the long-term health of an organization's infrastructure.

Painless System Configuration

Double-click the System icon in the Control Panel to open the System Properties dialog box. This looks very similar to the same dialog box in Windows NT Workstation 4.0. Here's a description of each tab:

- **General**   Unchanged since Windows NT Workstation 4.0—provides general information about the computer, including the registered owner and CPU type.
- **Network Identification**   New to Windows 2000 Professional—allows users to change the computer's name and domain membership.
- **Hardware**   Combines the Hardware Profiles tab, which allows users to set multiple hardware configurations for the computer, from Windows NT Workstation 4.0's System Properties dialog box with the new Add/Remove Hardware Wizard and the Device Manager.
- **User Profiles**   Unchanged since Windows NT Workstation 4.0—allows users to remove profiles, change profile types, and copy profiles.
- **Advanced**   Combines the Performance, Environment, and Startup/Shutdown tabs from Windows NT Workstation 4.0's System Properties dialog box—allows users to fine-tune Windows 2000 Professional, including virtual memory and how the operating system starts and shuts down in the event of errors.

After installing Windows 2000 Professional, some users might want to adjust a few settings in the System Properties dialog box. Some users change their virtual memory settings, but doing so is necessary only in the most unusual circumstances. However, I do recommend that users bump up the amount of space allocated to the registry by clicking Performance Options button in the Advanced tab and then clicking the Change button—24 MB is a good number. Also, as a matter of personal preference, I typically move the Temp folder to a location beneath *systemroot* by clicking the Environment Variables button in the Advanced tab.

Centralized Computer Management

The Computer Management console provides administrators with a single location for a variety of administrative tools. Open the Computer Management console by double-clicking the Administrative Tools icon in the Control Panel, and then double-clicking the Computer Management icon. A quicker way to open the Computer Management console is to add the Administrative Tools folder to the Start menu as described in Chapter 4, "Simpler User Interface." Then you can choose Programs from the Start menu, and choose Administrative Tools and Computer Management from the submenus.

Microsoft Management Console (MMC) is a program that acts as a host for consoles such as the Computer Management console. You'll learn more about MMC in Chapter 19, "Better Management Tools," but acquaint yourself with some terminology before continuing. The top level displayed by MMC is called a *console* and the outline in the left pane is called the *console tree*. The Computer Management console, or tool as it's also called, shown in Figure 5-7 has three *nodes* at the first level: System Tools, Storage, and Server Applications And Services. The right pane contains snap-ins, monitor controls, tasks, wizards, and documentation to manage a variety of hardware, software, and networking components in Windows 2000 Professional. You can add items to any existing console, and you can even create new consoles and configure them for specific administrative purposes.

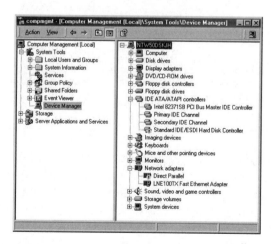

Figure 5-7
The Device Manager opened in the Computer Management console.

Most of the tools in the Computer Management console work exactly as they did in Windows NT Workstation 4.0. However, some tools—such as the Device Manager shown in Figure 5-7—are new to Windows 2000 Professional. Table 5-2 describes all the tools in the Computer Management console, most of which are unchanged from Windows NT Workstation 4.0. The System Information tool is new and provides information about the computer's hardware and software. The Group Policy tool is similar to the System Policy Editor in Windows NT 4.0, but it has many new policies and an improved user interface. The Device Manager is new and allows users to inspect and configure each device installed on the computer. Note that while the Server Applications And Services node has only one tool in Windows 2000 Professional, it has numerous tools in Windows 2000 Server.

Node	Tools
System Tools	Local Users and Groups
	System Information
	Services
	Group Policy
	Shared Folders
	Event Viewer
	Device Manager
Storage	Logical Drives
	Disk Management
Server Applications and Services	Indexing Service

Table 5-2
Nodes and tools in the Computer Management console.

There are a handful of tasks users might want to complete in the Computer Management console immediately after installing Windows 2000 Professional. First, it's a good idea to double-check the computer's disk configuration to make sure it reflects the user's view of reality. Second, users should check the event log and note any serious problems. Last, they might add local users to the computer's user database. Users should shy away from adding themselves to the local computer's Administrators group, however enticing the thought may be, because doing so opens the computer to viruses that take advantage of such situations. In addition, if you are a network domain administrator, discourage users from adding a local user account if you prefer that they log on to the domain. Even if the domain is unavailable to validate users' credentials, Windows 2000 Professional will use cached information to log them onto the computer.

Adding Users to the Local User Database

Windows 2000 Professional provides two different entry points for adding users to the local user database. The Local Users And Groups tool in the Computer Management console is the more advanced method and is roughly the same as the User Manager in Windows NT Workstation 4.0. The Users And Passwords icon in the Control Panel provides a simpler method that addresses the basic needs of most users. It can be used to add users, assign them to groups, and to set passwords. That's about it.

The following figure shows the Users And Passwords dialog box. It's missing many capabilities found in the Local Users And Groups tool. You, as an administrator of the local computer, can't assign profiles or edit groups, nor can you add a user to more than one group. Note that you can use this dialog box to add a domain user to a local group. For example, you might want to assign certain users from the domain to the local Administrators group. Doing so allows those users to administer the local computer without having administrator rights on the domain.

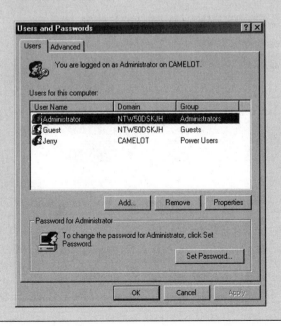

Easier Program Installation

The new Add/Remove Programs dialog box is friendlier than the ones in Windows NT Workstation 4.0 and Windows 98. The traditional tasks—installing and removing programs—are similar. Other capabilities are a bit beyond the traditional; for example, users can install applications directly from the network or the Internet. Figure 5-8 shows this new dialog box, and the following list summarizes some of the dialog box's additional capabilities:

- **Sorting** Users can sort the programs by size, frequency of use, and time of last use.

- **More feedback** More information is provided about each application, such as the amount of disk space it consumes and how frequently it gets used.

The Add/Remove Programs dialog box uses the new Windows Installer Service, which makes installing, removing, changing, and repairing applications easier. More important, this service makes each of these tasks more complete. For example, removing a program with the Windows Installer Service causes every last one of the program's files to be removed—even the odd DLL files that programs tend to scatter around the computer's hard disk. Chapter 10, "Most Reliable and Stable," provides many details about this service.

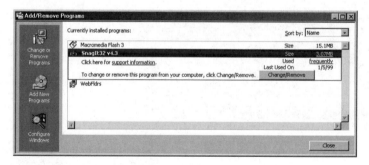

Figure 5-8
The new Add/Remove Programs dialog box.

> NOTE: Administrators can set policies that give the Add/Remove Programs dialog box access to network installation points based upon users' credentials. They can make different applications available for different groups of users. Administrators can also assign some applications, making them mandatory, and publish other applications that users can install as needed.

More Flexible Task Scheduling

The Task Scheduler was part of Internet Explorer 4, but users had to make a round trip to the Web in order to install it. Given that fact, most users did not install the Task Scheduler, so I'll cover it here as though it were a new feature.

The Scheduled Tasks folder is visible in Windows Explorer's hierarchy tree (name space). To open the Scheduled Tasks folder, users double-click the Scheduled Tasks icon in the Control Panel. They double-click the Add Scheduled Task icon to start the Scheduled Task Wizard, which guides them through scheduling a task. A task icon appears, and users can choose Properties from the icon's pop-up menu to change the task's more advanced options.

The Task Scheduler provides features similar to Windows NT's At command, which Windows 2000 Professional still supports. Users can schedule tasks to run daily, weekly, and monthly, as well as when the computer is idle or each time Windows 2000 Professional starts. Unlike the At command, Task Scheduler uses a graphical user interface to collect information about each job. Also unlike the At command, users can create multiple, overlapping schedules for a single task, and the operating system stores tasks as files in the Scheduled Tasks folder rather than in the registry. Keep in mind, too, that the Task Scheduler can work together with the At command. After scheduling a task using the At command, the task appears in the Scheduled Tasks folder. Users can change the task's properties in the Scheduled Tasks folder but, after doing so, users no longer access the task via the At command. Users specify the user account for tasks scheduled with the At command by choosing AT Service Account from the Scheduled Tasks folder's Advanced menu.

> TIP: Windows 2000 Professional's Maintenance Wizard is the quickest way to schedule tasks that should be a part of all configurations. It schedules ScanDisk to scan each hard disk for errors once a week and Disk Cleanup to remove unused, temporary files once a month. Users start the Maintenance Wizard from the Welcome screen, which Windows 2000 Professional displays the first time they start the operating system. Alternatively, users can choose Run from the Start menu and type *tuneup* in the Open box.

CHAPTER SIX

Better Mobile Computing Support

Mobile users have special needs that challenge an operating system. The most obvious difficulty is that mobile users are not connected to the network full time, but they still need access to important network files. They tend to like using their computers in odd places—30,000 feet in the air or sitting in a hotel lobby—where sustainable power isn't available. They pull a computer off a docking station and expect the operating system to reconfigure itself. They expect to connect to the network from any hotel room in the world. And when a computer stops working, they expect the administrator to fix it no matter where in the world they are.

Microsoft Windows 2000 Professional is a big boon for mobile users, going much further than even Windows 98 did by supporting an entirely new class of mobile computing requirements. Connecting to remote networks is much easier. Making files available offline is more intuitive. Users can undock a computer and the operating system reconfigures itself. Computers get more life out of their batteries. Configuring Windows 2000 Professional's mobility features is very easy, adding little or no complexity, since most of the features have wizards or are automatically configured. In fact, in the January 1999 issue of *Windows Magazine,* Scot Finnie describes Windows 2000 Professional's mobility features as "vastly improved." I agree.

This chapter describes Windows 2000 Professional's support for mobile users. Don't be alarmed if you notice that this chapter overlaps Chapter 5 a small bit. For example, this chapter also covers the Network Connection Wizard, but it does so specifically through the eyes of a mobile user.

Easy Dial-Up Network Connections

Most office users are accustomed to unabridged access to network resources, files, and printers. Mobile users aren't connected to the network full-time, but they can rely on dial-up network connections for temporary connections to the network. People who travel are traditional users of dial-up network connections, but even people who work at home can link to a corporate LAN, maintaining a connection to the organization.

Windows 2000 Professional supports dial-up connections to private networks, dial-up connections to the Internet, and direct connections between two computers. And dial-up network connections are well integrated into the operating system's architecture, so the operating system treats them just like any other network adapter. That means that mobile users use the network no differently than users who are connected to the LAN with a network interface card (speed being the exception). For more information about browsing a network using the My Network Places folder, see Chapter 4, "Simpler User Interface."

Dial-up network connections can be used with any networking components that the operating system supports. That is, if users can connect to a network physically using a network interface card, they can connect to it remotely. Windows 2000 Professional uses the industry standard Point-to-Point Protocol (PPP) or Serial Line Internet Protocol (SLIP) to connect to a remote access server. Both protocols are sometimes called *connection* or *over-the-wire* protocols because they transmit, with a network protocol such as Transmission Control Protocol/Internet Protocol (TCP/IP), over traditional telephone wire. The operating system also supports the Point-to-Point Tunneling Protocol (PPTP), the Layer 2 Tunneling Protocol (L2TP), and Internet Protocol security (IPSec) for establishing secure, virtual connections to private networks through an existing Internet connection. Figure 6-1 illustrates the differences between connection protocols such as PPP and tunneling protocols such as PPTP. For more information about the networking components that Windows 2000 Professional supports, see Chapter 15, "Advanced Networking Capabilities."

> NOTE: At this writing, Windows 2000 Professional does not include support for Novell's NetWare Remote Node (NRN) protocol, a requirement for connecting to NetWare Connect servers. Windows 98 does support this connection protocol, and you can be sure that NetWare will make it available as Windows 2000 Professional goes to market.

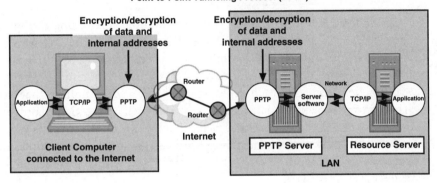

Figure 6-1
PPP and PPTP connections.

The Network Connection Wizard

You can create connections using the Network Connection Wizard, which is in the Network And Dial-Up Connections folder in the Control Panel. To start the wizard, double-click the Make New Connection icon. This section describes features of the Network Connection Wizard that are useful to mobile users. See Chapter 5, "Easier Setup and Configuration," for details about using this wizard for other purposes. The Network Connection Wizard can create the following types of remote connections:

■ **Dial-up** connections through traditional telephone wire that use a network protocol such as TCP/IP to transmit information. Note that the wizard distinguishes between connections to the Internet and connections to private networks; however, the interfaces that result are the same. Dial-up connections can be made using a modem, an ISDN (Integrated Services Digital Network) device, or X.25.

■ **Virtual private networks (VPNs)** are secure connections to private networks through the Internet. Windows 2000 Professional supports two tunneling protocols, PPTP and L2TP, both of which encrypt any data that is transmitted with one of the common protocols. Internal IP addresses are secure, too, since internal IP addresses are also encrypted and the Internet only sees external IP addresses.

■ **Direct** connections without network cards or telephone lines. Direct connections allow a cable—serial or parallel—to replace a traditional network interface card in the connection. Direct connections also support infrared links.

Windows 2000 Professional supports multiple networking configurations for a single device. This speaks to the need that many users have to use the same device to access multiple, differently configured connections, such as using a single modem to connect to both a corporate network and an Internet service provider. Instead of each device maintaining a configuration that has to be changed to allow access to different networks, each connection maintains configurations for all the devices that use it. Each connection stores its own information about those devices, including passwords, security settings, scripts, network protocols, and network settings. Thus, users no longer have to reconfigure the device for each network.

Each dial-up connection in the Network And Dial-Up Connections folder has the following features:

■ **Scripting** Some Internet service providers require users to manually type their names and passwords when logging onto the Internet. In the Security tab of a connection's Properties dialog box, shown in Figure 6-2, users create a script or select an existing script. Windows 2000 Professional provides scripts for CompuServe, hosts using a PPP menu system, hosts using SLIP, and hosts using a SLIP menu system. Windows 2000 Professional includes a file called Script.doc in the *systemroot*\System32\Ras folder that describes how to write scripts.

■ **Phone numbers and dialing rules** Users can specify alternative phone numbers for a connection, and Windows 2000 Professional will try each number in the list until it finds one that works. Also, the operating system allows users to create simple or even complex dialing rules that determine how it dials a phone number. "Phone and Modem Options," later in this chapter, describes these dialing rules.

■ **Dialing and redialing**   In the Options tab of a connection's Properties dialog box, users can configure the interface they see when the
operating system dials a connection. For example, they can choose
whether the operating system prompts them before dialing or displays
the dialing progress. They can also customize redialing by indicating the number of redial attempts and the time between each redial
attempt.

■ **Security settings**   Each connection maintains its own security settings. In the Security tab of a connection's Properties dialog box,
shown in Figure 6-2, the user can specify whether the connection
uses an unsecured password, a secured password, or a Smart Card to
verify their identity. If the typical settings aren't appropriate, the user
can select the Advanced Security Settings option button to specify
the exact types of password security the connection uses. Choices
include Password Authentication Protocol (PAP), Shiva Password
Authentication Protocol (SPAP), Challenge Handshake Authentication Protocol (CHAP), Microsoft CHAP (MSCHAP), and Microsoft
CHAP version 2 (MSCHAPV2). In all cases, the user can specify
whether or not the connection uses their Windows credentials.

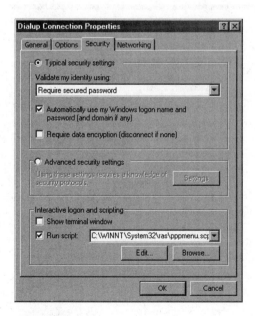

Figure 6-2
The Security tab of the Dialup Connection Properties dialog box.

■ **Multilink** In the Networking tab of a connection's Properties dialog box, users click the Settings button to enable channel aggregation. This feature allows a connection to combine two or more devices to increase its bandwidth. For example, a connection can combine two 56-Kbps modems to effectively create a 112-Kbps connection. Users determine what devices the connection uses in the Options tab in the Multiple Devices area.

The Network And Dial-Up Connections Folder

Double-click the Network And Dial-Up Connections icon in the Control Panel to open the Network And Dial-Up Connections folder. In addition to the Make New Connection icon, this folder contains a single icon for each network interface card installed on the computer as well as a single icon for each connection users create using the Network Connection Wizard. When users click a connection icon, the left side of the pane indicates the name, the type, the status, the device name, and the owner of that connection. When a connection isn't selected, the left side of the pane contains instructions for performing a variety of common tasks such as establishing a network connection or changing the computer's identification.

Administering Connections with Windows 2000 Server

Microsoft Windows 2000 Server changes the administration model for remote access on the server. In addition to applying systemwide settings to all users who log on to the server via remote access, Windows 2000 Server allows network administrators to control each user. Settings that network administrators can control on a per-user basis include access permissions, caller-ID verification, callback options, static IP addresses, and static routes. Administrators manage all of this from the Microsoft Management Console (MMC) Active Directory Users And Computers snap-in.

An additional capability is rules-based policies. The operating system matches connections to rules regarding such things as the time of day and the user group. When a connection matches a rule, the operating system places that rule's controls on the connection. This improvement provides significantly more control over incoming connections than network administrators had in previous server products.

Each connection's icon provides access to all the tools necessary to manage the connection, freeing users from having to look elsewhere in the Control Panel or Start menu for other tools. Each connection's Properties dialog box contains its entire configuration (as you learned in the previous section), including the modem, dialing, and password configurations. Users access the connection's status by choosing Connect from the icon's pop-up menu. Alternatively, users can view a connection's status by pointing to the connection's button in the taskbar. This status report includes information such as connection duration and throughput. However, users must explicitly indicate that they want to view the connection's status on the taskbar, and they do that by checking the Show Icon In Taskbar When Connected check box in the connection's Properties dialog box.

NOTE: Administrators can use policies to populate the Network And Dial-Up Connections folder with connections suitable to each user or group.

Phone and Modem Options

Dial-up connections dial telephone numbers to establish a connection through a modem. Windows 2000 Professional provides the Phone And Modem Options icon in the Control Panel to help users configure each modem and describe how the operating system should dial different telephone numbers. The Phone And Modem Options dialog box combines Windows NT Workstation 4.0's Modems and Telephony Control Panel icons and extends the features of each.

Users install modems in the Modems tab of the Phone And Modem Options dialog box by clicking the Add button. Since Windows 2000 Professional is a Plug and Play operating system (see Chapter 12, "Easy Device Installation"), the operating system automatically detects and installs most modems. Note also that Windows 2000 Professional prompts users to install a modem if they try to establish a dial-up network connection or try to run a communications program and they haven't already installed a modem. If the operating system fails to recognize the modem, users might need to configure the COM port using the Add/Remove Hardware Wizard.

Dial locations set rules that determine how Windows 2000 Professional dials telephone numbers depending on the current area code. For example, users might require the operating system to dial the area code when calling from 972 to 972, as happens in the Dallas, Texas, area, and they might require the operating system to dial 1 plus the area code when calling from 972 to specific exchanges within the same area code. Traditionally, these scenarios have been difficult for users to configure, requiring users to disable dial locations altogether so that they can provide explicit telephone numbers. Windows 2000 Professional's answer to this problem is to provide dialing rules, which can be as simple or as complex as the user requires. To create these dialing rules, users click the New button in the Phone And Modem Options dialog box. Then they can create a new location or select an existing location and click the Edit button. In the Edit Location dialog box, users click the Area Code Rules tab (shown in Figure 6-3); then they add new dialing rules by clicking the New button, or they edit an existing rule by selecting the rule in the Area Code Rules list and clicking the Edit button. As shown in Figure 6-3, the first rule specifies that all prefixes within the 214 area code require the operating system to dial the area code. The second rule specifies that some prefixes in the 972 area require 1 plus the area code, and the third rule specifies that the remaining 972 prefixes only require the area code.

The following list describes other essential dialing features that users configure in the Edit Location dialog box:

- **Outside lines**   Each dialing rule defines how users access an outside line for local and long-distance calls. Users can also disable call waiting, if necessary, and configure whether the location uses tone or pulse dialing. Users configure all of this in the General tab of the Edit Location dialog box.

- **Calling cards**   Travelling users frequently use calling cards for long-distance connections. They configure those connections in the Calling Card tab of the Edit Location dialog box. Users can choose one of the predefined calling card types—such as AT&T via 1010ATT0 or MCI via 10102220—or create their own. Having chosen a calling card type, users provide the card numbers and PINs (personal identification numbers). The Calling Card tab shows an example of what it's going to dial at the bottom of the dialog box.

TIP: You can't connect your computer's modem directly to a PBX (private branch exchange) system—doing so will fry it. While modems are analog devices, most PBX systems are digital. However, a few companies sell adapters that allow you to connect a modem to a PBX system; Innovative Trek Technology Pte Ltd (*http://www.ittrek.com/npkeyxs.html*) and TeleAdapt (*http://www.teleadapt.com*) are two such companies. An alternative to using an adapter to connect to a PBX system—particularly when taking your portable computer on visits to another company—is to look for a fax machine, which uses an analog phone line, and ask whether you can borrow its line for a few moments.

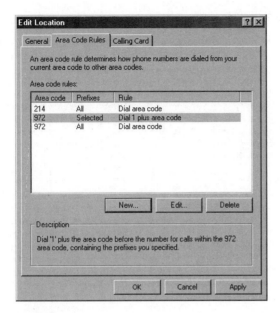

Figure 6-3
The Area Code Rules tab of the Edit Location dialog box.

Offline Files and Folders

Mobile users generally find themselves in one of two situations: either they're connected to the network and have full access to the files on it, or they're not connected to the network and must have some way to take those files with them. Well, one of Windows 2000 Professional's biggest innovations is offline files and folders. This feature provides similar functionality to the Briefcase from Windows NT Workstation 4.0 and Windows 98, but it's far more complete and definitely more intuitive.

Users make any network file or folder available offline by choosing Make Available Offline from its pop-up menu. Windows 2000 Professional copies those files to the portable computer and will endeavor to keep them synchronized with the network. And, unlike Briefcase, users can select a shared folder and make it available offline. That's all there is to it. Offline files remain in their original *namespace* whether the computer is offline or not. That means that users can find their offline files in My Network Places, as shown in Figure 6-4 on the following page, just as if they were still connected to the network. Even though many more files and folders might be available on the network when connected to it, when not connected to the network, users only see those files and folders that they chose to make available offline. Notice too how Windows Explorer

131

indicates that a file or a folder is available offline by putting a small overlay on the bottom left of each icon.

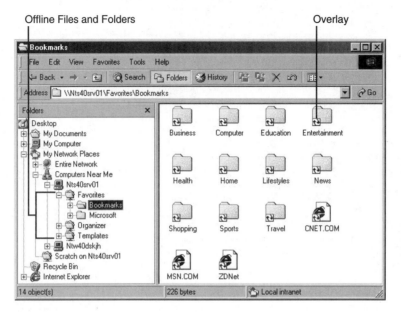

Figure 6-4
Offline files and folders in Windows Explorer.

The first time users make a file available offline, Windows 2000 Professional starts a wizard that explains offline files and folders and helps users configure how this feature works. Users can choose to display reminders about their connection status in the taskbar. They can choose to automatically synchronize with the network each time they log on to or log off the computer. All of these options are configurable in the Offline Files tab of the Folder Options dialog box (available via Windows Explorer's Tools menu). Users can also determine how much space the operating system sets aside for offline files, remove offline files from the local computer, and determine how the operating system behaves when the computer goes offline.

Going Offline

When the operating system loses the network connection, Windows 2000 Professional notifies the user by displaying a ScreenTip next to the Offline Files button in the taskbar. This ScreenTip tells users that they're no longer connected to the network but they can continue working offline. If configured properly, the operating system displays this ScreenTip on a regular basis—every 60 minutes by default—to remind users that they're working offline. If users want more information than was provided by the ScreenTip, they can click the Offline Files button on the taskbar to display the Offline Files Status dialog box shown in Figure 6-5. This dialog box indicates the connection that's offline as well as its current status. If the computer is available and users want to go back online, synchronizing their offline changes, they click Synchronize.

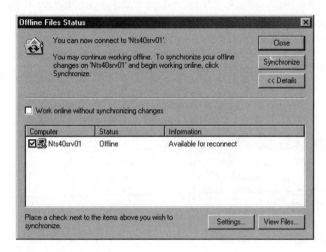

Figure 6-5
The Offline Files Status dialog box.

> NOTE: Administrators and users who share folders can control whether other users can make a file or a folder available offline. They can also configure a shared folder so that Windows 2000 Professional automatically makes available offline any file a user opens. Administrators and users can configure these options by clicking Caching in the Sharing tab of a folder's Properties dialog box.

Synchronizing Offline Files

By default, Windows 2000 Professional synchronizes offline files and folders each time users log on to and log off a network connection. They choose Synchronize from the Windows Explorer Tools menu to display the Items To Synchronize dialog box. This dialog box shows each shared folder—not each connection— containing offline files, and users can clear the check boxes next to each shared folder that they don't want to synchronize. Users then click Synchronize, and the operating system compares each offline file to the corresponding file on the network, making one or the other current. If the operating system finds a new file in an offline folder (on the network or on the local computer), it copies it to the other location.

Synchronization is highly configurable, allowing users to determine when Windows 2000 Professional synchronizes each offline file and folder. That is, users can create schedules that are appropriate for each shared folder. Users schedule synchronization for each network connection by clicking Setup in the Items To Synchronize dialog box. This displays the Synchronization Settings dialog box shown in Figure 6-6. Users have three choices: synchronizing files when they log on to and log off the network, when the computer is idle, or at a scheduled time (daily, weekly, or at regular intervals). In all cases, users can choose the network connection and shared folders to which the settings apply. Users can also choose what files and folders to synchronize based upon the type of connection.

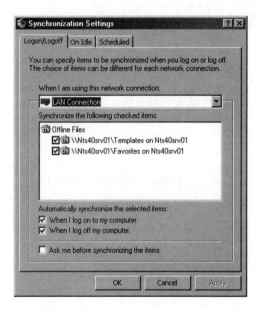

Figure 6-6
The Synchronization Settings dialog box.

The following list contains additional notes about using files offline:

- If users add files to an offline folder, Windows 2000 Professional copies those files to the network when it synchronizes the folder. Files added to the network folder are also copied to the local computer when the operating system synchronizes the folder.

- If users delete a file from an offline folder (and no one else has made changes to the network file), Windows 2000 Professional will remove the file from the network folder when it synchronizes the folder.

- Windows 2000 Professional performs file-level synchronization. If both versions of a file change, users can choose whether to preserve the network version or the local version, or they can choose to keep both. If users keep both versions, the operating system prompts them to rename the local version, and both versions appear in both locales.

- If users make a folder available offline and that folder contains shortcuts to other documents on the network, Windows 2000 Professional makes the documents that the shortcuts point to available offline. However, if an offline folder contains a shortcut to another folder, Windows 2000 Professional does not make that folder available offline.

- Permissions remain the same. When working with offline files, Windows 2000 Professional enforces permissions as though the computer was still connected to the network.

Briefcase as an Alternative

Briefcase was a great idea, but it has several drawbacks. Files can get out of synch easily. Users aren't able to make synchronization copies of shared folders; they have to copy subfolders instead. And the biggest drawback is that files don't show up in their original namespaces; users have to copy them to a Briefcase folder. Users often have files and folders from several different shared folders all in one Briefcase. Still, considering that little else was available in the base operating system, Briefcase was an easy way to pack files up for the road.

Briefcase hasn't changed in Windows 2000 Professional. On a folder's pop-up menu, users choose New and then choose Briefcase. After creating a Briefcase, they copy files to it from the network. Synchronizing the Briefcase means choosing Update All from its pop-up menu. Similar rules apply both to synchronizing Briefcases and to synchronizing offline files and folders. The operating system updates changed files and new files in offline folders. If a file changes in both locations, users can choose between overwriting either file or skipping the file.

With Windows 2000 Professional's offline files and folders, users have little reason to use Briefcase. There are exceptions, of course. Briefcase is better over a direct cable connection. Briefcase is the only choice if users want to put shared files on a floppy disk, take the disk with them, and then synchronize the disk when they return.

Dynamic Hardware Support

Windows 2000 Professional enables users to squeeze out every capability their portable computers can provide. For example, the operating system has the most advanced support for Plug and Play, allowing it to dynamically reconfigure the computer while it is running. This means that the operating system recognizes when users install or remove devices such as batteries, PC Cards, and other removable devices such as floppy disks and CD-ROM drives. The operating system also has built-in support for portable computers' special hardware requirements, including docking stations and power management.

The following list describes the Windows 2000 Professional features in which mobile users will be most interested, and you'll learn more about each of these in the following sections:

- **PC Cards** Users can insert and remove PC Cards, and Windows 2000 Professional dynamically configures the computer without requiring a restart.

- **Power management** Windows 2000 Professional manages the computer's power so mobile users get more life out of their computers' batteries.

- **Hardware profiles** Windows 2000 Professional maintains separate hardware configurations for when a portable computer is docked and undocked.

You should make sure that your computer is fully capable of using Windows 2000 Professional's hardware features. Some portable computers will require a Flash BIOS upgrade, for example. And, as noted by Mark Minasi in the December 1998 issue of *Windows NT Magazine,* make sure that the new portable computer you purchase supports the Advanced Configuration and Power Interface (ACPI). According to Minasi, "ACPI machines are still scarce. Don't assume that because you pay $6000 for a newly released machine, it'll work with [Windows 2000]." Minasi also points out that Microsoft favors ACPI over APM 1.2 because the ACPI standard is defined better than Advanced Power Management (APM) and is much easier to support.

PC Cards

PC Cards are the most exciting technology to hit portable computers since their invention. PC Cards allow users to insert a credit-card–sized device into a card slot, and then the operating system dynamically configures it, making that device immediately available. Users can insert a PC Card network adapter, for example, and the operating system configures the device, loads the network drivers, and connects to the network—emitting a satisfied "bleep" that lets you know that the operating system has done its job well. The operating system then notifies Windows Explorer of the change, and Windows Explorer updates its window to include the new network connection. When users remove the network adapter, the operating system reconfigures the computer, disconnects from the network, and unloads the network drivers.

ACPI versus APM Portable Computers

With a computer that has an ACPI BIOS, Windows 2000 Professional delivers the following features:

- Hibernation
- Low-power system states (sleep states)
- Low-power processor states
- Low-power device states
- Battery management, including support for:
  - ❑ Multiple batteries
  - ❑ Dynamic battery/alternating current (AC) changes
- Hot and warm docking and undocking
- Hot-swapping of Integrated Drive Electronics (IDE) and floppy devices
- Hot-swapping of PC Cards and CardBus cards

Windows 2000 Professional includes support for legacy portable computers that don't have an ACPI BIOS. The operating system supports hibernation, suspend and resume, and basic battery level reporting by way of the APM BIOS. The operating system also recognizes hardware by way of the Plug and Play BIOS, but only when it boots, and it also supports cold docking and undocking via hardware Profiles. Note that Microsoft ships Windows 2000 Professional with APM disabled, but users can enable it using the Power Options Properties dialog box.

Windows 2000 Professional's PC Card support covers hundreds of devices, including modems, network adapters, SCSI (Small Computer System Interface) adapters, multifunction adapters, and many more. Hot-swapping PC Card devices works only on an ACPI portable computer, but the operating system does recognize PC Card devices on an APM portable computer when it boots. The operating system ships with drivers for most of the PC Card devices that the operating system supports (thus, I recommend that users take their Windows 2000 Professional CD-ROM with them when they travel). Some devices don't have drivers on the Windows 2000 Professional CD-ROM, but you can certainly download them from the manufacturer's Web site or call the manufacturer's help desk. For more information about Windows 2000 Professional's Plug and Play implementation as well as its support for PC Cards, see Chapter 13, "Broader Hardware Support." The following list summarizes what you'll learn in that chapter and describes what makes these features so suitable for portable computers:

- **Dynamic reconfiguration**   Windows 2000 Professional recognizes when users install or remove devices such as PC Cards and then dynamically reconfigures the computer.

- **Resource allocation**   Windows 2000 Professional automatically assigns resources to each device as the operating system enumerates it. If required, the operating system can reallocate other devices' resources in order to free those resources for a particular device.

- **Driver loading**   Windows 2000 Professional determines the drivers required by each device and automatically loads them. If the operating system doesn't find the drivers already installed, it asks the user for a disk or other location where it can find them.

- **Device notifications**   Windows 2000 Professional notifies programs of certain Plug and Play events, allowing them to adjust themselves accordingly. For example, the operating system notifies Windows Explorer when users insert a network adapter.

Power Management

Battery life—it's the answer most mobile users give when they're asked what their biggest computing problem is. Windows 2000 Professional improves battery life.

The ACPI gives Windows 2000 Professional direct control over power management and Plug and Play functionality. This is in lieu of the APM BIOS controlling these features. The operating system provides a general method for handling power management, docking, Plug and Play, and other events. It takes over battery management policy from the APM BIOS, and it can manage batteries that have a Smart Battery subsystem interface or a Control Method Battery (CMBatt) interface. In addition to battery management, the ACPI enables three levels of power management, as the following list describes:

- **System power management**   Windows 2000 Professional can suspend the computer. The operating system also has the capability to control how devices wake the computer.

- **Device power management**   Windows 2000 Professional is capable of putting devices in lower-power states based on how much they are used by applications. For example, PC Card modems quickly drain a portable computer's battery but, by putting a PC Card modem in a low-power state, Windows 2000 Professional limits the modem's impact on battery life.

Traveling with Windows 2000 Professional

Users should prepare properly before traveling with Windows 2000 Professional. First, they should back up important files to the network or a tape drive. Storing those files in the My Documents folder makes that task easier. Users should also make network files available offline if they want to use those files on the road. It's always a good idea to test those files to make sure they open properly.

My next two recommendations help make sure that you won't run into any surprises. Make certain you've prepared the dial-up network connections you'll need and have tested that they work. On the road, you might not have the telephone numbers, the Domain Name System (DNS) addresses, or other information available. Also make sure you pack the Windows 2000 Professional CD-ROM in your briefcase or, alternatively, copy the installation files to the computer's hard disk— a bit of added insurance.

There are just a couple of things I recommend you do when you arrive at your destination. First, set the time zone so that it reflects your current location. Second, change your dial location. Both actions help ensure that the operating system will behave as you expect.

■ **Processor power management** While Windows 2000 Professional is idle but not sleeping, it can put the processor in a lower-power state, conserving more power.

Users configure battery-management policy and other power management features using the Power Options Properties dialog box shown in Figure 6-7. In the Control Panel, users double-click the Power Options icon. The following list describes the primary features in this dialog box that will interest users:

■ **Power schemes** Users can choose or create new power schemes that set how much idle time must pass before the operating system suspends the computer. They can also set how much idle time must pass before the operating system spins down the hard disk or turns off the monitor. Each of these settings is separate, and users configure them in the Power Schemes tab of the Power Options Properties dialog box.

■ **Advanced behaviors** In the Advanced tab of the Power Options Properties dialog box, users can select whether to display the power status on the taskbar and whether the operating system prompts them for a password when the computer awakens.

■ **Support for hibernation** Some portable computers support hibernation, which means that the computer stores everything in memory to disk and then powers down. When users power up the computer, everything returns to its previous state. Hibernation requires an amount of free disk space equivalent to the amount of RAM. Users configure hibernation in the Hibernate tab of the Power Options Properties dialog box.

■ **Support for APM** If users' computers support APM, users can enable support for it in the APM tab of the Power Options Properties dialog box. Enabling APM allows the operating system to suspend the computer when it's idle for a certain period of time. If users don't enable APM on a computer that doesn't support ACPI, they won't see the System Standby list in the Power Schemes tab.

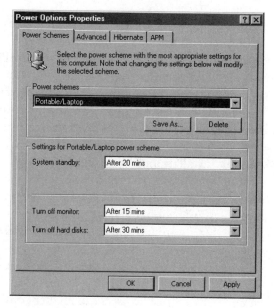

Figure 6-7
The Power Schemes tab of the Power Options Properties dialog box.

Hardware Profiles

Windows 2000 Professional has built-in support for docking stations (and port replicators). This provides users the mobility of a portable computer and the extensibility and versatility of a desktop computer. Many corporations are turning to the combination of portable computers and docking stations as replacements for desktop computers.

A typical portable computer has a couple of PC Card slots. Users might keep a modem in one of the slots. In order to connect to the network, they must insert a PC Card network adapter in the other slot. Both slots are then gone, and users are inconvenienced by having to unplug the network adapter before packing up the computer to go. In this scenario, users don't have the benefit of a large monitor, and they have to plug in and unplug additional devices (such as a keyboard and a mouse) from the back of the computer. Docking stations present a very different scenario. Users insert the network adapter in one of the docking station's PC Card slots. They plug the monitor, the keyboard, and the mouse into the docking station, too. When they're ready to go, they simply suspend the computer and lift it from the docking station. When they return, they put the computer back on the docking station and the network adapter, the monitor, the keyboard, and the mouse are available once again. In either case, Windows 2000 Professional automatically reconfigures the computer.

Part of what makes "hot docking" work is hardware profiles. In essence, a hardware profile tells the operating system which devices to start and how to configure each one. The operating system creates two hardware profiles for portable computers: Docked, used when the user connects the computer to the docking station, and Undocked. In the scenario described earlier, Docked would enable the network adapter, the monitor, the keyboard, and the mouse; Undocked would not. For desktop computers, the operating system creates a single hardware profile called Profile 1. Profile 1 initially contains all of the devices that the setup program detects during installation. Users can, of course, alter an existing hardware profile or create new hardware profiles. To alter a hardware profile, users specify whether a device is enabled or disabled in that profile.

To configure hardware profiles, users double-click the System icon in the Control Panel, then they click the Hardware tab and click the Hardware Profiles button. They then see the Hardware Profiles dialog box shown in Figure 6-8. There isn't a New button in this dialog box; to create a new hardware profile, users copy an existing profile by clicking the Copy button and then rename it by clicking the Rename button. Mobile users can further configure a profile by selecting the profile in the Available Hardware Profiles list and clicking Properties. In the hardware profile's Properties dialog box, they can specify that they're using a portable computer and whether the profile applies to a docked or undocked configuration.

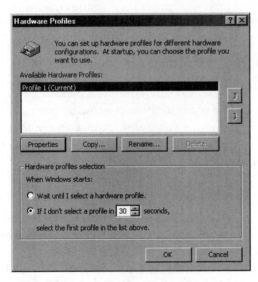

Figure 6-8
The Hardware Profiles dialog box.

Users determine which devices are enabled in each profile by using the Device Manager. To open the Device Manager, users click Device Manager in the Hardware tab of the System Properties dialog box. They double-click a device to open its Properties dialog box. Then they check or clear the check box next to a hardware profile to enable or disable the device in that profile. If users disable a device in a hardware profile, Windows 2000 Professional does not load drivers for that device and does not allocate resources to it. The operating system stores information about each hardware profile in the registry.

Enhanced Security for Mobile Users

In addition to battery life and portable computer configurations, security is a concern for mobile users. BIOS password protection keeps prying eyes away from important documents only until somebody figures out how to reset the password. Windows 2000 Professional's logon security keeps most other marauders away. File encryption keeps the more clever bandits at bay. However, for mobile users, security means more than just protecting important documents from intruders. Security also means backing up those files in case of failure. In addition, security means protecting the computer from viruses, which can wreak untold havoc on a computer's file system.

Windows 2000 Professional's new Backup utility is greatly enhanced over Windows NT Workstation 4.0's Backup utility. It has a wizard that walks users step by step through the backup process. And users can use it to back up files to the network before packing up their portable computers. To make it easy to back up those crucial documents, my recommendation is that users store all documents in the My Documents folder. Doing so means that there is a single folder to back up. Note that if the portable computer participates in a Windows 2000 network—see Chapter 20, "Lower Total Cost of Ownership with Microsoft Windows 2000 Server"—Windows 2000 Professional can automatically mirror documents on the server, making it unnecessary to manually back up those files.

Virus Protection

Viruses are another matter with no easy answer. And yet, with the number of disks that mobile users swap and the amount of time they spend on the Internet, most users' computers are at significant risk for contracting viruses. The best defense includes more than one action:

■ **Education** Users should understand the various ways that viruses can and cannot spread. That is, they should understand that their computer can catch a virus from a program they downloaded off the Internet, but not from the text of an e-mail message (unless they open an infected message). They should also know the traditional symptoms of viruses, which include erratic behavior, unusual error messages, lost files, or a computer that fails to start properly.

■ **Virus scanners**   A virus scanner is the only physical weapon users have for combating viruses. Virus scanners come in two flavors. Some actively monitor all access to the file system for any activity that suggests a virus; for example, this type of scanner would leap on a program that writes data to the master boot record (MBR). Others work on demand, examining every file on the user's computer for signatures that indicate the presence of a virus. Still other virus scanners combine both methods.

Encrypting File System

Windows 2000 Professional's Encrypting File System (EFS) encrypts files on the disk. EFS encrypts files using a randomly generated key, which is stored in non-paged memory to ensure that the operating system never stores the key in the paging file. EFS supports encryption for individual files, as well as for all of the contents of an entire folder. For more information about EFS, see Chapter 11, "Strongest Local and Network Security."

The entire encryption process is transparent to users once they've configured it. In other words, they work with encrypted files just as they do with any others. Users don't have to decrypt files in order to use them—EFS handles that process automatically. To enable encryption for a file or a folder, users choose Properties from its pop-up menu. In the General tab of the file's or folder's Properties dialog box, users click the Advanced button to display the Advanced Attributes dialog box as shown in Figure 6-9, and then check the Encrypt Contents To Secure Data check box. If users encrypt a folder, Windows 2000 Professional asks them if they want to encrypt the files in that folder only or the files in that folder and all its subfolders.

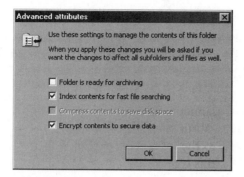

Figure 6-9
The Advanced Attributes dialog box for managing the contents of a folder.

Although Windows 2000 Professional allows users to encrypt individual files, I recommend that users encrypt entire folders. Doing so ensures that the operating system encrypts all files in that folder, including new files that users create as well as temporary files that programs create in the same folder as the original document. The following list suggests what specific folders mobile users should encrypt:

- **My Documents**   Mobile users should encrypt the My Documents folder, since that's where the operating system stores their documents by default.

- **Temp**   Encrypt the Temp folder so that no one can read the temporary copies of documents that most programs create while you're editing them. The Temp folder is in *systemdrive* by default.

Additional notes about EFS:

- File compression and file encryption are mutually exclusive.

- Users can encrypt files only on the NTFS file system, and they cannot encrypt system files.

- The user who encrypts a file or a folder is the only person who can open it.

- Copying files to a folder that's not encrypted decrypts the file.

- Users must move files into an encrypted folder using Cut and Paste instead of Drag and Drop. Drag and Drop does not automatically encrypt files when moving them.

- Users can encrypt files and folders on a remote computer as long as the administrator enables remote encryption.

- Encrypted files are not encrypted as they're transmitted over a network.

- Administrators can use a recovery policy to recover encrypted files if users lose their file encryption certificate or private key.

CHAPTER SEVEN

Superior Multilingual Support

Microsoft Windows 2000 Professional's language support is superior to that of any of its predecessors. Far and away the most significant enhancement is that all language editions are built on a single set of compiled components, so they all contain the same application programming interfaces (APIs), fonts, keyboard layouts, etc. The new operating system also implements Unicode 2, which you will learn about in this chapter.

All of this enables a variety of capabilities depending on the version of Windows 2000 Professional you use. There are three categories of Windows 2000 Professional that provide multilingual support: the English version, a collection of fully localized versions, and the new multilanguage version. There are more than 20 fully localized versions in the second category. The most basic capability is that users can read documents written in a variety of languages. Next, users can write multilingual documents. Other versions of Windows—including Windows 95, Windows 98, and Windows NT Workstation 4.0—had both of these capabilities, although the capabilities were limited in scope.

Windows 2000 Professional, Multilanguage Version (available separately), goes two steps further: first, by removing the limitations that existed in previous versions of Windows and second, by allowing users to change the language that the operating system uses to display its user interface (UI). The UI language-changing capability requires the multilanguage version of the operating system, and it means that any user can log on to a workstation and use the operating system in his or her preferred tongue. This new multilanguage version of Windows 2000 Professional will provide users with the maximum flexibility to choose the language in which they want to work, while reducing the management burden on network administrators.

For the network administrator, the multilanguage version means simplicity and reduced total cost of ownership (TCO). Now the administrator only needs to manage, support, and do service pack updates with one operating system code base. Before, network administrators had to maintain separate versions of the operating system, depending on the particular languages used in the organization. The multilanguage version now provides a simple, cost-effective solution for managing multilingual computing environments.

This chapter tells you more about these capabilities. It first describes the different language editions available. Then it describes the multilingual capabilities built into Windows 2000 Professional and how users can take advantage of them. Finally, it tells how best to administer Windows 2000 Professional on a multilingual network, and it makes specific recommendations for domain, machine, and user names.

Language Edition Availability

The goal of Windows 2000 Professional's language support is to enable multilingual networks, computing environments, and documents. Microsoft will ship 24 language editions—slightly fewer than Windows 98—and each of those language editions will support the input, display, processing, and output of text in all the languages supported by Windows 2000 Professional. All language editions should be available within three months of the English edition, with the exception of the Arabic and Hebrew editions, for which you should allow up to six months.

In addition to the various language editions, Microsoft will ship Windows 2000 Professional, Multilanguage Version. This edition provides the resources necessary to display the user interface in any supported language; for example, allowing one user of a computer to use it in French and another user logging on to the same computer to use it in German. Windows 2000 Professional, Multilanguage Version, is available through volume licensing programs such as Microsoft Open License Program (MOLP), Microsoft Select Agreement, and Microsoft Select Enterprise Agreement. The multilanguage version can also be obtained preinstalled on a new computer via an OEM license program.

Expect an initial release of Windows 2000 Professional, Multilanguage Version, to ship within six to eight weeks of the English edition; it will be updated with additional languages approximately four to six months later.

Stop! Learn These Important Concepts

The following sections describe important concepts that are essential for understanding Windows 2000 Professional's support for international users. This list summarizes those concepts:

- **Locale** is the information that the operating system maintains about the user's language, country, and cultural conventions.

- **Character encoding** relates binary values to alphanumeric characters, punctuation, and symbols. Other names for character encoding are *character set* and *code page*.

- **National language support** is an API that allows applications to manipulate the locale and the settings that relate to character encoding.

- **Localizable resources** are units of program code, strings, images, and icons that are kept separate from an application's main code. Localizable resources are kept in resource files that can be easily translated from one language to another.

Locale

A *locale* is the collection of information that the operating system maintains about the user's language, country, and cultural conventions. The language might be French, for example, and the sub-language might be French as it's spoken in Canada, France, or Switzerland. Even though a locale is presented as a combination of a language with a country, it is not a language setting. Some elements of a locale can be set and stored on a per-user basis; others (international or national standards data such as the name of the country or language or the ISO country code) are static and cannot be changed. The locale also includes default values for the following:

- Currency symbol
- Date, time, and number formatting
- Localized days of the week and months of the year
- Abbreviation for the name of the country
- Character encoding information
- Sorting and searching rules

Sorting and searching rules (the last item in the previous list) are more complex than most other international issues. Sorting and searching algorithms must follow the proper language rules for the locale in which users are using the information. For example, in the Spanish alphabet, CH is a unique character between C and D. In French, diacritics are sorted from right to left instead of from left to right, as they are sorted in English. A locale defines sorting and searching rules.

Windows 2000 Professional defines three types of locales:

- **System locale**   Every installation of Windows 2000 Professional has a default *system locale*. The system locale specifies which code pages the operating system uses by default and therefore determines which non-Unicode applications will work properly. The system locale only affects non-Unicode applications and is a per-machine setting. It is specified during setup, and post-setup changes require a reboot.

- **User locale**   In addition to a system locale, the operating system keeps a *user locale* for each user. The user locale affects date, time, and number formatting and is a per-user setting. Users can change locales without rebooting via the Regional Options icon in the Control Panel.

- **Input locale**   An *input locale* is the pairing of a language with a means of inputting that language. The implementation of an input locale could be in the form of a simple keyboard layout or in a more complex form such as an input method editor (IME). For example, the combination of the English language with a French keyboard layout would be an input locale. This determines what language is being used and how the text of that language is being entered. The rationale behind input locales is that most users who type text in multiple languages prefer to do so with a single keyboard layout whenever possible. Thus, a French user might prefer to write English, Spanish, and German text, all with the same keyboard layout: French.

Character Encoding

The tables that define character encoding are frequently known as *code pages*. Each numeric value (*code point*) in the table represents an alphanumeric character, a punctuation mark, or a symbol. Think of a code page as a table that relates binary numbers to the characters used to represent a given set of languages. Programs exchange information using encoded characters, then they render those characters on the screen using fonts. The American National Standards Institute (ANSI) defines several code pages. There are also several OEM (original equipment manufacturer) code pages that were originally designed for the needs of specific computer hardware. Here are a few examples of code pages and the language groups they represent:

Code Page	Type	Language
437	OEM	United States English
855	OEM	Cyrillic
864	OEM	Arabic
866	OEM	Russian
932	ANSI	Japanese
1250	ANSI	Central European
1254	ANSI	Turkish

Single-byte character sets include a maximum of 256 code points. The first 128 code points are defined as the standard ASCII (American Standard Code for Information Interchange) characters. The second 128 characters depend on the language. For instance, the first 128 characters of a set used for Greek are the standard ASCII characters, and the second 128 characters are those required to represent Greek text. All versions of Windows support the OEM and the ANSI single-byte character sets.

A *multibyte character set* uses combinations of either 8 bits or 16 bits to define each character. These character sets are primarily used for Asian languages, where 256 characters are not enough. Various vendors define different standards for multibyte character sets. Examples of multibyte character sets include Shift-JIS, GB 2312, and Big5.

Unicode is a double-byte character encoding where each character is represented by 16 bits (2 bytes). Unicode is the character encoding used by the Windows NT family and by Windows 2000 Professional

National Language Support

In Windows 2000 Professional, *National Language Support* is the set of system functions that applications access through the National Language Support API (NLSAPI). Through these functions, applications gain access to information such as the following:

- Locale information such as formats for date, time, number, and currency

- Localized names of countries, or names of days and months

- Character mapping tables that map ANSI or OEM code pages to Unicode

- Character typing information such as whether a code point represents a letter, a number, a spacing character, or a punctuation symbol

- Sorting rules and algorithms that define how to sort text in a particular language

- Font information such as which fonts are supported for various sections of the Unicode character set

- Keyboard layout information

Localizable Resources

Localizable resources are bits of information in a program that change from one locale to another. Generally, user interface elements such as the text on menus or in dialog boxes are localizable resources. Other localizable resources might include rules for spelling or hyphenation. Localizable resources are usually stored within resource files, which are text files with the RES file extension. The developer compiles a resource file and affixes it to the application's executable file. Windows 2000 Professional itself is an application that makes use of localizable resources. Recall that all language editions of Windows 2000 Professional share the same core of compiled program code. The only things that change from edition to edition are the localizable resources.

Windows 2000 Professional's Core Program Code

Windows 2000 Professional's predecessors were worldwide smashing successes. Such success has placed a heavy burden on Windows, however, as the requirements put upon the operating system have fragmented its code base. That's also true of applications designed for Windows. European language editions use single-byte character sets. Far Eastern language editions use multibyte character sets. Middle Eastern language editions use single-byte character sets, but require complex bi-directional layout and rendering technology. Each language edition includes specialized code and changes to existing code that enable it to handle each type of character set or special feature. For instance, the Asian and Middle Eastern editions are supersets of the core U.S. and European editions, containing additional APIs to handle more complex text input and layout requirements.

That has been the story up until now.

For Windows 2000 Professional, Microsoft distributes a global set of compiled components for all language editions—that is, Microsoft has combined the disparate code bases. In addition to the consolidation that the global program code brings to the new operating system, the existence of this common core allows developers to more easily build global applications that support multilingual documents and interfaces without using special tools; without using multiple editions of the operating system; and without resorting to specialized, proprietary code. The global components include all the APIs, flags, locales, fonts, and character sets required for all supported languages. Here are additional notes about Windows 2000 Professional's global components:

- All language editions are created from the same core code base.

- Each language edition contains all the international APIs (see "International APIs" below).

- Each language edition contains all the components necessary— including IMEs—to enter text in all languages that the operating system supports.

- Each language edition comes with the components necessary— including at least one font to represent each language—to display and format text in all languages that the operating system supports.

N O T E : An *input method editor* (IME) translates multiple keystrokes into single characters. For example, an IME allows users to input the thousands of characters in Asian languages with a standard 101-key keyboard. The IME consists of a dictionary of commonly used ideographs and an engine that converts keystroke combinations into phonetic and ideographic characters. In previous versions of Windows, only the language editions that required IMEs provided them. In contrast, each language edition of Windows 2000 Professional provides the necessary IMEs to enter text in all supported languages.

International APIs

Application developers can write generic code to handle data input, storage, and display for a large number of languages. Two APIs make this possible: the National Language Support API and the Multilingual API (MLAPI), both of which come with every language edition of Windows 2000 Professional. The Microsoft Developer Library provides the details of each API, but here's a brief summary:

- The NLSAPI contains functions for transforming strings, retrieving and manipulating code page information, and retrieving and manipulating locale information. The NLSAPI allows programs to query the system for information that changes depending on the language, country, or code page. Applications that fully utilize the NLSAPI will automatically change behavior based upon the information carried in the operating system's tables.

■ The MLAPI allows applications to handle different keyboard layouts and languages as well as on-the-fly changes to either—all of this with generic code. This API handles text layout (vertical versus horizontal text), keyboard layout changes, and so on. This is the API that enables transparent support for multilingual documents.

Unicode 2 Support

OEM character encoding was introduced with MS-DOS. ANSI character encoding was introduced with Windows 3.1. Unicode, a more recently developed double-byte encoding scheme, is in widest use today, and you can learn more about it at the Unicode Consortium's Web site: *http://www.unicode.org/*. The following table describes the evolution of character sets throughout Microsoft's operating systems:

Operating System	Character Sets
MS-DOS	OEM
Windows 3.0 and Windows 3.1	ANSI
Windows 95 and Windows 98	ANSI
Windows NT	OEM
	ANSI
	Unicode
Windows 2000 Professional	OEM
	ANSI
	Unicode 2

Unicode is almost as simple to use as ASCII, but it supports far more than the Latin alphabet. Characters are a fixed 16 bits wide, providing code points for more than 65,000 characters—enough to cover all the world's known characters, including those used in some of the world's oldest and most historic scripts. The Unicode language list includes Arabic, Armenian, Bengali, Chinese, Cyrillic, Devanagari, Georgian, Greek, Gujarati, Gurmukhi, Hebrew, Japanese Kanji, Japanese Kana, Kannada, Korean Hangul, Korean ideographs, Latin, Lao, Malayalam, Oriya, Tamil, Telugu, Thai, and Tibetan. The Unicode Consortium plans to add many more in the near future, including Braille, Burmese, Canadian Syllabics, Cherokee, Ethiopic, Khmer, Sinhala, and Syriac. Aside from the scripts required to represent each language, Unicode includes punctuation marks, diacritics, mathematical symbols, technical symbols, arrows, dingbats, and more. To date, Unicode defines codes for about 39,000 characters from all the world's alphabets, ideograph sets, and symbol collections. Figure 7-1 on the following page illustrates how a variety of scripts fit into the range of Unicode code points.

All products built on Windows NT technology have always used Unicode as their base character encoding. That means that, internally, Windows NT products represented all character strings with Unicode. Follow-up releases of Windows NT products used Unicode for the file system, the user interface, and network communication. Windows 2000 Professional uses the latest incarnation of Unicode—version 2. The operating system has additional code pages that facilitate translation between Unicode and other encoding schemes such as Macintosh, EBCDIC (Extended Binary Coded Decimal Interchange Code), and ISO (International Organization for Standardization). It also contains translation tables for the UTF-7 and UTF-8 (Unicode Translation Format) standards, which the operating system uses to exchange Unicode-based messages on networks and on the Internet. Additional advantages of Windows 2000 Professional's language and character support include the following:

- Provides a Unicode-based application environment

- Includes forward migration tools for existing non-Unicode data

- Allows unambiguous plain text, removing the requirement that applications tag text strings with code page information

- Supports Asian languages without all the programming tricks required to support variable-width character encodings

- Simplifies sharing data in mixed-language environments

- Supports conversion tables that allow non-Unicode applications to run in Windows 2000 Professional and also allow Unicode-enabled applications to operate in Windows 95 and Windows 98

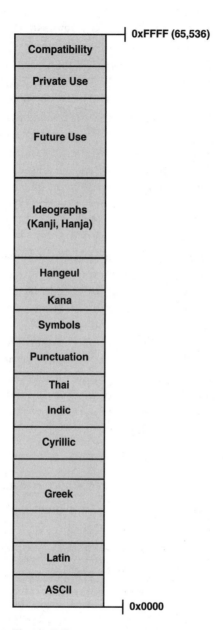

Figure 7-1
The arrangement of scripts in the Unicode range of code points.

Windows 2000 Professional doesn't abandon non-Unicode applications. It can imitate the Win32 application environment of any non-Unicode language edition of Windows, such as any edition of Windows 95 or Windows 98. For example, a Win32 application that uses code page 1251, which is a non-Unicode Russian character set, can run on a Spanish version of Windows 2000 Professional. System locales enable this functionality. For this to work properly, the appropriate *language group* (in this case, Cyrillic) must be installed. A language group is a software component that controls which system locales, user locales, and input locales the user can select. Microsoft provides 17 language groups, any combination of which can be installed at a given time.

Windows 2000 Professional does not allow two applications that use different languages to run at the same time if they use different (non-Unicode) code pages, since the operating system requires the user to restart the computer before changing the code page. Note that Unicode-based applications don't have this limitation, so users can run any two Unicode-based applications—regardless of the languages involved—side by side without having to reset the system locale. While this allows users to run localized Unicode applications, the major benefit is for developers, who can test a variety of localized applications on a single machine.

> **NOTE:** Sometimes a user might need to run an application intended for a different language edition of Windows 2000 Professional. For instance, a user might need to run a Greek non-Unicode application on the English edition of Windows 2000 Professional. The operating system supports this scenario. To do so, the user changes the system locale to Greek, restarts the computer, and runs the application. The operating system simulates the appropriate Win32 environment. While the user interface remains in English, the application runs just fine since the Greek code pages and fonts are loaded.

User Locale and Regional Settings

When users change the user locale, Windows 2000 Professional automatically updates regional settings such as the formats of numbers, currencies, times, and dates. The changes that the operating system makes reflect the appropriate country, language, and cultural conventions. For instance, when users choose English (United States), the currency symbol is the dollar sign ($), but when they choose English (United Kingdom), the currency symbol is the pound sign (£).

After users change the user locale, they can override any of the settings in the Numbers, Currency, Time, or Date tabs of the Regional Options dialog box. The following list describes the contents of each tab. Note that each tab shows an example at the top, allowing users to preview their changes before applying them.

- **Numbers** (see Figure 7-2) defines the format for numbers, including the character used for the decimal point, the character used for grouping digits, and the system of measurement (metric or U.S.).

- **Currency** defines the format for currency, including the currency symbol, the character used for grouping digits, the number of digits to the right of the decimal, and the format for negative values. Windows 2000 Professional includes support for the new euro symbol.

- **Time** defines the format for times, including the hour and minute separator as well as the symbols used for AM and PM.

- **Date** defines the format for dates, including the date separator and the formats for short and long dates. If the locale supports it, users can change calendar types.

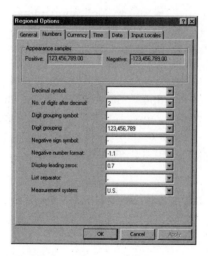

Figure 7-2
The Numbers tab of the Regional Options dialog box.

NOTE: The Date tab in the Regional Options dialog box allows users to determine how the operating system and applications interpret two-digit dates. That is, users specify a 100-year range in which the operating system considers all two-digit dates to fall. For instance, if users specify that two-digit dates fall between 1965 and 2064, 55 would mean 2055 and 65 would mean 1965. This option has no impact on four-digit dates. Not all applications rely on this feature, so it's not a total safeguard against the dreaded Year 2000 problem.

Support for Multilingual Documents

Users who communicate internationally often need to read documents written in languages other than their own. For instance, a user with the French edition of Windows 2000 Professional might want to read a document written in Chinese. Earlier versions of Windows presented various roadblocks to such users, requiring them to run a variety of operating system editions and a corresponding variety of applications. Another more-complex scenario involves creating a single document that contains more than one language. Instruction manuals that contain steps written in multiple languages are one example of this. Another example is the need that a supervisor might have to translate meeting minutes into several different languages for distribution around the world.

Previous versions of Windows had several limitations that made these scenarios difficult. Sometimes, developers came up with clever solutions to these problems, but the solutions usually led to complex, proprietary code that was difficult to maintain. The following problems were at the top of the list:

- File formats varied from one language edition of an application to the next.

- Editing Asian languages required IMEs that didn't exist in English or European editions of the operating system.

- Multilingual documents were possible only when the text was tagged with font and code page information, eliminating the possibility of mixed languages in ordinary text files.

- Multilingual documents were limited to scripts of similar types, preventing users from combining languages such as Arabic, Greek, Russian, and Japanese in a single document.

Installing Additional Languages

With Windows 2000 Professional, users can read and write multilingual documents as long as the applications use the operating system's international APIs and the appropriate language groups are installed on the computer. An administrator (of the computer running Windows 2000 Professional) must install the appropriate language groups, as users can't install language groups unless they have administrative permissions. In the Control Panel, double-click the Regional

Options icon. In the General tab, in the Language Settings For The System list, check the box next to each language group you want to install. After installing a language group, you must restart the computer.

> NOTE: Microsoft Internet Explorer 5 allows users to view Web sites that contain content in different languages. You can choose the languages you want to use in Internet Explorer 5 by choosing Internet Options from the Tools menu. In the Internet Options dialog box, click the Languages button; then, in the Language Preference dialog box, click the Add button and select the language you want to add. Adding a language to this list requires that the computer also have the appropriate font installed. You can install each language yourself, as described elsewhere in this chapter, or you can enable Internet Explorer to install languages on demand by clicking the Advanced tab on Internet Explorer's Options dialog box and then selecting Enable Install On Demand.

Customizing the Input Locales

The installed language groups allow users to read multilingual documents, but if users want to edit multilingual documents, they must create and install the appropriate input locales. Recall that an input locale is the pairing of a language and an input method. A keyboard layout is a table that maps certain keys on the keyboard to certain characters in Unicode. An input locale tells an aware application the language of the incoming text and tells Windows which table to use to map the keys on the keyboard to character codes. An example would be one input locale that pairs the French keyboard layout with the English language and another that pairs the same French keyboard layout with the German language. The user would then use the French keyboard layout to input both English and German text. Windows 2000 Professional stores input locales as part of the user's profile; therefore, each user configures his or her own.

Adding input locales is simple. In the Control Panel, double-click the Regional Options icon. In the Input Locales tab, shown in Figure 7-3, click the Add button to select a language and a keyboard layout (or an IME). Click the OK button to add the pair to the list of available input locales. To remove an input locale, select it and then click the Remove button. To change the keyboard layout or IME associated with a language, select the input locale and click the Properties button to display the Input Locale Properties dialog box; then, in the Keyboard Layout/IME list, select the keyboard layout you want to use. Windows 2000 Professional also allows users to customize how they switch between locales. That is, they can specify key sequences that automatically switch between one input locale and another, and they can specify whether the indicator appears on the taskbar. The following table describes these tasks, all of which can be performed in the Input Locales tab:

To Accomplish This	Do This
Set the default input locale	In the Installed Input Locales list, select the input locale you want to be the default, then click Set As Default.
Choose how to toggle Caps Lock	Do one of the following: Select the Press CAPS LOCK Key option button Select the Press SHIFT Key option button
Set a hot key for an input locale	In the Hot Keys For Input Locales list, select an input locale and then click the Change Key Sequence button.
Enable the input locale indicator	Check the Enable Indicator On Taskbar check box.

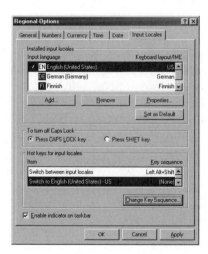

Figure 7-3
The Input Locales tab of the Regional Options dialog box.

Editing Multilingual Documents

While editing a document in an application that supports multilingual documents, users can switch between input locales in one of three ways, two closely related. First, they can use a hot key to change input locales. Windows 2000 Professional uses a default definition of Left Alt+Shift to alternate through each of the user's input locales. However, users can also associate hot keys with each individual input locale, or they can change the default used for toggling through all installed input locales for that user, as described in the previous section. Last, users can choose the input locale from the taskbar indicator. Clicking the taskbar indicator opens a menu, shown in Figure 7-4, from which users can choose an input locale. This taskbar indicator also reflects the current input locale when users press Left Alt+Shift to cycle through each. The following list summarizes the different methods for switching between input locales:

- Cycle through the input locales by pressing Left Alt+Shift until the taskbar indicator shows the desired input locale.

- Press the hot key associated with that input locale. For example, if you have associated Ctrl+Shift+0 with a locale, press that hot key.

- Click the taskbar indicator, then choose the desired input locale.

When users change input locales, the operating system notifies the current application that this event occurred. Note that the operating system notifies the current application, not all applications, because users can use a different input locale with each application they open on the desktop. An aware application uses the locale ID given to it by the operating system to tag its text with a language property. As a result, the application reacts appropriately to the keyboard, and the text that users see on the screen is appropriate. Not only that, but many applications have multilingual spell checkers and those also behave correctly. Applications can even use different input locales for different portions of a single document. As users move through a multilingual document, the application automatically changes the input locale to reflect the language to which the user is currently pointing.

Figure 7-4
The Input Locale taskbar indicator.

Windows 2000 Professional, Multilanguage Version

Large international organizations often require users to use more than one language. These companies must frequently install many different language versions of an operating system, instead of a single version with the same release date and the same set of service packs. The usual situation is that the organization dedicates a single computer to a single language—for example, an English system running English applications to handle English data. Users who need to communicate using more than one language are therefore forced to use multiple computers. A situation in which two users speak different languages and want to use the same computer is unthinkable. Each user would want the operating system's user interface to appear in their preferred language.

Previous versions of Windows—including Windows 95, Windows 98, and Windows NT Workstation 4.0—enabled an application to change its user interface's language and user locale on the fly. The developer created multiple language versions of each localizable resource and tagged them with language IDs. When users chose a language—typically through a menu—the application noted the user's choice and then specified a language ID to the Win32 API when retrieving resources. Thus, the application was able to display the user interface in the user's choice of language.

Windows 2000 Professional, Multilanguage Version, goes a step farther. Not only can users specify the language of an application's interface, but they can choose the language that the operating system uses to display its user interface. An administrator of a computer running Windows 2000 Professional, Multilanguage Version can install the user interface languages from a special CD-ROM that contains the required language resources and administrative tools. The program presents the administrator with a list of available languages, and the administrator chooses which ones to install: German, Russian, Spanish, Chinese, and so on. The program then copies the required resource files to the computer and updates the registry to reflect the languages available on the computer. As you learned at the beginning of this chapter, an initial version of Windows 2000 Professional, Multilanguage Version, will be available within six to eight weeks of the English edition, and additional languages will follow about four to six months later.

Once the administrator (of the local computer) has installed the chosen user interface languages, users will see the Menus And Dialogs Language list in the Regional Options dialog box. In this list, they can click the language they want the operating system to use. Changing the user interface language requires the current user to log off and log back on. Note that the user interface language is a per-user property and is part of each user's profile, so different users can use different languages. For example, you can configure the local Administrator account to always use English, regardless of the languages other users choose.

Network Administration Notes

The following list contains notes to help you better administer Windows 2000 Professional on a mixed-language network:

■ Windows 2000 Professional, Multilanguage Version, supports any upgrade path that the English edition supports. However, you can't upgrade from a localized edition of Windows 2000 Professional or Windows NT Workstation to the multilanguage version.

■ The ability to share multilingual data depends on the language groups installed on each computer, not on the network's domain structure. That said, homogeneous Windows 2000 networks are best for mixed-language environments, and grouping clients by language makes for easier administration.

■ In a mixed-language network, choose names carefully. A homogeneous environment uses UTF-8 for Domain Name System (DNS) names. For down-level clients, use ASCII for machine, domain, and user names.

■ Users can't log on to a computer that can't produce the characters needed for their user names and passwords. Windows 2000 Professional does allow users to change keyboards layouts when they log on, but only if the appropriate language groups were installed by an administrator (of the local computer). An administrator can add language groups with the Regional Options dialog box (available in the Control Panel) or during the setup process with the Advanced Settings dialog box. Chapter 3, "Setup Guide," describes this dialog box.

Comparison to Windows 98

Windows 98 and Windows 2000 Professional have many features in common. First, both support the NLSAPI and the MLAPI. Both handle input locale switching and multilingual input. Also, Microsoft produces multiple language editions of each operating system, although it releases a few more for Windows 98.

However, the two operating systems do have quite a few differences with regard to their multilingual support, mostly due to the fact that Windows 98 evolved from Windows 3.1. Windows 98 doesn't have native support for Unicode; it uses ANSI code pages instead. The lack of native Unicode support makes sharing data between machines running different code pages more difficult. Windows 98 can still run Unicode applications, but the applications must translate Unicode data to ANSI before making system calls. Other differences between the two operating systems include:

■ Windows 98 doesn't support multilingual user profiles or thread-based locales; thus, mechanisms for automatically changing an application's language don't exist.

■ Windows 98 doesn't support the ability to change the language it uses to display its own user interface, requiring users to maintain separate environments for each language in which they want to work.

■ The various language editions of Windows 98 don't share a single global set of compiled components; for example, Asian and Middle Eastern editions are supersets of the European edition. This means that IMEs are not available in the European edition of Windows 98.

More Imaging and Printing Capabilities

Microsoft Windows 2000 Professional's imaging and printing capabilities are subtle and easily overlooked, but they are some of the most important user-centered enhancements to the operating system. They make locating and adding printers much easier. Color documents look as users expect, due to Image Color Management (ICM) 2.0. And Windows 2000 Professional has support for a variety of new imaging devices, including scanners and digital cameras. The remaining imaging and printing features—the ones that are hard to improve upon—remain mostly as they were in Windows NT Workstation 4.0.

In addition to making it easier for users to create and print great documents, these new imaging and printing capabilities lower support costs. A bold statement, to be sure—but since users can easily find and install printers themselves, they no longer have to tie up the support desk's phone lines or, worse yet, clamor for the administrator's attention. The ability to search the organization for printers that have the appropriate features, or for printers that don't have long waiting lines, or for printers that are near the user's office means that the organization's resources are better used. In addition, network administrators will find that they have much better control over the network's printing resources and can even assign certain printers to individuals or groups of users. Steve Rigney said in the October 1998 edition of *PC Magazine,* "Network printing is the bane of every administrator's existence, and Microsoft appears to be trying to make this task easier."

This chapter describes these new imaging and printing capabilities, including the new Add Printer Wizard, the Point and Print feature, and the new Print dialog box. It describes one of the most innovative new features, Internet Printing, and a handful of others such as OpenType fonts, ICM 2.0, and support for scanners and cameras. Last, this chapter briefly touches on some features that are largely unchanged from Windows NT Workstation 4.0, just to assure you that they're still in working order.

Easier Printer Installation

Windows 2000 Professional supports both local and network printers. Network printers include those that are attached to a print server and those that are attached to the network with internal or external network interface cards. In short, users who are running any version of Windows that supports file and printer sharing can connect to any network printer that's shared—whether it's shared from a print server or from a peer computer. What catches many people by surprise is that Windows 2000 Professional can also connect to printers on the Internet (more on this feature later).

In order to connect to a printer—local or remote—you must install the drivers required to communicate with that printer. If you're using a local printer, or a printer on a network to which the computer is already connected, the communication problem is licked. There are three different ways to install printer drivers in Windows 2000 Professional: using the Add Printer Wizard, allowing the operating system to detect a Plug and Play printer, or using Point and Print to install a printer from the network. You will learn about each of these methods in the following sections.

The only "gotcha" is permissions. Permissions come into play for two different reasons. First, connecting to a network printer requires that the user has permission to do so. Assigning rights to a printer is up to the person who creates the network share. No other special permissions are required if the printer's driver files are available on the server or are already installed on the client. Second, the user must be a member of the local computer's Administrators group if the driver files need to be installed from another source, such as a floppy disk or a CD-ROM. The reason is that installing printer drivers requires permission to install trusted code, which only members of the local computer's Administrators group have. For more information about trusted code and how it enhances the operating system's security, see Chapter 10, "Most Reliable and Stable."

After installing a local printer in Windows 2000 Professional, you can share it with others, assuming that the network administrator hasn't implemented policies to prevent you from doing so. Sharing a printer also requires that you have Manage Printer permission on your computer. To share a printer, choose Sharing from the printer's pop-up menu; then, in the Sharing tab of the dialog box, select Shared As and type a name for the printer. You can also install additional drivers—so that other users with different versions of Windows can install drivers using Point and Print—by clicking the Additional Drivers button. After sharing a printer, Windows 2000 Professional can publish the shared printer to Active Directory if the computer participates in a Windows 2000 Server domain running the Active Directory service.

The Add Printer Wizard

Installing a local printer using the Add Printer Wizard isn't much different than doing the same in Windows NT Workstation 4.0. However, installing network printers is much easier, and the Add Printer Wizard also allows users to connect to printers on the Internet (more on this in "New Internet Printing," later in this chapter).

The Add Printer Wizard is in the Printers folder. As always, users can open this folder by choosing Settings from the Start menu and then choosing Printers. However, Windows 2000 Professional has changed the actual location of the Printers folder. In the Folders bar of Windows Explorer, it no longer appears under My Computer; it appears under Control Panel instead. This change makes sense and consolidates a variety of folders used for configuration purposes, such as the Fonts folder and the Scheduled Tasks folder.

To install a printer, click the Add Printer icon in the Printers folder, then follow the wizard's instructions. Figure 8-1 on the following page shows what it looks like when browsing the network for a printer. The wizard works a bit differently depending on whether Active Directory is available or not:

- **Active Directory Available** The wizard allows the user to search Active Directory for a printer based upon a variety of characteristics. "Better Ways to Find a Printer," later in this chapter, describes how to perform this feat.

- **Active Directory Unavailable** Users can install a printer using its UNC (uniform naming convention) path or its URL (Uniform Resource Locator). If installing a network printer, they specify its path in the form of *servername\printername*. If installing a printer from the Internet, they specify the path in the form of *http://*servername/ printername. Users can't direct the Add Printer Wizard to search for a printer if Active Directory isn't available; however, the wizard will allow them to browse the network if they click the Next button without specifying a UNC path or a URL.

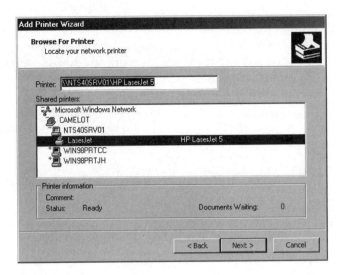

Figure 8-1
The Add Printer Wizard.

Plug and Play Printer Detection

Windows 2000 Professional includes more than 2500 printer drivers that are new or revised since Windows NT Workstation 4.0 was released. These drivers include support for all of the latest printers but, at the manufacturers' request, Microsoft has dropped support for most of the outdated ones.

Many of these printers are Plug and Play. Users plug the printer into the computer's parallel port and Windows 2000 Professional automatically detects the printer and installs the appropriate drivers. Most of the time, users have to restart the computer in order for the operating system to detect the printer. If the operating system doesn't automatically detect the printer, users can always use the Add Printer Wizard to install it, but this requires the user to know the printer's manufacturer and model. Note that a user has to be a member of the local computer's Administrators group in order to install printer drivers from a CD-ROM or a floppy disk. For more information about Windows 2000 Professional's Plug and Play implementation, take a look at Chapter 12, "Easy Device Installation."

Point and Print Printing

Point and Print is the easiest way to install a printer from the network. Users locate a printer in the My Network Places folder or by searching Active Directory. After locating a printer, users choose Connect from the printer's pop-up menu. Alternatively, users can drag a printer icon from the My Network Places folder to the Printers folder or open the printer's queue by typing its UNC path in the Run dialog box available from the Start menu. Windows 2000 Professional will copy the printer's drivers from the network and add an icon for the printer to the Printers folder.

If users are running Windows 2000 Professional, and if they are installing printers from a Windows 2000 Server domain, Point and Print works with no effort on the part of the network administrator. Other networks might provide support for Point and Print, so the network administrator should check the vendors' documentation. In order to make printer drivers from a Windows 2000 Server domain available to clients running operating systems other than Windows 2000 Professional, the network administrator must install the additional drivers required by those clients.

Better Ways to Find a Printer

The traditional method for users to locate a network printer is to browse the network. They must examine every server, hoping to find a shared printer, or they must have some prior knowledge about the printer such as the printer's UNC path. However, if Active Directory is available on the network, users can search this directory to locate printers near them, printers that have certain features, and so on. For more information about the benefits of Active Directory and how Windows 2000 Professional uses it, see Chapter 20, "Lower Total Cost of Ownership with Microsoft Windows 2000 Server."

In order to search Active Directory for a printer, a directory service must be installed on the local computer. If a directory service is not installed, Windows 2000 Professional will not be successful when users ask it to search for a printer. Even without a directory service, users can still connect to a printer in the My Network Places folder, in the new Printers dialog box, or by specifying the printer's UNC path or URL in the Run dialog box available from the Start menu.

There are two ways to search for a printer. Choose Search from the Start menu and then choose Find Printers. This opens the Find Printers window. Alternatively, click the Search For Printers hyperlink at the bottom of Windows Explorer's Search bar. This changes the Search bar so that it collects basic information about the printer. Both methods allow users to search for printers of a specific model or in a specific location. However, the Find Printers window also allows users to search for printers meeting additional criteria:

- Does the printer support double-sided printing?
- Can the printer staple its output?
- Can the printer print color documents?

■ Does the printer use a certain paper size?

■ Does the printer support a minimum resolution?

■ What is the printer's minimum speed?

Windows 2000 Professional displays the results in the Search Results list. Users can double-click a printer to view its queue. They can right-click a printer to install it.

NOTE: Administrators have significant control over how Active Directory publishes information about printers. For example, they can set policies to automatically point users to specific printers. They can also prevent Active Directory from publishing information about a specific printer or printers attached to a particular computer.

Similar Printer Configuration and Management

In Windows NT Workstation 4.0, users can set personal printing preferences. Doing so in Windows 2000 Professional is only slightly different. The menu command is different—it is Printing Preferences now instead of Document Defaults, which makes the feature more accessible thanks to a name that makes more sense. Users choose Printing Preferences from a printer's pop-up menu to display the printer's Printing Preferences dialog box as shown in Figure 8-2.

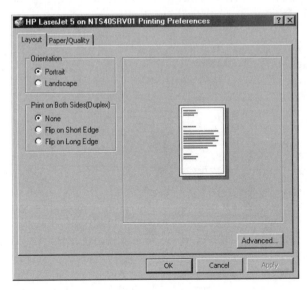

Figure 8-2
The Printing Preferences dialog box.

Users can change the printer's paper orientation, specify duplex printing, set the paper source, and configure a variety of other advanced features.

Like setting printer preferences, configuring the printer is much the same as it was in Windows NT Workstation 4.0. Figure 8-3 shows a printer's Properties dialog box, which users can display by choosing Properties from the printer's pop-up menu. Users can change the printer's properties only if they have Manage Printers permission. The following list describes the typical tabs you'll find in a printer's Properties dialog box:

- **General**   General properties
- **Sharing**   Printer share name and permissions
- **Ports**   Port selections and properties
- **Advanced**   Document scheduling and spooling properties
- **Security**   Security settings
- **Device Settings**   Device-specific properties

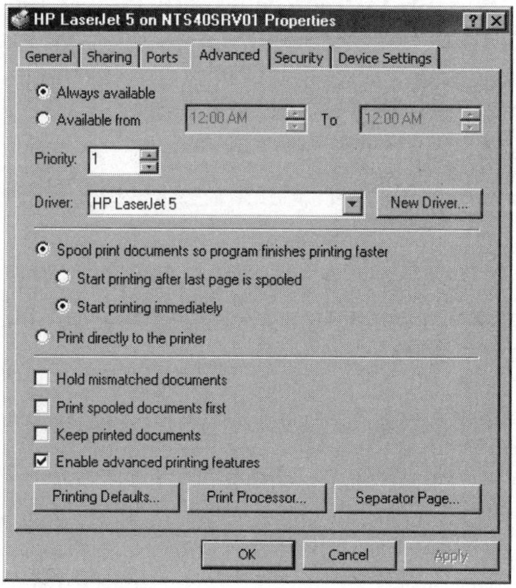

Figure 8-3
A typical printer Properties dialog box.

All users can pause, resume, restart, and cancel their own print jobs. They can also change a print job's priority if they have Manage Documents permission. Users double-click a printer's icon in the Printers folder to view its queue, as shown in Figure 8-4. If a printer shortcut had been created on the desktop previously, they could double-click that instead. The print queue shows information about each print job such as the document's name, its status, its owner, and the number of pages. Users can get a general overview of the printer's status by selecting the printer's icon in the Printers folder. This causes Windows Explorer to display that information beside the list of printers.

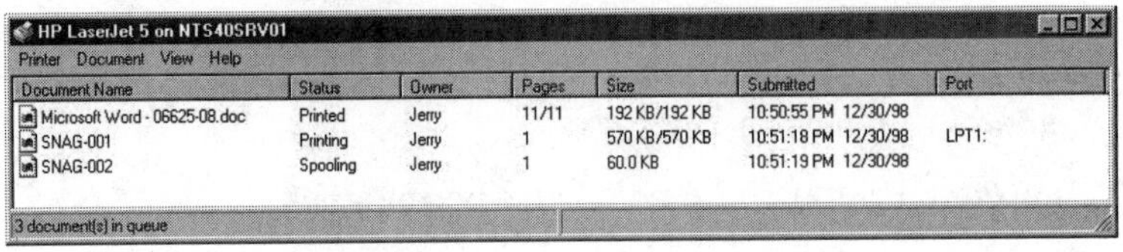

Figure 8-4
Managing the print queue.

Better Document Printing

Windows 2000 Professional has many different ways that a user can print a document:

- Choose Print from an application's File menu.

- Choose Print from a document's pop-up menu.

- Drag a document icon to a printer icon on the desktop or in the Printers folder.

- Add a shortcut for the printer to the Send To folder, which is in the user's profile, then choose Send To from the document's pop-up menu and choose the printer's shortcut.

When printing a document from within an application (by choosing Print from the application's File menu) users see the new Print dialog box. This dialog box is greatly enhanced over earlier versions. Figure 8-5 shows you what it looks like. Here's an overview of what users can do in the Print dialog box:

- In the Select Printer list, point to a printer to see its status in a ScreenTip.

- In the Select Printer list, select the printer that will print the document.

■ Click Find Printer to search Active Directory or browse the network for a printer.

■ Click the Layout tab or the Paper/Quality tab to change preferences for the document.

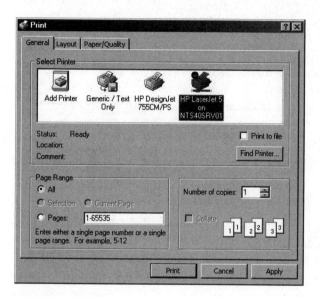

Figure 8-5
The new Print dialog box.

New Internet Printing

Internet Printing is a hot new feature that allows users to connect to printers on the Internet. Consider it an alternative to fax, overnight mail, or e-mail attachments. Users might print a reservation on a hotel's printer, for example, rather than faxing the reservation. This feature is based on the new *Internet Printing Protocol (IPP)*. It creates remote procedure call (RPC) connections to printers on the local area network and HTTP connections to printers on the Internet.

Working with Internet printers is similar to working with any printer on a network. Users can install the printer using Point and Print. Windows 2000 Professional copies the printer drivers from the printer's URL. Alternatively, users can install an Internet printer using the Add Printer Wizard; they just provide the printer's URL instead of a UNC path. They send a document to an Internet printer just as they would to any other printer. Applications don't even know that they're communicating with a printer on the Internet, as it looks like any other local or network printer. The one difference with Internet printers is that Windows 2000 Professional displays the printer's URL instead of its name in the Printers folder and in the Print dialog box.

For a printer to be accessible via the Internet, it must be attached to a Windows 2000 server that is accessible from the Internet. First, administrators must install Internet Information Services (IIS) on the server. Then, they must install and share the printer. That's all there is to it. From then on, any user can connect and send output to the printer. Since this feature is based on HTTP security schemes, server administrators can, of course, limit access to the printer. If administrators restrict the printer, the server will authenticate users before allowing them to print, manage print jobs, or manage print queues. Print drivers are signed, too, ensuring the client of their integrity.

Users can view the status of a printer on the Internet. To browse the printers available on a server on the Internet, users open *http://*servername/*printers* in a Web browser. To view a particular printer, users open *http://*servername/ sharename. Windows 2000 Server maintains Active Server Pages that generate HTML views of the available printers as well as print queue and print job information for each printer. Of course, the printers that users see or can access are limited to those for which they have permission. An alternative to viewing this information in a Web browser is to select a printer's icon in the Printers folder; after connecting to an Internet printer, Windows 2000 Professional adds an icon for it to the Printers folder. Windows Explorer displays information about the printer beside the list of printers. The following list describes the pages available when users do connect to a printer server across the Internet or intranet using a Web browser:

- **Server View**   Lists printers and the status of each

- **Printer Job Queue**   Shows the queue for a specific printer and the status of each printer

- **Printer Properties**   Displays properties for a printer such as model, status, location, paper types, and so on

- **Detailed Status**   Displays details of a printer's status, including errors and wait time

Improved Precision Color Matching: ICM 2.0

Different devices produce colors differently, making it difficult to generate the output users expect. For example, chartreuse might look a bit odd on the color printer as compared to the screen display. Image Color Management (ICM) 2.0 is an API that helps ensure colors are faithfully reproduced across most output devices. In other words, ICM 2.0 makes color portable across applications, platforms, and devices that support it. It's particularly valuable for Web designers who have to deal with color fidelity across multiple platforms. Windows 2000 Professional includes support for ICM 2.0 on scanners, monitors, and printers.

ICM 2.0 provides a means for software and devices to communicate. It uses color profiles to communicate color characteristics of a device to the color management system. Applications, such as publishing software and image editors, use this information to make the adjustments necessary to produce accurate colors on each device. Adobe PhotoShop is an example of an application that has long provided support for color management; most amateur-oriented image editors, on the other hand, have not provided this support. In most cases, color management just works. That is, it works after the output devices have been associated with the appropriate color profiles. Windows 2000 Professional comes with a variety of color profiles. Some vendors provide additional profiles that you can use. Several color profiles are listed below; note, however, that the sRGB Color Space profile can be used with any device that supports ICM 2.0:

- Diamond Compatible 9300K G2.2

- Hitachi Compatible 9300K

- NEC Compatible 9300K G2.2

- sRGB Color Space Profile

- Trinitron Compatible 9300K G2.2

All of these profiles are in the folder *systemroot*\System32\Spool\Drivers\ Color. To enable a color profile, users choose Install Profile from the profile's pop-up menu. The icon's color changes from gray to white. Then, users associate devices with the profile by choosing Associate from the profile's pop-up menu. In the Associate Device tab (shown in Figure 8-6 on the following page) of the dialog box, they click Add and then select the device they want to associate with the profile. Users can associate more than one device with each profile.

Any device—a color printer or monitor, for example—that supports ICM 2.0 has the Color Management tab in its Properties dialog box. This tab allows users to associate a color profile with that device.

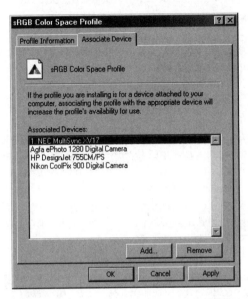

Figure 8-6
The Associate Device tab of a color profile's dialog box.

Improved Font Types and Management

The new addition to Windows 2000 Professional's font arsenal is OpenType fonts. OpenType is a new universal font format that combines leading technologies such as TrueType and Type 1 fonts. It handles all fonts with a unified registry so that both TrueType and Type 1 fonts are supported across all platforms. Features such as subsetting and compression make OpenType fonts especially relevant to the Internet and the World Wide Web, as they make for a really quick download.

OpenType fonts are digitally signed; doing so ensures the integrity of the font. Digital signatures are only available for OpenType fonts, and a signature is required for a font to actually be considered OpenType. In order for a font to be signed, it must meet the requirements of the digital signature table in the OpenType specification. It must also pass tests that verify the integrity of the hinting algorithms the font contains. Applications check the digital signature using the WinVerifyTrust API. A user can verify that a font's signature is valid by right-clicking the font's icon, choosing Properties, clicking the Digital Signatures tab, selecting the font in the Signature list, and clicking the Details button. The dialog box that appears is shown in Figure 8-7.

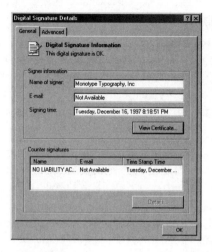

Figure 8-7
Verifying the validity of an OpenType font's digital signature.

> **NOTE:** Any language edition of Windows 2000 Professional can open fonts from any other locale. For example, you can use a Japanese font on an English edition of the operating system. For more information about the operating system's multilingual features, see Chapter 7, "Superior Multilingual Support."

Installing Fonts

As it does with many features in Windows 2000 Professional, drag and drop makes installing fonts easy. Users simply drag any font from any other disk or folder to the Fonts folder in the *systemroot* directory. The operating system will automatically install the font and add the appropriate information to the registry. Other methods are available for installing fonts—none of them as elegant as drag and drop—and those methods are given in the following list:

- ■ **Copying** Use the Copy command to copy fonts to the Fonts folder. The Fonts folder must be active in Windows Explorer for the operating system to automatically update the folder and registry, allowing the font's icon to be displayed. If the Fonts folder isn't active, Windows 2000 Professional will update the folder and registry the next time the user opens the folder.

- **Dialog box installation** This method is antiquated, a remnant from Windows 3.1, and it's certainly not the easiest way to install fonts. With the Fonts folder open in Windows Explorer, choose Install New Font from the File menu. Use the Add Fonts dialog box to locate the font files. Select the fonts you want, and click OK.

- **Automatic and unattended installation** The operating system automatically installs a variety of OpenType, TrueType, and raster fonts when you install it. Some applications and printers install additional fonts, too. Note that administrators can specify that fonts be installed during unattended setups and can control which fonts users can access.

- **Cartridge installation** Windows 2000 Professional treats font cartridges as device fonts. Users select font cartridges in the Device Settings tab of a printer's Properties dialog box. The Hewlett-Packard Printer Control Language (HPPCL) minidriver that comes with Windows 2000 Professional supports all of the known HP font cartridges. If users need to install a cartridge that isn't already supported, they need to supply a printer cartridge metrics file, which describes the font's characteristics to the operating system. Users install a printer cartridge metrics file just as they would any other font.

- **Soft font installation** Downloadable soft fonts are fonts that reside on the hard disk but are downloaded to the printer as needed. Users install soft fonts in the same way as cartridge fonts—by right-clicking the printer's icon, choosing Properties, and using the Device Settings tab in the dialog box.

To remove a font, the user simply deletes that font's file from the Fonts folder. This action removes the font file as well as the information associated with it in the registry.

Managing Installed Fonts

The primary user interface for managing fonts is the Fonts folder. Users can view each font's properties by choosing Properties from the font's pop-up menu. They can view samples of a font by double-clicking the font's icon. Take a quick peek into the Fonts folder, and you'll notice different icons and different file extensions. Each file extension represents a different type of font file, as described in Table 8-1.

Extension	Type	Description
TTF	TrueType font file	TrueType or OpenType font
TTC	TrueType collection	Collection of TrueType or OpenType fonts used in the Far East
FOT	Font resource file	Descriptive information about a TrueType font that contains a path to an actual TTF file—basically a shortcut to a TTF file
FON	Raster font file	Raster or vector font data
AFM	Adobe Font Metric	Information needed to create a Type 1 font—used in conjunction with INF and PFB files
INF	Initialization file	Information needed to create a Type 1 font—used in conjunction with AFM and PFB files
PFM	Printer Font Metric	Header information for a Type 1 font—used in conjunction with PFB files
PFB	Printer Font Binary	Glyph information for a Type 1 font—used in conjunction with a PFM file, or with AFM and INF files
OTF	OpenType file	Information required for an OpenType font that has PostScript outlines

Table 8-1
Font file extensions and their meanings.

Viewing a Font's Properties

Choose Properties from a font's pop-up menu to view information about it. The font's Properties dialog box contains three or four tabs, depending on the type of font:

- ■ **General** Statistics related to the font

- ■ **Digital Signatures** Information about the font's digital signature and verification that the signature is valid

- ■ **Version**   Information about the font's owner, version, and copy-right—only available for non-OpenType and non-TrueType fonts

- ■ **Security**   Security settings for the font file

- ■ **Summary**   Summary information about the font file

NOTE: Microsoft's typography site—*http://www.microsoft.com/ typography*—has a utility that allows users to view additional information about fonts. This information includes the font's origin, copyright, type sizes to which hinting and smoothing are applied, code pages supported by the font's extended characters, and so forth.

Fonts and the Computer's Resources

Dating all the way back to Windows 3.1, users have heard warnings about the amount of resources that fonts can take up. Users were frequently told that the mere installation of a font gobbled up huge amounts of memory, since the operating system always loaded every font it found on the system—so they were told.

Fonts do gobble up resources, but only when they're actually used in a document. Some users have been so brazen as to include hundreds of fonts in a single document—never mind the fact that this violates every known design principle—without causing too many problems. A typical font can use up to 250 KB of memory when loaded by the operating system. A Far Eastern font can use as much as several megabytes of memory, but remember this is only when it's actually used.

Windows 2000 Professional does several things to minimize the impact that large fonts have on the system's performance and memory use. For example, large Far Eastern fonts might be split into subsets before the operating system sends them to the printer server. This means that the operating system only spools those glyphs that are required to produce the document. Another thing that might impact a font's effect on memory consumption and performance is the fact that the operating system doesn't spool fonts if they're available on the printer server. In this case, print jobs are spooled as metafiles that are interpreted on the printer server, and the rasterization of OpenType fonts is performed on the printer server.

New Device Classes Such As Scanners

Windows 2000 Professional supports a number of new imaging devices. Scanners, digital still cameras, digital video cameras, and other image-capturing devices are among the highlights. In most cases, since these devices are usually Plug and Play, Windows 2000 Professional automatically detects them and installs the appropriate drivers. For more information about Windows 2000 Professional's implementation of Plug and Play, see Chapter 12, "Easy Device Installation."

Figure 8-8 shows the Scanners And Cameras Properties dialog box, which you open by clicking the Scanners And Cameras icon in the Control Panel. Install an imaging device by clicking Add to start the Scanner And Camera Installation Wizard. The Scanners And Cameras Properties dialog box can link a device to a program, too; for example, scanning a document can automatically open the document in an associated program. To associate a program with an imaging device, select the device in the list, then click the Properties button. In the Events tab, click the event with which you want to link the application. If you don't see the Events tab, the device doesn't support this feature. Click the application to which you want to send the event, then click Send To This Application. Note that you only see applications that support this feature in the list.

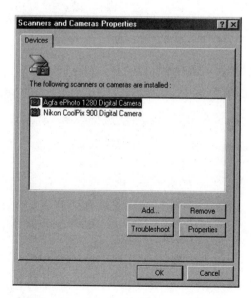

Figure 8-8

The Scanners And Cameras Properties dialog box.

TIP: The new My Pictures folder makes viewing scanned images outside of an image editor very easy. Store the scanned image in a file in the My Pictures folder, then select the image file; Windows Explorer will display a preview of the image. To learn more about the My Pictures folder, see Chapter 4, "Simpler User Interface."

PART III

FAST, SAFE,
AND SECURE

CHAPTER NINE

Best Performance

Microsoft Windows 2000 Professional performs better than any previous version of Microsoft Windows. Enhancements to the kernel make applications run more smoothly. New storage features, such as content indexing and disk optimization, provide quicker access to information. Many subtle improvements in the operating system's performance are due to an extensive makeover of its storage subsystems and a variety of enhancements to its primary file system, NTFS. The end result is that users finish tasks more quickly and have a more positive experience.

This chapter describes features that improve Windows 2000 Professional's performance. In the course of describing enhancements to the storage subsystem as well as new storage features, this chapter also touches on a number of features that don't necessarily impact the operating system's performance but do make it easier and less expensive to manage. For example, volume mount points remove drive letter limitations, making the operating system more flexible. Link tracking ensures that a user's shortcuts are always accurate—even after the user unwittingly moves a shortcut's target file—saving users time and aggravation.

What you won't find in this chapter is information about performance features that are unique to Microsoft Windows 2000 Server. For more information about Windows 2000 Server, see *Introducing Microsoft Windows 2000 Server*, Microsoft Press, 1999. In addition to the storage features you'll learn about in this chapter, *Introducing Microsoft Windows 2000 Server* describes the new Microsoft distributed file system (Dfs), which significantly improves the manageability of network storage.

Volume Management

The volume management architecture, shown in Figure 9-1 on page 189, is responsible for the creation, deletion, alteration, and maintenance of storage volumes. New for Windows 2000 Professional is the Logical Disk Manager (LDM)—not to be confused with the Disk Management snap-in—which manages dynamic disks. The operating system maintains the existing fault-tolerant disk manager (FT Disk) for basic disks. In addition to LDM and FT Disk, Windows 2000 Professional supports third-party disk managers and provides interfaces for remote administration using Microsoft Management Console (MMC) snap-ins. This list describes the two types of disks supported by Windows 2000 Professional:

- **Basic disks**   FT Disk manages basic disks, just as it did in Windows NT Workstation 4.0. A basic disk is a physical disk that contains primary partitions, extended partitions, and logical drives. Windows 2000 Professional can use volume, mirror, and stripe sets with or without parity that were created in Windows NT Workstation 4.0 or earlier, but it can't create them. Also, Windows 2000 Professional can't extend a basic disk online, so changes to a basic disk require the operating system to reboot. MS-DOS, Windows 98, and Windows NT Workstation 4.0 can all use basic disks.

- **Dynamic disks**   LDM manages dynamic disks, which are physical disks that contain dynamic volumes—not partitions and logical drives—that users create with the Disk Management snap-in. Dynamic disks can contain a large number of volumes. Use dynamic disks if the computer runs only Windows 2000 Professional and if you want to take advantage of features such as online volume extension, fault tolerance, disk mirrors, and disk striping. Note that administrators can configure dynamic disks online, meaning that changes to a dynamic disk do not require the operating system to reboot.

Dynamic disks contain dynamic volumes, which can be simple, spanned, mirrored, striped, or striped with parity (RAID-5)—RAID stands for redundant array of independent disks. A simple volume is not fault-tolerant. It can contain the space on a single physical disk, using a single region or multiple regions linked together, or it can span multiple disks. A simple volume that spans multiple disks is called a spanned volume. Striped volumes store data in alternating stripes across two or more physical disks. They significantly improve the file system's performance by allowing multiple disks to do the work of one. Mirrored volumes are fault-tolerant; they provide redundancy. That is, they duplicate data on two physical disks so that, if one disk fails, the operating system continues to function. Mirrored disks do affect the operating system's performance but protect against hardware failure. Only Windows 2000 Server supports the remaining type of dynamic volume, RAID-5, but you can create a RAID-5 volume on a server from Windows 2000 Professional. RAID-5 volumes stripe data and parity across three or more physical disks, allowing the operating system to recreate data on a failed portion of a disk from the remaining data and parity.

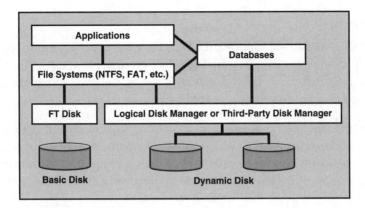

Figure 9-1

The volume management architecture.

Administrators manage basic and dynamic disks with the Disk Management snap-in. You can add this snap-in to any MMC console, but it's already available in the Computer Management console. In the Control Panel, double-click the Administrative Tools icon followed by the Computer Management icon. Figure 9-2 shows the Disk Management snap-in with two disks: a dynamic disk with NTFS and a basic disk with the CD-ROM File System (CDFS). The features that were available in Windows NT Workstation 4.0's Disk Manager are still here—you access them from a disk's or a volume's pop-up menu. For example, to upgrade a basic disk to a dynamic disk, choose Upgrade To Dynamic Disk from the disk's pop-up menu—not from the volume's pop-up menu.

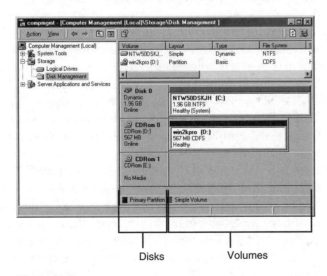

Figure 9-2

The Disk Management snap-in.

File System Support

Windows 2000 Professional supports multiple file systems on basic and dynamic disks. Although the operating system introduces a new file system (Universal Disk Format) and extends NTFS to version 5, it continues to support older file systems as described in this list:

- **FAT16**   Since the original version of MS-DOS, Microsoft operating systems have supported the FAT16 file system. Windows 2000 Professional continues to support FAT16 as an upgrade path from earlier operating systems. Note that under Windows 2000 Professional, the maximum partition size for FAT16 is 4 GB.

- **FAT32**   Windows 95 OSR2 and Windows 98 introduced the FAT32 file system. Windows 2000 Professional also supports this file system. FAT32 uses smaller clusters than FAT16, freeing between 20 and 30 percent more disk space. The maximum partition size is 2 TB. While Windows 2000 Professional will use any FAT32 partition created in Windows 98, for performance reasons the operating system will create FAT32 partitions up to 32 GB only.

- **CDFS**   CDFS stands for CD-ROM File System. The operating system uses CDFS to read CD-ROM devices. CDFS adheres to the International Organization for Standardization (ISO) 9660 specification.

The Universal Disk Format (UDF) file system is new for Windows 2000 Professional. Defined by the Optical Storage Technology Association (OSTA), it's compliant with the ISO-13346 specification and is intended to be the successor to CDFS. This file system is for use by digital video discs (DVDs), CD-ROMs, and data interchanged among incompatible operating systems. Features include long and Unicode file names, access control lists (ACLs), streams, reading and writing (not just mastering), and bootability. Windows 2000 Professional doesn't support writing to a UDF file system, but it will in the future. The most current version of UDF is 1.5, and this version is supported by Windows 2000 Professional. The OSTA has recently approved a draft of UDF 2.0, and Windows 2000 Professional will support this version at a later date.

The NTFS file system was introduced in the original release of Windows NT. It's the file system that Microsoft recommends to all Windows 2000 Professional users, except when formatting the system partition of a Compaq Alpha computer or when configuring a computer to start more than one operating system. NTFS has features that FAT doesn't. It's secure, controlling access to files and folders through ACLs. It supports native file compression. Transaction logs and fault-tolerant volumes make files recoverable. All in all, comparing NTFS to FAT is like comparing dynamite to firecrackers. And Windows 2000

Professional introduces NTFS 5, which contains a plethora of new features that you'll learn about later in this chapter.

For help choosing a file system, see Chapter 3, "Setup Guide." Chapter 3 describes the differences between the file systems. It also describes Windows 2000 Professional's file system requirements for those users who want to install and choose among multiple operating systems.

Compatibility Issues

Upgrading to Windows 2000 Professional from Windows NT Workstation 4.0 results in the conversion of all NTFS 4 volumes to version 5. In addition, if the computer isn't configured to boot multiple operating systems, Windows 2000 Professional automatically converts FAT16 boot volumes to NTFS 5. If the computer can boot both Windows 2000 Professional and Windows NT Workstation 4.0, keep in mind that users must install Service Pack 4 in order for Windows NT Workstation 4.0 to use NTFS 5 basic volumes. Even with Service Pack 4, Windows NT Workstation 4.0 can't use dynamic disks. The following list describes limitations with using NTFS 5 volumes in Windows NT Workstation 4.0:

- Reparse points don't work.
- Disk quotas are ignored.
- Encrypted files are inaccessible.
- Sparse files are inaccessible.
- The change journal is ignored.

If users of a dual-boot configuration mount an NTFS 5 volume in Windows NT Workstation 4.0 and return to Windows 2000 Professional, Windows 2000 Professional will clean up the file system. For example, it will clean up quota information, and if users exceed their quota, all further allocations will fail. Windows 2000 Professional will reset change journals to indicate that the information in them is incomplete. Encrypted and sparse files don't require this process, since these files are inaccessible to Windows NT Workstation 4.0.

Improved NTFS File System

Windows 2000 Professional extends NTFS to version 5. NTFS 5 still supports all of version 4's features. Both versions of NTFS are extremely reliable and include fault-tolerant features such as mirrored and striped sets. Both are easy to administer. But, as the following list describes, NTFS 5 goes further than version 4:

■ **More flexibility** NTFS 5 is more flexible than version 4. For example, mount points allow administrators to mount a volume to any path on another volume, increasing the size of the first volume while making the second more accessible.

■ **Enhanced security** NTFS 5 includes the Encrypting File System (EFS). EFS uses public key security to encrypt files on an NTFS 5 volume, preventing unauthorized users from accessing those files.

■ **More efficiency** NTFS 5 provides features that make more efficient use of disk space. Support for sparse files means that extremely large files containing sparse data can use very small amounts of disk space.

■ **Improved performance** Aside from improvements to the storage subsystems, NTFS 5 enables features that make more dramatic impacts on performance. The best example of such a feature is the Disk Defragmenter snap-in, which you'll learn about later.

Some storage features require the operating system to update NTFS 4 volumes to NTFS 5. Thus, Windows 2000 Professional automatically updates each NTFS volume to version 5 as soon as it's mounted. The operating system will also upgrade any boot volume formatted with FAT16 to NTFS 5, unless the computer is configured to start more than one operating system.

Reparse Points

Reparse points, and Installable File System (IFS) filter drivers, are the technology behind many of Windows 2000 Professional's new storage features. Directory junctions, mount points, native structured storage (NSS), and EFS are features that you'll learn about in this chapter, and all of them rely on reparse points. Reparse points allow software vendors to have a consistent mechanism for extending the storage subsystem's functionality, eliminating the need for vendors to write proprietary code. And since many of the operating system's features rely on reparse points, it's wise to understand them.

Reparse points are file system objects that carry a specialized attribute and can trigger extended functionality in the storage subsystem. Each portion of a path can have a reparse point attribute. For example, the path C:\MyFolder\MySubfolder\Myfile.ext has locations for as many as four reparse points: the root folder, MyFolder, MySubfolder, and Myfile.ext. Windows 2000 Professional implements this extended functionality using IFS filter drivers. Microsoft assigns a unique reparse point tag to each IFS filter driver. Thus, a reparse point tag identifies a specific IFS filter driver. When, during pathname resolution, Windows 2000 Professional encounters a file system object that has a reparse tag, it allows each IFS filter driver to examine the reparse point. If the reparse point tag matches a filter driver's tag, that driver intercepts the reparse point. Each IFS filter driver is responsible for implementing specific functionality; for example, its purpose might be to decrypt a file (with EFS) or to retrieve a file from remote storage (with RSS).

Figure 9-3 shows an example of how reparse points work, and here's a blow-by-blow description of what's going on in this figure:

1. The user double-clicks a file or folder that has a reparse point tag.

2. The call goes to the file system, which recognizes the reparse point attribute.

3. Each IFS filter driver examines the reparse point tag and intercepts the call if there is a match; otherwise, it passes it on to the next IFS filter driver.

4. The IFS filter driver implements its specific functionality; for example, mounting a volume or retrieving a file from offline storage.

5. Control returns to the calling application, which may then need to reflect the work done by the IFS filter driver. The filter driver might change Windows Explorer's namespace, for example, and Windows Explorer would update itself accordingly.

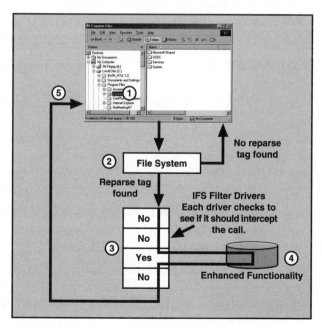

Figure 9-3
An example of how reparse points work.

Directory Junctions

Directory junctions allow Windows 2000 Professional to join folders. They use a special type of reparse point that can map a directory to any local target directory. That is, they can graft any directory onto any other directory. This feature is similar to mount points (discussed later in this chapter), but mount points can only graft the root of another volume onto a directory. An example is in order to help you better understand directory junctions.

Imagine a volume with two folders, C:\First and C:\Second, with a third folder called D:\Folder. The operating system can create a directory junction in each of the first two folders, which grafts D:\Folder onto it. The result is the existence of subfolders in both C:\First and C:\Second that resolve to D:\Folder. Thus, C:\First\Folder and C:\Second\Folder are one and the same. The actual names of the directory junctions are arbitrary and don't have to be the same in both folders.

With a few differences, directory junctions are similar to Dfs shares on Windows 2000 Server. This list describes the differences:

- Dfs functionality is integrated with Active Directory.

- Dfs is designed to graft network shares into a single namespace, but directory junctions are tools for grafting local storage into a single namespace.

- Dfs offers load balancing and fault tolerance via replication across systems, but directory junctions have no inherent load-balancing or fault-tolerance features.

- Dfs works across file systems, but directory junctions are a feature of NTFS 5.

- Dfs requires a client component, but directory junctions don't.

Sadly, Windows 2000 Professional provides no user interface for directory junctions. This feature is available only to developers. I do anticipate that Microsoft will give this extremely useful feature a user interface in the near future.

Volume Mount Points

Volume mount points are similar to directory junctions. And, like directory junctions, mount points rely on reparse points and therefore require NTFS 5. Rather than allowing the operating system to graft one directory onto another, they allow the operating system to graft an entire volume onto a directory. Placing a mount point on a directory causes the file system to resolve the directory to the root of a specific local volume. Mounting is transparent and doesn't require a drive letter. In short, mount points graft the root of a volume onto a directory.

Useful? Extremely. Mount points simplify storage management for administrators, allowing them to add storage without disturbing a volume's namespace and without the restrictions caused by drive letters. For example, administrators can scale storage by mounting additional physical disks to a mount point on an existing volume. And mount points are "sticky." That is, changes in the device name of the target volume, caused by changing the hardware configuration, don't cause a problem. The operating system identifies the device by its mount point just like you'd identify a device by its drive letter.

The administrative purposes for mount points aren't too important for Windows 2000 Professional users. A more common scenario is a user with two disk volumes who wants to access the second volume through a folder on the first. Maybe that user stores personal documents on the second volume and wants to access them through My Documents\Personal. Here's another example. To better manage storage space used by applications, users can mount a second volume to C:\Program Files so that the applications look like they're in C:\Program Files but they're actually on the second volume.

Mounting volumes requires administrative-level rights, meaning that an administrator has to do the task for the user or the user has to have administrator rights on the local computer. In the Disk Management snap-in, which members of the local computer's Administrators group can access from the Computer Management console, choose the Change Drive Letter And Path command from a volume's pop-up menu. (This command isn't available on a disk's pop-up menu.) The Drive Letter And Paths dialog box, shown in Figure 9-4 on the following page, displays a list showing each mount point for the volume. Click the Add button to assign a drive letter to the volume or to create an additional mount point for the volume.

Take a closer look at Figure 9-4 and you'll notice that this volume—a CD-ROM drive—doesn't have a drive letter associated with it. It's mounted on two different folders—C:\Documents And Settings\Administrators\Desktop\CD-ROM and C:\Windows 2K—and it doesn't show up in Windows Explorer as a separate drive letter (drive E, shown in Figure 9-4, is a second CD-ROM drive). This is a key feature of mount points: they eliminate administrators' frustration with drive letter limitations. Rather than mounting volumes to drive letters, administrators can mount volumes to folders.

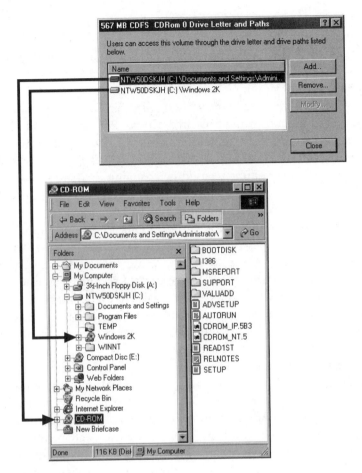

Figure 9-4
The Drive Letter And Paths dialog box.

Distributed Link Tracking

Distributed Link Tracking maintains the integrity of a shortcut's reference, allowing the referenced object to move about the file system transparently. To experience link tracking yourself, create a shortcut to any file on the computer; then, move the original file to another folder or, if the computer is part of a Windows 2000 domain, to any location on the network domain. Open the shortcut that references the original file and notice that it automatically tracks the file to its new location.

While the most visible example of Distributed Link Tracking is shortcuts, it's available to any client application that subscribes to it. Applications such as Microsoft Word and Microsoft Excel are examples. Thus, in the situation where a Word document contains a link to an Excel spreadsheet, Distributed Link Tracking would automatically update the link if the user moved the spreadsheet. Distributed Link Tracking works in the following situations:

- The name of the target file has changed.

- The target file has been moved within the same volume.

- The target file has been moved between two volumes on the same computer.

- The target file has been moved between two computers on the same domain.

- A volume has been physically moved from one computer running Windows 2000 Professional to another computer running Windows 2000 Professional on the same network domain.

- A computer running Windows 2000 Professional has been renamed.

- The name of the network share containing the target file has changed.

The Encrypting File System

NTFS 5's new Encrypting File System generates a lot of interest. You'd think that with Windows 2000 Professional's security, encryption wouldn't be necessary. However, anyone can still remove a disk from a user's computer and mount it in another. Once mounted, an administrator can take ownership of the data on that disk, effectively bypassing NTFS security. If that doesn't sound feasible for desktop computers, think about portable computers. Lose a portable computer to witlessness or thievery, and the files on its disk are open game to anyone who knows how to get to them.

EFS uses 128-bit (40-bit internationally) Data Encryption Standard (DES) encryption to encrypt individual files and folders. Encryption keys are implemented on a Windows 2000 domain or—in the case of a standalone computer—locally. The operating system generates a recovery key so administrators can recover encrypted data in the event that users lose their encryption key or if they leave the company. For more information about EFS, see Chapter 11, "Strongest Local and Network Security." Chapter 11 describes how to enable encryption for files and folders as well as how to recover encrypted files.

File Compression

Storage compression remains unchanged in NTFS 5. Just note that storage compression and EFS are mutually exclusive. The compression algorithm that Windows 2000 Professional uses is very similar to the algorithms in DoubleSpace and DriveSpace 3—the compression tools in Windows 98. But unlike either of these compression tools, which compress entire volumes, NTFS 5 can compress individual files and folders. In addition, NTFS 5's compression feature doesn't significantly degrade Windows 2000 Professional's performance, though the same thing cannot be said of compression's effect on Windows 2000 Server's performance.

You can compress a file or folder by choosing Properties from its pop-up menu. Then, in the General tab, click the Advanced button to display the Advanced Attributes dialog box, shown in Figure 9-5, and check the Compress Contents To Save Disk Space check box. To compress an entire volume, choose Properties from the volume's pop-up menu. Then, in the General tab of the volume's Properties dialog box, check the Compress Drive To Save Disk Space check box.

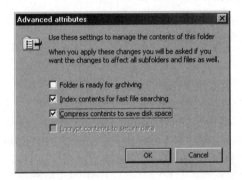

Figure 9-5
The Advanced Attributes dialog box for a folder.

Disk Quotas

Disk quotas allow administrators to manage the amount of disk space allotted to individual users, charging users only for the files they own. Windows 2000 Professional enforces quotas on a per-user and per-volume basis, so administrators can't issue quotas for individual network shares or folders. Note that disk quotas are smart enough to take sparse and offline files into account when calculating the amount of disk space consumed by users.

While administrators typically use quotas to control the disk space used on the network, they can also use quotas for a similar task on a local computer. For example, in the case of four users sharing a single computer, the administrator (of the local computer) can allocate a fixed amount of disk space to each user. As users approach their limits, the operating system gives them a warning. When they go over their limits, the operating system prevents them from using any more space on the disk.

Figure 9-6 shows the Quota tab of a disk's Properties dialog box. Administrators can enable disk quotas by checking the Enable Quota Management check box. After enabling disk quotas, administrators can specify the amount of disk space allocated to each user and the threshold at which the operating system warns users that they're getting close to their limits. Administrators can also specify which events the operating system logs in the event log. If they want more granular control over quotas, such as specifying limits for individual users, they can click the Quota Entries button. The Quota Entries dialog box reports the amount of disk space allocated to each user, and double-clicking a user in the list opens the Quota Settings dialog box. Administrators use the Quota Settings dialog box to set individual limits. After enabling or disabling quotas, there will be a long pause while the operating system scans the volume and applies the quotas.

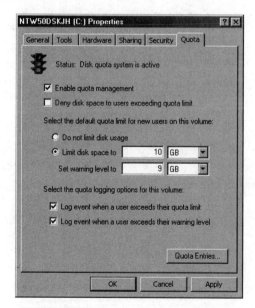

Figure 9-6
The Quota tab of a disk's Properties dialog box.

Enabling Technology

NTFS 5 provides many more new features than you've read about in this chapter. Most are inconsequential to users, as they're features that developers use to create world-class storage applications but they don't provide user interfaces.

Native Structured Storage (NSS) improves the performance and efficiency of ActiveX compound documents. Rather than storing all the parts of an ActiveX compound document in a single data stream, NSS allows each embedded object to be stored in a separate data stream. NSS uses reparse points to indicate that a file has multiple data streams and to translate multiple data streams into a single data stream when the file migrates to file systems other than NTFS 5.

A sparse file is a file with a special attribute that causes NTFS to interpret the file's data based on allocated ranges. NTFS allocates meaningful, non-zero data on the file system. Any non-meaningful, zero-filled data is not allocated. When NTFS reads the file, allocated and unallocated data is returned to the application as though all of it were allocated on the file system. An example of using a sparse file is a scientific application that might use 1 TB to store an extremely large matrix. The matrix might include very little meaningful data, maybe 1 MB. With the sparse file attribute set, NTFS would not allocate zero-filled space; it would allocate space for meaningful data only—1 MB in this case.

The change journal, new for Windows 2000 Professional, tracks activity on NTFS volumes by tracking added, deleted, and modified files. The change journal is a more efficient way to track changes than time stamps or notifications. NTFS implements the change journal as a sparse file. Software vendors can use this feature to provide enhanced features—such as file system indexing engines, content replication engines, and storage archiving—in their applications. Many of the operating system's new features rely on the change journal; examples include the Indexing Service, the Remote Storage Service, and the Backup utility.

The Indexing Service

A feature that Windows 2000 Professional borrows from Internet Information Services (IIS), the Indexing Service is now an integral part of the operating system. It indexes the content of files in local and network storage, enabling the file system to become a rich data store. Through a simple user interface—the Search bar in Windows Explorer—users can find files faster. For more information about using the Search bar in Windows Explorer, see Chapter 4, "Simpler User Interface."

The Indexing Service indexes a file's contents and properties. For example, users can search the index for all documents that contain the words "Windows 2000," or search for all documents written by Jerry. In order for the Indexing Service to index a file, a document filter must be available. While most vendors will provide filters if appropriate for their applications, the Indexing Service provides filters for HTML files, text files, Microsoft Office documents, and Internet e-mail files.

The Indexing Service pretty much does its own thing. It requires very little interaction from users. The service runs continuously, indexing new and changed files. Windows 2000 Professional does not enable the Indexing Service in a default installation, but users can easily enable it by clicking the Indexing Service hyperlink in Windows Explorer's Search bar. Administrators can further manage the Indexing Service using the Indexing Service snap-in, which administrators can add to an MMC console or access via the Computer Management console. Figure 9-7 shows you what it looks like.

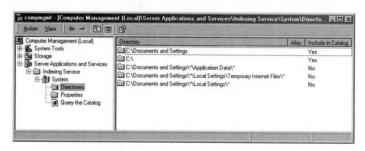

Figure 9-7
The Indexing Service snap-in.

Catalogs

The Indexing Service stores an index in a catalog. After installing Windows 2000 Professional, the Indexing Service creates a default catalog called "System" that includes all the local, non-removable storage devices on the computer. Administrators can change the configuration of this catalog, or even add new catalogs, using the Indexing Service snap-in. Each catalog contains two types of information:

- **Document contents** The catalog contains each document's contents. The Indexing Service omits words that aren't useful for searching, such as articles, prepositions, common nouns, and verbs. Most of the space in a catalog goes to the document contents portion, which is roughly 30% of the original documents' total size.

- **Document properties** The catalog contains information about each document, including the date created, the last date modified, and so forth. Some applications create additional properties: author, number of characters, and editing time are examples. The Indexing Service supports an application's custom properties as well as the META tags found in HTML documents.

Scanning

The Indexing Service scans directories to inventory their contents. Scanning—the process of creating or updating an inventory of files that need to be indexed—is not the same as indexing, which is the process of collecting information about a file. By default, the Indexing Service automatically scans all directories on all local volumes, but administrators can limit its activities to certain directories. The Indexing Service performs two different types of scans:

- **Full scan** The Indexing Service performs a full scan the first time it runs, when administrators add a new folder to the catalog, or as part of a recovery process in the event of serious errors.

- **Incremental scan** If some event stops the Indexing Service, it automatically does an incremental scan after it restarts. This means that the Indexing Service adds to its inventory those files that changed since it was last running.

During day-to-day operations, the Indexing Service doesn't perform either type of scan. The operating system notifies it the moment that files change; as a result, the Indexing Service can index files without scanning. The Indexing

Service never receives change notifications for files on remote computers, so it periodically scans folders on remote computers.

Indexing

The Indexing Service uses a document filter to gather a document's contents and properties, storing both in the catalog. After extracting a document's contents, the Indexing Service performs additional processing:

- The Indexing Service determines the language in which the document was written so that it can break the document into words.

- The Indexing Service removes words that aren't useful for searching. Articles, prepositions, common nouns, and common verbs are on the exception list.

Searching

Administrators can search the catalog using the Indexing Service snap-in, but the user interface is a bit clunky. The best user interface for searching is Windows Explorer's Search bar, shown in Figure 9-8, which is available to administrators and users alike. Chapter 4, "Simpler User Interface," describes this feature but doesn't tell you much about the types of queries users can enter.

Figure 9-8
Searching using Windows Explorer's Search bar.

Free-text and vector queries are a bit esoteric, and I refer you to Windows 2000 Professional's Help for more information about them. Conventional queries can be as simple as a keyword or a phrase that a document must match. Less technically savvy users will stick to simple, keyword queries. Queries are not case-sensitive, and the Indexing Service treats any words it finds in the exception list as placeholders. For example, the query *learn to swim* will match *learn to swim* and *learn and swim*, since the word *to* is in the exception list. Users can further refine their queries using the following techniques:

- **Boolean operators** Boolean operators include *AND* (*&*), *OR* (|), and *NOT* (*!*). For example, *Windows AND 2000* matches documents that contain both words, while *Windows OR 2000* matches documents that contain either word. *Windows AND NOT 2000* matches documents that contain the first keyword and not the second.

- **Proximity operators** The *NEAR* operator indicates that two words should appear near each other in a matching document. For example, *Windows NEAR 2000* matches documents that contain both keywords, preferably near each other. The Indexing Service will match all documents that contain both keywords, but it will assign a higher weight to the documents in which the two keywords are closer.

- **Wildcards** A wildcard (*) helps match words that begin, end, or begin and end with certain characters. For example, *Win** matches Windows, winning, and winter. *Stemming* matches documents that contain variations of a word. For example, *run*** (two asterisks) matches run, ran, and running. The first character of a wildcard query must be an exclamation mark (*!*).

- **Property-value queries** Queries can find documents that have properties matching certain values. For example, *@DocAuthor = "Jerry Honeycutt"* matches all documents authored by Jerry Honeycutt and *@Size > 10000* matches all files that are larger than 10,000 bytes in size. Property-value queries also support regular expressions by prefixing a property with a number sign (#) instead of the at sign (@). For example, *#DocAuthor = Jer** matches all documents whose author's name begins with Jer. Table 9-1 describes properties that are available for many documents.

Property Name	Description
Access	Last time a document was accessed
All	All properties in a document
AllocSize	Disk space allocated to a document
Attrib	File attributes
ClassId	Class ID of document object
Characterization	Abstract of a document generated by the Indexing Service
Contents	Contents of a document
Create	Time a document was created
Directory	Physical path to a document, not including its filename
DocAppName	Name of the application that created a document
DocAuthor	Author of a document
DocByteCount	Number of bytes in a document
DocCategory	Type of document, such as memo, schedule, etc.
DocCharCount	Number of characters in a document
DocComments	Comments about a document
DocCompany	Name of the company for which a document was written
DocCreatedTm	Time a document was created
DocEditTime	Total time spent editing a document
DocHiddenCount	Number of hidden slides in a Microsoft PowerPoint document
DocKeywords	Document keywords
DocLastAuthor	Most recent user who edited a document
DocLastPrinted	Time a document was last printed
DocLastSavedTm	Time a document was last saved
DocLineCount	Number of lines in a document
DocManager	Name of the author's manager
DocNoteCount	Number of pages with notes in a Microsoft PowerPoint document
DocPageCount	Number of pages in a document
DocParaCount	Number of paragraphs in a document

Table 9-1
Document properties available for queries.

(continued)

Table 9-1. *continued*

Property Name	Description
DocPartTitles	The names of spreadsheets in a Microsoft Excel document; the names of slides in a Microsoft PowerPoint document; and the names of documents in a Microsoft Word master document
DocPresentationTarget	Target format of a Microsoft PowerPoint presentation
DocRevNumber	Current version number of a document
DocSlideCount	Number of slides in a Microsoft PowerPoint document
DocSubject	Subject of a document
DocTemplate	Name of a document's template
DocWordCount	Number of words in a document
FileIndex	Unique ID of a file
FileName	Documents filename
HitCount	Number of hits in a document
HtmlHRef	Text of an HTML link
HtmlHeading1 … 6	Text of HTML headings: *H1* through *H6*
MediaEditor	Name of a file's primary editor
MediaOwner	Owner of a file
MediaProduction	Date the media was produced
MediaProject	Project to which the file's contents belong
MediaRating	Rating of quality or content
MediaSequence_No	Sequence number of the media file in the group
MediaSource	Name of the file's source
MediaStatus	Status of the file in a project workflow: 0 Draft 1 Edit 2 Final 3 In Progress 4 New 5 Normal 6 Other 7 Preliminary 8 Proof 9 Review

Property Name	Description
MediaSupplier	Name of the file's source
Path	Physical path to a document, including its filename
Rank	Rank of a match (0 through 1000), with larger numbers indicating a better match
RankVector	Ranks of individual parts of a vector query
ShortFileName	Document's 8.3 filename
Size	Size of a document in bytes
Vpath	Full virtual path to a document, including its filename
WorkId	Internal ID for a file
Write	Time a document was last modified

Table 9-1
Document properties available for queries.

The Disk Defragmenter Snap-In

The utility that provides the biggest performance advantage for Windows 2000 Professional users is the Disk Defragmenter snap-in. Each file contains one or more clusters—sometimes thousands. Ideally, the operating system would always store these clusters on the same area of the disk, making it quick to access the file. Over time, however, the operating system must store a file's clusters in different places. This usually occurs because the next free space in the file system isn't big enough to hold all of the file's clusters. The operating system stores a portion of the file's clusters in that location, and then moves on to the next free space. Loading a fragmented file takes longer than loading an unfragmented file.

As shown in Figure 9-9 on the following page, the Disk Defragmenter snap-in increases the computer's performance by collecting each of a file's fragments and storing them on a contiguous area on the disk. It also consolidates the disk's free space so that creating new files is quicker. It can defragment FAT16, FAT32, and NTFS 5 volumes. The Disk Defragmenter snap-in is not available in the Computer Management console, but you can easily add it to any MMC console by choosing Add/Remove Snap-In from the Console menu.

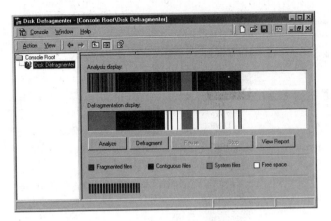

Figure 9-9
The Disk Defragmenter snap-in.

Disk Cleanup

Unused temporary files are the bane of most users. Those files sit around in the file system, gobbling up precious resources and offering nothing in return. Going on a rampage and deleting a bunch of files isn't safe, as the chances of deleting an important file are quite high. But hold on! The Disk Cleanup Wizard can safely remove temporary files, freeing up additional disk space. It isn't available on the Start menu. Choose Properties from a disk's pop-up menu; in the General tab of the disk's Properties dialog box, click the Disk Cleanup button. The Disk Cleanup Wizard (see Figure 9-10) calculates the amount of disk space it can free up, and then it allows you to choose which of the following tasks you want to perform:

- Removing offline files
- Emptying the Recycle Bin
- Compressing unused files
- Removing Windows 2000 Professional temporary files
- Removing downloaded program files (ActiveX controls and Java applets)
- Removing temporary Internet files
- Removing unused Windows 2000 Professional components
- Removing unused programs

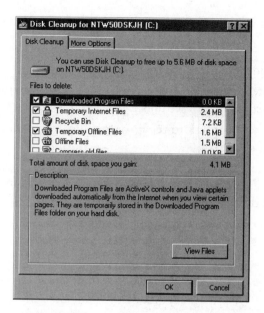

Figure 9-10
The Disk Cleanup Wizard.

TIP: After using the Disk Cleanup Wizard to remove temporary files, analyze the disk with the Disk Defragmenter snap-in to see if the disk will benefit from defragmentation. The disk's performance probably will benefit from this process if the Disk Cleanup Wizard removed a large number of files.

Backup

The Backup utility (shown in Figure 9-11 on the following page) is greatly improved in Windows 2000 Professional. It sheds the clunky user interface of its predecessor, adopting the tabbed look of Windows 98's Backup utility. It also includes a handful of new wizards that make backup and restoration operations much easier.

The Backup utility's improvements are much more than skin deep. It includes support for Active Directory (Windows 2000 Server), Automated System Recovery (ASR), RSS, disk-to-disk operations, and a host of other new storage features. The following list describes the tasks that the Backup utility can perform:

- Archive files and folders and restore them as necessary
- Prepare for automated system recovery, which helps users recreate each volume and restore system settings if the hard disk fails
- Create an emergency repair disk to repair system files if they become corrupted or are missing
- Make a copy of the computer's system state, including the registry, system boot files, Active Directory (Windows 2000 Server), and the Certificate Services database
- Make a copy of any offline RSS data and mounted disks

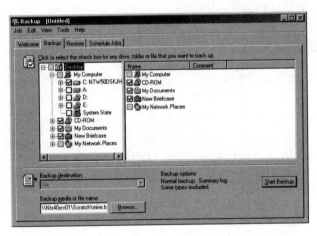

Figure 9-11
The Backup dialog box.

CHAPTER TEN

Most Reliable and Stable

Unreliability and instability have many symptoms. Untested device drivers can cause the computer to crash frequently or force users to reboot their computers too often. Everyone exhales loudly after successfully installing an application, and faulty uninstall programs can bring a computer to its knees. These symptoms aggravate users and administrators, but they also cost companies money. A computer crashes, and a user is no longer working. Applications need upgrades, and administrators are walking the halls.

Microsoft Windows 2000 Professional doesn't fix the symptoms—it fixes the problems (at least, many of them). This operating system is more reliable and more stable than any previous version of Windows. For example, device driver signing ensures that users install the highest quality drivers. The operating system doesn't need to reboot as often now, which ensures that it's always up and productive. But the biggest contribution to reliability and stability is the Windows Installer Service. It's responsible for making sure that applications install correctly, continue to work reliably, and don't adversely impact the stability of the operating system—and when they are no longer needed, can be completely and safely removed from the system.

The Windows Installer Service has two sides to it—with and without Active Directory. In Windows 2000 Professional, the service can install, upgrade, repair, and remove applications. These are the features that users care about. In conjunction with Windows 2000 Server, the Windows Installer Service allows network administrators to publish applications in Active Directory, and then use policies to make those applications available to different groups of users or even assign mandatory applications to certain users. You'll learn about the first aspect of the Windows Installer Service in this chapter. This chapter also provides a brief overview of how the Windows Installer Service can be leveraged in a Windows 2000 Server Active Directory environment. However, for more information about publishing applications in Active Directory and using policies to deploy applications, see *Introducing Microsoft Windows 2000 Server*, Microsoft Press, 1999.

Device Driver Signing

Digitally signed device drivers ensure the quality of device drivers that ship with Windows 2000 Professional. In fact, Microsoft ships with the operating system only those device drivers that have a Microsoft digital signature—and all device drivers that users install from the Windows Update Web site will have a Microsoft digital signature. The result is an operating system that's easier to support and costs less to own.

Driver signing (code signing) uses existing digital signature cryptographic technology to store authenticating information in a security catalog (.CAT) file. The process doesn't change the device driver's program code; driver signing stores a hash of the driver's program code, along with other relevant information, in the CAT file. The information in this file indicates that the device driver was tested by the Windows Hardware Quality Lab (WHQL) and passed. Then, Microsoft signs the CAT file. The operating system is able to verify the device driver's integrity because of the values stored in the CAT file, and it verifies the integrity of the CAT file with its digital signature. Microsoft creates a CAT file for each device driver package. The driver's INF file references the CAT file. After installing the device driver, the operating system continues to maintain the CAT file.

Users can view security catalogs, which are in the *systemroot*\System32\ CatRoot folder. Double-click a CAT file to display the Security Catalog dialog box. While this dialog box contains a lot of information, the only useful bit might be the file's digital signature. Click the View Signature button to view the CAT file's signature and the certificate used to sign the CAT file. Note also that users can view any file's digital signature, including digitally signed OpenType fonts, by choosing Properties from the file's pop-up menu and then clicking the Digital Signatures button. If users are interested in viewing the public key certificate associated with a file's digital signature, they can look it up in the Certificate Manager. For more information about the Certificate Manager and Windows 2000 Professional's public key security features, see Chapter 11, "Strongest Local and Network Security."

> **NOTE:** Network administrators can use policies to control driver installation on a Windows 2000 domain. They can prevent Windows 2000 Professional from installing unsigned drivers. They can cause the operating system to warn users when they're installing unsigned drivers. They can, at their discretion, allow the operating system to install all device drivers, signed or unsigned. Administrators use the Computer Management console's Group Policy snap-in to set this policy.

Fewer Reboots: From Fifty Cases to Seven

Many configuration changes that require a reboot when running Windows NT 4.0 no longer require a reboot when running Windows 2000 Professional. The following list describes many of the scenarios that no longer require users to reboot the computer:

- Adding new disks
- Adding disk space to an NTFS volume
- Configuring Plug and Play devices
- Changing an IP address to resolve an IP address conflict
- Changing video display attributes such as color resolution
- Changing the mouse
- Adding and removing network protocols
- Adding a new page file
- Increasing a page file's size
- Installing File and Print Services for NetWare
- Changing the server name for AppleTalk Workstations
- Switching MacClient network adapters and viewing shared volumes
- Removing Microsoft Transaction Services
- Installing Microsoft SQL Server (7.0)
- Installing Exchange ("Platinum")

There are a few configuration changes that continue to require a reboot when running Windows 2000 Professional. The following list describes some of those:

- **Changing the ISA adapter configuration**   Installing Industry Standard Architecture (ISA) devices requires a reboot only if the operating system can't bring the device online dynamically or if the INF file or class installer specifically requests a reboot.

- **Changing the system font**   Changing the system font requires the operating system to reinitialize the USER and GDI (Graphics Device Interface) objects from scratch—difficult to do on a running system.

- **Adding and removing communication ports**   After configuring the computer's communication ports, Windows 2000 Professional requires users to reboot the computer to avoid resource conflicts when the ports require a jumper change.

- **Changing the default system locale**   Since the boot loader loads the translation tables associated with the system's default code page, the operating system must reboot.

- **Changing the computer's name**   Changing the computer's name requires users to reboot the computer, but changing the computer's domain membership does not.

- **Installing service packs or hotfix patches**   Service packs and hotfix patches usually replace core program code, requiring users to reboot the computer.

The Windows Installer Service

The Windows Installer Service defines a standard for installing, repairing, removing, and updating applications. That is, it provides for the total life cycle of an application—from installation to upgrade to removal. The big picture is that the Windows Installer Service is a key part of Microsoft's Zero Administration Windows initiative, reducing the cost of operating each desktop. For example, the service eliminates the need for network administrators to visit each desktop in order to install, upgrade, repair, or remove applications; they can perform those activities from the server. The Windows Installer Service reduces total cost of ownership by utilizing just-in-time installation. This means that users get the features of their applications when they need them—and installation is totally transparent in many cases. That's the big picture; the following list provides a few more details about the Windows Installer Service's features and how it makes the operating system so much more reliable:

- **DLL conflicts**   DLL (dynamic-link library) conflicts are the bane of most users and, even more so, administrators. The Windows Installer Service reduces those conflicts by placing DLLs in their own folders, treating them as part of a component that's not to be shared with other components. Additionally, the Windows Installer Service does a better job of managing shared components.

- **Application repair**   Each application that's designed for the Windows Installer Service specifies a list of critical files. The operating system monitors those files and automatically replaces them if they're missing or corrupt. You'll frequently see this capability described as *self-repairing* or *self-healing* applications.

■ **Failed installations**   If an installation fails, the Windows Installer Service can restart the installation at the point of failure or remove changes made up to that point, restoring the computer to the state it was in before the installation.

■ **Software updates**   The Windows Installer Service tracks the original installation, and this makes upgrading each of the application's components more reliable and automatic.

■ **Application removal**   The Windows Installer Service tracks an application's components. Components include files, registry entries, and shortcuts. Tracking each component allows the service to completely remove the application, including all of its DLLs.

■ **Componentization**   The Windows Installer Service allows authors to build their applications as collections of discrete components—sometimes down to the feature level. Users can then pick and choose the components, or features, that they want to install.

Most users have no idea that the Windows Installer Service even exists—nor should they. They certainly don't care about the service's administrative angle, which you'll learn about following this section. However, users do care about installing, upgrading, and removing applications. They do care about the user interfaces they see, which—unbeknownst to them—are courtesy of the Windows Installer Service. And what they see is, first of all, the new Add/Remove Programs dialog box shown in Figure 10-1 on the following page. You learned about this dialog box in Chapter 5, "Easier Setup and Configuration." Users use it to install, remove, and modify applications.

Users can utilize the Windows Installer Service in two other ways, if they are in a Windows 2000 Server Active Directory environment. First, if users try opening a file that has no association with an application already installed on their system, but Windows 2000 Professional finds a suitable application has been published or assigned in the Windows 2000 Server Active Directory, the Windows Installer Service can automatically install the application.

Second, if a network administrator assigns an application to a user, Windows 2000 Professional puts a shortcut for the application on the user's Start menu without actually installing the application. When the user chooses that application from the Start menu, the operating system automatically downloads and installs it. These two capabilities are collectively known as "just-in-time installation."

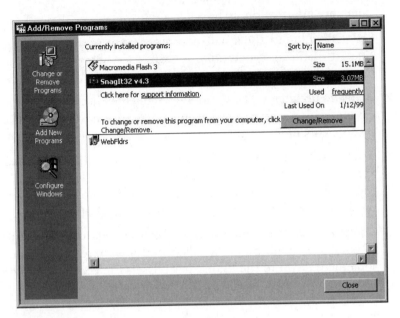

Figure 10-1
The new Add/Remove Programs dialog box.

NOTE: Microsoft has announced plans to make the Windows Installer Service available for Windows NT Workstation 4.0, Windows 95, and Windows 98. However, the company has not announced a timeframe for its availability.

Windows Installer Service Packages

Application developers can use native authoring tools and administrators can use repackaging tools to create a Windows Installer Service package. Windows Installer Service packages contain all the information necessary to describe how to install an application in every conceivable situation. Scenarios include installation on different platforms, installation of different product features, installation from different sources, and so forth. Each package also includes information about the application's components, including what files must be present for a particular feature to work properly. More specifically, Windows

Installer Service packages are files (with an MSI extension) that contain the following information:

- **Summary information** The application's version, date, and vendor

- **Installation instructions** Instructions that describe what files, registry entries, shortcuts, etc. are installed and under what conditions they're installed

- **Application files** References to the actual application files and components (In some cases, the package can contain actual compressed source files.)

To take full advantage of the Windows Installer Service, software developers must specifically design their applications to use it. Authoring tools will be available from third-party sources to help vendors comply. Administrators can repackage existing applications, although repackaged applications won't take full advantage of the Windows Installer Service. Windows 2000 Server includes WinInstall LE (limited edition) for this purpose. Repackaged applications are treated as a single feature, or component, so they won't have the manageability and flexibility of an application with native support for the Windows Installer Service.

Publishing

Windows 2000 Professional and Active Directory allow network administrators to publish applications. Windows 2000 Server provides the Software Installation snap-in as an extension to the Computer Management console's Group Policy snap-in. The Software Installation snap-in makes it easy for network administrators to manage the software for their organization. Using this tool, administrators can assign or publish applications to a Group Policy object that's associated with an Active Directory container: site, domain, organizational unit, etc.

Network administrators can choose to assign or publish an application. The following list describes the differences between the two approaches:

- **Assigned** Administrators can assign an application to a group of users who need that application to perform their jobs. Additionally, administrators can assign an application to a computer. Applications that are assigned to users will be installed, using the Windows Installer

Service the first time a user starts the application. Applications that are assigned to computers will be installed the next time the computer starts up. Users can't completely remove an assigned application, however—it is resilient. Administrators can also assign a new version of the application, and the upgrade automatically installs the next time users choose the application from the Start menu or open a document associated with the application.

■ **Published**   Administrators publish applications that might be useful to some users, but aren't mandatory. Users can use the Add/Remove Programs dialog box, available in the Control Panel, to install published applications. When users try opening a file that a published application can open, the operating system offers to install the application for the user. After installation, a published application behaves like an assigned one, except that users can remove it if they want to.

The Microsoft Windows Logo

Many will deny my assertion that one of the biggest contributors to reliability is the Microsoft Windows logo. However, I stand by my assertion, and—other than the occasional shareware application—I won't touch an application that doesn't proudly display that logo on its box. The Windows logo doesn't necessarily ensure that the application does what it's supposed to do. Rather, its purpose is to signify that the application works and plays well with the operating system and with other applications.

VeriTest, Inc., a third-party testing company, tests applications on a variety of points. Only after passing muster can vendors license the logo from Microsoft and display it on their applications' packaging.

The technical specification for the Windows logo identifies what an application must do to work effectively with Windows 2000 Professional. The specification is written so that applications that meet the criteria will also work with previous versions of Windows. The following describes the qualifications for receiving the logo:

■ The application functions normally after the operating system is upgraded to Windows 2000 Professional.

■ The application provides a consistent, accessible user experience to reduce support and training costs.

- The application uses the Windows Installer Service to ensure a robust, self-repairing installation. This helps ensure that the application will interoperate with other applications, and that the application will properly uninstall.

- The application supports OnNow/ACPI capabilities to deliver the best mobile computing experience possible.

- The application is IntelliMirror-enabled, properly maintaining user preferences and computer settings. This ensures a good "roaming user" experience and support for multiple users per machine.

- The application runs in a secure Windows environment and complies with system policies.

CHAPTER ELEVEN

Strongest Local and Network Security

Microsoft Windows 2000 Professional is a secure operating system. This means that the operating system can discretely control access to system resources. The operating system can record and audit all access to the system. All access to the operating system requires a password and leaves an audit trail. These features are traditional strengths of the Microsoft Windows NT product family and—other than their location in the user interface—they have changed very little.

Still, Windows 2000 Professional adds a plethora of new security features to its arsenal. The Encrypting File System (EFS) protects users' files from prying eyes. Windows 2000 Professional includes many new authentication protocols, including Kerberos, which the operating system uses to provide a single sign-on (SSO) to the network, and the Extensible Authentication Protocol (EAP). Smart Cards allow users to authenticate themselves using tamper-resistant credentials, and Windows 2000 Professional integrates Smart Cards with Kerberos, supporting multifactor authentication. Finally, network communications are more secure with the Layer 2 Tunneling Protocol (L2TP)—a new virtual private network (VPN) protocol—and new protocols for encrypting data transmitted on the network, including Internet Protocol security (IPSec). You'll learn about all of these features in this chapter.

Some features are more interesting to Windows 2000 Professional users than others. The EFS and VPNs are particularly useful, whether users use a standalone computer or connect to a local area network (LAN). Many other features work behind the scenes and users rarely know about them, but those features are still critical components of the operating system's security. Even though these features don't require user intervention, they often require administration on a Windows 2000 domain—a topic this book doesn't cover. If you want to learn more about administering these features, see *Introducing Microsoft Windows 2000 Server* (Microsoft Press, 1999).

Public Key Security

A key component used by most of Windows 2000 Professional's security features is public key security. A few concepts will come in handy as you learn about those features, and the most important one is the difference between private key and public key encryption:

- **Private key encryption,** also known as symmetric or shared-secret encryption, uses the same secret key to encrypt and decrypt data. When two parties exchange information that's encrypted using symmetric encryption, one uses the private key to encrypt the data while the other uses the exact same private key to decrypt it. The Data Encryption Standard (DES) is an example of private key encryption.

- **Public key encryption,** also known as asymmetric encryption, uses two different keys, one public and one private. Each key is mathematically related to the other. What one key does, only the other key can undo. For example, data encrypted by the public key is decrypted by the private key, and vice versa. Likewise, data that's digitally signed by the private key can be verified using the public key, and vice versa. Most of the security features you'll read about in this chapter rely on some form of public key encryption.

With symmetric encryption, both parties share a single secret key, meaning that each party trusts that the other will keep the secret key, well, a secret. With asymmetric encryption, however, one party uses the private key to encrypt or digitally sign data while the other uses the public key to decrypt or verify the digital signature, and vice versa. Users publish their public key, explicitly or implicitly, and keep their private keys to themselves. For example, users can digitally sign an outgoing e-mail message with their private key, and the recipients can verify the source of the message using the sender's public key. Similarly, users can send a message encrypted using the recipient's public key, and the recipient decrypts the message using his or her private key. I've limited this discussion to e-mail messages, but network connections, file encryption, and other security features use a similar process.

Certificate Authenticity

One of the big problems with symmetric encryption is that both parties must have the secret key. Asymmetric encryption doesn't work that way. The sender encrypts a message using the private key and sends the public key, which the recipient uses to authenticate the message, along with the message. Sending the public key along with the message seems odd—as though anyone could pose as the sender by including the public key with the message. Remember, though, that once the sender encrypts a message with the private key, only the public key can decrypt the message, and the public key is registered with a trusted certificate authority. Thus, if the public key (verified by the certificate authority) received with the message matches the private key used to encrypt the message, the message is authentic—assuming that the sender managed to keep the private key safe.

To ensure the integrity of the public key, users publish the key with a *certificate* (public key certificate). The certificate contains information such as the key's name, its intended purpose, its owner, its expiration date, and the name of the certificate authority, as well as the public key itself. A certificate authority— VeriSign is one of the best-known certificate authorities—digitally signs the certificate. Users can verify the digitally signed certificate using the certificate authority's public key but, in actuality, software performs that process on behalf of users. For example, an e-mail program automatically verifies the authenticity of the sender's public key and notifies the recipient if it suspects foul play. Likewise, a secure network connection uses the server's public key to verify the identity of the server.

In summary, the following list describes the conditions under which an operating system or application accepts a certificate as proof of identity:

- The certificate hasn't expired.

- The certificate authority has not revoked the certificate.

- The intended purpose of the certificate matches how the certificate is used.

- The software trusts the certificate authority that issued the certificate.

- The certificate is authentic, as determined by its digital signature.

Certificate Purposes

In Windows 2000 Professional, certificates have many purposes, most of which are described in the following list:

- Allow data on disk to be encrypted

- Allow data to be signed with the current time

- Allow a recovery agent to recover encrypted data

- Allow secured communication over the Internet

- Allow you to digitally sign a Certificate Trust List
- Ensure e-mail came from the sender
- Ensure software came from a software publisher
- Ensure the content of e-mail cannot be viewed by others
- Guarantee the identity of a remote computer
- Guarantee your identity to a remote computer
- Protect device drivers and system components from tampering
- Protect e-mail from tampering
- Protect software from tampering after publication
- Verify the source of device drivers and system components

The Certificate Manager

Most users will never have to manage certificates using the Certificate Manager. Regardless, Windows 2000 Professional provides the Certificate Manager to manage certificates. Users can remove certificates. They can import certificates from or export certificates to backup files. Users can also request new certificates from enterprise and standalone certificate authorities. Users open the Certificate Manager in the Control Panel by double-clicking the Users And Passwords icon and then clicking the Certificates button in the Advanced tab of the Users And Passwords dialog box. The Certificate Manager, shown in Figure 11-1, has four tabs—Personal (hidden in the figure), Other People, Intermediate Certification Authorities, and Trusted Root Certification Authorities—each corresponding to a *certificate store.*

The most common task for Windows 2000 Professional users is to export certificates to a backup file. First, making backup copies of personal certificates ensures that users can recover them if they are lost. Second, users should always back up and remove recovery certificates—these allow recovery of encrypted files when a certificate or private key gets lost—to prevent unauthorized users from decrypting their files (more on that later). To export a certificate, users select the certificate and then click the Export button. The Certificate Manager Export Wizard prompts users for the file format, whether they want to export the private key with the certificate, and a password that the Certificate Manager Export Wizard uses to protect the private key. Even though the export file is password-protected, users should still take special precautions for protecting it.

Figure 11-1
Trusted Root Certification Authorities in the Certificate Manager.

Authentication

Authentication is the process of validating users' credentials, which are usually names and passwords. By authenticating themselves, users prove their identities. After being authenticated, users are allowed access to the local computer, the network, etc., based upon the rights and privileges assigned to them by the administrator. For example, when users log on to the local computer, Windows 2000 Professional authenticates them against its own local user database. When users log on to a Windows 2000 domain, the operating system authenticates them against the network domain's user database. An Internet service provider authenticates users before allowing them to connect to the Internet. Any situation where access to a resource requires a name and a password is a situation that requires authentication.

Windows 2000 Professional supports a variety of authentication protocols for connecting to a remote access server. Each protocol handles authentication a bit differently, and some are more secure than others. Users configure a connection's authentication protocol in the Network And Dial-Up Connections folder (see Chapters 5 and 6 if you're not familiar with this folder). They choose Properties from the connection's pop-up menu and click the Security tab. Users rely on the default configuration by selecting the Typical Security Settings option button. They select the Advanced Security Settings option button and then click the Settings button to display the Advanced Security Settings dialog box, shown in Figure 11-2, in which they can fully configure the authentication protocols. In all cases, the remote access server must support at least one of the authentication protocols enabled in the connection.

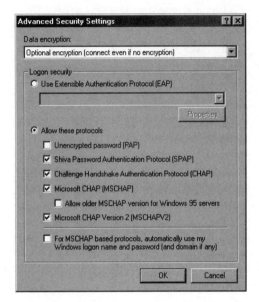

Figure 11-2
The Advanced Security Settings dialog box.

Each dial-up or VPN connection in the Network And Dial-Up Connections folder can use any of the following authentication protocols (those at the bottom of the list are stronger than those at the top):

- **Password Authentication Protocol (PAP)** uses clear-text passwords and is the simplest form of authentication. Use this protocol only when the remote access server doesn't support more advanced authentication protocols, such as when connecting to an Internet service provider.

- **Shiva Password Authentication Protocol (SPAP)** allows Shiva clients to connect to computers running Windows 2000 Server.

- **Challenge Handshake Authentication Protocol (CHAP)** negotiates a secure authentication. This authentication protocol can prove to the remote access server that you know your password without actually sending the password. It does so by transforming the password using the Message Digest 5 (MD5) hashing scheme (see Figure 11-3). Most third-party Point-to-Point Protocol (PPP) servers support CHAP and MD5.

- **Microsoft Challenge Handshake Authentication Protocol (MSCHAP)** is similar to plain CHAP, but it's specifically designed for Microsoft products.

- **Microsoft Challenge Handshake Authentication Protocol Version 2 (MSCHAPV2)** is the latest version of MSCHAP. It provides mutual authentication, stronger initial data encryption keys, and different encryption keys for sending and receiving data.

- **Extensible Authentication Protocol (EAP)** is an extension of PPP that provides remote authentication using third-party security protocols and devices such as Kerberos, Smart Cards, retina scan, voiceprint, and many more. In other words, it provides a method for supporting additional authentication protocols within PPP. Windows 2000 Professional relies on EAP to protect VPNs from brute-force, dictionary, and password-guessing attacks. Windows 2000 Professional provides two flavors of EAP: MD5, which you learned about earlier in this list, and Transaction-level Security (TLS), which is a stronger authentication method based on public key security.

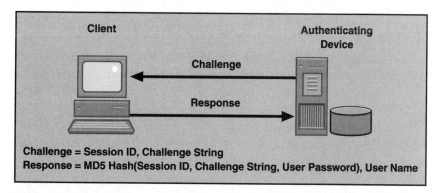

Figure 11-3
The Challenge Handshake Authentication Protocol.

Windows 2000 Professional doesn't use the authentication protocols you just read about when it connects to a LAN. The operating system uses the NTLM protocol (formerly called the Windows NT LAN Manager), a legacy authentication protocol, when it connects to a LAN. NTLM in Windows 2000 is no different than in Windows NT Workstation 4.0: it's slow, and every access to a secure resource requires authentication. Windows 2000 Professional also uses a new authentication protocol called Kerberos. Kerberos is much faster than NTLM and it supports SSO.

Single Sign-On (Kerberos)

Windows 2000 Professional's single sign-on (SSO) capability allows users to access all network resources after a single authentication. The network validates a user's credentials once, the first time she or he accesses the network. The integrated SSO capability is easy to use, it improves users' productivity, it reduces the cost of maintaining the network, and it improves network security through the built-in Kerberos protocol. The following list describes additional benefits of SSO:

- **Simpler administration** Rather than requiring administrators to perform SSO-specific tasks, SSO is a transparent part of the operating system.

- **Better administrative control** Windows 2000 stores all SSO information in Active Directory, which provides a single repository for all information about each user's rights and privileges.

- **Improved user productivity** Users no longer have to authenticate themselves multiple times, and they don't have to remember multiple passwords. Even better: the help desk will need to answer fewer calls about forgotten passwords.

- **Better network security** SSO prevents the most common source of security violations. With a single set of credentials, users no longer have to write their passwords down on sticky notes and, since all SSO information is in Active Directory, administrators know the status of each user account.

- **Consolidation of heterogeneous networks** SSO allows administrators to combine separate networks, consolidating administrative efforts and applying security policies uniformly across all the networks.

The Kerberos protocol, which Windows 2000 Professional uses to implement SSO, uses encrypted data packets called *tickets* to validate users' identities. A special computer serving as a Key Distribution Center (KDC) issues tickets in its area of authority (realm). On a Windows 2000 domain, each domain controller is a KDC and the domain is its realm. Figure 11-4 shows how Kerberos works. When users log on to the domain, the KDC provides an initial ticket called a *ticket granting ticket* (TGT). When users need to use a network resource, the operating system gives the TGT to the KDC and requests a *service ticket* (ST) for that particular resource, which the operating system presents to the resource.

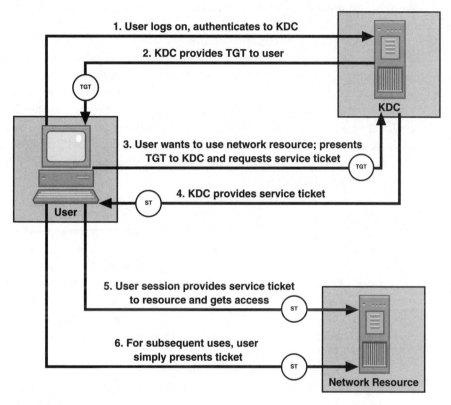

Figure 11-4
The Kerberos protocol.

Windows 2000 Professional users don't do anything special to enable SSO. Obviously, when running on standalone computers, SSO isn't an issue. On Windows 2000 domains, however, SSO administration is performed in Active Directory. For more information about these topics, I refer you to *Introducing Microsoft Windows 2000 Server.*

Smart Card Authentication

Smart Card technology is fully integrated into Windows 2000 Professional. It provides features similar to SSO, described in the previous section, but it allows the operating system to authenticate users using the private and public keys stored on a card. Smart Cards provide a tamper-proof location for storing credentials, and unlocking those credentials requires that users provide a personal identification number (PIN).

As opposed to Kerberos authentication, which uses shared-secret cryptography (the password is the shared secret), Windows 2000 Professional implements Smart Card technology via asymmetric cryptography (encryption and decryption require two different keys, private and public). When users log on to the operating system using a Smart Card, the card's private and public keys replace the user's password. The KDC encrypts the user's session key with the user's public key, while the client decrypts the session key with the user's private key. For more information about asymmetric cryptography, see "Public Key Security," earlier in this chapter.

Windows 2000 Professional automatically detects Smart Card readers and installs support for them. After enabling support for Smart Cards, users see an icon on the Windows 2000 Professional splash screen that looks like a Smart Card reader. To log on to the computer using a Smart Card, users insert the Smart Card in the reader and type their PIN. When used in combination with dial-up and VPN connections, Smart Cards present a formidable barrier against intrusion. Users configure a dial-up network connection to use a Smart Card by configuring it in the Network And Dial-Up Connections folder. In the Security tab of the connection's Properties dialog box, users select Smartcard in the Validate My Identity Using list.

Windows 2000 Professional supports the Gemplus GemSAFE and Schlumberger Cryptoflex Smart Cards. Gemplus GemSAFE Smart Cards are white with an oval-shaped metal contact. Schlumberger Cryptoflex Smart Cards are white or gray with a rectangular metal contact.

> NOTE: Other than configuring a dial-up network connection to validate users' credentials with a Smart Card, users don't need to do much in order to enable Smart Cards in Windows 2000 Professional. However, network administrators must create a certificate and prepare the card. For more information about enrolling for a certificate and storing it on a card, see *Introducing Microsoft Windows 2000 Server.*

The Encrypting File System

Windows 2000 Professional's Encrypting File System (EFS) is based on public and private key encryption and the CryptoAPI architecture. While EFS can use any symmetric encryption algorithm to encrypt files, the initial release of EFS uses DES—128-bit in North America and 40-bit internationally. Future releases of EFS will allow users to install alternative encryption algorithms.

Users can begin using EFS right away, as EFS is mostly transparent. The file system automatically generates an encryption certificate for the user along with an associated private key, if these items don't already exist. Users can encrypt individual files or entire folders. If users add files to an encrypted folder, EFS automatically encrypts the new files. If users move an encrypted file from one folder to another, the file remains encrypted since each file carries its own encryption key. Users don't have to decrypt files before using them, either, as EFS automatically detects an encrypted file, locates the user's private key, and decrypts the file as it reads the file's contents from disk.

Not only is EFS easy to use, it is also easy to administer. Windows 2000 Professional provides administrative tools to provide advanced features as well as recovery keys and policies, which allow administrators to recover encrypted files if a user loses his or her encryption certificate and associated private key or if he or she leaves the organization. Network administrators can configure recovery policies on the domain. Users with computers that aren't connected to a network domain can also recover encrypted files. EFS generates a self-signed recovery certificate, including its associated private key, the first time a user logs on to the computer as the administrator, making that user the default *recovery agent* (the user capable of restoring encrypted files).

Encrypting Files

Users encrypt files and folders in Windows Explorer. They choose Properties from the item's pop-up menu to display its Properties dialog box. Then, they click the Advanced button to display the Advanced Attributes dialog box (see Figure 11-5 on the following page) and check the Encrypt Contents To Secure Data check box. If they are encrypting a folder, Windows 2000 Professional asks them if they want to encrypt that folder only or that folder and all of its subfolders. Even if the folder is devoid of subfolders, users should choose to encrypt the folder and its subfolders if they want the operating system to encrypt new subfolders. Users permanently decrypt files and folders by going through the same process and clearing the Encrypt Contents To Secure Data check box.

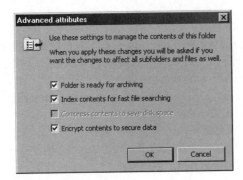

Figure 11-5
The Advanced Attributes dialog box for a file or folder.

Alternatively, users can use Cipher.exe at the MS-DOS command prompt to encrypt files and folders. If the user does not provide any command line options, Cipher.exe reports the encryption status of the current folder. The following table describes the command line options for Cipher.exe:

```
cipher [/e | /d] [/s:dir] [/i] [/f] [/q] [dirname [...]]
```

/e	Encrypts the specified directories. EFS will encrypt any files that users add to the folder.
/d	Decrypts the specified directories. EFS will no longer encrypt files that users add to the folder.
/s:dir	Specifies the directory to encrypt or decrypt.
/i	Continues encrypting or decrypting a folder even after Cipher.exe encounters errors.
/f	Forces Cipher.exe to encrypt all specified directories, even if they are already encrypted. By default, Cipher.exe skips directories that are already encrypted.
/q	Causes Cipher.exe to report only essential information.
dirname	Specifies a pattern or a directory.

If users want to protect their documents from intrusion, they should encrypt the My Documents folder, including all of its subfolders. Users should also encrypt the Temp folder, since many programs create, in that folder, temporary copies of the documents users edit. Regardless, users should always encrypt an entire folder, rather than individual files, since many programs create backup copies of a document in the document's original location, and encrypting the entire folder ensures that Windows 2000 Professional also encrypts those backup copies.

NOTE: EFS does not allow users to encrypt files in the *systemroot* folder, which is Winnt by default. They can still encrypt files in their user profiles, however, since Windows 2000 Professional stores user profiles in the *systemdrive*\Documents And Settings folder.

Using Encrypted Files

A user who encrypts files can access them as though they were not encrypted. EFS automatically locates the user's private key and decrypts each file as it reads the file from disk. File encryption is so transparent that some users might wonder whether or not their files are indeed encrypted. They can easily verify that fact by selecting the file or folder in Windows Explorer and noting the attributes that it displays on the left side of the pane. Users can browse other users' encrypted folders, but they can't open files in them. If they try to open a file encrypted by another user, they see the "Access Denied" error message.

The user who encrypted a file can copy it as they would any other file. If users copy a file to a file system that doesn't support EFS (for example, FAT16 or FAT32), the file is not encrypted in its destination location. If an administrator enables encryption on a remote computer, the user who encrypted a file can copy that file to the remote computer and it remains encrypted. Files are not encrypted as they're transmitted across the network, however, but users can use a protocol such as IPSec to protect data as it traverses the network. Similar to copying files, users move files as they would any other file. One warning is that if users had access to an encrypted file or folder before it was encrypted, they can remove the file even though it is now encrypted. That is, encryption does not protect files from deletion by other users. Backing up files using the Copy command has the same limitations as described earlier: files can end up decrypted if the user who encrypted the files copies them to a file system that doesn't support encryption. The new Backup utility does handle encrypted files correctly, regardless of the destination, and the backup operator doesn't need access to the user's private key to do the backup.

The following list includes additional notes about working with encrypted files:

- File compression and file encryption are mutually exclusive.

- Users can encrypt files only on the NTFS file system, and they can't encrypt system files.

- The user who encrypts a file or folder is the only person who can open it.

- Copying files from an encrypted folder to a folder that's not encrypted decrypts the files.

- Users must move files into an encrypted folder using Cut and Paste instead of Drag and Drop. Drag and Drop does not automatically encrypt files when moving them.

- Users can encrypt files and folders on a remote computer as long as the administrator enables remote encryption.

- Encrypted files are not encrypted as they're transmitted over a network.

- Users can't share encrypted folders on the network.

- Protocols such as IPSec can protect data through a network transmission.

- Administrators can use a recovery policy to recover encrypted files if users lose their file encryption certificate or private key.

Roaming with EFS

Moving to a different computer presents a special problem. Moving encrypted files to the other computer isn't enough, as users need to install their encryption certificate and associated private key in order to use those files on the other computer. EFS provides two solutions. First, users can use roaming profiles, a feature that administrators must enable on the network domain, so that users' encryption certificates and private keys are available on any computer running Windows 2000 Professional.

A less elegant method is to manually move the encryption certificates and private keys from one computer to another. Use the Certificate Manager, described earlier in this chapter. In the Personal tab, observe the certificate's intended purpose as shown in the Certificate Intended Purpose area; it should be "Encrypting File System." Then click the Export button. After exporting the encryption certificate to a file, users can take the file to another computer and import it using the Certificate Manager.

> **NOTE:** By default, Windows 2000 Professional doesn't install the Certificate Manager in the Computer Management console, but users can easily add it by opening the file *systemroot*\System32\ Compmgmt.msc in Microsoft Management Console (MMC) and choosing Add/Remove Snap-In from the Console menu. For more information about using MMC and the various snap-ins that Windows 2000 Professional provides for it, see Chapter 19, "Better Management Tools."

Recovering Encrypted Files

If users lose their encryption certificate and its associated private key, or if an employee suddenly leaves the organization, a recovery agent—a user designated to recover encrypted files—can recover encrypted files on a computer using a *recovery policy*. Recovery policies are in the Computer Management console's Group Policy snap-in, as shown in Figure 11-6. EFS will not work if a recovery policy doesn't exist; thus, emptying the Encrypted Data Recovery Agents folder disables EFS. Windows 2000 Professional creates a default recovery policy locally for all standalone computers, and the local administrator is the recovery agent.

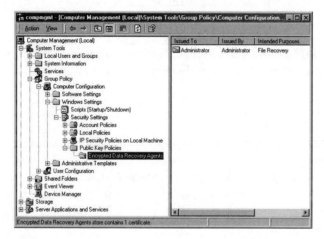

Figure 11-6
Recovery policies in the Group Policy snap-in.

In order to recover encrypted files, the user must log on to the computer as the recovery agent and then decrypt the files.

If a user doesn't have access to the certificate and private key, he or she must rely on another recovery agent. Users back up the encrypted files using Backup or a similar backup utility. Then, they e-mail the backup files to a recovery agent, who then decrypts the files using the recovery agent's own recovery certificate and then e-mails the files back to the user.

To protect the recovery certificate and its associated private key, recovery agents should remove the recovery certificate from the Certificate Manager after they export it to a backup file, as described in the previous section. Doing so prevents other people from gaining access to the recovery certificate and private key. Recovery agents can identify the certificate to be removed because the Certificate Manager describes its intended purpose as "File Recovery." After exporting the recovery certificate to a PFX file, they can remove it from the Certificate Manager; this ensures that the exported PFX file contains the only copy of the private key. They should put the PFX file in a safe place and import it into the Certificate Manager only when they must recover encrypted files on the computer.

> **NOTE:** The information in this section describes the default recovery policy created for a standalone computer. In a Windows 2000 domain, the server administrator creates recovery policies at the domain, the organizational unit, or the computer level. In this case, the default recovery agent is the domain administrator. Domain administrators should secure the recovery certificate and associated private key by exporting it and then deleting it from the Certificate Manager. The exported PFX file should then be stored in a safe place. Also, in a Windows 2000 domain, administrators can create additional recovery certificates and designate certain users as recovery agents.

Virtual Private Networks

Windows 2000 Professional has built-in support for virtual private network (VPN) connections. A VPN allows users to securely connect to a private network through a public network such as the Internet. A VPN, which provides the same level of security as any private network, is the logical equivalent of a wide area network between two different sites. VPNs have numerous advantages, as the following list describes:

- **Lower cost** Rather than using expensive 800 or long-distance telephone numbers, users connect to a VPN through the Internet by placing a local call to an Internet service provider.

- **Easier administration** Administrators don't have to worry about additional equipment or administrative issues, since the Internet service providers and the telephone companies provide the equipment required to connect users to the remote access server.

- **Better security** A VPN connection is secure, even though the connection is through the Internet. Not only does the connection encrypt data sent over the wire, but Windows 2000 Professional also provides numerous authentication protocols, as described in "Authentication," earlier in this chapter.

■ **Support for existing protocols** VPN connections support the most common protocols, including TCP/IP, IPX/SPX, and NetBEUI. Existing applications can therefore work across VPN connections.

■ **IP address security** The data transmitted through a VPN connection, including internal Internet Protocol (IP) addresses, is encrypted. All the Internet sees is the external IP addresses required to route data to the remote access server.

VPN connections communicate through an IP connection—usually the Internet. That Internet connection can be through a dial-up connection to an Internet service provider, illustrated in Figure 11-7, or through a more permanent connection. In the first case, which is more common for client computers running operating systems such as Windows 2000 Professional, the operating system establishes a PPP connection to the Internet service provider. Then, the operating system establishes the VPN connection, called the PPTP or L2TP tunnel, through the PPP connection. In the case of a more permanent connection, which would be commonly used to connect two networks, an Internet connection is already available, through a LAN or a service such as an asymmetric digital subscriber line (ADSL), and the operating system establishes the VPN connection through it. In either case, after establishing the VPN connection, users have secure access to the private network. For more information about creating and configuring VPN connections in the Network And Dial-Up Connections folder, see Chapter 6, "Better Mobile Computing Support."

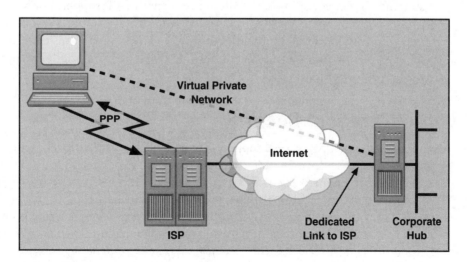

Figure 11-7
A virtual private network connection through the Internet.

Windows 2000 Professional supports two different tunneling protocols: Point-to-Point Tunneling Protocol (PPTP) and Layer 2 Tunneling Protocol (L2TP), both of which you'll learn about in the following section. PPTP was available in Windows NT Workstation 4.0 and Windows 98. L2TP is an extension of PPTP and is available in Windows 2000 Professional. Microsoft's implementation of both tunneling protocols provides a complete solution, including the following features:

- **Authentication**   Both protocols authenticate users' identities.

- **Address management**   Both protocols protect internal IP addresses.

- **Data encryption**   Both protocols encrypt data carried over the public network.

- **Key management**   Both protocols manage and refresh the encryption keys used by both the client and server computers.

- **Multiprotocol support**   Both protocols can encapsulate the most commonly used networking protocols, including IP, IPX, and NetBEUI.

While PPTP and L2TP provide similar features, the two protocols do have some differences. PPTP supports only IP networks, while L2TP supports IP, Frame Relay, X.25, and Asynchronous Transfer Mode (ATM) connections. Note that, at this time, Windows 2000 Professional's L2TP implementation only supports IP networks. Another difference is that PPTP supports only a single tunnel between the client and the server, while L2TP supports multiple tunnels, allowing for different qualities of service. The last major difference is that L2TP provides tunnel authentication, while PPTP does not. Still, if either tunneling protocol is used with IPSec, IPSec provides tunnel authentication.

Internet Protocol Security

Windows 2000 Professional supports Internet Protocol security (IPSec). IPSec simplifies the deployment and management of network security. Designed by the Internet Engineering Task Force (IETF) for the Internet Protocol, IPSec supports network-level authentication, data integrity, and encryption. In short, IPSec provides machine-level encryption and authentication, securing both data and passwords. For more information about implementing IPSec on a Windows 2000 domain, see *Introducing Microsoft Windows 2000 Server*.

PART IV

BEST OF
WINDOWS 98

Easy Device Installation

The primary design goal of Plug and Play is to make computers easier to use. Users no longer have to fiddle with jumpers and resource conflicts. They simply plug a device into the computer—and it works. Administrators spend less time tearing computers apart and more time administering the network. Vendors can create more innovative products and spend less time writing device drivers. As you can see, everyone benefits from Plug and Play.

Up to now, Plug and Play has been absent from the Microsoft Windows NT product line. Windows 95 introduced it. Windows 98 bettered it. Windows NT Workstation 4.0 did not contain it.

Plug and Play finds its way into Microsoft Windows 2000 Professional in the form of the OnNow design initiative. In layperson's terms, OnNow is a system-wide approach to configuration and power management. Part of OnNow is the Advanced Configuration and Power Interface (ACPI) specification, which takes over system configuration from the Plug and Play BIOS (basic input/ output system). It also takes over power management from the Advanced Power Management (APM) 1.2 BIOS. Windows 98 and Windows 2000 Professional both implement the ACPI.

This chapter describes how OnNow and—more specifically—the ACPI make computers easier to use. You'll learn about Plug and Play, power management, and the new Win32 driver model (WDM). You'll also learn about some features specific to Windows 2000 Professional, such as its new diagnostic boot options, which Windows 98 has had for some time now. This chapter describes the technology that makes devices easy to install. For more information about the devices that Windows 2000 Professional supports, see Chapter 13, "Broader Hardware Support."

OnNow

The OnNow design initiative makes computers immediately available and easier to use. Before OnNow, computers had to boot when users turned them on; with OnNow, computers are immediately available after waking from a low-power state. When not in use, a computer seems to be off, but the computer can still respond to events in its environment. Programs adjust their behavior as the computer's power state changes, ensuring that those programs don't interfere with the computer's power management. Also, all devices participate in the computer's power management.

OnNow encompasses changes to hardware, software, and operating systems that allow them to work together to manage the power of the system:

- **Operating system** The operating system assumes control of system configuration and power management from the Plug and Play BIOS and the APM BIOS.

- **Unified driver model** Windows 98 and Windows 2000 Professional implement a unified driver model that supports Plug and Play and per-device power management.

- **System interfaces** Through interfaces between the operating system and the system board, each device driver manages its device's power. OnNow defines new software and hardware abstraction interfaces for Plug and Play and power management.

- **Power management standards** OnNow standardizes power state definitions and power management interfaces, making class drivers responsible for their devices.

- **Application architecture** Applications play a key role in power management by adjusting their behavior based on the state of the computer and each device. They must also inform the operating system about their own state: idle, working, etc.

Figure 12-1 provides a simplified view of the Windows 2000 Professional components that are within the domain of the OnNow initiative. Through the ACPI, the operating system is responsible for Plug and Play and power management, which includes allowing applications to participate in the process. The WDM provides a unified driver model. You'll learn about these technologies in the remainder of this chapter.

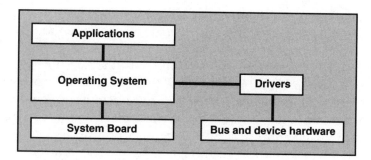

Figure 12-1
Components within the domain of the OnNow initiative.

> NOTE: Much confusion exists regarding OnNow and the ACPI. Just remember that OnNow is an *initiative*, not a technology. That is, there isn't a Windows 98 or a Windows 2000 Professional feature called "OnNow." However, OnNow does influence many of Windows 2000 Professional's features through specifications such as the ACPI, which is jointly defined by the companies participating in the OnNow initiative.

Plug and Play

Plug and Play is a combination of hardware and software components that recognize a computer's hardware and adapt to changes in the computer's configuration. Plug and Play does the work, requiring little interaction from users. For example, rather than users setting a network interface card's jumpers, Plug and Play automatically assigns resources to the card. Rather than users juggling resources, ensuring that no two devices are in contention for them, Plug and Play arbitrates conflicts. From users' perspectives, their computers just work.

A Plug and Play system requires the interaction of a computer's operating system, BIOS, devices, and device drivers. Windows 2000 Professional extends the existing Windows NT I/O infrastructure to support Plug and Play as well as power management. It's optimized for portable, desktop, and server computers that have ACPI system boards. It also provides a common device driver interface called the Win32 driver model, which you'll learn about later in this chapter. As you see, Windows 2000 Professional meets the requirements of a Plug and Play system.

The level of Plug and Play support that Windows 2000 Professional provides depends on the computer's devices and device drivers. For full Plug and Play functionality, users should use Plug and Play devices with Plug and Play device drivers, both of which must comply with the OnNow design initiative and the ACPI. Non–Plug and Play devices used in combination with Plug and Play device drivers will be partially supported by Plug and Play. Plug and Play won't automatically recognize such devices (users use the Add/Remove Hardware Wizard shown in Figure 12-2 to install them), but it can manage those devices' resources and power. And, with Plug and Play drivers, non–Plug and Play devices show up in the Device Manager along with Plug and Play devices. Without a Plug and Play driver, the operating system provides no Plug and Play support for a device, regardless of whether it is a Plug and Play device. This means that legacy drivers continue to work as before—they won't have Plug and Play support. If all of this is a bit much to remember, take a look at Table 12-1:

	Plug and Play Driver	Non–Plug and Play Driver
Plug and Play Device	Full Plug and Play Support	No Plug and Play Support
Non–Plug and Play Device	Partial Plug and Play Support	No Plug and Play Support

Table 12-1
Levels of Plug and Play support.

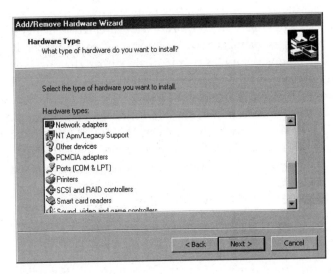

Figure 12-2
The Add/Remove Hardware Wizard.

The Configuration Process

Windows 2000 Professional's Plug and Play process works similarly to Windows 98's Plug and Play process. Each time the operating system starts, it goes through a process similar to this:

1. Identify each device installed on the computer.

2. Determine each device's resource requirements.

3. Create a configuration with no resource conflicts.

4. Assign resources to each Plug and Play device.

5. Load the drivers required for each device.

6. Notify the operating system of configuration changes.

The Evolution of Plug and Play

Recall Windows 3.1? Installing anything but standard devices on a computer running Windows 3.1 wasn't easy. Simply configuring a communications port was troublesome for most users. More advanced hardware such as tape drives, digital cameras, and scanners were out of reach for anyone but technically savvy users. And for that matter, many modern devices weren't even feasible for Windows 3.1 because of the monolithic device drivers that were difficult to develop.

Windows 95 introduced Plug and Play. It relied on a Plug and Play BIOS. Although "plug and pray" jokes abounded, Windows 95 Plug and Play worked. It automatically detected and configured the computer's standard devices, including communications ports, and it made installing more advanced hardware a no-brainer for most users. Windows 98 maintains support for the Plug and Play BIOS, but it also supports the ACPI.

Windows 2000 Professional implements Plug and Play through the ACPI. It does not fully support Plug and Play via the Plug and Play BIOS. The ACPI specification defines the requirements for the computer's system board and BIOS. It defines new interfaces for Plug and Play that include power management and new configuration capabilities, all of which are under the operating system's control. Windows 98 also uses this specification.

When Windows 2000 Professional starts, it identifies every device on the computer. Identifying and recognizing are two separate things, however, as some devices might continue to be unrecognized by the operating system even after it identifies that they exist. Devices that aren't required to start the computer remain inactive until after the operating system starts, ensuring that resource conflicts don't render the computer useless. The process of identifying a computer's devices is called *enumeration*.

After identifying each device, Plug and Play determines each device's resource requirements. Note that device drivers do not assign resources to the devices they control. Instead, Plug and Play identifies each device's requirements and, based upon those requirements, assigns resources to it. The resources it assigns include I/O ports, interrupt requests (IRQs), direct memory access (DMA) channels, and memory locations. Plug and Play stores the computer's configuration in the registry. For example, a device might require one IRQ and an I/O port. After inventorying the requirements of all the devices, Plug and Play determines that IRQ 7 and I/O port 300h are available (a typical configuration for some network adapters) and assigns those resources to the device. A key part of this process is that, while creating the computer's configuration, Plug and Play makes sure no two devices are using the same resources, thus avoiding the conflicts that once plagued users. After configuring the devices, Plug and Play identifies the device drivers required by each device and loads them.

During the course of normal operations, Plug and Play is still "doing its thing." It provides an interface between the system and the device drivers. The interface consists of I/O routines, Plug and Play I/O request packets (IRPs), driver entry points, and the registry. It also handles Plug and Play events and power management events such as the insertion or removal of a PC Card device. For example, Plug and Play recognizes when users dock or undock their computers, reconfiguring the computer as necessary. Last, Plug and Play enables applications to register for notification of certain Plug and Play and power management events.

Changes to the Windows NT Code Base

The addition of Plug and Play to Windows 2000 Professional is responsible for numerous changes to the Windows NT code base. These changes were dictated by the ACPI specification, which defines a new interface between the operating system and the computer's Plug and Play and power management features. Other specifications also contribute to the changes in the operating system; you can learn more about those specifications at *http://www.microsoft.com/hwdev*. The following list describes the most prominent changes:

- Windows 2000 Professional includes changes to existing user-mode components so that they support device installation and removal. Changed components include the Spooler, class installers, Control Panel applications, and the setup program. In addition, Windows 2000 Professional has new user-mode Plug and Play components.

- Windows 2000 Professional includes new APIs for reading from and writing to the registry. In addition, Microsoft has changed the registry structure to accommodate Plug and Play while providing backward compatibility with previous versions.

Windows 2000 Professional continues to support legacy device drivers, but these drivers have no Plug and Play or power management functionality. Vendors who want to support Plug and Play must write new drivers that take into account the changes described in this section. And if they want to write drivers that work in Windows 98 as well as in Windows 2000 Professional, they must write WDM drivers as described later in this chapter.

Plug and Play Architecture

Figure 12-3 on page 249 illustrates Windows 2000 Professional's Plug and Play architecture. The top portion of the figure illustrates the user-mode components. User-mode components cooperate with kernel-mode components to provide dynamic configuration and to provide interfaces with other components (such as the setup program and the Control Panel) that must participate in Plug and Play. The bottom portion of the figure illustrates the kernel-mode components. These support boot-time Plug and Play activity and provide interfaces between the hardware abstraction layer (HAL), the executive, and the device drivers.

The following list describes the most important components in Figure 12-3, going from top to bottom, left to right:

- **Plug and Play components (user-mode)**   The user-mode Plug and Play Manager and the other user-mode components are 32-bit extended versions of Windows 98's Configuration Manager APIs. The user-mode components expose functionality from the user-mode Plug and Play Manager. The Setup program installs drivers.

■ **Plug and Play Manager (kernel-mode)** The kernel-mode Plug and Play Manager controls the Plug and Play process and directs bus drivers to enumerate and configure devices connected to them.

■ **I/O Manager** The I/O Manager provides core services for device drivers. It's the kernel-mode component that translates user-mode read and write commands into read and write IRPs and it manages all other operating system IRPs. The I/O Manager is in Windows NT Workstation 4.0, too, which means that users can manually install a Windows 2000 Professional Plug and Play driver in Windows NT Workstation 4.0.

■ **Power Manager** The Power Manager coordinates power events and generates power management IRPs. It works in conjunction with the Policy Manager, which monitors the computer and integrates user, application, and device statuses into power policies.

■ **More Windows NT interfaces** Windows 2000 Professional provides interfaces other than the WDM interface for legacy device drivers, hardware detection, and other capabilities that WDM doesn't support. Device drivers that use these interfaces are no longer compatible with Windows 98; thus, if vendors must create device drivers that are compatible with both operating systems, they should stick to the WDM interfaces.

■ **The WDM interface** Windows 2000 Professional provides a layered architecture for device drivers. Two or more device driver layers exist for any given device. The layers include a bus driver, a function driver, and an optional filter driver. More information about each follows in this list.

■ **WDM bus drivers** WDM bus drivers control bus power management and Plug and Play features. WDM bus drivers enumerate the devices on a bus, report dynamic events to the operating system, respond to Plug and Play and power management IRPs, multiplex access to a bus, and administer each device on a bus. Microsoft provides WDM bus drivers for buses such as Peripheral Component Interconnect (PCI), universal serial bus (USB), PC Card, and IEEE 1394.

■ **WDM function drivers** WDM function drivers, also known as device drivers, are usually implemented as class driver and minidriver pairs. Microsoft provides most class drivers, which implement functionality required by all devices of a particular class. Vendors provide their own minidrivers, which provide device-specific functionality.

■ **WDM filter drivers** Optional filter drivers are above or below function drivers and add features to or modify the behavior of a device. Original equipment manufacturers (OEMs) and independent hardware vendors (IHVs) provide filter drivers.

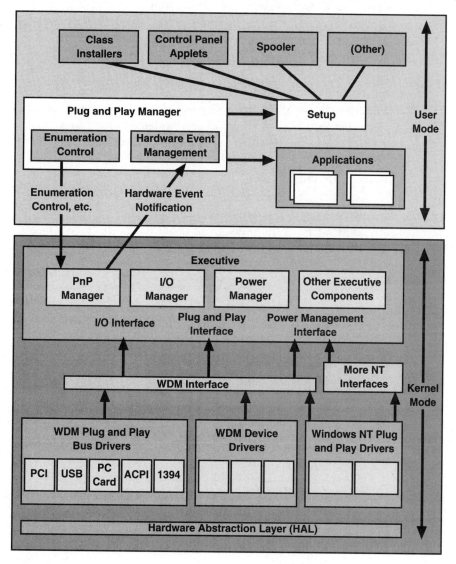

Figure 12-3
Windows 2000 Professional Plug and Play architecture.

The Device Manager

The Plug and Play Manager maintains a device tree, which users can see in the Device Manager shown in Figure 12-4, that keeps track of the computer's active devices, including each device's configuration. The Plug and Play Manager updates the device tree as the computer's configuration changes. For example, it updates the device tree when users insert a PC Card device or when it reallocates resources.

To open the Device Manager, double-click the System icon in the Control Panel. Then (in the System Properties dialog box) click the Hardware tab followed by the Device Manager button. The device tree is hierarchical—it represents devices on a bus as children of the bus adapter or controller. For example, in Figure 12-4, an S3 Trio32/64 video adapter plugs into a PCI bus and an NEC MultiSync XV17 plugs into the video adapter. Also shown in this figure are two CD-ROM drives that plug into a secondary Integrated Drive Electronics (IDE) channel, which is connected to the same PCI bus as the video adapter. Note that the Device Manager doesn't normally present this view of the device tree, a view that more accurately reflects how the operating system stores the device tree in the registry. In order to see this view, choose the Devices By Connection command from the Device Manager's View menu.

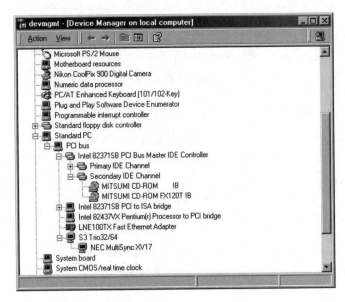

Figure 12-4
The Device Manager.

Using the Device Manager, you can change a device's configuration. Double-click any device to open its Properties dialog box. Figure 12-5 on the following page shows such a dialog box for a network interface card. The following list describes the tabs found in just about every device's Properties dialog box:

- **General** This tab displays the device's status and allows users to choose the hardware profiles (see Chapter 6, "Better Mobile Computing Support") in which the device works. Users click the Troubleshooter button to diagnose problems with the device.

- **Driver** This tab displays information about the device's drivers, including the provider, date, and version. Click the Driver Details button to see the name of each file. Click the Update Driver button to choose a new driver for the device.

The Good BIOS List

Since early in the development process, Microsoft has maintained a list of ACPI BIOSs that are known to work with Windows 2000 Professional. This list contains the name of each ACPI machine and BIOS that Microsoft tested and verified as stable and ready to support ACPI when running Windows 2000 Professional. In Windows 2000 Professional, the Good BIOS list is in a file called Txtsetup.sif.

Running Windows 2000 Professional on a computer that's on the Good BIOS list assures the user that they won't need to upgrade the BIOS. The operating system will install and enable support for ACPI; it will provide network and modem connectivity; it will report information about battery life; and it will provide functionality involving the capability to suspend, hibernate, and resume. However, if a computer isn't on the Good BIOS list, the operating system won't install support for ACPI, and users will have to upgrade the BIOS in order to use those features. Even without a proper BIOS, the operating system will provide enough functionality for users to connect to the Internet and update their computers.

Microsoft closed testing for the Good BIOS list well before finishing development on Windows 2000 Professional. However, the operating system will automatically treat a BIOS with a date later than January 1, 1999, as good. To catch those that failed Microsoft's testing after this date, the operating system also keeps a Bad BIOS list. The operating system will not enable support for ACPI if the BIOS is on this list.

■ **Resources** This tab displays the resources assigned to each device. In most cases, users should leave these settings alone. If changing these settings is necessary, users clear the Use Automatic Settings check box and then select a configuration from the Setting Based On list, or change individual settings by clicking the Change Settings button. The bottom portion of this tab describes any resource conflicts with other devices.

Many devices have additional tabs in their Properties dialog boxes that contain device-specific options. For example, a disk controller might have an Advanced tab that provides options for the master and slave devices. A mouse's Properties dialog box might have an Advanced tab that contains a sample rate and input buffer. And a communications port might have a Port Settings tab that contains the device's speed, data bits, parity, stop bits, and flow control.

Figure 12-5
A device's Properties dialog box.

Power Management

Windows 2000 Professional manages the computer's power. In compliance with the OnNow design initiative, the operating system's power management features conserve energy while the computer is working and put the computer to sleep when it's not working. The operating system's power management features include the following:

- **System power management** The ACPI defines mechanisms for putting the computer to sleep and waking it up, allowing any device to wake the computer.

- **Device power management** Windows 2000 Professional can put individual devices into low-power states based upon how much those devices are getting used by applications. The ACPI separates decision-making from implementation, making sure the component best able to specify a device's power state is the one doing so.

- **Processor power management** Windows 2000 Professional can control the processor's power state, meeting conservation, thermal, and audible noise goals.

- **System events** The ACPI defines an event handling mechanism for thermal events, power management events, docking, device insertion and removal, and so on.

- **Battery management** The ACPI moves battery management from the APM BIOS to Windows 2000 Professional. For example, the operating system determines battery-warning thresholds. It also calculates the remaining battery capacity.

The criteria for deciding how to conserve energy and when to put a computer to sleep are part of the operating system's power policy. Different aspects of power policy have different policy owners. Windows 2000 Professional owns the power policy for the computer as a whole, determining when the computer should go to sleep and how to operate the processor to conserve energy, meet thermal goals, and meet audible noise goals. Each device class has a separate policy owner (usually a WDM driver) that has intimate knowledge of how that device gets used. Each policy owner makes power management decisions for its class and works with the operating system's power policy to put the computer to sleep. While power policies are in the domain of policy owners, power control—actually controlling each device's power consumption—is the responsibility of each device driver.

You can configure power management features with the Power Options Properties dialog box, shown in Figure 12-6. To open this dialog box, double-click the Power Options icon in the Control Panel. The following list describes the primary features that interest users in the Power Options Properties dialog box:

- **Power schemes**   Users can choose or create new power schemes that set how much idle time must pass before the operating system suspends the computer. They can also set how much idle time must pass before the operating system spins down the hard disk or turns off the monitor. Each of these settings is separate, and users configure them in the Power Schemes tab.

The ACPI in a Nutshell

The ACPI is responsible for a host of Windows 2000 Professional's new hardware features. Specifically, it:

- Enables power management *and* Plug and Play
- Integrates system board devices into driver-based power management
- Makes computers more robust with central control of power management
- Eases driver development

And, if you're wondering, Windows 2000 Professional maintains limited support for the APM BIOS. However, the ACPI is far superior to APM. The APM BIOS manages power in a black box but, with the ACPI, the operating system manages power and communicates changes to applications and hardware. The APM BIOS has poorly defined power states and event handling, but the ACPI has strictly defined power states and event handling. Finally, there are hundreds of different APM BIOS versions, while the ACPI is chipset-based and there are fewer than 10 chipsets. Have no doubt that Microsoft is tending away from APM and towards the ACPI because it's far better defined and controlled.

■ **Advanced behaviors** In the Advanced tab, users can select whether to display the power status on the taskbar and whether the operating system prompts them for a password when the computer awakens.

■ **Support for hibernation** *Hibernation* means that the computer stores everything in memory to disk and then powers down. When users power up the computer, everything returns to its previous state. Hibernation requires an amount of free disk space equivalent to the amount of RAM. Users configure hibernation in the Hibernate tab.

■ **Support for APM** If users' computers support APM, they can enable support for it in the APM tab. Enabling APM allows the operating system to suspend the computer when it's idle for a certain period of time. If users don't enable APM on a computer that doesn't support the ACPI, they won't see the System Standby list in the Power Schemes tab.

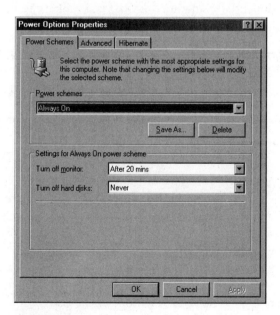

Figure 12-6
The Power Options Properties dialog box.

The Win32 Driver Model

The Win 32 driver model (WDM) has four distinct features:

- WDM provides binary compatibility between Windows 98 and Windows 2000 Professional, allowing vendors to develop a single driver for both operating systems.

- WDM contributes to Plug and Play in Windows 2000 Professional by defining new IRPs, used in both Windows 98 and Windows 2000 Professional, that communicate events to kernel-mode device drivers.

- WDM provides power management IRPs to comply with OnNow and the ACPI.

- WDM expands the class/minidriver model that proved so successful with SCSI (Small Computer System Interface) and NDIS (network driver interface specification) drivers. Microsoft writes class drivers that provide functionality for an entire device class while vendors write device-specific minidrivers.

You've already learned about most of these features in this chapter, but that last bullet requires more explanation. In a pre-WDM world (with the exception of SCSI and NDIS drivers), each device driver carried with it all the code required

Too Good to Be True?

WDM sounds wonderful, but there are caveats of which you should be aware: Many device classes don't have WDM support and still require separate Windows 98 and Windows 2000 Professional device drivers. Examples include video and printer drivers.

WDM doesn't give developers a guarantee that the device drivers they write for Windows 2000 Professional will automatically work in Windows 98, either. In fact, most developers find quite the opposite. In addition, the operating systems usually require that developers use separate sections in an INF file, one for each operating system.

And what about all those Windows 95 users? Windows 95 doesn't support WDM, which means that developers must still write device drivers for Windows 95 if they intend to support customers who are using it.

to control a device. Even with similar devices connected to similar buses, vendors repeated the same code—and the same mistakes—that every other vendor repeated in their device drivers. The solution to the problem is to put code that's common to all devices of a particular class in a component, while vendors develop a small device driver that picks up the slack. And that's what WDM does—it divides device drivers into two separate components. Class drivers provide functionality for all devices in a class, and Microsoft provides them for just about every class of device that has a well-defined standard. Minidrivers, supplied by vendors, are smaller than class drivers and provide functionality for a specific device—functionality that the class driver does not provide. The bottom line is that vendors don't need to expend as much effort to produce drivers for their products, since most of the work is done in the class driver. And users get higher-quality device drivers, since much of the code, and the potential for error, is isolated in one place. Figure 12-7 illustrates this concept:

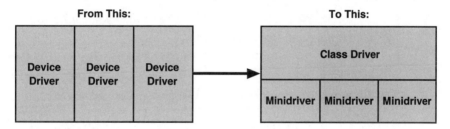

Figure 12-7
Class driver/minidriver architecture.

Windows 2000 Professional includes WDM support for a variety of device types: USB, HID (human interface device), digital audio, and so forth. For more information about the specific types of devices supported by the operating system, see Chapter 13, "Broader Hardware Support."

Much of that support comes from the WDM Streaming class driver, which the operating system uses for audio and video capture devices. This driver uses an interface that interconnects device drivers to optimize the flow of data within the kernel. It functions on hardware cards and external buses such as USB. The key thing you should know abut the WDM Streaming class driver is that it provides a single driver model for MPEG (Moving Pictures Experts Group), video capture, USB audio and video, IEEE 1394 audio and video, and other types of streaming hardware. Developers create specific drivers based on the WDM Streaming class driver, which means that they can use a single driver model for working with all types of data.

Diagnostic Boot Options

If Windows 2000 Professional does not start properly, users can usually start it in safe mode. Safe mode is an operating mode that uses only basic files and drivers. That is, in safe mode, Windows 2000 Professional loads the minimum device drivers required to start the computer: mouse, monitor, keyboard, basic video, etc. Windows 2000 Professional provides the following safe mode options:

- **Safe Mode**   Starts Windows 2000 Professional with the minimum files and drivers. If the computer doesn't start using this option, users might need to use their Automated System Recovery disks to repair the computer.

- **Safe Mode with Networking**   Starts Windows 2000 Professional as described in the previous item, but includes network connections as well.

- **Safe Mode with Command Prompt**   Starts Windows 2000 Professional with the minimum files and drivers, and displays the command prompt.

- **Enable Boot Logging**   Starts Windows 2000 Professional normally, but logs all the drivers and services that the operating system loads or doesn't load. The operating system stores this log in *systemroot*\ Ntbtlog.txt.

- **Enable VGA Mode**   Starts Windows 2000 Professional using the basic VGA (Video Graphics Array) driver.

- **Last Known Good Configuration**   Starts Windows 2000 Professional using the configuration that the operating system saved before it shut down most recently. Since this restores the registry to the state it was in when the operating system last shut down, any recent changes to the computer's configuration are lost.

- **Directory Services Restore Mode**   Doesn't apply to Windows 2000 Professional.

- **Debugging Mode**   Doesn't apply to Windows 2000 Professional.

To start Windows 2000 Professional in safe mode, press F8 when the boot loader prompts for an operating system. If the boot loader doesn't prompt for an operating system—which will be the case if Windows 2000 Professional is the only operating system installed on the computer—hold down an arrow key

as the computer starts. From the following Options Menu screen, choose
an option:

```
Windows 2000 Advanced Options Menu
Please select an option:



Safe Mode
Safe Mode with Networking
Safe Mode with Command Prompt

Enable Boot Logging
Enable VGA Mode

Last Known Good Configuration
Directory Services Restore Mode (Windows NT domain controllers only)
Debugging Mode
```

CHAPTER THIRTEEN

Broader Hardware Support

Microsoft Windows 2000 Professional supports a broader set of hardware than any previous version of Microsoft Windows NT. The operating system now supports more than 6500 devices—and that includes support for 65 percent more legacy devices than were supported by Windows NT Workstation 4.0. That also includes expanded support for legacy printers, scanners, and digital cameras.

Windows 2000 Professional supports a whole new breed of hardware, too, due in large part to the architectural changes you read about in Chapter 12, "Easy Device Installation." Windows 2000 Professional supports Plug and Play and power management, including support for the Advanced Configuration and Power Interface (ACPI). One of the most important technologies that OnNow and the ACPI spawned is the Win32 driver model (WDM). WDM enables independent hardware vendors (IHVs) to develop better device drivers more quickly—drivers that are compatible with Windows 98 and Windows 2000 Professional. WDM also allows device drivers to participate in the Plug and Play and power management processes. WDM supports many of the new device classes you'll read about in this chapter.

This chapter rehashes neither Plug and Play nor power management. Instead, it describes the new types of hardware that the operating system supports, and it describes the operating system's expanded support for legacy devices. The chapter starts off describing the buses that the operating system supports, including the new universal serial bus (USB) and the IEEE 1394 bus, and it follows that with descriptions of the different hardware classes.

Universal Serial Bus (USB)

USB is a hot-pluggable Plug and Play serial interface that provides a low-cost, industry-standard port for installing external devices. Most desktop computers sold today have two USB ports, and most portable computers have at least one.

USB has significant advantages over legacy I/O ports. First, all USB devices use the same I/O connector, eliminating the different cables and connectors used by different types of devices. USB also supports *hot plugging*, which means that users can install or remove a USB device while the computer is running, and the operating system automatically reconfigures itself accordingly. The last advantage is one of the biggest—USB minimizes an inherent flaw in the Intel architecture that limits the number of resources (IRQs and I/O ports, for example) available to devices and therefore limits the number of devices installed in the computer. With USB, users can plug multiple USB devices into a single USB port. The industry already produces, or plans to produce, a variety of USB devices fitting into the following broad categories:

- **Input**   Keyboards, joysticks, and pointing devices
- **Storage**   Hard disks, CD-ROM drives, and removable media
- **Communications**   Modems, ISDN adapters, and network adapters
- **Output**   Monitors, printers, and audio devices
- **Imaging**   Scanners and digital cameras

USB uses a tiered topology, allowing users to attach up to 127 devices to the bus. Currently, USB supports up to five tiers, with each device located no further than five meters from a hub. Figure 13-1 illustrates a USB topology, and the following list describes the terminology associated with USB topologies:

- **Host**   The USB host is built into the computer's system board or is installed as an adapter card on the computer. The host controls all traffic on the bus and usually acts as a hub. Root, root tier, and root hub are less frequently used terms for a host.
- **Hub**   A hub provides a port through which users attach a device to the bus. Hubs detect devices that users attach to them. They're also responsible for providing power management to devices.
- **Device**   USB devices attach to the bus through a port, or hub. Many USB devices can also be hubs. For instance, a USB keyboard can have ports for attaching additional USB devices such as a mouse.

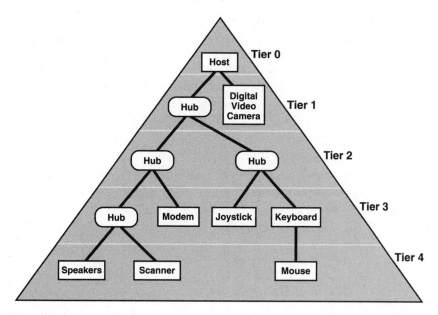

Figure 13-1
A sample USB topology.

Hold Out for USB Devices

My personal experience with USB has been very good. That's why I recommend that you make your next hardware purchase a USB device. Most modern computers have one or more USB ports, and a tour through your local computer store or favorite computer catalog will turn up several different types of devices. I've found USB mice, speakers, keyboards, joysticks, and more.

USB devices are incredibly easy to install—easier than comparable devices that use legacy ports. For example, I've often had problems configuring an external mouse PS/2 port for use with my portable—but after plugging a USB mouse into the port, the operating system immediately recognized it and installed drivers for it. USB also allows me to extend my computers without using up additional resources, which is terrific, since installing the required hardware—network, sound, video, and Small Computer System Interface (SCSI) adapters—usually depletes any interrupts left over by the system.

USB supports two different maximum transfer rates, which the host chooses based on the amount of bandwidth a device needs. Devices that don't require large amounts of bandwidth, such as mice and keyboards, operate at up to 1.5 megabits per second (Mbps). Devices that require higher bandwidths, such as modems and speakers, use a 12 Mbps isochronous transfer rate. The exact transfer rate that a host uses for a device depends on its transfer mode. Isochronous and interrupt transfer modes guarantee communication at a particular rate. Bulk and control transfer modes use whatever rate is available.

In Windows 2000 Professional, USB is supported by WDM through the WDM Streaming class driver. Windows 2000 Professional provides USB host controller minidrivers for the Open Host Controller Interface (OHCI) and the Universal Host Controller Interface (UHCI). It also includes a USB class driver, a USB hub driver, and a Peripheral Component Interconnect (PCI) enumerator.

IEEE 1394 (FireWire)

IEEE 1394 (FireWire) is a high-speed, Plug and Play–compliant serial bus designed to complement USB, and it's especially suitable for streaming video, desktop teleconferencing, and other applications requiring fast throughput. IEEE 1394 provides for 100 Mbps, 200 Mbps, and 400 Mbps transfer rates—and the 1394 Trade Association, which looks after the 1394 standard, is working on speeds in excess of 1 Gbps (gigabits per second). The consumer-electronics industry has readily adopted this technology, as evidenced by the fact that most middle- to high-end computers come with IEEE 1394 ports built into the system board. IEEE 1394 is the bridge that brings computers and consumer electronics together. The industry is now shipping digital VCRs, digital camcorders, and digital satellite receivers with IEEE 1394 interfaces. Thus the convergence begins—for example, consumers can use digital VCRs to view movies *and* store computer data, and they can record scenes using a digital camcorder and edit those scenes on their computers.

Users can connect up to 63 devices to a single IEEE 1394 bus, and they can connect up to 1023 buses to format a large network of over 64,000 devices. Each device can have up to 256 terabytes of memory, all of which is addressable over the bus. Figure 13-2 shows a sample IEEE 1394 topology. The following list describes frequently used IEEE 1394 terminology:

■ **Splitter**   A splitter provides additional IEEE 1394 ports.

■ **Bridge**   A bridge isolates traffic within a specific area of the IEEE 1394 bus.

- **Repeater**   A repeater extends the range between devices by retransmitting signals.

- **Device**   Each IEEE 1394 device usually has 3 ports, but can have up to 27, and users can daisy-chain up to 16 devices. In a tree topology, users can connect more devices.

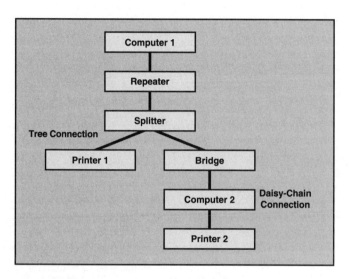

Figure 13-2
A sample IEEE 1394 topology.

IEEE 1394 supports three different transfer rates: 93.304 Mbps (S100), 196.608 Mbps (S200), and 393.216 Mbps (S400). Users can interconnect devices that use different transfer rates, and the maximum transfer rate will be the highest rate supported by the slowest device. Like USB, IEEE 1394 supports an isochronous transfer mode where the transfer rate is guaranteed. It also supports an asynchronous transfer mode, which transmits data whenever no isochronous traffic is on the bus.

IEEE 1394 is supported by WDM in Windows 2000 through the WDM Streaming class driver. The operating system includes an IEEE 1394 bus class driver; minidrivers for IEEE 1394 system board connections; minidrivers for a number of IEEE 1394 adapters, such as those manufactured by Adaptec and Sony; and the OHCI in the hardware layer. While Windows 98 supports the PCILynx IEEE 1394 adapter, Windows 2000 Professional does not. Digital video capture and editing applications communicate with the device drivers through DirectShow, which includes the DV and MPEG2 codecs, as shown in

Figure 13-3. In turn, each device driver communicates through the IEEE 1394 port using the IEEE 1394 class driver as well as the appropriate minidriver.

NOTE: A codec (compressor/decompressor) is a driver that converts data from one format to another, usually involving compressed and uncompressed formats. One of the standard codecs is MPEG2. MPEG stands for Moving Pictures Experts Group.

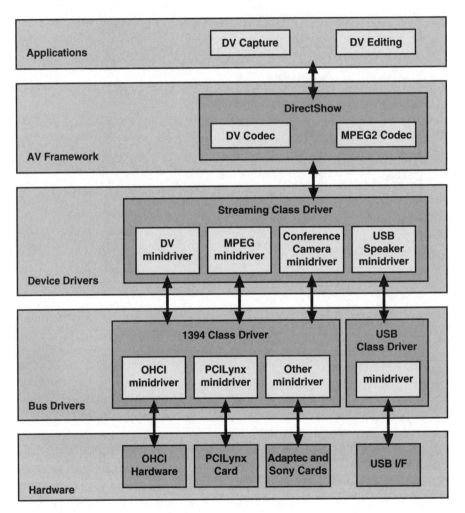

Figure 13-3
IEEE 1394 for audio/visual devices.

Windows 2000 Professional implements support for IEEE 1394 storage devices, printers, and scanners using Serial Block Protocol 2 (SBP2). The hardware and bus drivers form an architecture similar to the one shown in Figure 13-3, but the SBP2 port driver appears above the IEEE 1394 bus drivers, providing support for storage devices, printers, scanners, human interface devices (HIDs), and audio devices.

NOTE: According to Microsoft, the current interfaces for hard disk drives, the most popular of which is Integrated Drive Electronics (IDE), have reached the end of their useful lives. Accordingly, Microsoft suggests that vendors start preparing for a transition to IEEE 1394 storage devices. Consider that a hint of things to come: hard drives will be faster and, more importantly, they'll have hot-plugging capabilities.

New Device Classes

The following sections describe Windows 2000 Professional's new and enhanced support for a variety of devices. All of the devices discussed in this section are supported by WDM, and Windows 2000 Professional also maintains support for legacy versions of the same. Note that most of these devices—with the exception of HIDs and still image devices—are enabled via the WDM Streaming class. For more information about the WDM Streaming class, see Chapter 12, "Easy Device Installation."

Here's an overview of what's discussed in the remainder of this chapter:

- Digital audio devices connected to USB ports
- DVD and the Universal Disk Format (UDF)
- HIDs connected to USB ports
- Still image devices such as scanners and digital cameras
- Video capture devices such as camcorders
- New video display technologies such as Accelerated Graphics Port (AGP)

Audio

While Windows 2000 Professional continues to support legacy audio devices, WDM provides support for a new breed of devices that are part of Microsoft's digital audio initiative. The goals of this initiative are to solve problems caused by complicated configurations and to improve the performance of internal and external audio devices. In the first case, configuring audio hardware is a process that stumps most users—and even if Plug and Play correctly configures devices, using audio hardware with MS-DOS applications presents special problems. In the second case, previous versions of Windows did a poor job of mixing multiple software and hardware sources, meaning that users could only hear sound generated by one application at a time. For example, if they were playing a DirectX-based game that was monopolizing the audio device, users wouldn't hear "You've got mail" when new mail arrived.

In Windows 2000 Professional, digital audio is supported by WDM. WDM can handle multiple streams of audio, meaning that two applications can output sound at the same time and users can hear both. This architecture also makes it possible to perform audio management in software. That is, kernel-mode components handle mixing and routing rather than the analog hardware. And Windows 2000 Professional can redirect audio to any available output, including USB and IEEE 1394 devices. Redirecting audio output to external devices has two big advantages:

- **Higher fidelity**   Preserving signal fidelity is difficult with internal audio devices because of the high amount of radio-frequency noise that exists. Digital audio travels to an external device with no signal degradation.

- **Device visibility**   Plug and Play might configure an internal audio device, but it doesn't guarantee that the speakers are connected to it. However, USB speakers are visible to Plug and Play, so the operating system knows if they're not connected. Moreover, the controls on the speakers, such as volume, bass, and treble, can work in sync with the operating system's volume control.

Figure 13-4 illustrates Windows 2000 Professional's architecture for its implementation of the digital audio initiative. The System Audio Device component determines how to format and combine digital audio streams. The Mixer component actually mixes each stream. Combined, the two components allow multiple audio applications to play sounds at the same time. The WDM Streaming class driver, in combination with USB and IEEE 1394 minidrivers, supports digital audio through USB and IEEE 1394 devices. The Audio Port class driver supports internal Industry Standard Architecture (ISA) and PCI audio devices. The Audio Port class driver is a container for a collection of port drivers. This component works in conjunction with the Adapter driver, which is a container for a collection of miniport drivers.

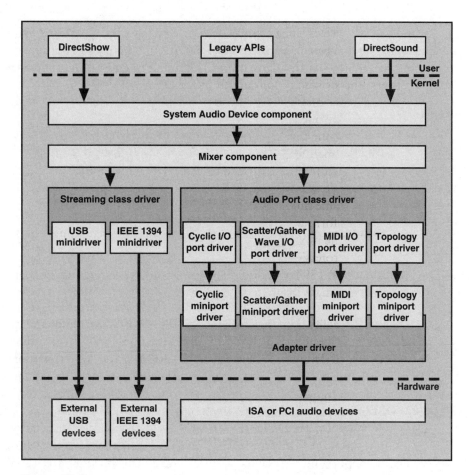

Figure 13-4
Architecture for WDM audio.

> **NOTE:** Microsoft encourages all vendors to implement external digital audio using the USB and IEEE 1394 buses. Both provide an excellent means to deliver a high-quality conversion to and from analog. USB is best for the near future, but Microsoft anticipates the consumer-electronics industry to move towards IEEE 1394 for audio processing.

DVD

DVD (interpreted as either "digital versatile disc" or "digital video disc") is the natural progression of the CD-ROM. It fosters a new breed of optical disc storage technologies for a wide variety of consumer electronics and computer devices. In other words, DVD can provide digital storage for audio, video, and data—and it's also a replacement for laser disc, audio CD, CD-ROM, VHS videotape, and dedicated game technologies. It's not merely an extension of CD-ROM technology—it's designed from beginning to end for multimedia applications and the storage of full-length movies.

Several types of DVD are in use:

- **DVD-Video** A DVD disc that contains full-length movies that a DVD-Video player or a computer's DVD-ROM drive can play back.

- **DVD-ROM** A DVD disc that contains computer data and is read by a computer's DVD-ROM drive. Double-sided, double-layered discs can hold up to 17 gigabytes.

- **DVD-WO** A DVD disc that supports one-time recording, similar to CD-R.

- **DVD-RAM** A DVD disc that supports multiple recording capabilities, similar to magneto optical discs.

Figure 13-5 illustrates how Windows 2000 Professional implements support for DVD, portions of which WDM supports with the WDM Streaming class driver. The operating system provides a DVD-ROM driver, which supports the DVD-ROM industry-defined command set (known as the Mt. Fuji command set), including commands for copyright protection. For more information about the WDM Streaming class driver, which plays an important role in the operating system's support for DVD, see Chapter 12, "Easy Device Installation."

Windows 2000 Professional supports DVD with more than just device drivers. It supports movie playback, for example. This includes a DVD-Video player that has a rich set of features, and the quality of movies played on a computer is significantly higher than when played on standard DVD-Video devices. The operating system also supports DVD as a storage device and will support writable devices in the future.

The file system on DVD discs is the Universal Disk Format (UDF). Defined by the Optical Storage Technology Association (OSTA), it's compliant with the ISO-13346 specification and is intended to be the successor to the CD-ROM File System (CDFS). Features include long and Unicode file names; access control lists (ACLs); streams; reading and writing (not just mastering); and bootability. Windows 2000 Professional doesn't currently support writing to a UDF file system, but it will in the future. The most current version of UDF is 1.5, and this version is supported by Windows 2000 Professional. OSTA has recently approved a draft of UDF 2.0, and Windows 2000 Professional will support this version at a later date.

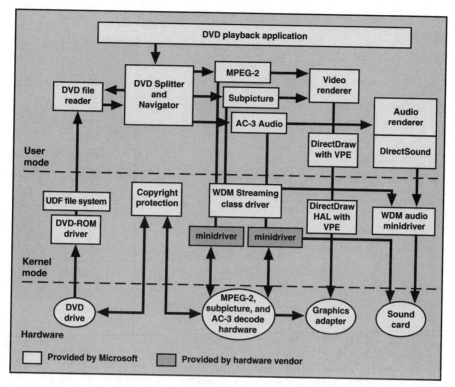

Figure 13-5
Architecture for DVD.

Human Interface Devices

Windows 2000 Professional supports a uniform, cross-platform method for accessing input devices. HIDs—based on the USB Implementers Forum's USB Device Class Definition for HIDs—include a variety of controls for vehicle simulation, virtual reality, sports equipment, appliances, and games. Windows 2000 Professional provides Plug and Play and power management for USB HIDs and requires no additional drivers.

HIDs are supported by WDM. More specifically, the operating system provides the HID class driver, the HID minidriver, and the HID parser. Figure 13-6 on the following page shows the relationships among these components. As indicated in the figure, Windows 2000 Professional includes support for HID keyboards, mice, and joysticks. Windows 2000 Professional also provides HID support for devices connected to legacy ports and traditional support for legacy applications that don't make use of the HID interface at all.

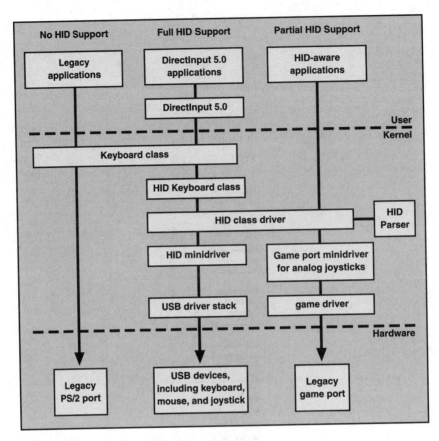

Figure 13-6
Architecture for HIDs.

Still Image

Windows 2000 Professional is the first member of the Windows NT product family to provide support for still image devices. The still image architecture is the first step in providing a common solution for supporting devices such as flatbed scanners, sheet feed scanners, handheld scanners, and digital cameras.

WDM provides support for still image devices, as shown in Figure 13-7. An independent software vendor (ISV) provides the application, and an independent hardware vendor (IHV) provides the user-mode minidrivers. The kernel-mode drivers depend on the type of device. WDM supports SCSI, IEEE 1394, and USB digital still image devices. Support for infrared and serial still image devices (connected to standard COM ports) comes from the existing infrared and serial interfaces. And, initially, Windows 2000 Professional won't support network or parallel still image devices. Windows 2000 Professional does provide the remaining components, including the still image control panel, the event monitor, and the control center:

- ■ **Still image control panel**   Windows 2000 Professional provides the Scanners And Cameras icon in the Control Panel. In the Scanners And Cameras Properties dialog box, users can install and remove non–Plug and Play still image devices. They can also test devices and control associations between specific devices and events. For more information about this dialog box, see Chapter 8, "More Imaging and Printing Capabilities."

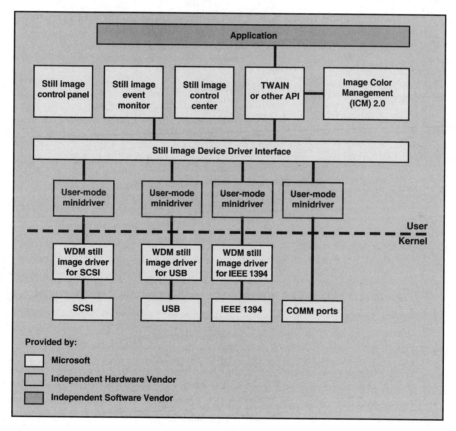

Figure 13-7
Architecture for still image devices.

- **Still image event monitor and control center** Windows 2000 Professional supports push model behavior by detecting a still image device's events and dispatching them to the still image control center. Using policies that define how to distribute events, the still image control center distributes events to applications.

- **Still image DDI** The still image device driver interface (DDI) is the link between the user-mode minidrivers and other components. It supports enumeration, device information, data and command I/O, event notification, and color management.

Video Capture

While continuing to support legacy video capture technologies, Windows 2000 Professional provides additional capabilities via WDM:

- Supports USB and IEEE 1394
- Supports multiple, simultaneous streams
- Allows television tune and input selection
- Supports field capture and field display
- Shares a class driver architecture with DVD devices
- Works with DirectShow and the WDM Streaming class
- Manages video input through DirectDraw video port extensions (VPEs)

While Windows 2000 Professional provides the WDM Streaming class, it doesn't provide any minidrivers. Each IHV must provide the appropriate minidrivers: PC or VPE for analog video capture and USB or IEEE 1394 for digital video capture.

Video Display

Windows 2000 Professional maintains support for legacy video adapters, but it adds new support for Intel's AGP specification. For more information about AGP, see Chapter 14, "Awesome Multimedia and Graphics."

CHAPTER FOURTEEN

Awesome Multimedia and Graphics

Microsoft Windows 2000 Professional includes support for a variety of new and exciting multimedia technologies. Users have anticipated some of these technologies—such as a full implementation of Microsoft DirectX—for quite some time. They need wait no longer.

Aside from a full implementation of DirectX 7, which you'll learn about in this chapter, Windows 2000 Professional also supports other new capabilities. It supports the OpenGL 1.2 specification. It supports advanced display standards such as Accelerated Graphics Port (AGP). Users can install multiple display adapters and monitors to increase their screen real estate. This chapter describes all of these new capabilities—and don't forget the new hardware support you learned about in Chapter 13, "Broader Hardware Support," which includes multimedia storage, display, and audio devices.

Microsoft DirectX

DirectX is a group of enabling technologies that transform computers running Microsoft Windows into multimedia powerhouses for gaming, video conferencing, high-end business applications, and more. DirectX provides enhanced full-color graphics, video, 3D animation, and surround sound. A whole class of applications that could not run on Microsoft Windows NT Workstation 4.0 can run on Windows 2000 Professional. This includes the thousands of DirectX games available on the market. Windows 95 and Windows 98 also include DirectX.

Usually a component that sits behind the scenes, providing users with an exciting multimedia experience, DirectX has two purposes. First, via the DirectX Foundation layer, it enables developers to create multimedia applications that run on any version of Windows that supports DirectX, regardless of the computer's hardware, taking full advantage of the computer's high-performance features.

In other words, DirectX provides developers better access to the computer's hardware without the developers having to worry about which display adapter, sound card, or 3D accelerator chip is installed on the computer. Second, through the DirectX Media layer, DirectX simplifies creating multimedia content and integrating a wide range of multimedia elements. The following list provides a bit more meat about each layer:

- **The DirectX Media layer** The DirectX Media layer provides high-level application programming interfaces (APIs) for animation, media streaming, and interactivity. The purpose of the DirectX Media layer is to help developers integrate different types of multimedia effects. It does so by providing a single set of APIs for combining multimedia elements, as well as providing a time-based approach for specifying the relationship between multimedia elements such as sound and animation.

- **The DirectX Foundation layer** The DirectX Foundation layer provides a single set of APIs to developers, which they can use to access the computer's high-performance features. These APIs allow developers to interact directly with low-level functions that control graphics acceleration; input devices such as joysticks, keyboards, and mice; and sound mixing and output. The DirectX Foundation layer provides a hardware abstraction layer (HAL), which places drivers between hardware and software, and a hardware emulation layer (HEL), which emulates capabilities that the computer's hardware might not provide.

For more information about DirectX than is provided in this chapter, visit Microsoft's DirectX Web site: *http://www.microsoft.com/directx.* This site provides detailed white papers that discuss how DirectX works and how programmers use it.

The DirectX Media Layer

The DirectX Media layer provides three APIs: Microsoft DirectShow, Microsoft DirectAnimation, and Microsoft DirectX Transform. Taken together, these APIs provide new ways for developers to create animation, behaviors, streaming, etc. Figure 14-1 illustrates the DirectX Media layer, and the following list describes its major components:

- **DirectShow** DirectShow was once known as Microsoft ActiveMovie. It's a media-streaming architecture that enables high-quality capture and playback of multimedia streams, including audio and video. Developers can compress a variety of formats into a DirectShow stream, including Apple QuickTime, AVI (Audio Video Interleaved), MPG, and WAV. Capture is based on Video For Windows or the Win32 driver model (WDM). The visible user interface for DirectShow is the Windows Media Player.

■ **DirectAnimation**   Animation, streaming, and integration of multimedia effects are what DirectAnimation is all about. It allows developers to integrate 2D vector graphics, 3D graphics, sprites, audio, and video. The term *developer* doesn't imply traditional programmers, either, since DirectAnimation is accessible to a wide variety of people who create content, including HTML and Dynamic HTML authors. Users typically experience DirectAnimation when viewing animations in Microsoft Internet Explorer.

■ **DirectX Transform**   DirectX Transform opens up DirectX, allowing developers to extend the DirectX platform. It simplifies implementing transforms and allows applications to better integrate with DirectX. Examples of transforms would be adding textures to images or blending two images together. A user's experience with DirectX Transform is typically through DirectAnimation, which is a host environment for DirectX Transform. Dynamic HTML authors who use Internet Explorer 5's filter style are doing so thanks to DirectX Transform.

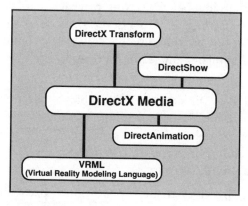

Figure 14-1
The DirectX Media layer.

The DirectX Foundation Layer

Figure 14-2 illustrates the DirectX Foundation layer. The following list describes each component:

- **Microsoft DirectDraw**   DirectDraw is a memory manager for graphics and video images. It allows developers to go around the traditional layers associated with programming video output by providing direct access to the display's memory and hardware features. DirectDraw supports a large variety of display hardware and enables many of the intense, action-packed games on the market today.

- **Microsoft Direct3D**   Direct3D has two different modes. Immediate Mode allows developers to port high-performance multimedia applications such as games to Microsoft Windows. Retained Mode helps developers build and animate 3D worlds.

- **Microsoft DirectInput**   DirectInput provides an interface that by-passes the operating system, working directly with drivers for a variety of input devices. Those devices include joysticks, flight yokes, head-gear, multibutton mice, and a whole new breed of input/output devices known as *force-feedback*. Force-feedback devices provide effects such as a kickback when users squeeze the trigger, vibration, and resistance—all of which make game play more realistic.

- **Microsoft DirectSound**   DirectSound is the audio part of DirectX. It provides features such as low-latency mixing playback, hardware acceleration, and 3D positioning. It allows developers to mix multiple audio signals and it can provide direct access to the sound hardware. DirectSound emulates any features not supported by the sound hardware.

- **Microsoft DirectSound 3D**   DirectSound 3D enables applications to position sounds anywhere in a 3D space, going beyond the limits of left-right balancing. For example, games can simulate 3D effects such as rolloff and Doppler shift. DirectSound 3D emulates this feature if it's not available in the sound hardware.

- **Microsoft DirectPlay**   DirectPlay enables applications—particularly games—to communicate over the Internet, a modem link, or a network. The tools that DirectPlay provides allow players to find game sessions and sites to manage the information that flows between hosts and players. So many games on the market do support head-to-head competition because DirectPlay makes implementing it easy for developers.

■ **Microsoft DirectMusic**   DirectMusic, the newest addition to DirectX, allows developers to create musical backgrounds that DirectX composes in real time based upon the application's changing requirements. In other words, the music that users hear is always original, not the repetitive music that some games play. Microsoft provides DirectMusic Producer, which authors can use to create DirectMusic objects, including styles, personalities, templates, and Downloadable Sample (DLS) instruments.

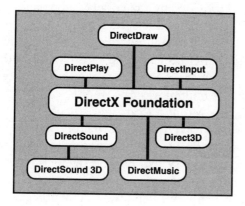

Figure 14-2
The DirectX Foundation layer.

OpenGL 1.2

Windows 2000 Professional includes support for the latest version—1.2—of OpenGL. The following list describes the key features of OpenGL 1.2:

■ Improved support for Windows

■ Improved performance

■ Improved visual 3D quality by separating specular color

■ Significant new capabilities and functionality for developers

Support for Multiple Display Devices

Windows 2000 Professional supports multiple monitors, increasing the size of users' desktops. Users can connect up to 10 individual monitors to the same computer. They can put one window on each desktop, stretch windows across multiple desktops, and so forth. Imagine the possibilities! Web authors can view their Web sites on one monitor while editing the HTML on another. Business users can see views of related data on separate monitors; for example, they can view a portfolio on one monitor while viewing a stock ticker on another. Presenters can display their presentations on one monitor while viewing their notes on another. Administrators can work on one monitor while viewing network performance information on another. You get the idea.

Windows 2000 Professional provides multiple display support for Peripheral Component Interconnect (PCI) and AGP video adapters. Users can attach each display to its own video adapter, or multiple displays to a single video adapter that has multiple outputs. After installing the hardware, users double-click the Display icon in the Control Panel to activate the Display Properties dialog box where they can configure multiple displays. In the Settings tab of the dialog box, they click the Additional Monitor icon at the top of the dialog box and select Extend My Windows Desktop Onto This Monitor. Each display can have its own resolution and color depth. One monitor always serves as the primary display; that's where the operating system displays the logon dialog box when you start the computer, and where most programs display their windows when you first open them. Users can move windows to any other display or stretch them across multiple displays.

The following list describes additional features that are available when using multiple monitors in Windows 2000 Professional:

- Users can arrange the monitors in order to determine how items move from monitor to monitor. They can do so in the Settings tab of the Display Properties dialog box by positioning each monitor's icon in relationship to the other monitors' icons.

- Users can change the primary monitor at any time. The primary monitor is the device on which Windows 2000 Professional displays the logon dialog box. It's also the device on which most applications open their initial windows.

- Users can move windows from one display to another by simply dragging the window through the top, right, bottom, or left edge of the monitor.

- Users can also choose to display the same information on all monitors.

Accelerated Graphics Port

Typical computers have two types of buses: Industry Standard Architecture (ISA) and PCI. Most modern adapter cards use the newer PCI bus. And, up until now, PCI video adapters were the choice for high-performance displays. However, Intel has introduced AGP—an expansion slot designed just for video cards. To use an AGP video adapter, a computer must have an AGP graphics controller and a compatible chipset, such as the Pentium II LX chipset. Figure 14-3 illustrates where AGP fits within a computer's architecture.

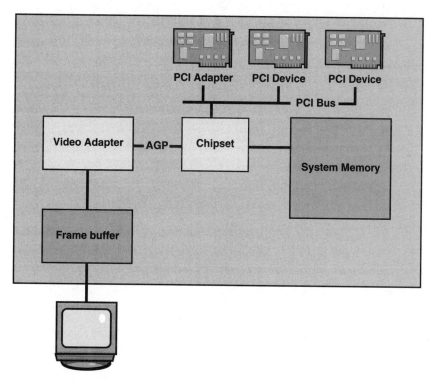

Figure 14-3
How AGP fits into a computer's architecture.

AGP has these advantages over PCI video adapters:

- AGP's peak bandwidth is up to four times higher than PCI's, and it has higher sustained rates due to sideband addressing and split transactions.

- AGP is a dedicated bus, reducing contention with other devices. This means that AGP operates concurrently with and independently from devices on the PCI bus.

- AGP allows the CPU to write directly to shared system memory, rather than to local memory. The CPU can write to shared system memory much faster than to local memory.

- AGP can read textures from shared system memory while reading and writing other data from local memory, improving performance of high-resolution 3D scenes.

- AGP can execute graphics data directly from system memory, instead of having to first move graphics data into video memory before executing it.

CHAPTER FIFTEEN

Advanced Networking Capabilities

According to Bernard Aboba, a Senior Program Manager at Microsoft Corporation, this is the "golden age of networking." Computers are faster. Network interface cards (NICs) are faster. More bandwidth is available. Networked applications such as NetMeeting are more commonplace. Users' awareness of networking is higher. For that matter, some folks talk about home-based networks as though they were common appliances. Part of what has brought all this about is the Internet, Internet Protocol (IP), and the Web—the technologies that have captured the world's attention and imagination.

Microsoft Windows 2000 Professional makes taking advantage of the latest networking innovations much easier. For instance, it makes configuring and using networking technology simpler, reducing the cost for businesses and removing barriers that prevent consumers from using home-based networks. It reduces the complexity of network infrastructure by making it easier to configure and maintain, and it makes networking more secure. This chapter describes the new and improved networking technologies that Windows 2000 Professional includes. It does not cover technologies that were previously available in Windows NT Workstation 4.0, nor does it discuss new features such as the My Network Places or the Network And Dial-Up Connections folders. For more information about Windows 2000 Professional's user interface for networking features, see Chapter 4, "Simpler User Interface," and Chapter 5, "Easier Setup and Configuration."

Advanced Protocol Support

Windows 2000 Professional maintains support for the same clients, protocols, and services found in Windows NT Workstation 4.0. That includes the Microsoft Network and NetWare clients; File and Printer Sharing for Microsoft Networks;

and the TCP/IP, IPX/SPX, NetBEUI, and AppleTalk networking protocols. The most significant enhancements to the operating system's networking capabilities are to the TCP/IP protocol stack, however, and the remainder of this section focuses on them.

Transmission Control Protocol/Internet Protocol (TCP/IP) is the suite of Internet Engineering Task Force (IETF) standard protocols that carry traffic across the Internet. Microsoft has adopted TCP/IP as the strategic network transport for all members of the Windows product family. Support for a standards-based TCP/IP protocol makes Windows 2000 Professional Internet-ready, and it allows the operating system to work with a broad range of third-party networking solutions. Windows 2000 Professional installs TCP/IP by default, so configuring a computer to connect to an IP network is easier.

Figure 15-1 illustrates Microsoft's implementation of TCP/IP and relates each of the protocol's four layers (Application, Transport, Internet, and Network Interface) to the Open Systems Interconnection (OSI) model. The Network Interface Layer puts TCP/IP packets on the network device and receives TCP/IP packets from the device. Since TCP/IP is independent of any actual network access method, frame format, or medium, the operating system can use it to connect to different network types: Ethernet, Token Ring, X.25, Frame Relay, and Asynchronous Transfer Mode (ATM). The Internet Layer addresses, packages, and routes TCP/IP packets. It includes four core protocols: Internet Protocol (IP), Address Resolution Protocol (ARP), Internet Control Message Protocol (ICMP), and Internet Group Management Protocol (IGMP). The Transport Layer provides the Application Layer with session and datagram communication services and includes two core protocols: Transmission Control Protocol (TCP) and User Datagram Protocol (UDP). Last, the Application Layer allows applications to access the services of the other layers. Application Layer protocols include Routing Information Protocol (RIP) and Simple Network Management Protocol (SNMP).

Table 15-1 gives an overview of Windows 2000 Professional's TCP/IP features, which include several performance enhancements over Windows NT Workstation 4.0's implementation of TCP/IP. In the sections that follow, you'll learn about the operating system's TCP/IP performance improvements, including support for larger, scalable receive windows; Selective Acknowledgments (SACK); better roundtrip estimation; and Fast Retransmit. These performance enhancements make TCP/IP a better transport protocol for networking in high-bandwidth LAN and WAN environments.

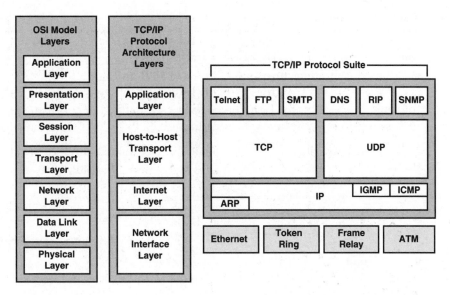

Figure 15-1
Windows 2000 Professional's TCP/IP architecture.

Type	Description
Standard Features	Automatic discovery of the path maximum transmission unit (PMTU)
	Dead gateway detection
	Duplicate IP address detection
	Internal IP routing
	IP Multicasting—Internet Group Management Protocol 2
	Internet Protocol security (IPSec)
	Logical and physical multihoming
	Multiple default gateways
	Multiple network interface cards (NICs) bound to different media types
	Quality of Service (QoS)
	Virtual private networks (VPNs)

Table 15-1   *(continued)*
Windows 2000 Professional's TCP/IP features, enhancements, and services.

Figure 15-1 *continued*

Type	Description
Performance Enhancements	Protocol Stack tuning
	Selective Acknowledgments (SACK)
	TCP scalable window sizes (RFC 1323)
	TCP Fast Retransmit
Services Available	Basic TCP/IP utilities (FTP, Telnet, etc.)
	Dial-Up Networking (PPP/SLIP)
	Domain Name System (DNS)
	Dynamic Host Configuration Protocol (DHCP)
	Microsoft Internet Information Services (IIS)
	NetBIOS interface
	Network Dynamic Data Exchange (NetDDE)
	Point-to-Point Tunneling Protocol (PPTP)
	Remote procedure call (RPC) support
	Simple Network Management Protocol (SNMP) agent
	TCP/IP network printing
	TCP/IP management tools (ARP, IPconfig, tracert, etc.)
	Wide Area Network (WAN) support
	Windows Internet Naming Service (WINS)
	Windows Sockets version 2 (Winsock2)

NOTE: Proposed standards for TCP/IP are submitted as documents called Requests for Comments (RFCs). The Internet Architecture Board (IAB) is the committee responsible for managing the process of publishing RFCs. This chapter refers to RFC 1323 (TCP scalable window sizes) and RFC 793 (retransmission timing).

Large Window Support

The TCP receive window size determines the amount of data that a connection can buffer at one time. That is, the sending host can transmit a set amount of data before waiting for an acknowledgment and a window update from the receiving host. Windows 2000 Professional's implementation of TCP/IP provides better performance by adjusting itself to different environments. It can use a larger window size than previous versions of the operating system—so, instead of using a hard-coded receive window size, TCP adjusts during the session:

1. The connection request advertises a window size of 16 KB.

2. After establishing the connection, TCP adjusts the window size to the nearest multiple of the maximum segment size (MSS), which both hosts negotiate while setting up the connection. If the window size isn't at least four times the MSS, TCP adjusts the window size to four times the MSS, with a maximum size of 64 KB.

3. TCP continues to adjust the window size in even increments of the MSS. By matching the window size to even increments of the MSS, TCP increases the percentage of full-sized TCP segments used in bulk data transmissions.

To further improve performance on high-bandwidth, high-delay networks, Windows 2000 Professional supports RFC 1323. This RFC describes a scalable window size, allowing TCP to negotiate a scaling factor for the window size when establishing the connection. This feature allows for a receive window of up to 1 GB.

Selective Acknowledgments

Selective Acknowledgments (SACK) is a new performance-related feature that's important for network connections that use large TCP window sizes. Without SACK, a receiving host can only acknowledge the latest sequence number of contiguous data that it has received. That is, the receiving host can only acknowledge the left edge of the receive window. With SACK enabled, the receiving host can also acknowledge individual blocks of data. The result is that the receiving host is able to inform the sending host of exactly which data it has received and which data it has not received. This allows the sending host to selectively retransmit missing data without requiring it to retransmit data that the receiving host already has. Better performance is the bottom line, particularly on lossy networks such as those formed by Internet service providers.

Roundtrip Estimation

Windows 2000 Professional's TCP/IP stack includes support for TCP timestamps (as defined by RFC 1323). This is an important feature for connections that use large window sizes. Timestamps help TCP accurately measure roundtrip time so that it can adjust retransmission time-outs. Windows 2000 Professional enables support for timestamps by default.

Fast Retransmit

TCP starts a retransmission timer for each outbound segment it passes to IP. If, before the timer expires, TCP doesn't receive an acknowledgment from the receiving host that the segment was received, TCP retransmits the segment. For new connection requests, the retransmission timer is set to three seconds and, by default, Windows 2000 Professional resends the segment up to two times. During the session, TCP recalculates the retransmission time using the Smoothed Round Trip Time (SRTT) algorithm described by RFC 793. Doing so, TCP tunes itself to the delays found in most TCP connections over high-delay links.

The Fast Retransmit algorithm allows TCP to retransmit data prior to the retransmission timer expiring. When a receiving host that supports Fast Retransmit receives data with a segment number higher than what it expects, indicating that holes might exist in the data, it sends an ACK (acknowledgment) to the sending host that indicates the sequence number it was expecting. When

NDIS 5.0

The Network Driver Interface Specification (NDIS) describes how transport protocols and NICs communicate with each other. NDIS 3.1 provided the basic abilities for a protocol to communicate with an NIC, and NDIS 4.0 added several new features such as high-speed sending and receiving of packets.

Windows 2000 Professional supports NDIS 5.0, the latest version of NDIS, which adds several significant new features. Examples include power management, Plug and Play, and support for Windows Management Instrumentation (WMI). NDIS 5.0 also includes mechanisms for off-loading certain tasks to intelligent hardware—tasks such as TCP/IP checksum calculation, IPSec encryption, TCP message segmentation, and Fast Packet Forwarding. In addition to a deserialized miniport that improves performance on multiprocessor computers, NDIS 5.0 includes support for native access to connection-oriented media such as ISDN (Integrated Services Digital Network) and ATM, including ATM/ADSL (asymmetric digital subscriber line) and ATM/cable modem. NDIS 5.0 also supports Quality of Service (QoS) when the media support it. For more information about NDIS 5.0, see Microsoft's Web site: *http://www.asia.microsoft.com/hwdev.*

the sending host receives a series of ACKs indicating the same sequence number, it immediately resends the segment that the receiving host is expecting, without waiting for the retransmission timer to expire for that segment, in order to fill gaps in the data. Implementation of the Fast Retransmit algorithm greatly increases the performance of TCP/IP on lossy networks such as the Internet.

Automatic Private IP Addressing

Microsoft Automatic Private IP Addressing (APIPA) makes creating small private networks easy. APIPA automatically assigns unique IP addresses to computers and peripherals connected to the local area network (LAN). And since it assigns IP addresses without any work on the part of users or administrators, it eliminates the need for administrators to assign static IP addresses or manage IP addresses using the Dynamic Host Configuration Protocol (DHCP) or a Domain Name System (DNS) server. In a nutshell, APIPA does for networking what Plug and Play does for hardware management.

Globally unique IP addresses aren't necessary on private networks. Thus, APIPA uses blocks of IP addresses that the Internet reserves for private networks (169.254.0.0 through 169.254.255.254 with the subnet mask 255.255.0.0). APIPA automatically assigns these reserved IP addresses to hosts on the private network. It also makes sure that no two hosts on the private network have duplicate IP addresses. Since these addresses aren't globally unique beyond the private network, hosts cannot use them across the Internet. Even so, a network address translator (NAT) or a Microsoft Proxy Server can allow hosts on the private network to access the Internet.

The following list describes the key benefits of APIPA:

- **Works with DHCP servers**   Each time Windows 2000 Professional starts, it looks for a DHCP server. If it finds one, it retrieves an IP address from the DHCP server; otherwise, APIPA assigns an IP address to the host. In either case, APIPA periodically checks to make sure that the host's IP address is unique on the network and it establishes a new address for the host if not.

- **Works with Microsoft Proxy Server**   Proxy Server allows hosts on a private network to access the Internet. In other words, Proxy Server provides access to the Internet on behalf of hosts on a private network. See the description of network address translators in the next bulleted item.

■ **Works with network address translators** Independent hardware vendors (IHVs) such as Cisco Systems, Ascend, and Rampnet provide NATs that allow networks with private IP addresses to use DHCP to connect transparently to the Internet. An NAT translates each host's private IP address to a public address obtained from an ISP, which is globally unique, so that other hosts can access it across the Internet.

■ **Supports NetBIOS Name Service** APIPA uses NetBIOS Name Service (NBNS) for name-to-address resolution. This allows private networks to gradually evolve toward using other name services such as DNS, WINS, and so on. If a host discovers the presence of a name service such as DNS, however, the host starts using it.

■ **Supports legacy systems** A number of legacy clients don't use NBNS. These computers keep name-to-address bindings in a Hosts file. Network administrators can use a legacy client's Hosts file to assign it a static IP address, and APIPA will use a Hosts file for name resolution if it does not receive an answer from DNS or NBNS. This allows Windows 2000 Professional to communicate with legacy clients.

Universal Plug and Play

Microsoft recently announced a new initiative called Universal Plug and Play, with the goal of enabling users to build home networking solutions for communication, entertainment, home automation, and personal productivity. Home networking allows numerous intelligent consumer appliances and computers to connect as peers and share resources in the home. Home networking allows families to share resources such as printers and files, and it provides shared access to the Internet from multiple computers. Home networking isn't limited to computers, either, as a broad range of devices can be enhanced to support connectivity to the home network and the Internet. For more information, see *http://www.microsoft.com/homenet.*

■ **Opens up new opportunities for IHVs** IHVs such as 3Com and Intel offer inexpensive networking kits, which they've designed for small office and home networks. These provide a number of NICs and an inexpensive hub. IHVs that enable APIPA in their hardware can take advantage of Windows 2000 Professional's networking support. That is, APIPA-enabled hubs allow users to create simple networks that the operating system automatically configures.

Enhanced Quality of Service

Real-time multimedia applications are extremely sensitive to bandwidth restrictions and time delays. In order to deliver multimedia streams over IP networks well, the application must have certain guarantees:

■ **Bandwidth** Multimedia data—particularly video—requires more bandwidth than traditional networks can provide. For example, an uncompressed NTSC (National Television Standards Committee) video stream requires up to 200 megabits per second and, even when compressed, a handful of multimedia streams can overpower all other network traffic.

■ **Latency** Latency is the amount of time it takes a multimedia packet to get from the sending host to the receiving host. It has a serious impact on the quality of the multimedia stream. Transmission delays, queuing delays, and delays in host protocol stacks all contribute to latency.

■ **Jitter** Whereas the order that regular network traffic arrives at the receiving host isn't always important, multimedia data must arrive in sequence at the receiving host in order to be any good to the user. Jitter in the transmission signal causes dropped packets and gaps in the multimedia stream.

■ **Coexistence** Multimedia traffic is different than regular network traffic, which usually arrives at the receiving hosts in unpredictable bursts. Large amounts of these bursts can clog routers and cause gaps in multimedia streams.

Windows 2000 Professional's support for QoS helps guarantee the bandwidth, latency, jitter, and coexistence requirements of real-time multimedia applications. It assures the timely transfer of large amounts of data, and it allows multimedia traffic to coexist with traditional traffic on the same network. The operating system implements QoS as an extension to the Winsock2 programming interface, called Generic QoS (GQoS), providing a method for applications to reserve network bandwidth between the sending and receiving hosts. The mechanism it uses to implement QoS includes the following:

- Resource Reservation Protocol (RSVP)

- Local traffic control: packet scheduling and the IEEE 802.1p protocol

- IP Type of Service and Data Terminal Ready (DTR) header settings

Resource Reservation Protocol

RSVP is an IETF standard designed to support resource reservations on networks. RSVP propagates an application's QoS requests to all routers along the data path, and the network or internet reconfigures itself to provide the required level of service. Understanding how RSVP works is best done by looking at the steps it uses to establish a network flow:

1. A sending host that wants a certain quality of service broadcasts *path messages* toward the intended receiving hosts using an RSVP-enabled Winsock service provider. These path messages describe the bandwidth requirements and are propagated to each router along the path.

2. A receiving host confirms the flow and network path by sending *reserve messages* through the network or internet. These reserve messages describe the bandwidth characteristics of the data the receiving host wants to receive and are propagated to each router along the path back to the sending host.

3. Each router determines whether it chooses to accept the proposed reservation. If it chooses to do so, the router commits its resources and sends reserve messages to the next hop along the path.

Figure 15-2 illustrates the steps you just read about. The sending host transmits the path message, while the receiving host transmits the reserve message. You can think of the result as a data pipeline that has a quality of service guarantee suitable to the type of data the sending host is transmitting.

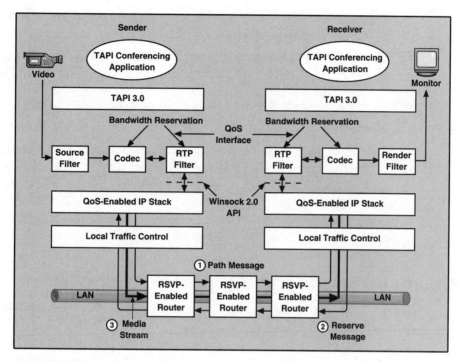

Figure 15-2
Resource Reservation Protocol.

Local Traffic Control

Windows 2000 Professional implements local traffic control using three different mechanisms:

- **Packet scheduling** Packet scheduling can be used with or without RSVP. It identifies network traffic as belonging to a particular flow, and it schedules the packets in each flow according to its traffic control parameters. Traffic control parameters include a scheduled rate, which paces the transmission of packets, and a priority, which determines the order in which packets are submitted when congestion occurs.

- **802.1p** The IEEE 802.1p protocol specifies methods for prioritizing network traffic. Windows 2000 Professional allows network traffic that's traversing 802.1p LANs to receive preferential treatment. Traffic control can determine the 802.1p user priority value to associate with each packet, and 802.1p-enabled switches can give prioritized service to certain packets.

- **Layer 2 signaling mechanisms** Depending on the specific underlying data link layer, the QoS service provider can invoke additional traffic control mechanisms.

IP Type of Service

Each IP packet has a three-bit precedence field, indicating the priority of the packet. Each packet can also have an additional field that indicates a delay, throughput, or reliability preference to the network. Local traffic control sets these bits in the IP headers of packets on particular flows, and network devices will treat them appropriately. The precedence and additional fields are similar to 802.1p priority settings, but higher-layer network devices interpret them.

Advanced Telephony Support

TAPI 3.0 (Telephony Application Programming Interface) uses an open standard to move multimedia traffic over any IP network. In this case, *multimedia* is a broad term that includes voice, data, and video collaboration. The choice of physical media is flexible and includes Plain Old Telephone Service (POTS) lines, ADSL, ISDN, leased lines, coaxial cable, satellite, and twisted pair. The result is that the same IP networks that carry Web, e-mail, and data traffic can allow individuals, businesses, schools, and governments throughout the world to communicate in a variety of new forms.

TAPI 3.0 helps organizations lower the cost of existing services, including voice and broadcast video, while broadening organizations' ability to communicate using video conferencing, application sharing, and whiteboard tools. Organizations tend to deploy separate networks for voice, data, and video traffic. Each network has different transport requirements, and each is expensive to install and maintain. In addition, since each network is physically separate, integrating them is difficult if not impossible. TAPI allows organizations to integrate the different voice, data, and video networks on a single IP network. Figure 15-3 illustrates the convergence of IP and PSTN (public switched telephone network) networks. By collapsing the disparate networks, organizations reap lower costs, easier management, and more productivity—not to mention a whole new breed of collaboration tools that were previously impossible to build. For example, TAPI enables applications for telecommuting, real-time document collaboration, distance learning, employee training, video conferencing, video mail, and video on demand.

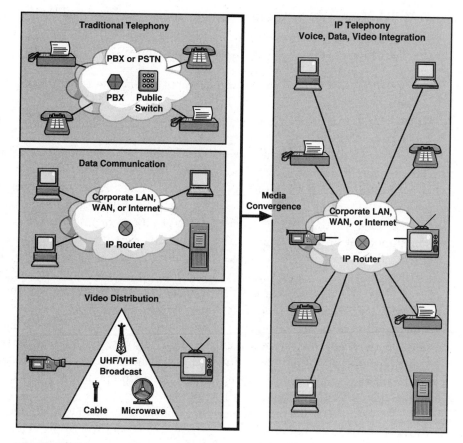

Figure 15-3
IP network, PSTN telephony, and media convergence.

TAPI 3.0 is an architecture that provides methods for making connections among two or more computers. Programmers can use any language—including Java, C++, and Microsoft Visual Basic—to create TAPI applications. In Windows 2000 Professional, TAPI 3.0 provides support for the classic telephony providers as well as the H.323 standard for conferencing and IP multicast conferencing. In addition, TAPI 3.0 integrates with Active Directory in order to simplify deployment, and it supports QoS to improve conference quality.

Asynchronous Transfer Mode

Asynchronous Transfer Mode (ATM) is emerging as an important worldwide standard for transmitting information of all types, including real-time multimedia streams that are sensitive to time delays. For example, many cable modems use

ATM. Telephone companies and enterprise customers are readily adopting ATM, making it the newest generation of LAN switching. And ATM enables a whole new class of applications that would either be impossible or impractical with conventional LAN technologies.

ATM does not rely on any specific type of physical transport; it's compatible with existing physical networks, including twisted pair, coax, and fiber optics. Unlike conventional LANs, no speed limit is designed into ATM LANs. ATM networks are limited only by the speed of the physical network layer. ATM is also compatible with existing networks, including Ethernet and Token Ring, allowing administrators to build homogenous ATM networks incrementally.

Traditional LAN technologies are connectionless. A protocol driver simply addresses a packet and sends it on its way. Each host examines the packet to determine whether the packet is addressed to it and, if so, takes the packet. The important bit to remember about connectionless networks is that, after placing the packet on the network, the sending host is out of the loop. This process partially explains why connectionless networks are prone to latency and jitter. However, a homogenous ATM network is connection-oriented. Instead of addressing a packet and sending it, the sending host requests a call to the ATM address of the receiving host, providing service access point (SAP) information that identifies a particular application running on the receiving host. In other words, an application on the sending host establishes a connection to an application on the receiving host through the ATM adapters on both hosts. This connection is also called a virtual circuit (VC).

A VC supports services such as QoS, since the VC allows an application to specify the quality of connection it requires. In fact, ATM provides QoS guarantees that other transport systems simply can't. Yes, 100-megabit Ethernet can provide bandwidth similar to ATM, but only ATM can provide the QoS guarantees required for real-time telephone and video streaming, smooth videoconferencing, and other multimedia streams that require low latency and jitter. And while the QoS mechanisms you read about earlier in this chapter provide some capability to reserve resources on an IP network, ATM was designed from the ground up to support QoS. That is, QoS is not an afterthought that has to be retrofitted into ATM.

For more information about ATM, including an outstanding white paper that explains how ATM works, see *http://www.microsoft.com/ntserver/commserv.*

Authentication Protocols

Windows 2000 Professional supports a variety of authentication protocols. Most of the protocols in the following list were included in Windows NT Workstation 4.0, but Layer 2 Tunneling Protocol (L2TP), Extensible Authentication Protocol (EAP), and Remote Authentication Dial-In User Service (RADIUS) are new to Windows 2000 Professional:

- **Password Authentication Protocol (PAP)** uses clear-text passwords and is the simplest form of authentication. Use this protocol only when the remote access server doesn't support more advanced authentication protocols, such as when connecting to an Internet service provider.

- **Shiva Password Authentication Protocol (SPAP)** allows Shiva clients to connect to computers running Microsoft Windows 2000 Server.

- **Challenge Handshake Authentication Protocol (CHAP)** negotiates a secure authentication. This authentication protocol can prove to the remote access server that you know your password without actually sending the password. It does so by transforming the password using the Message Digest 5 (MD5) hashing scheme (see Figure 11-3). Most third-party Point-to-Point Protocol (PPP) servers support CHAP and MD5.

- **Microsoft CHAP (MSCHAP)** is similar to plain CHAP, but is specifically designed for Microsoft products. MSCHAP version 2 is the latest version of MSCHAP. It provides mutual authentication, stronger initial data encryption keys, and different encryption keys for sending and receiving data.

- **Extensible Authentication Protocol (EAP)** is an extension of PPP that provides remote authentication using third-party security devices, such as Kerberos, Smart Cards, retina scan, voiceprint, and many more. In other words, it provides a method for supporting additional authentication protocols within PPP. Windows 2000 Professional relies on EAP to protect virtual private networks (VPNs) from brute-force, dictionary, and password-guessing attacks. Windows 2000 Professional provides two flavors of EAP: MD5, which you learned about earlier in this list, and Transaction Level Security (TLS), which is a stronger authentication method based on public key security (used for Smart Card authentication).

■ **Remote Authentication Dial-In User Service (RADIUS)** supports auditing by third-party accounting and auditing packages.

Tunneling Protocols

Microsoft first introduced VPNs in 1996 with PPTP. Windows 2000 Professional adds two new protocols to its arsenal: L2TP and Internet Protocol security (IPSec). The following list describes all three protocols. You learned how to configure them in Chapter 11, "Strongest Local and Network Security."

■ **Internet Protocol security (IPSec)**   IPSec is an IETF-proposed standard that Windows 2000 Professional supports. Windows 2000 Server tightly integrates IPSec with system policy management to transparently enforce encryption between hosts. Organizations can use IPSec to tunnel through private and public networks.

■ **Layer 2 Tunneling Protocol (L2TP)**   Supported only by Windows 2000 for client-to-server and server-to-server tunneling, L2TP is an IETF draft for transmitting non-IP traffic through IP networks. It uses IPSec to provide optional encryption, and it supports dynamic IP address assignment to simplify management.

■ **Point-To-Point Tunneling Protocol (PPTP)**   PPTP is a mature tunneling technology that's available for Windows 95, Windows 98, Windows NT Workstation 4.0, and Windows 2000 Professional. It's a good alternative to L2TP and IPSec for organizations that don't want to install and manage a public key infrastructure for VPNs.

UNIX Interoperability

Windows 2000 Professional makes integrating with UNIX resources easier, and it also makes moving to a single desktop solution possible. Rather than using two computers—one running Windows 2000 Professional for productivity tasks and one running UNIX for technical tasks—users can use a single desktop to perform all their tasks. Windows NT Services for UNIX v.1, an add-on pack for Windows 2000 Professional, provides core network interoperability with UNIX environments. New and improved features include the following:

■ **NTFS client and server**   Windows NT Services for UNIX supports the NTFS file system versions 2 and 3, the standard file protocol for

UNIX environments. It also supports letter case sensitivity for server, folder, and filenames.

■ **Telnet client and server** Windows NT Services for UNIX supports new Telnet terminal types, including VTNT, VT100, and ANSI. To verify users' credentials, it also provides support for Windows NT LAN Manager (NTLM) authorization. The Telnet client looks and feels like UNIX, making it easier to use for users who are already familiar with UNIX.

■ **UNIX scripting commands** Windows NT Services for UNIX provides a Korn Shell and 25 other UNIX bins such as ls, touch, and tee. Doing so helps users leverage their existing infrastructure and investment in UNIX scripts.

■ **One-way password synchronization** Users can use Windows NT Services for UNIX to synchronize Windows 2000 Professional passwords on UNIX systems, ensuring that users have secure access to UNIX resources. That is, any changes users make to their Windows 2000 Professional passwords are automatically changed on the UNIX side. This feature includes support for standalone workstation, server, or domain password synchronization. Windows NT Services for UNIX supports Solaris and HP-UX, as well as the rlogin method where no UNIX code exists.

For more information about Windows NT Services for UNIX, see *http:// www.microsoft.com/ntserver/nts/exec/overview/sfu.asp*. At this URL, you'll find a good overview of Windows NT Services for UNIX as well as links to more technical information, including a reviewer's guide.

Network Integration

Windows 2000 Professional is a very flexible network client, whether working with Windows 2000 Server, Windows NT Server 4.0, Novell NetWare, or UNIX. Users in any of these environments will see the same visual components, such as the My Network Places folder and Windows Explorer. In support of NetWare networks, for example, Windows 2000 Professional includes a NetWare client and the IPX/ SPX protocol stack. Windows 2000 Professional includes support for the services traditionally found on Microsoft networks, too, including DHCP and WINS. The operating system's built-in support for a variety of networks—including the client, protocol, and various services— enables users to connect to a whole host of network environments.

Integrated Web and Desktop

To fully integrate the Web into the user's desktop, Microsoft Internet Explorer 5 is built into Microsoft Windows 2000 Professional. Outwardly, users will notice few changes between Internet Explorer 4 and Internet Explorer 5. The menus are roughly the same. The toolbars are similar. Dialog boxes, too, are similar in both versions of the popular Web browser. Sure, Internet Explorer 5 changes some aspects of the user interface—but those changes are so subtle as to be missed by a user's casual inspection. The improvements that users will find after a more-thorough inspection are incremental enhancements to existing features, and the inclusion of improved AutoComplete and AutoCorrect features, similar to those found in Microsoft Office.

The main enhancements to Internet Explorer 5 are for developers, allowing developers to build better applications that provide a richer experience for the user. Fixed tables give developers more control over page layout (tables are frequently used to lay out columns of text), and they allow Web pages to load faster. A feature called Client Capabilities allows a developer to determine some of the hardware and software capabilities of the client machine and it ensures that Web pages appear as the developer intended. The new Behaviors feature makes Dynamic HTML more accessible to developers, so users are likely to see more-engaging content on the Web. A variety of performance enhancements allow developers to build enterprise-class applications that meet users' expectations. The list goes on—and users will notice these enhancements on the Web page, not on the browser's toolbar.

This chapter covers mostly what's new in Internet Explorer 5. It offers a brief reminder about features that continue from Internet Explorer 4 to version 5. It covers in more detail the user interface enhancements in Internet Explorer 5, and it uses the rest of the space to describe new features for developers and administrators. Note also that this chapter does not describe how Internet Explorer 5 integrates the Web into the user's desktop. For more information about how the browser makes using the local computer easier, see Chapter 4, "Simpler User Interface."

The Best of Internet Explorer 4

The jump from Internet Explorer 3 to Internet Explorer 4 was like graduating from your father's golf clubs to a pristine set of titanium golf clubs. Internet Explorer 4 was an innovative Web browser that not only beat its predecessor in a feature-by-feature comparison but that also won all major reviews, beating all other Web browsers hands down. It brought the Internet onto users' desktops, making the Web an accessible and powerful tool that they could use while performing their jobs. Explorer bars made searching easier, and they made the Favorites and History lists more available. Internet Explorer 4 included new and innovative security features for increased privacy and protection. It integrated well with other programs: Internet mail, UseNet newsgroups, etc. Millions of users, including myself, have learned to depend on Internet Explorer 4's awesome features and would miss them if they were gone.

As you read in this chapter's introduction, little has changed between Internet Explorer 4 and Internet Explorer 5—visually. Both offer similar power and flexibility, and both are easy to use. Features made popular by Internet Explorer 4 are still around in Internet Explorer 5. (Incidentally, Internet Explorer 5 does drop support for the separate Channels bar, a feature that was never popular with users, and instead integrates it into Favorites.) Some features have improved user interfaces in Internet Explorer 5, but they work the same way in most cases. The following list describes some of the features that Internet Explorer 5 carries forward from Internet Explorer 4, and later in this chapter you'll learn about how Internet Explorer 5 enhances them:

- **A single Explorer**   Internet Explorer removes most distinctions between using Windows Explorer to browse the local computer and using Internet Explorer to browse the Internet. That is, users browse the local computer with the same interface as they do networks, intranets, and the Internet.

- **A Web-savvy taskbar**   As shown in Figure 16-1, Internet Explorer makes the taskbar and Start menu into Web browsing tools. The Favorites command is available on the Start menu. Users can add the Address bar to the taskbar. Users can further customize the contents of toolbars and the Start menu.

- **Offline browsing**   Users subscribe to Web pages, and then Internet Explorer automatically downloads their content as a background task. This allows users to view content while they're not connected to the Internet, spending as little time connected to the Internet as possible.

As you'll learn later in this chapter, Internet Explorer 5 expands this feature to make it even easier to use.

■ **Easy navigation**   The AutoComplete feature helps users type URLs quicker and more accurately. New Forward and Back buttons keep track of recent sites. Internet Explorer 5 makes navigation even easier with a variety of enhancements that you'll learn about later.

■ **Explorer bars**   Explorer bars provide a convenient way for users to search the Web, choose a favorite Web page, or return to sites they've already visited. Users pick sites from the left pane while viewing them in the right pane. Internet Explorer 5 extends all three Explorer bars (Search, Favorites, and History) by adding more capabilities.

■ **The Internet Connection Wizard**   Internet Explorer's Internet Connection Wizard simplifies the process of signing up with an Internet service provider (ISP). It helps users choose an ISP and then set up an account. After setting up an account, the wizard automatically configures the computer to connect to the ISP.

■ **Security zones**   Security zones provide advanced protection for the computer as well as privacy. They do so without interrupting users with repeated warnings, as long as users are visiting sites that they've indicated are trusted.

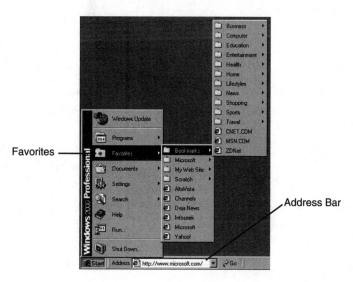

Figure 16-1
The Web-savvy taskbar and Start menu.

New and Improved in Internet Explorer 5

Internet Explorer 5 provides numerous enhancements to Internet Explorer 4. The following sections describe these enhancements in detail, but the following list will help you take a quick inventory of them:

- **Searching** The new Search Assistant helps users search for all types of information, including Web pages, phone numbers, UseNet messages, and much more. It automatically searches using all available search engines, so that a user can quickly switch between different sets of search results.

- **Navigating** Navigation is even easier for novice users, due to the introduction of the Go button and the AutoCorrect feature. Advanced users will enjoy more-powerful navigation tools.

- **Forms** Internet Explorer allows users to recall previous form input. In fact, the browser saves users' form input with the Web page in the cache, freeing users from having to reenter the same information time and time again.

- **Favorites** The Organize Favorites dialog box is greatly improved, making it easier for users to organize their favorite sites. Favorite sites can also be imported from and exported to Netscape Navigator and Communicator.

- **Offline Web pages** Offline browsing is more-intuitive and better integrated, and Microsoft has removed the unpopular separate Channels bar from the browser and instead integrated it with Favorites.

- **Internet connections** Users can create Internet connections on a per-user, per-connection basis, making it easy to connect to the Internet through different networks.

- **Error handling** Internet Explorer provides more feedback with better error messages, and it avoids the annoying script error messages that confound most users.

- **Performance** Features such as fixed tables and an improved Dynamic HTML–rendering engine make the browser more responsive than it ever was before.

- **Integration** Internet Explorer 5 is better integrated with other Internet tools.

Better Searching

Internet Explorer 5 supports the Search bar, shown in Figure 16-2, which users open by clicking the Search button on the toolbar. The Search bar provides one-stop searching for the user, including looking for Web pages, people, companies, maps, encyclopedias, UseNet newsgroups, and more. Users select the type of search they want to perform and provide keywords, and Internet Explorer 5 displays the results. A new feature for Internet Explorer 5 is that it highlights the keywords in the list of results, making it easier to locate appropriate Web pages.

Users can also customize the options that are available in the Search bar. For each type of search, they choose the search providers that they want available in the Search bar as well as the order in which they appear. Of course, users can continue to search using traditional search engines, such as Yahoo and Infoseek, but those same search providers are available in the Search bar and are better integrated with the browser.

One nice improvement is the background searching done using multiple search engines. If users search for a particular topic using one search engine and don't find the results they're looking for, they can simply switch to the next search engine and see the results of its search, and then on to the next search engine if necessary. All engines search simultaneously, so that users only need to state their search request once, and then they can view multiple sets of results.

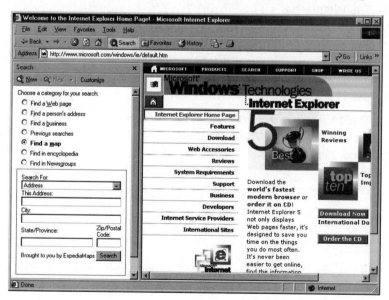

Figure 16-2
The Search bar appears in the left pane of the Internet Explorer 5 window.

Easier Navigating

Internet Explorer 5 adds the following navigational features, each of which makes moving from Web page to Web page easier for novices and experts alike:

- **The Go button** The Address bar works as it always has: a user types the URL and then presses Enter. However, Internet Explorer 5 adds the Go button, which serves the same purpose as pressing Enter on the Address bar. This feature was introduced after usability labs discovered that new Web users frequently will type in a URL and then end up staring at the Address bar, unaware that they need to press the Enter key.

- **AutoCorrect** AutoCorrect automatically corrects commonly misspelled URL conventions, including http://, www, com, net, and org.

- **Explorer bars** Figure 16-2, earlier in this chapter, shows what an Explorer bar looks like. Internet Explorer 5 provides the Favorites, History, and Search bars. These three Explorer bars have a similar user interface, and the Web browser can save the state of each Explorer bar between sessions.

- **The History bar** The History bar provides multiple views of the user's history: By Date, By Site, By Most Visited, By Order of Visit, and so forth. And within each view, the History bar organizes Web sites by domain name, rather than by the first portion of the URL ("honeycutt" rather than "www"). In addition, users can search the History list.

- **Toolbar customization** Users can customize Internet Explorer 5's toolbars. Although the most useful buttons are already on the toolbar, users can add buttons such as Folder, Cut, Copy, and Paste. Customizing the toolbar allows users to build a more-comfortable environment, making navigation easier.

- **The FTP folder** Internet Explorer presents FTP sites the same way that Windows Explorer presents local folders. This makes navigating FTP sites much easier.

- **An approved sites list** Administrators and parents can control what sites users are allowed to visit, and doing so doesn't require depending on sites to rate themselves. Administrators and parents can approve and disapprove sites using the Approved Sites tab of the Content

Advisor dialog box; to activate this dialog box, they choose Internet Options from the Tools menu, select the Content tab, and then click the Enable button.

Simpler Form Input

The AutoComplete feature for forms helps users fill out forms on a Web page using previous input. For example, after filling out a form the first time, users can recall their input the next time they use the same form. AutoComplete for forms supports single-line text boxes, and username and password fields. Internet Explorer 5 stores users' input on the local computer, and the information is inaccessible by other users.

Improved Favorites

Internet Explorer 5 has a new Organize Favorites dialog box. Shown in Figure 16-3, this dialog box makes creating new folders, moving favorites from one folder to another, and renaming favorites easier. It also provides additional information about each favorite Web site, including its URL, the number of visits, the date last visited, and whether the Web site is available for offline use. To open the Organize Favorites dialog box, choose Organize Favorites from Internet Explorer's Favorites menu.

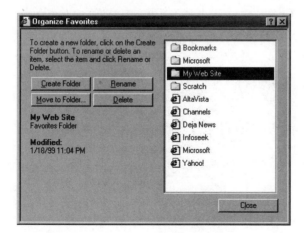

Figure 16-3
The Organize Favorites dialog box.

In addition to helping users organize their favorite Web sites, Internet Explorer 5 makes smart choices when users designate a page containing a set of frames as a favorite. The browser automatically recognizes the entire frameset arrangement instead of simply defaulting to the outermost URL.

The last enhancement to the Favorites feature is for those users who use Netscape Navigator in conjunction with Internet Explorer 5. Microsoft added to Internet Explorer 5 the ability to import and export favorites. Users can import Navigator bookmarks into Internet Explorer 5 as easily as they can export favorites to Navigator. To do so, users choose the Import And Export command from Internet Explorer's File menu.

Enhanced Offline Viewing

Offline browsing is one of the biggest improvements to Internet Explorer 5. Microsoft makes this feature much easier to use than it was in Internet Explorer 4. For example, users can now save a Web page to disk along with all of the images referenced in the Web page. They can then use that Web page offline or e-mail it to other users.

The ability to save an entire Web page to disk is small potatoes compared to the full set of services Internet Explorer 5 provides for offline Web pages. When adding a Web page to the Favorites list, users check the Make Available Offline check box in the Add Favorite dialog box (see Figure 16-4). Internet Explorer 5 downloads the Web page on a regular schedule, which users are free to customize as they see fit. If the computer is offline when they try to view the Web page, Internet Explorer 5 uses the offline version of the Web page. If the computer is online, however, the Web browser retrieves the Web page from the Internet.

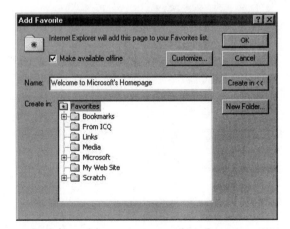

Figure 16-4
Making a Web page available offline.

Users manage offline Web pages using the Windows Synchronization Manager. They choose Synchronize from Internet Explorer's Tools menu. The Windows Synchronization Manager is the central location where users manage all of the computer's synchronization tasks, including Web pages, Internet mail, offline files and folders, etc. For more information about synchronization, including using offline files and folders, see Chapter 6, "Better Mobile Computing Support."

Yet one more thing that Internet Explorer 5 does much better than Internet Explorer 4 is let users know when a Web page is not available offline. The Web browser disables any Web pages in the Favorites list or in the History bar that aren't available.

Easier Internet Connections

Internet Explorer 5 supports multiple connections, and each connection has an independent configuration that includes passwords, security, scripts, network protocols, network settings, and proxy servers. Figure 16-5 shows the new Connections tab in the Internet Options dialog box. Note that Internet Explorer 5 moves the Internet Options command from the View menu to the Tools menu. If users don't yet have an Internet connection, they can click the Connect button and the Internet Connection Wizard will walk them through setting up an account, if necessary, as well as configuring the computer to connect to the Internet.

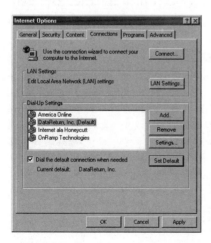

Figure 16-5
The Connections tab in the Internet Options dialog box.

Internet Explorer 5's ability to use multiple connections eliminates the need for users to reconfigure the network settings for different types of connections: private network, Internet, etc. Users create connections based on the network to which they're connecting rather than based on the devices they're using. For instance, a connection called "My ISP" might use the same modem as a connection to the user's corporate network but require a totally different configuration. (When dialing via an ISP, typically there is no proxy setting, whereas when connecting via a corporate network, proxys are common.) The bottom line is that users no longer have to manually reconfigure their settings for each different type of connection they make to the Internet.

For proxy server users, Internet Explorer 5 supports the Web proxy AutoDiscover (WPAD) protocol. This protocol helps the operating system automatically locate the proxy server and configure the browser to access the Internet through it.

Improved Error Handling

Figure 16-6 shows one of Internet Explorer 5's new error messages. Rather than simply displaying the cryptic HTTP 404 error when the URL doesn't exist, the Web browser displays an error message that suggests where users can find the site for which they're looking. The example shown in the figure suggests that the user check the URL, visit the site's home page, or click the Back button. Note that when users connect to the Internet through a proxy server, they continue to see the proxy server's error messages rather than Internet Explorer 5's.

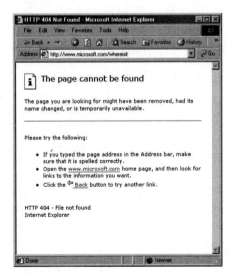

Figure 16-6
Internet Explorer 5's HTTP 404 File Not Found error message.

In addition to better HTTP error messages, Internet Explorer 5 provides more-descriptive script error messages. Users can decide which script errors they want to see in the future and which script errors they don't want to see. While users probably don't care about script error messages and would like to avoid them all, developers will appreciate the more-informative error messages.

Performance Improvements

Internet Explorer 5 provides numerous performance improvements, all of which provide a better experience to users:

- **Fixed tables** Fixed tables display much faster than normal tables—up to 100 times faster. You'll learn more about fixed tables later in this chapter.

- **A new Dynamic HTML rendering engine** Internet Explorer 5 has a new rendering engine that makes Web pages with Dynamic HTML and data binding render faster.

- **HTTP-Expires** Internet Explorer 5 no longer second-guesses developers when they specify an expiration date for a Web page. The Web browser won't automatically check the network when an object from the cache hasn't yet expired; it will use the cached copy of the object instead. Enforcement of the expiration date reduces network traffic and improves performance by preventing unnecessary trips to the Web server.

Integration with Other Tools

Internet Explorer 5 integrates well with other Internet tools, providing the following features:

- **Smart editing** Users edit HTML documents in the programs that created them. For example, if an HTML document was created using Microsoft Word or Microsoft Excel, then Internet Explorer 5 automatically invokes the correct program when a user starts to edit the Web page.

- **A default HTML editor** Users can designate a default HTML editor, and can choose additional editors from the drop-down menu of the toolbar's Edit button.

- **Web-based e-mail integration** Internet Explorer 5 supports Web-based e-mail clients such as MSN Hotmail and Yahoo. It can use the Web-based e-mail client for Mail To links as well as for the Read Mail and Send Page commands.

New Tools for HTML Developers

Microsoft listened to its customers and what did it hear? That developers need support for creating enterprise-ready Web applications—and for the latest, most important Internet standards. Dynamic HTML needs to be more accessible to them. And developers need a fully componentized architecture that enables the easy development of powerful Internet applications, not just Web pages.

The first issue—support for creating enterprise-ready Web applications—implies that developers need better performance and stability. That is, Internet Explorer needs to be fast enough for serious applications. To that end, Internet Explorer 5 includes numerous changes to improve the Web browser's performance as well as its stability. Microsoft optimized the internal algorithms to perform basic tasks faster. The most notable improvements apply to viewing very large documents and Web pages that are bound to a database. A new Dynamic HTML rendering engine makes Web pages that use Dynamic HTML snappier, and developers can provide hints—similar to declaring the height and width of an image—to Internet Explorer 5 that will make it display their Web pages faster.

Speaking to the second issue, support for the most important Internet standards, Internet Explorer 5 has support for the following standards, many of which the World Wide Web Consortium (W3C) defines:

- HTTP 1.1

- Dynamic HTML, including DOM (Document Object Model) and ECMA-262 (European Computer Manufacturers Association) scripting

- Dynamic HTML Behaviors (recently submitted to W3C)

- Cascading style sheets (CSS) 1.0, CSS level 2, and CSS positioning

- Dynamic Properties (recently submitted to W3C)

- XML 1.0 (Extensible Markup Language), including a parser, an object model, and a data source object model

- Platform for Internet Content Selection (PICS)

- Portable Network Graphics (PNG)

The following sections address the remaining issues, such as more-accessible Dynamic HTML. You'll learn about fixed tables, dynamic behaviors, persistence, and more. You'll also learn about other features that help developers create more-robust applications.

Fixed Tables

Prior to fixed tables, a Web browser examined an entire table before determining how to lay it out and size each cell—a very slow process. Even though developers could specify column widths, the Web browser still examined the entire table and would often ignore the developer's hints. While tables with few rows and columns displayed relatively quickly, large tables, data bound tables, and nested tables were slow. All in all, tables were a frustrating experience for both developers and users.

Developers create a fixed table by adding *table-layout:fixed* to the table's style. Then they provide hints about the table's dimensions using the Colwidth attribute or the <Col> or <Colgroup> tag. By relying on the hints a developer provides, rather than by examining the table to determine its size, Internet Explorer 5 renders the table much more quickly. The performance is up to two orders of magnitude faster than with normal tables. That means a large table that normally takes 100 seconds to display will display in about one second as a fixed table.

An additional benefit is that fixed tables are an easier tool to use for laying out text. Developers frequently use a table to format columns of text on a Web page. This proves to be a frustrating experience, however, as the Web browser sometimes "does its own thing." With a fixed table, developers can be reasonably sure that when they specify a table whose first column is 200 pixels wide with a second column that uses the remaining width of the client area, that's what they're going to get.

> **NOTE:** At this moment, Internet Explorer 5 is the only Web browser that supports fixed tables. While down-level browsers will display the Web page, ignoring the *table-layout* property, the table might not look as the developer intended. Many of the remaining features that you'll learn about in this chapter are also unique to Internet Explorer 5—for now.

Dynamic HTML

Dynamic HTML is the rave these days. What is it? My definition of Dynamic HTML is the separation of content, format, and behavior using technologies such as HTML, cascading style sheets, and scripts. In a more general sense, Dynamic HTML is the API for HTML, allowing developers to create full-scale, Web-based applications. Developers can use the processing power of the client computer to create interactive Web pages rather than relying on round trips to the Web server each time the content changes.

So if Dynamic HTML is the cat's meow, why do so few Web sites use it? Certainly, you can find plenty of sites with cute rollover effects that change text and images when a user points to them. What you don't find much of are Web sites that fully utilize the capabilities of Dynamic HTML. The reason is that Dynamic HTML is just too difficult for most developers to use effectively. Well, Internet Explorer 5 makes Dynamic HTML much more accessible to all developers. For example, behaviors completely separate functionality from content. Developers no longer have to write complicated scripts to use Dynamic HTML. Changing code is easier than before because the Web page's HTML file doesn't have to include scripts anymore—in other words, scripts are not intermingled with HTML. For that matter, Web developers can purchase third-party behaviors and hook them up to their Web pages without ever seeing a single line of script. Once and for all, content, format, and behavior are now completely separate.

Dynamic behaviors deserve more explanation. Just as cascading style sheets separate content from format, dynamic behaviors separate content from behavior. Developers build reusable scripts (called behaviors) and custom XML tags, and then refer to them from their Web pages. In the long term, dynamic behaviors will allow separate roles: programmers will worry about scripts, designers will worry about formatting, and writers will worry about content. This componentized approach allows each contributor to a Web page to focus on their own core competency. Internet Explorer 5 includes several built-in behaviors, but many more will be available from third-party sources. To associate a behavior with an element, developers add *behavior: url* (for example, *behavior: mybehavior.sct*) to the element's style. An SCT file is much like an HTML file; it contains scripts and a set of XML elements, objects, methods, and events.

Cascading Style Sheets

Cascading style sheets separate content from format. Developers specify styles in a <Style> tag and associate those styles with individual elements. Using CSS is not unlike using document templates in Microsoft Word—they specify the format of paragraphs and characters in different situations. Internet Explorer 4 supports CSS level 1 and CSS positioning, and Internet Explorer 5 adds support for CSS level 2.

Internet Explorer 5 extends CSS level 2 with new capabilities, which Microsoft has submitted to the W3C for review:

■ **Current style**   Each element on the Web page has the CurrentStyle property, which exposes all of the element's CSS properties, whether the developer assigned a value to that property or not. For example, developers can use the CurrentStyle property to determine an element's font size even though they didn't explicitly set the font size.

■ **Multiple CSS classes**   Developers can apply more than one CSS class to an element. This makes applying multiple behaviors to an element much easier.

■ **Dynamic properties**   Developers can assign a function to a CSS property. For example, *font-size: function(this.clientWidth/20)* sets the style's font size to a twentieth of the width of the client window. Internet Explorer 5 recalculates dynamic properties each time the Web page changes, using an intelligent recalculation engine that's similar to the technology used in spreadsheets. In short, dynamic properties make setting up complex layouts trivial, eliminating the need for the developer to write complex scripts to accomplish the same feat.

Client Capabilities

With client capabilities, the developer can determine the Web browser's features to see what components are and are not available. For example, does the browser support DHTML? Developers can provide content that's appropriate for the user's Web browser, making sure that Web pages appear as the developers intended. Developers can also query for information about the computer's configuration. For example, the server might serve up more dynamic content on faster processors or less dynamic content on slower ones. Developers can serve up static content if a user has disabled scripts.

Browserless Applications

Internet Explorer 5 enables developers to create browserless applications. One example is a calculator application that actually looks like a calculator. Browserless applications have an HTA file extension and are missing the Web browser's traditional user interface: menus, toolbars, icons, title information, and so forth. None of these items appear in the window unless the developer creates them. The bottom line is that browserless applications pack all the power of Internet Explorer 5 (object model, protocol support, rendering power) without the strict security model and user interface of the browser.

Internet Explorer 5 returns the client's capabilities in response to an HTTP request for this information. Server-side scripts use this information to serve up appropriate content. Performing this task on the server is more efficient than doing the same on the client, allowing the server to make decisions about content before transmitting it to the client. Internet Explorer also supports client capabilities via the clientCaps behavior so that developers can make content decisions on the client, if necessary.

Full Drag-and-Drop Functionality

Internet Explorer 5 supports full drag-and-drop functionality. You can use drag and drop to move objects between frames and to move objects between Internet Explorer 5 and the desktop or other applications. Developers now have full control over cursors and drag initialization, and Internet Explorer 5 provides support for the Clipboard.

Internet Explorer 5 provides a number of new capabilities that further enable developers to support drag and drop on their Web pages. First, it features new mouse capture events and methods such as ReleaseCapture and SetCapture. Second, it allows elements to switch between relative and absolute positioning on the fly.

Persistence

Internet Explorer 5 can maintain the state of any element on a Web page so that, when users return to that page, it appears as they last saw it. For example, when a user returns to a page that contains a collapsible outline, the Web browser can restore the outline to the state it was in when the user last saw it. Other elements that can be restored include form data, positions of objects, page content, styles, and script variables.

Developers used to rely on cookies to perform this feat, but cookies are terribly inefficient. Internet Explorer 5 provides an XML-based method for retaining an element's state that avoids the limitations of cookies. It uses a local store for persistent data that it protects from unauthorized cross-domain access—developers control access to the storage. And this storage isn't restricted by the 4K limit imposed on cookies. Persistence is implemented through the following dynamic behaviors:

- **saveHistory** Captures and restores a Web page's state during the session

- **saveFavorite** Captures and restores a Web page's state between sessions

- **saveSnapshot** Saves any arbitrary element's state between sessions

Development Support

Internet Explorer 5 provides two features that make creating Web pages easier for developers:

- **Compatibility mode** Developers can test sites using Internet Explorer 4 as well as Internet Explorer 5, making sure their sites work in down-level browsers.

- **Debugging messages** Internet Explorer 5 provides a developer mode that displays greatly improved error messages (see Figure 16-7). These error messages give more details about script errors, HTML structure errors, etc. and they help diagnose application errors. By default, the Web browser turns off this feature.

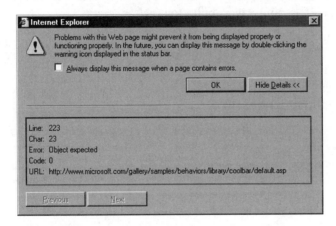

Figure 16-7
An example of a script error message.

Extensible Markup Language

Extensible Markup Language (XML) is a tag language that describes structured data. Just as HTML provides a universal way to view data, XML provides a universal way to work with data. I like to think of XML as a self-describing, text-based database format. It separates structured data from the user interface, allowing developers to integrate data from diverse sources in their user interfaces. In the long run, XML will enable more-precise content declaration, more-meaningful searches, and a whole new way to view and manipulate data.

Internet Explorer 5 supports the following key XML features:

- Developers can use XML as an additional markup language on their Web pages. They can mix XML and HTML in the document stream, and they can apply CSS or Extensible Style Language (XSL) directly to XML elements, controlling how they look.

■ The high-performance, validating, XML engine fully supports W3C XML 1.0 and namespaces, which allow developers to uniquely qualify element names on the Web, avoiding conflicts between elements with the same name.

■ Based on the W3C XSL working draft, Internet Explorer 5 allows developers to apply style sheets to XML data. XSL has pattern-matching capabilities that allow developers to programmatically locate information within an XML data set.

■ XML schemes describe how an XML document is formed, including allowable element names, rich data types, allowable element combinations, and attribute availability for each element.

■ XML can be processed on the server, allowing developers to support browsers that don't do XML and providing a way to pass data between multiple distributed application servers. Processing XML on the server avoids similar processing on the client, but it requires a return trip to the server in order to change views.

■ The XML DOM is a standard API that gives developers control over the XML document's content, structure, format, etc. Internet Explorer's implementation of the XML DOM includes full support for the W3C XML DOM recommendation and is accessible from scripts and other programming languages.

Ease of Administration

Many companies now view Web browsers as productivity tools on a similar level with operating systems. In fact, more and more companies distribute a Web browser as part of the standard desktop and rely on their intranets as a tool for disseminating information. Thus, administrative control of employees' Web browsers is important, prioritized immediately below control of the desktop operating systems.

The Internet Explorer Administration Kit (IEAK) 5 provides administrators with the capability to customize Internet Explorer 5, to deploy it, and to manage it after it's installed on users' computers. Administrators can create custom, branded installations of Internet Explorer 5 using the Configuration

Wizard, preconfiguring user settings for proxy servers, security, desktop, and so on. The IEAK Configuration Wizard allows administrators to lock down the desktop, as necessary, to ensure that only items that they choose appear on users' desktops. IEAK 5 also eases deployment by providing numerous methods for distributing Internet Explorer 5 to users, and by allowing administrators to build custom installation packages that they can distribute to the entire company or to a specific group of users. And last, IEAK 5 makes routine maintenance easier. Using the IEAK Profile Manager, administrators can make changes from a central location. They can change any and all desktop settings on any supported platform, including 32-bit Windows, 16-bit Windows, Macintosh, and UNIX. And when used in a Windows 2000 domain, IEAK Profile Manager works seamlessly with the Group Policy snap-in and is integrated with Active Directory.

For more information about IEAK 5, visit *http://ieak.microsoft.com*. The following list provides an overview of IEAK 5's features:

- **Preinstalled components**   IEAK 5 allows administrators to specify a customized set of components before installing Internet Explorer 5 on a machine.

- **Customized installation**   Administrators can choose which components are available using the Custom Install option, limiting users' choices.

- **Customized toolbars**   Administrators can customize Internet Explorer 5's toolbars to launch applications, run scripts, etc. This makes the browser fit the company better.

- **Favorites customization**   IEAK 5 allows administrators to customize the Favorites list, and to add, change, and delete favorite Web sites during automatic configuration.

- **Specified install folder**   Administrators can specify the installation folder.

- **Updated check page**   Even though a user might change their Start page, administrators can force the user's browser to periodically return to a specified URL. The interval of time allowed to pass before returning is configurable.

- **Feature selection mode**   Administrators can customize the IEAK Customize Wizard to cover the features they want to use when customizing Internet Explorer 5.

- **Automatic digital signing**   IEAK 5 will automatically sign the code it produces, and administrators can pick the certificate that IEAK 5 uses for that purpose.

- **Integrated deployment**   IEAK 5 allows administrators to integrate Internet Explorer 5's deployment with the Microsoft Office 2000 Custom Install Wizard, resulting in a single customization and deployment of productivity and Web tools.

CHAPTER SEVENTEEN

Wide Applications Support

Customers have given Microsoft clear, consistent feedback about the upgrade process. Some of their biggest concerns are about upgrading from Microsoft Windows 98 and Microsoft Windows NT Workstation 4.0 to Microsoft Windows 2000 Professional. What happens to the applications that users require for doing their jobs? Administrators don't want to have to visit each desktop in order to make applications work correctly—they just expect those applications to migrate properly. Upgrading from Windows 98 can be even more worrisome in this regard, particularly with so many customers considering—for the first time—replacing Windows 98 desktops with products built on Windows NT technology.

This chapter describes how Microsoft, in cooperation with independent software vendors (ISVs), is making this migration process as smooth as possible. First, ISVs can build upgrade packs that the setup program uses to update an application during the upgrade of the operating system, making sure that the application works properly in Windows 2000 Professional. Second, Microsoft is testing many more legacy applications for Windows 2000 Professional than it did for Windows NT Workstation 4.0. Last, Microsoft is enhancing the Windows logo program to ensure that new applications work well in Windows 2000 Professional. With all of these pieces in place, users are likely to find that the most popular applications will work well in Windows 2000 Professional.

Common Application Failures

Microsoft is putting considerable effort into testing a variety of applications with Windows 2000 Professional. Doing so isn't without its challenges, though. The sheer number of applications, along with the fact that some ISVs are not willing to update older versions of their applications, make this task much more difficult. In the process of testing applications that vendors have not updated, Microsoft has encountered a variety of problems. I share those problems with you in this chapter so that you will know what to expect.

Please note that most well-written applications are compatible with Windows 2000 Professional. Some applications will require minor modification, and many ISVs plan to provide patches for the most popular applications, so their users will not encounter these problems. The list below itemizes some of the most common application issues that can cause compatibility problems with Windows 2000 Professional. If users encounter any of the following problems, they should contact the application's vendor for an update:

- **Replacing system files** Some applications try to replace system files with older versions. This can cause stability problems for other applications as well as for the operating system. Windows 2000 Professional protects against such applications by monitoring its core system files. If an application tries to overwrite a system file, Windows 2000 will put the original pristine version back on the system. This will preserve the integrity of the operating system as well as any other applications that are using that file, but it is possible that the application that tried to replace the system file will fail.

- **Using version information improperly** Some applications fail to install because they interpret Windows 2000 Professional's version incorrectly. For example, some applications assume they won't work with any version of Windows that isn't version 4.0.

- **Using the incorrect installation path** Some programs write hard-coded paths to file locations that are not constant. For example, many applications assume that drive C is the system drive and/or assume that the users' program files are stored in "C:\Program Files"—which is not always the case. Applications should use the Win32 APIs—ideally the SHGetFolderPath API—to find the appropriate location for their files.

- **Applications that include software drivers** Applications such as antivirus, remote control, backup, disk defragmenter, and redirector programs might fail in Windows 2000 Professional if they haven't been updated. The worst-case scenario is that a poorly written driver causes a *blue screen*—a blue, character mode screen with a bunch of unintelligible data on it. Another likely scenario involves initialization errors. That is, a driver fails to start properly but doesn't warn users that it isn't working. Examples include antivirus programs that, unbeknownst to the user, are not working properly.

■ **Failing to install fonts properly** Microsoft tests reveal that some applications don't properly install their own fonts on the system. In these cases, the fonts aren't visible until after users restart the computer or until they open the Fonts folder.

■ **Relying on Windows 98 features** Applications that rely on files and program code specific to Windows 98 will fail. Users might see the Entry Point Not Found dialog box or another dialog box that reports a missing system file.

■ **Relying on the Windows 98 registry** Applications that rely on portions of the registry that are unique to Windows 98 will fail on Windows 2000 Professional. The error messages that users see will vary, but an example would be an application reporting that there isn't a default printer because of differences in the registry.

■ **Failing to register uninstallers** A few applications don't register an uninstaller, so users won't be able to remove them with the Add/Remove Programs dialog box. Still other applications that do register uninstallers might not uninstall properly. The uninstaller might hang or fail to remove all of the application's files, folders, and registry entries.

■ **Failing to close the application process** A few applications fail to close the application process even though the parent window does close. When this happens, users can't restart the application, and they receive messages that say the application is already running even though they can't see the application on the desktop.

■ **Failing to verify users** Applications that authorize computer accounts or domain users don't always accept valid users on trusted domains.

■ **Using excessive timeouts** Applications that wait for resources to become available might seem to hang. For example, an application that is waiting for a network connection might appear to hang if the computer isn't connected to the network.

■ **Failing to display help files** Some applications may not be able to display their own help files.

■ **Failing to use system resources** Some applications can't view and display system resources such as the Recycle Bin, CPU utilization, and the Event Viewer.

■ **Giving incorrect advice** Applications that advise users on required configuration changes might give users incorrect information. For example, backup applications that use their own tape drivers might give users incorrect information about disabling the system tape driver, since that function is now performed in the Computer Management console. Still other programs incorrectly report their status.

NOTE: Applications that rely on Microsoft Internet Explorer 4 components will probably need an update. Check with the applications' vendors. For example, Visual InterDev 6.0, a product that Microsoft designed to work with Internet Explorer 4, does not work correctly with Internet Explorer 5. Microsoft intends to update Visual InterDev 6.0.

The Microsoft Windows Logo

Ensuring applications' compatibility with Windows 2000 Professional is a complicated puzzle, and a significant piece of the puzzle is making sure that new applications work properly. To help put this piece in place, Microsoft has significantly updated the Windows logo requirements to take Windows 2000 Professional into account. The Windows logo signifies that an application works properly in Windows and plays well with other applications. In order to earn the Windows logo, a product must meet specific technical standards to ensure that it works well with the operating system. Only after passing these tests can vendors license the logo from Microsoft and display it on their applications' packaging.

Compliance testing for the Windows logo is performed by VeriTest, Inc., a third-party testing company. The following section describes the requirements of the Windows logo in general terms—but keep in mind that the requirements are much more stringent than this chapter would lead you to believe. For more information about the Windows logo, including the exact requirements that an application must meet, see *http://msdn.microsoft.com/developer/winlogo/win2000.htm.*

Some of the benefits of an application that conforms to the Windows logo guidelines are as follows:

■ The application's installation is robust and self-repairing, helping to minimize "DLL Hell" conflicts and enabling better interoperation of applications.

■ The application facilitates easy software deployment and management.

- The application is IntelliMirror enabled, properly maintaining user preferences and computer settings. This ensures a good "roaming user" experience, support for multiple users per machine, and desktop regeneration in machine replacement scenarios.

- The application runs in a secure Windows environment and complies with system policies.

- The application supports OnNow/ACPI capabilities to deliver the best mobile computing experience possible.

- The application provides a consistent, accessible user experience to reduce support and training costs.

- The application functions normally after the operating system is upgraded to Windows 2000 Professional.

Whereas the Windows logo is the piece of the puzzle that ensures new applications are compatible with Windows 2000 Professional, upgrade packs are the piece that helps vendors update existing applications so that they are compatible. Given the fact that Microsoft has made information about upgrade packs available since 1997, most vendors will be prepared—or possibly embarrassed. Microsoft plans upgrade packs for a variety of its applications: Microsoft Fax and the Outlook client are examples. Microsoft will also include upgrade packs from various vendors such as InstallShield. Note that many Windows 98 applications do not require an upgrade pack in order to work properly in Windows 2000 Professional.

Understanding Upgrade Packs

The goal of an upgrade pack is to make an application run in Windows 2000 Professional as well as it ran in Windows 98 or Windows 95. There are two different scenarios that upgrade packs address:

- **Applications incompatible with Windows 2000 Professional**   For these applications, an upgrade pack might replace Windows 98–specific program files or move Windows 98–specific settings to a more suitable place in the Windows 2000 Professional registry. In short, the upgrade pack does whatever is required to make the application compatible.

- **Applications compatible with Windows 2000 Professional**   Some applications are indeed compatible with Windows 2000 Professional. If they install differently on Windows 2000 Professional than they do on Windows 98, however, they won't work properly after users upgrade the operating system. Thus, an upgrade pack prevents users from having to reinstall an application. It does this by updating the application's files and changing its settings just as though the user reinstalled it in Windows 2000 Professional.

In the latter case, these upgrade packs are implemented as migration DLLs, which ISVs create using the information they find at *http://www.microsoft.com/ msdn/news/feature/110397/migration*. Migration DLLs range in size from about 100K to several MB, depending on the application's complexity, and they usually present no interface to the user. Vendors provide an INF file in addition to the migration DLL. The migration DLL and the setup program use the INF file to exchange information about the migration process. For example, the INF file reports the migration DLL's changes to the setup program.

Checking for Required Upgrade Packs

Windows 2000 Professional's setup program can generate a compatibility report that alerts users to significant problems—problems that might prevent them from using the computer properly. To generate a compatibility report without installing the operating system, users run Winnt32.exe with the /checkupgradeonly command line option. The setup program reports its results in a dialog box, and stores a more permanent copy of them in a log file called Upgrade.txt or Winnt32.log. To specify that the setup program check for the necessity of upgrade packs in unattended mode, users can provide the following answer file with Winnt32:

```
[unattended]
win9xupgrade=yes
[win9xupg]
ReportOnly=yes
SaveReportTo=UNC Path
AppendComputerNameToPaths=yes
```

Replace *UNC Path* with the network share in which you want to store the computer's upgrade report (\\Nts50srv01\reports is an example). The setup program always uses the same filename for the upgrade report, so if you want to use the same script on more than one computer, include the command *AppendComputerNameToPaths=yes*. This causes the setup program to create a unique folder for each computer.

The upgrade report will alert users to applications it thinks require upgrade packs. However, it won't catch every application that requires an upgrade pack.

For users to be sure that they will be able to use all their applications, they should check each ISV's Web site for information about whether the application requires an upgrade pack. In addition, Microsoft provides an Application Catalog on its Web site that lists applications that are compatible with Windows 2000 Professional and Server. This site is located at *http://www.microsoft.com/windows/pro/ compatible*. Another source of information will be other users' experience, which users can check by searching UseNet using a service such as DejaNews (*http:// www.dejanews.com*).

Getting Upgrade Packs from an ISV

Microsoft intends for ISVs to distribute upgrade packs via their Web sites at no charge. This choice makes sense, as the Web is already the method that vendors prefer to use for distributing updates, fixes, and so forth. Other options are available for vendors to distribute upgrade packs, including mailing diskettes and CD-ROMs to registered users, sending e-mail, etc.

Since Windows 2000 Professional's setup program uses upgrade packs to migrate applications during the upgrade process, users should collect the upgrade packs they require before they run the setup program. Users can specify additional upgrade packs during the setup process using the Provide Upgrade Packs dialog box shown in Figure 17-1. For more information about the setup process, see Chapter 3, "Setup Guide."

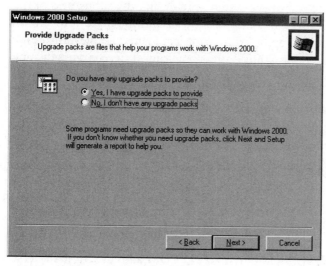

Figure 17-1
The Provide Upgrade Packs dialog box.

Legacy Applications

Windows 2000 Professional is Microsoft's preferred platform for 16-bit Windows and MS-DOS applications. Windows 2000 Professional protects the system from errant 16-bit applications, while Windows 98 only protects the system against 32-bit programs.

Windows 2000 Professional expands support for legacy applications over Windows NT Workstation 4.0. Microsoft is testing 50 percent more Win16 and MS-DOS applications than they did for Windows NT Workstation 4.0. These include 16-bit applications that shipped prior to Windows 95. Keep in mind that the final results will change after Windows 2000 Professional ships, but Microsoft estimates that it will test the top 500 legacy applications. Microsoft prioritizes the list of applications they're testing using data provided by Dataquest and PC Data as well as feedback that Rapid Deployment Program (RDP) customers provide.

Windows 2000 Professional supports 16-bit applications by emulating the environment in which they were designed to run. *Environment subsystems* emulate environments for OS/2 and POSIX (Portable Operating System Interface for UNIX) applications. *NT virtual DOS machines* (NTVDMs) provide environments for MS-DOS and Win16 applications. Each MS-DOS NTVDM and application runs as a separate process, and each MS-DOS and Win16 NTVDM runs in its own address space. This means that a failed MS-DOS application doesn't impact the rest of the system, preserving the robustness of the operating system. In addition, this design allows Windows 2000 Professional to pre-emptively multitask all applications, not just Win32 applications. Figure 17-2 illustrates how Windows 2000 Professional runs different types of applications, and the following list describes the processes in more detail:

- **Win32 subsystem**   The Win32 subsystem is the native environment for Windows 2000 Professional. All Win32 applications run on this subsystem.

- **MS-DOS NTVDM**   The environment for MS-DOS applications is implemented as an NTVDM, a 32-bit Windows application that simulates an Intel 486 computer running MS-DOS. Each MS-DOS application runs in a separate NTVDM, and Windows 2000 Professional can run a large number of them at the same time.

- **Win16 NTVDM**   The Win16 NTVDM adds additional layers to the MS-DOS NTVDM that emulate the 16-bit functionality of Windows 3.1. By default, Windows 2000 Professional runs all 16-bit Windows applications in a single, multithreaded NTVDM. Each application cooperatively multitasks in its own thread.

- ■ **OS/2 subsystem** The OS/2 subsystem runs 16-bit character-based OS/2 applications, emulating OS/2 version 1.3. It does not support OS/2 2.0 or later.

- ■ **POSIX subsystem** The POSIX subsystem runs applications written to the POSIX 1 standard. Applications must conform to POSIX 1 or the standards set by the International Organization for Standardization (ISO) and the International Electrotechnical Commission (IEC), collectively known as the ISO/IEC standards.

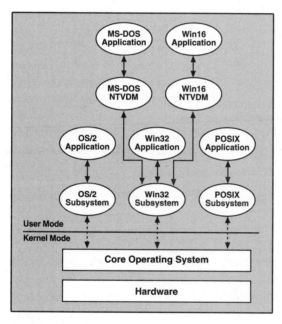

Figure 17-2
Application environments.

MS-DOS–Based Applications

As you read earlier, each MS-DOS application runs in a separate NTVDM. Within resource limits, Windows 2000 Professional can run any number of NTVDMs, each with its own address space. Also, each NTVDM has its own configuration files—Autoexec.nt and Config.nt—and users can create custom startup files for any MS-DOS application. While most MS-DOS applications work in Windows 2000 Professional, some do not. The following list contains some of the operating system features that might prevent an MS-DOS application from working in Windows 2000 Professional:

- Task-switching APIs
- Block-mode device drivers
- Internet 2F dealing with DOSKEY program callouts (AX=4800)
- Microsoft CD-ROM Extensions (MSCDEX) functions 2, 3, 4, 5, 8, E, and F
- The clipboard API (int 2k and func 17 commands)
- V*x*Ds

Win16-Based Applications

The environment that Windows 2000 Professional provides for Win16-based applications is similar to the enhanced-mode environment in Windows 3.1. Most Win16-based applications work well in Windows 2000 Professional. The exceptions are the same as for MS-DOS applications: task-switching APIs, block-mode device drivers, etc. Note that Windows 2000 Professional supports enhanced-mode applications on an Intel-compatible computer and, on a non–Intel-compatible computer, the operating system emulates the Intel 40486 instruction set. This allows many Win16-based applications to run on RISC-based computers.

PART V

LOWER COST
OF OWNERSHIP

CHAPTER EIGHTEEN

Easier Deployment

Without deployment tools, rolling out a new operating system is costly for big organizations. Administrators must manually preinstall the operating system and productivity applications on new computers before shipping them to users. Upgrading or installing an operating system on existing computers requires support staff to visit each computer, or to educate users about how to install and configure their own computers, leaving the organization at the mercy of users with differing capabilities. None of these circumstances is desirable, as they cost the organization big bucks.

Microsoft Windows 2000 Professional saves organizations money by automating the deployment process—a key step toward reducing total cost of ownership. Administrators can install the operating system on multiple computers with little or no user intervention. However, automating the setup process is only one step in the overall deployment process. Organizations must create a carefully thought-out deployment plan and then follow through on that plan. Microsoft publishes excellent deployment planning guides to help organizations be successful: *http://www.microsoft.com/ntworkstation/deployment/deployment*. Aside from saving money, automating the deployment process keeps people focused on their jobs and removes barriers to taking advantage of more-advanced technologies such as Windows 2000 Professional.

This chapter describes the three primary methods organizations can use to automate the setup process. First, the unattended installation process automatically installs Windows 2000 Professional on numerous computers while easily supporting many different hardware configurations. Second, disk image replication provides a way to quickly distribute already-working configurations to computers that have similar hardware. Third, the Remote Installation Service (RIS) allows predetermined configurations to be installed on multiple clients with varying hardware in a tightly controlled and secure manner. Note that this chapter does not describe the setup program, and it does not describe how to install the operating system on an individual computer. For more information on those topics, see Chapter 3, "Setup Guide."

Unattended Installation

Unattended installation allows administrators to totally or partially automate the process of installing Windows 2000 Professional on individual computers. The setup program uses a script called an answer file, which provides answers for questions that it would normally ask users. Installation is automatic and supports many different hardware configurations throughout the organization. Windows 2000 Professional provides the Setup Manager Wizard that administrators can use to generate answer files (see Figure 18-1).

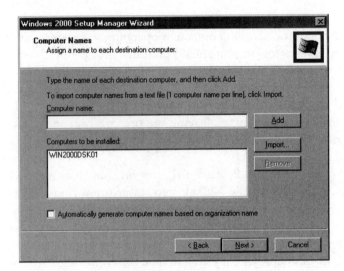

Figure 18-1
The Setup Manager Wizard.

NOTE: Answer files aren't just useful for deploying Windows 2000 Professional to large numbers of users. They're also the best way to create an unattended installation for a single computer. That is, you can use the Setup Manager Wizard to create an answer file; then, you can start the setup program with the answer file, walk away from the computer, and return after the setup program finishes installing the operating system. Also, if you're responsible for evaluating Windows 2000 Professional and find yourself installing the operating system repeatedly, an answer file can save you significant amounts of time.

Answer Files

An answer file contains multiple sections that describe the installation requirements. Unattend.txt is the typical filename of an answer file. It tells the setup
program how to interact with the distribution files and folders. More importantly, an answer file supplies answers for questions that the setup program
normally asks the user, allowing users to install Windows 2000 Professional
completely hands-free. The following script listing shows a complete answer
file that provides enough information for Windows 2000 Professional to be installed with no user intervention. The script specifies the name of the computer
(WIN2000DSK01), the display color depth and resolution, and the components
required to connect to the network:

```
;SetupMgrTag
[Unattended]
    UnattendMode=FullUnattended
    OemPreinstall=No
    TargetPath=Windows

[GuiUnattended]
    AdminPassword=password
    TimeZone=20

[UserData]
    ProductID=111111-111111-111111-111111-111111
    FullName="Jerry Honeycutt"
    OrgName="Jerry Honeycutt"
    ComputerName=WIN2000DSK01

[Display]
    BitsPerPel=16
    Xresolution=800
    YResolution=600
    Vrefresh=72

[LicenseFilePrintData]

[TapiLocation]
    AreaCode=972

[RegionalSettings]

[OEM_Ads]
```

```
[GuiRunOnce]
    Command0="rundll32 printui.dll,PrintUIEntry /in /n \\SRV\LJ

[Identification]
    JoinDomain=CAMELOT
    CreateComputerAccountInDomain=Yes
    DomainAdmin=Administrator
    DomainAdminPassword=password

[Networking]
    InstallDefaultComponents=No

[NetAdapters]
    Adapter1=params.Adapter1

[params.Adapter1]
    INFID=*

[NetClients]
    MS_MSClient=params.MS_MSClient

[params.MS_MSClient]
    RPCSupportForBanyan=No

[NetServices]
    MS_SERVER=params.MS_SERVER

[params.MS_SERVER]

[NetProtocols]
    MS_TCPIP=params.MS_TCPIP

[params.MS_TCPIP]
    DNS=Yes
    EnableLMHosts=Yes
    AdapterSections=params.MS_TCPIP.Adapter1

[params.MS_TCPIP.Adapter1]
    SpecificTo=Adapter1
    DHCP=Yes
    WINS=Yes
    WinsServerList=192.168.0.1
    NetBIOSOptions=0
```

The Setup Manager Wizard (setupmgr.exe) provides a graphical user interface (GUI) that makes creating answer files easy. It's available on the Windows 2000 Professional CD-ROM. The Setup Manager Wizard creates two files—an answer file called Unattend.txt and a batch file that automatically launches the setup program with the answer file. The batch file sets the AnswerFile environment variable to the location of the answer file and the SetupFiles environment variable to the location of the Windows 2000 Professional source files; then, it launches the setup program with the answer file as a command line argument.

While the simple way to create an answer file is to use the Setup Manager Wizard, you, as a network administrator, can also create answer files manually. Use a basic text editor—perhaps Notepad—and save the answer file as Unattend.txt (you can use any filename, but Unattend.txt is the norm). Alternatively, you can edit one of the sample answer files found on the Windows 2000 Professional CD-ROM. The file Unattend.txt contains comprehensive information about the contents of an answer file, including each section and each parameter. With this documentation, you can create answer files that are far more complex than those you can create using the Setup Manager Wizard.

Distribution Folders

For users to install Windows 2000 Professional using an answer file, network administrators must provide the source files and the Unattend.txt file for the users. Network administrators can distribute both of these items in a number of ways. First, administrators can create a distribution point on the network; then, copy the Windows 2000 Professional source files, the Unattend.txt file, and the batch file to the network share. Administrators can direct users to start the setup process themselves by e-mailing instructions to users, or they can make installation automatic by starting the setup program from users' logon scripts.

Second, you—as a network administrator—can distribute Windows 2000 Professional on a CD-ROM. Provide users with a retail copy of the Windows 2000 Professional CD-ROM, then provide them with the answer file. You can distribute the answer file on a bootable floppy disk that automatically starts the setup process, in an e-mail message that contains the script as an attachment, or by any other method. Alternatively, you can burn a CD-ROM that contains the Windows 2000 Professional source files along with the answer file. Ideally, the CD-ROM would be bootable so users could install the operating system by inserting the disc in the drive and restarting their computers. Otherwise, you can place a batch file on the CD-ROM to start the setup process. Note that you can also distribute Unattend.txt on a floppy disk and allow users to use that file with the Windows 2000 Professional CD-ROM.

If you, as a network administrator, are using a custom CD-ROM or a network distribution point to distribute Windows 2000 Professional, you must stick with the folder hierarchy that Microsoft recommends. On the network share, create a folder called i386 for the *x*86-based source files or—if the installation is for a Compaq Alpha computer—a folder called Alpha for Alpha-based source files. Copy the contents of a given folder from the Windows 2000 Professional CD-ROM to a folder with the same name on the network share. For example, copy i386 from the CD-ROM to i386 on the network share. The setup program looks for the following additional subfolders as well:

- **i386\OEM** Contains additional files required to complete pre-installation. The setup program copies files from this folder to the temporary folder that it creates during the text-mode portion of the process. This allows administrators to provide folders, files, and tools required for the automated installation process. This folder can also include a file called Cmdlines.txt, which contains commands that the setup program will run during the GUI portion of setup.

- **i386\OEM\textmode** Contains hardware-dependent files that the setup loader and setup program install during the text-mode portion of the setup process. This folder can include OEM hardware abstraction layers (HALs) as well as SCSI, keyboard, video, pointing, and other device drivers. A file called Txtsetup.oem indicates the components that the setup program will load and install. Additionally, the OEMBootFiles section of the Unattend.txt file can indicate components in this folder that the setup program should install.

- **i386\$OEM$*drive letter*** Contains a folder structure that the text-mode portion of the setup process copies to the root of the corresponding drive on the target computer. The setup program copies files in i386\$OEM$\C to the root of drive C, for example, and it copies files in i386\$OEM$\D\Example to the Example folder on drive D.

- **i386\$OEM$\$1** Similar in purpose to the Systemdrive environment variable. The setup program uses this folder to rearrange drive letters without creating errors in applications that point to hard-coded drive letters.

When installing from MS-DOS or Windows 3.1, files in the OEM folder—and in its subfolders—must use 8.3 (8 characters for the name, 3 characters for the extension) filenames. If administrators want to use long filenames, they can place a file called $$Rename.txt in a folder that indicates new names for some or all of the files in that folder; then, the setup program will rename those files when it copies them to the target computer. For example, an entry in $$Rename.txt that looks like *myfile.txt="This Is My File.txt"* will copy myfile.txt from the OEM folder to the target computer, but it will name the file This Is My File.txt on the target computer.

Deployment

The Setup Manager Wizard creates a batch file that automatically launches the setup program with the answer file as a command line parameter. The command line in this batch file has the following format:

```
Winnt[32] /unattend:answerfile /s:source [/syspart:targetdrive]
```

The /unattend command line option indicates the path to the answer file. The /s command line option indicates the path to the Windows 2000 Professional source files. In both cases, the path can be on the local computer or it can be a Uniform Naming Convention (UNC) path to a network share. The /syspart command line option copies boot and temporary files to the target drive and marks that drive as active. Note that this command line option is only useful for Winnt32.exe (not Winnt.exe), and only if the administrator intends to place the image on a target drive and then insert that drive into another computer as the primary drive. For more information about the setup program—particularly the command line options available for Winnt.exe and Winnt32.exe—see Chapter 3, "Setup Guide."

Disk Image Replication

Disk image replication is the process of duplicating a configuration on multiple computers, as illustrated in Figure 18-2 on page 341. Administrators install Windows 2000 Professional on a master computer, and use the System Preparation utility to prepare the hard disk for duplication. They can transfer the disk image to multiple target computers in a variety of ways, including duplicating the disk, distributing the image on a network share, creating a bootable CD-ROM, or using removable storage such as high-capacity tapes. Disk image replication dramatically reduces deployment time and is quickly becoming the most powerful way to set up new computers and to upgrade existing computers:

- **Comprehensive** Disk image replication is the only method that covers all key aspects of the computer's configuration, including the operating system, service packs, applications, and device and desktop settings.

- **Easy to deploy** Disk image replication is one of the easiest methods of deployment. Creating a reference system is easy, requiring no knowledge beyond that of installing the operating system, installing applications, and configuring the system.

- **Quick to install** Disk image replication is generally one of the fastest methods for deploying a standard desktop. Administrators can set up new computers in as little as five to fifteen minutes per desktop, after they create the distribution media.

- **Reduces costs** Disk image replication reduces calls to the help desk and ultimately reduces the total cost of ownership. Administrators can thoroughly test a configuration before deploying it. The help desk knows how each computer is configured so troubleshooting is easier, and the organization can proactively fix known problems on other computers that are built from the same image.

Disk image replication has limitations, however. The process only works with computers that have very similar hardware. For example, a disk image prepared on a computer with an older system board isn't likely to work well on a computer with a newer system board. This limitation keeps businesses with many different hardware configurations from using disk image replication, and it's a good argument for standardizing hardware configurations throughout an organization. Additionally, disk image replication might duplicate user-specific settings from the reference system to the target computer. For example, replicating an e-mail profile from the reference system causes all users to end up with the same e-mail account.

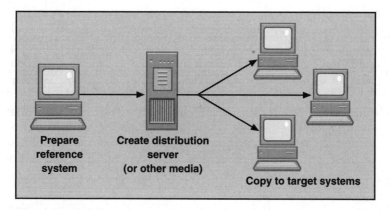

Figure 18-2
The disk replication process.

Availability

The tool that administrators use to prepare a disk for replication is called the System Preparation tool. Microsoft does not make the System Preparation tool available to customers who don't have a volume licensing agreement. However, it is available free to the following types of customers:

- **Microsoft Select** Business, government, and educational customers with more than 1000 desktops who are members of the Microsoft Select licensing program

- **Enterprise agreement** Select customers who use Microsoft's platform of products and who have committed to a fixed number of desktop licenses for a three-year period

- **Microsoft Open License Program (MOLP)** Small and medium-sized businesses, government, and educational organizations with 5 to 1000 desktops who participate in this simple volume-licensing solution

- **Microsoft Solution Providers** Independent Microsoft Certified Solution Providers licensed to use the System Preparation tool

For more information about the availability of the System Preparation tool, see *http://www.microsoft.com/ntworkstation/deployment/deployment.*

Disk Image Preparation

The *reference system* is the computer whose hard disk will be replicated. To prepare the reference system, install Windows 2000 Professional on it, including any service packs as necessary. Then, customize the desktop, implementing any management customizations such as preventing access to certain Control Panel icons or creating persistent network connections. Install the standard applications, templates, macros, and other tools that users require to do their jobs. Last, configure the computer to run any post-installation scripts or programs that are needed for the first time a user logs on to the operating system. For more information about preparing the reference system, see the documentation that comes with the System Preparation tool.

After the reference system is ready, network administrators use the System Preparation tool to prepare the disk image for duplication. The System Preparation tool's command has the following format:

```
Sysprep.exe [/quiet] [/nosidgen] [/pnp]
```

/quiet	Runs Sysprep.exe without displaying any messages.
/nosidgen	Runs Sysprep.exe without generating a new security identifier (SID). Use this option if you aren't going to clone the computer. This option is useful for systems that you're preparing for end users, so they can customize their systems.
/pnp	Forces a Plug and Play refresh on reboot, causing Plug and Play to redetect adapter cards such as network, modem, and video adapters.
/reboot	Automatically reboots the computer after running.

Disk Image Distribution

The following list describes how administrators can distribute the disk image after creating it:

- **Bootable CD-ROM**   This is the easiest method for users, and it doesn't gobble up network bandwidth. It does require administrators to distribute a physical disk.

- **Network distribution point**   Administrators can make the disk image available on a network share, but users must use a boot floppy to gain access to the network, and network bandwidth might suffer when too many users install at one time.

■ **Hard disk replication**   A variety of vendors provide disk duplication utilities that you can use to physically duplicate the contents of one hard disk onto another. Table 18-1 lists some of the most popular vendors and their Web sites.

Vendor	URL
Altiris (formerly KeyLabs)	*http://www.altiris.com*
Micro House International	*http://www.microhouse.com*
PowerQuest	*http://www.powerquest.com*
Symantec	*http://www.symantec.com*

Table 18-1
Utilities for duplicating a disk image.

The first time users start a computer using a hard disk prepared by the System Preparation tool, or when they install the disk image from the network or a CD-ROM, a minisetup program runs. This minisetup program finalizes the computer's configuration by prompting the user for information such as name, administrator password, and networking configuration; creates a unique security identifier (SID) for the computer; and adds the computer to the network domain. You can create an answer file, similar to Unattend.txt, to script the minisetup program. Once the minisetup program finishes configuring the computer, it reboots the computer and the user is ready to log on. The entire process can take as little as three to five minutes.

Remote Installation

The Remote Installation Service (RIS) ships with Microsoft Windows 2000 Server. It allows client computers to install Windows 2000 Professional from a special server called an RIS server. RIS uses remote-boot technology and server-based software, and it supports a variety of installation methods (prepared disk images, answer files, etc.), automatic client computer naming policies, and maintenance and troubleshooting tools. To better understand RIS, you should familiarize yourself with its terminology:

■ **RIS server**   A Windows 2000 Server that has RIS installed and configured to respond to remote-boot–enabled client computers.

■ **Pre-Boot Execution Environment (PXE)**   A DHCP-based (Dynamic Host Configuration Protocol) remote-boot technology that client computers use to remotely install the operating system from an RIS server.

■ **Boot ROM**   A BIOS-oriented chip on a network interface card that's responsible for initiating the sequence required to boot the client computer remotely.

■ **RIS client**   A NetPC or a computer with a boot ROM that adheres to the PXE specification—or any computer with a network card that the RIS boot floppy supports (see Table 18-2 later in this chapter).

Remote Installation Service

RIS uses PXE. A boot ROM or an RIS boot floppy initiates the network service boot. Then, the network service boot causes the client computer to receive an IP address through DHCP and it downloads the Client Installation Wizard. Following that, the Client Installation Wizard prompts the user to log on and provides the user with a menu offering various operating system options customized for that user.

Network administrators use the Remote Installation Preparation Wizard to prepare a disk image for RIS. To do so, they use a process similar to the System Preparation tool. Administrators prepare an existing computer running Windows 2000 Professional by installing the applications users require and by customizing the desktop. Administrators can configure the computer in a variety of ways, including specifying policies, setting colors, specifying a background bitmap, and disabling games. The Remote Installation Preparation Wizard configures the computer to a generic state, removing anything unique to the client computer such as its unique SID, computer name, and hardware settings in the registry. Doing so allows clients with different hardware configurations to use the same image. Last, administrators provide a friendly description of the image, and users see that description in the Client Installation Wizard.

Figure 18-3 shows the components used by RIS. RIS relies on Domain Name System (DNS) for locating the directory service and client computer accounts. It requires a DHCP server, which client computers use to get their IP addresses before contacting RIS. It also requires Active Directory for locating RIS clients. Installing RIS on the server causes the following additional services to start:

- **Boot Information Negotiations Layer (BINL)**   Listens for client computers' remote installation requests and manages RIS

- **Trivial File Transfer Protocol (TFTP)**   Used by RIS to download the initial files required to begin the remote installation process

- **Single Instance Store (SIS)**   Reduces the storage requirements of RIS by scanning the RIS volume for duplicate files and storing a single copy of each file in the SIS while leaving links in place of the original files

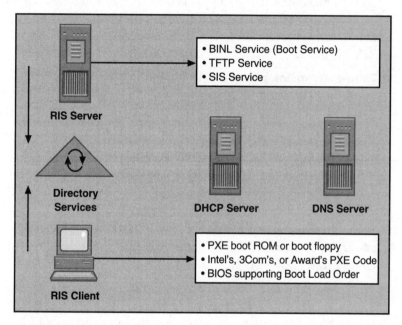

Figure 18-3
RIS components.

RIS Management Options

The following options are available for RIS administrators using the Microsoft Directory Services Manager snap-in:

- **Installation choices**   Administrators can set specific access permissions that guide users to the appropriate installation options.

■ **Automatic client computer naming format** Administrators can base computer names on the username or on the user's first and last name, or administrators can create a custom naming format specific to the organization.

■ **Active Directory location for computer accounts** Administrators can specify the default Active Directory location where all remotely installed client computer accounts are created during the setup process.

■ **Computer account pre-staging** Administrators can specify restrictions to make sure that RIS servers only service authorized computers on the network. They can specify computer names and default Active Directory locations, and which RIS servers will support which RIS clients.

■ **Third-party maintenance and troubleshooting tools** Administrators can provide access to third-party maintenance and troubleshooting tools. Examples include virus scanners, flash BIOS updates, and diagnostic tools.

■ **Additional operating system images** Administrators can add additional operating system versions or disk images to RIS servers. They can also add new installation templates to existing operating system images to provide more installation options.

■ **Remote configuration of RIS servers** Administrators can remotely configure RIS servers from Windows 2000 Professional, changing any configuration option.

■ **Rogue server prevention** Administrators can prevent unauthorized RIS servers from servicing client computers on the network by specifying which RIS servers can provide installations to remote-boot–enabled clients.

The Client Installation Wizard

When the boot ROM or RIS boot floppy starts the Client Installation Wizard, it presents four options to users:

■ **Automatic Setup** The easiest way to install Windows 2000 Professional, this option allows users to choose which image to install but doesn't prompt them for configuration settings during the setup process.

■ **Custom Setup**   This option allows network administrators to override the automatic computer naming process as well as the default location within Active Directory where the client computer accounts are created. It's most often used by help desk personnel to install a computer for someone else.

■ **Restart A Previous Setup Attempt**   This option restarts a failed installation.

■ **Maintenance And Troubleshooting**   Network administrators use this option to access third-party maintenance and troubleshooting tools, including flash BIOS updates and PC diagnostic tools. Note that RIS doesn't provide any of these tools.

The first option, Automatic Setup, is the option that users will use to install Windows 2000 Professional from the RIS server. Users choose which image or answer file they want to install, and the wizard requires no input from the user—not a single response. While users can choose the image that's most suitable for their role in the company, network administrators can limit the choices available to groups or individual users. Network administrators have additional controls available to them as well, including the ability to predefine an automatic machine-naming scheme and to specify the location within Active Directory where client computer accounts are created. This helps ensure that all computer accounts within the domain have appropriate names.

The requirements for a remote computer are similar for NetPC and non-NetPC computers. The recommended hardware requirements are the same as those you learned about in Chapter 2, "Meet the Windows Family." However, a NetPC computer must have a PXE DHCP-based boot ROM version .99c or greater. A non-NetPC computer must have a Peripheral Component Interconnect (PCI) Plug and Play network adapter with a PXE DHCP-based boot ROM version .99C or better. Table 18-2 on the following page lists a handful of network adapters that meet these requirements. The RIS boot floppy does not support Industry Standard Architecture (ISA), Extended Industry Standard Architecture (EISA), or Token Ring network adapter cards.

Vendor	Network Adapter
3Com Corporation	3C900 (Combo and TP0)
	3C900B (Combo, TPC, and TP0)
	3C905 (T4 and TX)
	3C905B (Combo, T4, and TX)
Advanced Micro Devices	AMD PC Net
	AMD PC Fast Net
Hewlett-Packard Corporation	HP DeskDirect 10/100 TX
Intel Corporation	Pro 10+
	Prop 100+
	Pro 100B
	E100B series
SMC Networks	SMC 8432
	SMC 9332
	SMC 9432
Compaq Corporation	NetFlex II
	NetFlex III

Table 18-2
RIS-compatible network adapters.

C H A P T E R   N I N E T E E N

Better Management Tools

Microsoft Windows 2000 Professional introduces a variety of management tools—most of which work on any type of network. The goal, of course, is to reduce the cost of owning and operating a set of computers. Tools that help organizations achieve this goal include Microsoft Management Console (MMC), Windows Management Instrumentation (WMI), and Security Templates.

Even though these and other Windows 2000 Professional management tools perform different tasks, they have a couple of things in common. They consolidate various administrative tasks in a single user interface so administrators no longer have to search for the right tool for a given job. They also add the power and flexibility that administrators require for doing the job their way. For example, MMC allows administrators to organize their tools by task, by schedule, or by any other criteria imaginable. The Security Templates snap-in allows administrators to build security templates, which they can apply or compare to a computer's security configuration.

This chapter describes many of the new Windows 2000 Professional management tools that work on any type of network. However, by using Windows 2000 Professional in combination with Microsoft Windows 2000 Server, organizations can realize greater benefits and lower costs. For more information about using Windows 2000 Professional with Windows 2000 Server, including a discussion of IntelliMirror, see Chapter 20, "Lower Total Cost of Ownership with Microsoft Windows 2000 Server." And for more information about these and other management tools, see *http://www.microsoft.com/management*.

Windows Update

Windows Update, shown in Figure 19-1on the following page, is an online extension of Windows 2000 Professional that helps keep computers current. Users can download enhancements such as device drivers, service packs, and new features that Windows Update selects to work with their computers. Users start Windows Update by choosing Windows Update from the Start menu. Then, they can choose to have Windows Update scan the computer and provide a list of enhancements that are specific to their computer's hardware and software configurations. For administrators who are concerned about users "doing their own thing," Windows Update allows administrators to maintain tight control of the update process:

- **Corporate IT catalog** Windows Update provides a searchable catalog for administrators. They can choose which downloads will be available to which users and download them to a server behind a firewall, making them available on the local network.

- **Disabling Windows Update** By manipulating group policies, administrators can remove the Windows Update icon from the Start menu, and prevent users from accessing the Windows Update Web site from anywhere within Windows 2000 Professional.

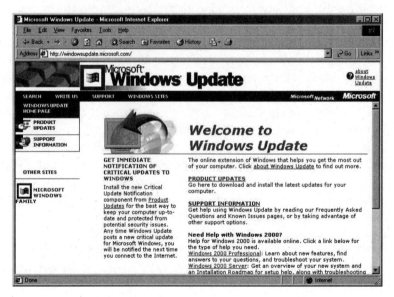

Figure 19-1
Windows Update.

Microsoft Management Console

Microsoft Management Console (MMC)—an extensible, common framework for management applications—does not supply any management behavior itself. Instead, it allows you to create consoles, which provide a common environment for snap-ins (sometimes called tools, plug-ins, etc.) that Microsoft and other independent software vendors (ISVs) develop using the Windows Software Development Kit (SDK). Snap-ins are ActiveX controls that provide the actual management behaviors, so administrators can create virtually any type of tool—and combine tools as they see fit—for use by other administrators and users. In short, MMC consoles are the management hosts, while snap-ins are the actual management tools.

MMC is the result of Microsoft's commitment to create better management tools. The goal was to simplify network administration through integration, delegation, task orientation, and user interface simplification—all of which are key problems for Microsoft's customers. The result—MMC—defines a common host for Microsoft's own administrative tools that also offers a generalized management framework to many ISVs. Going forward, MMC will be a key part of Microsoft's strategy for management tools. Most Microsoft development teams will use MMC to host future management applications for all versions of Windows as well as the Microsoft BackOffice family of products.

The initial release of MMC, included in Windows 2000 Professional, has the following goals:

- **Reduce total cost of ownership (TCO)** MMC allows network administrators to better organize their tools in a single user interface, delegate tasks, and simplify remote administration.

- **Facilitate task delegation** Administrators can group administrative tasks into composite tools and forward those tools to other administrators or subordinates for task completion.

- **Provide a single host for all management tools** While MMC doesn't replace existing management tools, it does allow administrators to package them as consoles so that they can access their tools from a single user interface.

As you just read, MMC does not replace existing management tools such as HP OpenView and IBM Tivoli Management Environment. MMC extends these tools by allowing administrators to package them as collections of snap-ins, which makes it possible to access all of the administrative management tools through a single user interface. In addition, existing management tools can communicate with MMC snap-ins. For example, a management tool can detect an event and send an alert to a snap-in; then, the administrator (or even the snap-in itself) can take appropriate action based upon the alert.

A Single User Interface

MMC is the primary management host for Windows 2000 Professional. It's a multiple-document–interface application that uses the operating system's Internet technologies extensively. MMC combines numerous client and server tools with a single user interface. For example, the tool with which administrators will be most familiar is called the Computer Management console. However, the operating system provides many other snap-ins, and ISVs can further extend MMC by writing their own snap-ins.

Administrators can create consoles that contain various snap-ins, and they can share those consoles with other administrators. For example, an administrator can create a console for basic workstation maintenance and then share that console with other administrators who are responsible for performing that task. In addition to creating consoles aligned with one-time tasks, administrators can create consoles for daily, weekly, and monthly tasks. The possibilities for organizing the tools that administrators use are endless.

The Computer Management Console

The Computer Management console consolidates a variety of other tools, such as Event Viewer, Device Manager, and Disk Manager. All of these tools are available with a single user interface, and network administrators can use them from any computer on the network. The Computer Management console has the following components, shown in Figure 19-2:

- **System Tools**   These tools are available on every computer running Windows 2000, including Professional and Server, and they include Local Users and Groups, System Information, Services, Group Policy, Shared Folders, Event Viewer, Device Manager, and other snap-ins.

- **Storage**   These tools include the Disk Management snap-in, which performs the same functions as Windows NT Workstation 4.0's Disk Manager utility.

■ **Server Applications and Services** These tools are optional or are only available in Windows 2000 Server. In Windows 2000 Professional, users see the Indexing Service and any optional services that they have installed.

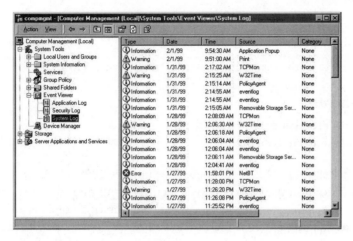

Figure 19-2
The Computer Management console.

Security Configuration Tool Set

Chapter 11, "Strongest Local and Network Security," described many of Windows 2000 Professional's excellent security features, all of which are built into the base operating system. A single sign-on allows users to access resources anywhere on the network. Security policies and account management, when used in conjunction with a network domain, provide flexible network configurations. The Encrypting File System allows users to protect their files from prying eyes. In the past, administrators and users configured all of these features using various graphical user interfaces. However, these user interfaces weren't centralized, which meant that an administrator might have to open many different tools to configure security on one computer.

The Security Configuration Tool Set speaks to the need for a single user interface for configuring security. It provides a framework for enterprise-level analysis and, more important, it reduces security-related administration costs by providing a single user interface where administrators can view, analyze, and adjust the computer's entire security configuration. Microsoft's goals for the Security Configuration Tool Set include allowing administrators to do the following:

- Configure security on one or more computers running Windows 2000

- Perform security analysis on one or more computers running Windows 2000

- Complete both tasks using a single user interface (MMC)

Tool Set Components

Windows 2000 Professional provides the following components as part of the Security Configuration Tool Set:

- **Setup Security** When users install Windows 2000 Professional, the setup program uses a predefined security configuration to set the computer's initial security. The initial configuration contains an initial security database, called the Local Computer Policy database. However, the setup program does not overwrite an existing security database when upgrading from Windows NT Workstation 4.0.

- **Security Configuration Service** This is the core engine of the Security Configuration Tool Set. It runs on every computer running Windows 2000 Professional, and it is responsible for all of the security configuration and analysis functionality.

- **Security Templates** Administrators use this MMC snap-in, shown in Figure 19-3, to define computer-specific security configurations, which the snap-in saves as INF files. Microsoft does not intend the Security Templates snap-in to replace the variety of system tools that address different portions of the computer's security. Rather, the Security Templates snap-in is designed to complement the system tools by providing a standard security template and by performing certain operations in the background. To learn more about this snap-in, see "Security Templates," later in this chapter.

- **Security Configuration and Analysis** Administrators use this MMC snap-in to import one or more saved security configurations to a security database. Importing a configuration builds a computer-specific security database that is a composite configuration. Administrators can apply the composite configuration to the computer or analyze the computer's current configuration against the composite.

■ **Security Settings extension to the Group Policy snap-in** This MMC snap-in extends the Group Policy snap-in. It allows administrators to define a security configuration as part of a Group Policy object. For more information about group policies, see Chapter 20, "Lower Total Cost of Ownership with Microsoft Windows 2000 Server."

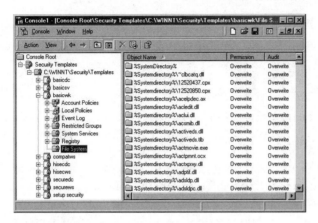

Figure 19-3
The Security Templates snap-in.

Security Templates

The Security Templates snap-in allows administrators to configure security at a macro level. That is, the snap-in allows them to define configuration settings and have Windows 2000 Professional implement those settings in the background. It groups security configuration tools in a central location—providing a uniform interface for the various tools—and automates them. Administrators no longer have to use many different user interfaces to monitor and adjust a computer's overall security configuration.

Security is a characteristic of the computer as a whole. That is, almost every operating system component is responsible for some aspect of security. Since administrators in the past had to examine many different user interfaces to analyze and configure the different aspects of security, questions such as "Is the computer secure?" were very difficult to answer. By providing a single user interface for configuring the computer's security, the Security Templates snap-in becomes a resource for answering those types of questions. For example, the snap-in allows administrators to configure and analyze all of the following:

■ **System security policies** Set policies that control access to the computer (password policies), object security, audit settings, and domain policies

- ▣ **User accounts** Assign group memberships, privileges, and user rights

- ▣ **System services** Configure the different services that run on the computer, including network transport services such as TCP/IP, NetBIOS, File Sharing, and others

- ▣ **System registry** Set security for the system registry

- ▣ **System store** Set security for elements of the local file system, such as files and folders

- ▣ **Directory security** Manage security of objects in Active Directory

The Security Templates snap-in also allows administrators to define templates that include settings for security attributes for the areas in the list above. Administrators can then apply those templates to the computer, configuring its security. Administrators can also perform security analysis on the computer using the templates as recommended configurations. Templates are text-based INF files that specify configuration information in different sections; the Security Templates snap-in's configuration engine parses the information in each of those sections. The snap-in includes a variety of predefined templates, but the architecture is flexible enough that administrators can create custom templates and add new sections to existing templates as required.

The Security Templates snap-in is easy to learn and use, contributing to an organization's lower TCO. It contains no complicated options, using a simple graphical user interface to define configuration templates and view security analysis data. In addition to an easy user interface, the Security Templates snap-in contains a command-line utility that allows administrators to perform configuration and analysis as part of a script (see "Windows Scripting Host," later in this chapter). Between the two user interfaces—graphical and command-line—the Security Templates snap-in easily fits into any administration model.

Secondary Logon Service

Until now, one of the biggest problems with respect to security has been that administrators always log on to the Administrator account and do privileged as well as unprivileged operations within the same logon session. This is primarily because it is far more convenient to log on once and do all the operations than to have to constantly log on and off based on the task being performed. This makes Windows 2000 Professional highly susceptible to "Trojan horse" attacks. The simple act of running Microsoft Internet Explorer and accessing a non-trusted Web site can be extremely damaging to the system if it's done within the administrative context. The Web page may have Trojan code that will get downloaded to the system and will execute in the administrative context; therefore it will be able to do such things as reformat the hard disk, delete all files, and create a new user with administrative access.

Secondary logon capability in Windows 2000 Professional addresses this problem by providing a mechanism to launch applications in different security contexts without the administrator having to log off. This capability is provided using the Secondary Logon Service. This service allows administrators to always log on to a nonadministrative account and still be able to perform administrative tasks by invoking trusted administrative applications in an administrative context. This requires system administrators to have two accounts: an ordinary user account, which is their own, and an administrative user account, which may be different for each administrator or shared among administrators.

Service Pack Integration

Service packs deliver updates (fixes and sometimes new features) to the originally released operating system. With Windows NT Workstation 4.0, this caused problems for administrators managing large numbers of workstations. There was no integration between the operating system and the service packs. The lack of integration caused significant problems because, when the system state was changed—for instance, when Remote Access Service (RAS) was installed—the entire service pack had to be reapplied. The operating system was not aware that a service pack had been applied, so a component such as RAS would be installed using the old files from the CD-ROM and not the files from the service pack. Other problems were common as well, and they constituted a significant impediment to the full deployment and use of service packs by corporations, original equipment manufacturers (OEMs), and end users.

Windows 2000 Professional provides the following two solutions to the problems that most organizations had with Windows NT Workstation 4.0 service packs:

- **Slipstreaming** A service pack is fully integrated with an updated version of the Windows 2000 Professional CD-ROM or network distribution share. The result of this is that any installations done from the CD-ROM or from the share automatically contain the appropriate files from the service pack, without anyone having to manually apply the service pack after first installing Windows 2000 Professional. Slipstreaming can be done either by Microsoft when shipping CD-ROMs or by a corporation wanting to "slipstream" their distribution share.

■ **Post-setup installation of a service pack** A service pack is installed on an existing Windows 2000 system. Once the service pack is installed, if the user changes the system state (for instance, adds RAS), Windows 2000 Professional will automatically install the correct files, whether those files are on the Windows 2000 installation CD-ROM or on the service pack media. This eliminates the administrative burden of constantly having to reinstall service packs.

The Repair Command Console

With Windows NT Workstation 4.0, administrators complained that there was no Microsoft-sanctioned way to access an NTFS file system volume unless the operating system had been started. However, in some cases, starting the operating system was impossible if a Windows NT Workstation 4.0 system file was corrupted or missing. The only solution in this case was either to do a parallel install of Windows NT or to run the repair process, both of which were time-consuming. Because of this difficulty, administrators often installed Windows NT Workstation 4.0 on a FAT partition, because they could always access the volume using an MS-DOS floppy disk.

With Windows 2000 Professional, administrators are able to start a command console that can read and write to NTFS volumes using the three Windows 2000 Professional boot floppies. This allows administrators to copy files, start and stop services, and repair the system in a very granular way. Functionality is also provided to repair the MBR/Boot sector, and to partition and format volumes. This console (known as the Repair Command Console) also implements security so unauthorized users cannot access NTFS volumes.

The Repair Command Console is integrated into Windows 2000 Professional text mode and can be started in the following ways:

1. Administrators can press F10 after starting the three Windows 2000 Professional boot disks or the Windows NT CD-ROM to the Welcome screen; alternatively, they can select the Repair Command Console from the Repair options.

2. Winnt32.exe will have a /cmdcons switch that will add an entry to the OS Loader for the console and copy the files (the Windows NT text-mode setup files) required to start the console. In this case, when the user starts the console, the system will boot straight to the console (the user does not need to press F10).

Windows Management Instrumentation (WMI)

Windows 2000 Professional includes WMI, which is a component based on the Desktop Management Task Force's Web-Based Enterprise Management (WBEM) standard. WMI, a kernel-level instrumentation technology, provides a common way for hardware, applications, and the operating system to report events. The WMI technology provides the following:

- Ability to monitor, command, and control any entity through a common, unifying set of interfaces, regardless of the underlying instrumentation mechanism.

- An application programming interface (API) that programmers can use to provide and access management information in their applications.

- Interoperability with other Windows management services. This approach simplifies developers' efforts to create integrated and well-built management solutions.

- A flexible architecture that allows vendors to extend the information model to cover managed objects such as devices and applications by writing code modules called providers (also called WBEM providers). Providers are the means to connect WMI with management information sources.

- Extensions to the Win32 driver model (WDM) to capture instrumentation data and events from device drivers and kernel-side components.

- A powerful event mechanism that allows management events to be asserted and associated with other management information. These notifications can also be forwarded to local or remote management applications.

- Device configuration by management applications. For example, a management application might need to reconfigure devices after receiving an event notification.

- A rich query language that enables detailed queries of the information model.

- A scriptable API that developers and administrators can use to create management applications. You'll learn about the Windows Scripting Host (WSH) later in this chapter.

WMI publishes information, configures device settings, and supplies event notifications from device drivers. Even though WMI is part of WDM, other types of drivers—such as Small Computer System Interface (SCSI) and network driver interface specification (NDIS)—can use it. The following list describes the types of information that WMI makes available to management applications:

- **Published data**   Windows 2000 Professional provides a standard set of WMI data for its port and class drivers.

- **Custom data**   OEMs and independent hardware vendors (IHVs) provide data through driver extensions.

- **Secure data**   Windows 2000 Professional security descriptors provide secure data for a designated use.

- **Expensive data**   Collecting some data can adversely impact a driver's performance, and WMI only collects this information when an application specifically requests it.

- **Event notifications**   Event notifications are a key feature of WMI. They allow drivers to detect hardware events and pass them to WMI for corrective action. For example, a disk driver that detects an unusually high number of errors can send an event notification to a disk management utility.

Windows Scripting Host (WSH)

WSH adds simple, powerful, and flexible scripting to Windows 2000 Professional. Before WSH, the only native scripting language supported by the Windows operating system was the MS-DOS command language in batch files. Although it is fast and small, MS-DOS has limited features as compared to WSH. WSH enables administrators to create more-advanced scripts that automate a variety of tasks such as configuring a user's computer and making network connections.

WSH, a language-independent scripting host for 32-bit versions of Windows, enables users to execute scripts directly on the desktop or in a command console (see Figure 19-4). Windows 2000 Professional provides two scripting engines with WSH: Visual Basic Scripting Edition (VBScript) and JavaScript. Microsoft anticipates that ISVs will provide scripting engines for additional languages such as Perl, REXX, TCL, and Python.

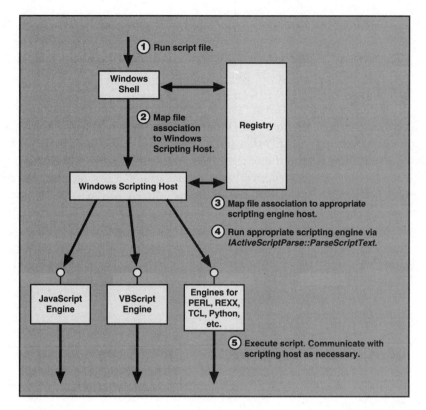

Figure 19-4
Windows Scripting Host architecture.

Administrators don't have to embed scripts in HTML documents in order for users to run them; instead, users run scripts directly from the desktop by double-clicking the script file icon or by typing the name of the script at the command prompt. WSH is ideal for noninteractive scripting requirements (including logon scripting and administrative scripting) as well as for interactive scripting requirements. WSH provides two different scripting hosts. The Windows-based scripting host is Wscript.exe, and it runs scripts that users launch from the desktop. The MS-DOS–based scripting host is Cscript.exe.

In addition to WSH, Microsoft provides two hosts for running scripts:

- ■ **Microsoft Internet Explorer** Developers use scripts to create dynamic Web pages. Scripts interact with the Web page to change its content in response to users' actions.

■ **Internet Information Services (IIS)**   Developers use scripts on Active Server Pages to choose the content that the server feeds to the Web browser. Active Server Pages and scripts allow developers to link Web pages to legacy applications and databases.

Administrators can create scripts at any level of complexity. Each scripting engine provides the statements that you'd expect to find in that language—*for* loops, *if* statements, and other statements. And WSH's object model provides comprehensive access to the operating system. Scripts can access the file system and the registry. They can control applications using COM; for example, administrators can create a script that opens a monthly status report in a word processor, updates links to various spreadsheets, and then e-mails the document to a manager. Administrators can also automate tedious tasks using WSH, including customizing users' environments after installation, and they can perform more-advanced logon script processing.

Lower Total Cost of Ownership with Microsoft Windows 2000 Server

Microsoft Windows 2000 Professional adds important management capabilities that enable organizations to reduce the cost of owning and operating their computers. Features such as Windows Management Instrumentation (WMI), Microsoft Management Console (MMC), and Security Templates make the operating system easier to manage in any networking environment.

However, combining Windows 2000 Professional with Microsoft Windows 2000 Server provides additional capabilities that make centralized change and configuration management flexible and easy to implement. Users get a reliable computing environment, while organizations have a hands-off way to keep users' computers running well. The bottom line is that using Windows 2000 Professional in a homogenous Windows 2000 network reduces an organization's total cost of ownership (TCO).

The capabilities that help organizations reduce TCO stem mostly from Windows 2000's IntelliMirror component. The idea of mirroring a file is to maintain synchronized copies of that file on the server computer and the client computer. IntelliMirror is capable of mirroring documents, security settings, configuration settings, and applications. Additional capabilities reinforce the organization's goal of reducing costs. Two technologies, both of which I present in this chapter, are key components used by IntelliMirror—these are Active Directory and Group Policy. While this chapter provides an overview of these features, *Introducing Microsoft Windows 2000 Server* (Microsoft Press, 1999) provides many more details. Also, for more information, see *http://www.microsoft.com/windows*.

Active Directory

Active Directory directory service is certainly the Windows 2000 Server feature that industry insiders discuss most. It provides a simple, centralized location for administering and managing large Windows 2000 networks, and it provides key capabilities that help organizations manage their infrastructures. Network administrators use it to manage user accounts, to manage printers, and to locate resources in a distributed computing environment. Capabilities include a hierarchical view of the directory, extensibility, scalability, distributed security, and multimaster replication. While Active Directory makes managing networks easier for administrators, it also makes accessing network resources easier for users. To meet customer requirements, Microsoft designed Active Directory to deliver value in all of the following roles:

- **User and network resource management**   By providing a scalable, hierarchical information repository to simplify tasks such as deploying applications, delegating administrative privileges, and locating network resources such as printers and file shares.

- **Security authentication and authorization services**   By providing flexible authentication and consistent authorization services that offer a new level of data protection while minimizing barriers to doing business over the Internet.

- **Directory consolidation**   By reducing the number of directories companies need. This improves information sharing and enables common management of users, computers, applications, and directory-enabled devices. For example, Active Directory enables companies to manage Windows 2000 users and Exchange mailbox information in one place.

- **Directory-enabled infrastructure**   By enabling elements such as networking devices and Microsoft's Distributed file system (Dfs) to offer enhanced quality of service and greater functionality through access to information about users (and their roles), machines, network elements, and management policies stored in the directory.

- **Directory-enabled applications**   By enabling simplified application deployment, simplified configuration and management, greater functionality, and synergy with other directory-enabled components of the network computing environment.

Traditional directory services are tools for organizing, managing, and locating resources on the network. Objects that a directory service manages include printers, documents, e-mail addresses, databases, user accounts, distributed components, and other resources. In short, traditional directory services are similar to a telephone book's white pages, which map inputs (names) to outputs (phone numbers). Directory services also function as yellow pages. For example, users can ask to see a list of all the printers on the network. However, Active Directory goes far beyond traditional directory services by providing the following features:

- **Scalability without complexity** Active Directory scales to millions of objects per partition, and it uses indexing technology and advanced replication techniques to speed performance.

- **Built around Internet standards** Active Directory provides access to all features through the Lightweight Directory Access Protocol (LDAP), and it uses a DNS-based namespace to simplify access in an Internet environment.

- **Flexible, simple security model** Active Directory supports multiple authentication protocols such as Kerberos, X.509 certificates, and Smart Cards, and it provides a security group model that works well in highly distributed environments.

- **Facilitates directory consolidation** Active Directory provides synchronization support through LDAP-based interfaces and scales to accommodate application-specific directory consolidation requirements. Additionally, leading interoperability and meta-directory vendors have announced that they will provide support in their products for Active Directory.

- **Provides a comprehensive feature set and development environment** Active Directory has attracted leading vendors such as SAP, Baan, Cisco, 3COM, and many more to ensure that Active Directory will be supported by the applications that customers already use.

Active Directory supports multiple indexes for fast retrieval and stores sparse objects (objects with many empty properties) efficiently. Active Directory supports multiple stores, and it can hold more than 10 million objects in each store—offering unmatched scalability while maintaining a simple hierarchical structure for easy administration. When combined with Dfs, Active Directory brings networks closer to the vision of a single global namespace.

Users don't experience Active Directory the same way that administrators experience it. For users, Active Directory works in the background, making it easier to find the computers, printers, and other network resources they want to use. Users experience Active Directory when they search for resources using Windows Explorer's Search bar or when they browse My Network Places. Users also unknowingly encounter Active Directory when they search for a printer in the Add Printers dialog box. For more information about searching the network, see Chapter 4, "Simpler User Interface." For more information about searching the network for printers, see Chapter 8, "More Imaging and Printing Capabilities."

Group Policies

Active Directory enables network administrators to create group policies. Network administrators use group policies to define almost anything about users' computing environments, including access to applications and resources, privileges, desktop settings, password policies, and other settings. The Group Policy snap-in, shown in Figure 20-1, provides a user interface for editing these policies. The Group Policy snap-in includes the following sections:

- **Account Policies**   Configure policies that apply to user accounts (local and domain) including password policies, account lockout policies, and the new Kerberos policy.

- **Local Policies**   Configure auditing policies, user rights, and various security options for computers running Windows 2000 Professional.

- **IP Security Policies**   Configure security policies for IP (Internet Protocol) traffic.

- **Public Key Policies**   Configure encrypted data recovery agents for the Encrypting File System (see Chapter 11, "Strongest Local and Network Security"), domain-wide root certificate authorities, trusted certificate authorities, etc.

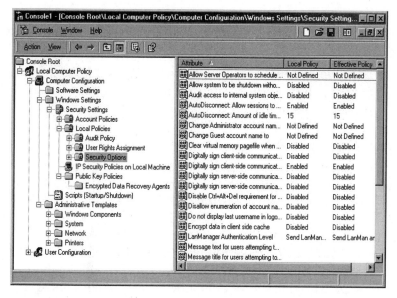

Figure 20-1
The Group Policy snap-in.

IntelliMirror

Windows 2000 Professional and Windows 2000 Server are a powerful combination. Together, they provide a whole new class of management capabilities, many of which were inconceivable just a few short years ago. IntelliMirror—the new name for these capabilities—provides the following benefits:

- **Reduced TCO** Using technologies such as Active Directory and Group Policy, IntelliMirror provides centralized, policy-based administration for the organization.

- **The ability to roam** IntelliMirror supports users who roam from computer to computer on the network. Users' documents, settings, and applications are always available.

- **Replaceable computers** The Remote Installation Service (RIS), enables a user to connect a computer to a server and install Windows

2000 Professional. IntelliMirror enhances this capability by restoring the user's documents, settings, and applications; thus, computers are quickly and easily replaced.

■ **Lifecycle management** IntelliMirror helps administrators manage each step in the software lifecycle, including installation, upgrades, repairs, and removal.

User Settings Management

The combination of Windows 2000 Professional and Windows 2000 Server provides users with a familiar computing environment wherever they log on to the network. User settings such as items on the Start menu, Favorites, desktop settings (wallpaper, fonts, colors, etc.), and printer paths follow users whether they're offline or using another computer that's connected to the network. This combination also allows network administrators to define specific computing environments for users and computers without actually visiting those desktops. In addition to managing software and documents, administrators can use the Group Policy snap-in, described earlier in this chapter, to define settings for individual users and groups of users. The following list provides a few examples:

■ **Desktop preferences** Control virtually anything related to the operating system's graphical user interface (GUI). They can also specify which settings will follow users to different computers; which settings users can change; preferences for specific applications; and scripts to run during logon, logoff, startup, and shutdown.

■ **Security settings** Determine what resources users or computers can access by applying access control lists (ACLs) to files and folders.

■ **Delegated administrative privileges** Allow administrative privileges to be assigned to other users, specifying who can set permissions on files and folders, who can publish items to the Active Directory database, and who can create new groups.

Document Management

IntelliMirror gives administrators a significantly easier and more flexible way to manage user data. Using Dfs, for example, they can redirect any folder to any server or combination of servers. This makes grouping and backing up important data easier. Administrators can also set disk quotas on either a per-user or a per-volume basis to manage how much disk space users can gobble up. Group policies allow administrators to determine how and where users can access documents. For example, administrators can specify that users must always save documents to the My Documents folder.

IntelliMirror makes document management easier for users, too:

- **More protection**   Windows 2000 Professional mirrors users' documents on both the client and the server. To minimize the impact on network traffic, Windows 2000 Professional opens both copies of a document, but makes edits only on the local copy. As users edit their documents, the operating system uses a write-through cache to keep the server copy of the document current.

- **Better availability**   Even if the network goes down, users can access their documents using the local mirrored copy. Changes are automatically synchronized when the network comes back online.

- **Data follows users**   Users have access to their important documents on any computer running Windows 2000 Professional that's attached to the network; they access the server's mirrored copy. Changes are automatically synchronized the next time they log on to their primary desktop computer. Windows 2000 Professional also protects a user's documents from other users.

Remote Windows Installation

You learned about the Remote Installation Service (RIS) in Chapter 18, "Easier Deployment." When combined with IntelliMirror, RIS comes as close as possible to the idea of a fully replaceable computer. That is, a user's computing environment—including the operating system, applications, documents, and settings—can be replicated with nothing more than a valid username and password. (This assumes that the user's computer supports RIS with a suitable boot ROM, either on the computer or on the network adapter card.)

Software Installation and Maintenance

The Windows Installer Service, which you learned about in Chapter 10, "Most Reliable and Stable," makes administering applications easier. For example, network administrators can use policies to install, upgrade, or remove applications based on the needs of users and groups. Network administrators can choose to assign mandatory applications to users or they can publish applications, allowing users to install them as needed. Windows 2000 Professional also makes the user's experience better:

- **Easier installation and upgrades**   Users use the Add/Remove Programs dialog box to view and install the applications that are available on the network.

- **No more unknown file types**   When users open a file for which an application isn't installed on the computer, the Windows Installer Service can install an application from the network that can open the document. For small programs, this procedure is almost transparent to users.

- **Applications follow users**   Administrators store applications as part of a user's profile, so users have easy access to their applications when they log on to any network computer running Windows 2000 Professional. Applications are only installed when invoked, even though they appear on the Start menu at all times during the session.

- **Fewer application errors**   Applications that take advantage of the Windows Installer Service can automatically repair themselves, replacing important files if necessary.

GLOSSARY OF TERMS

access control list (ACL)   Consists of access control entries (ACEs) that specify access or auditing rights to that object for one user or group. There are three ACE types: two for discretionary access control and one for system security.

ACPI   *See* Advanced Configuration and Power Interface.

Active Directory   The directory service included with Microsoft Windows 2000 Server. It stores information about objects on a network and makes this information available to users and network administrators. Active Directory gives network users access to permitted resources anywhere on the network using a single logon process. It provides network administrators with an intuitive hierarchical view of the network and a single point of administration for all network objects. *See also* directory service.

Active Directory Manager   An administrative tool designed to perform day-to-day Active Directory administration tasks. These tasks include creating, deleting, modifying, moving, and setting permissions on objects stored in the directory. These objects include organizational units, users, contacts, groups, computers, printers, and shared file objects. *See also* object.

administrator   A user of a computer running Windows 2000 Professional who has permission to configure that computer and to specify the types of access other users will have to that computer. This type of administrator is also called a *local administrator*. A *network administrator,* on the other hand, is a person who has permission to configure a network domain and to specify the types of access other users will have to the resources on that domain.

Advanced Configuration and Power Interface (ACPI)   An open industry specification that defines power management on a wide range of mobile, desktop, and server computers and peripherals. ACPI is the foundation for the OnNow industry initiative that allows system manufacturers to deliver computers that will start at the touch of a keyboard. ACPI design is essential to take full advantage of power management and Plug and Play in Windows 2000. If you are not sure if your computer is ACPI-compliant, check your manufacturer's documentation. *See also* Plug and Play.

ASR   *See* Automated System Recovery.

asynchronous communication   A form of data transmission in which information is sent and received at irregular intervals, one character at a time. Because data is received at irregular intervals, the receiving modem must be signaled to let it know when the data bits of a character begin and end. This is done by means of start and stop bits.

auditing   Tracks the activities of users by recording selected types of events in the security log of a server or a workstation.

authentication   The process by which the system validates the user's logon information. A user's name and password are compared against an authorized list. If the system detects a match, access is granted to the extent specified in the permissions list for that user. When a user logs on to an account on a computer running Microsoft Windows 2000 Professional, the authentication is performed by the workstation. When a user logs on to an account on a Microsoft Windows 2000 Server domain, authentication may be performed by any server of that domain. *See also* server, trust relationship.

Automated System Recovery (ASR)   A Windows feature that will recover and restore your hard disk and your Windows operating system if your hard disk fails or is damaged. You must first use the Windows Backup utility to prepare for ASR before you can use ASR to recover a damaged system. *See also* emergency repair disk.

backup media pool   A logical collection of data-storage media that has been reserved for use by Windows 2000 Backup. Windows 2000 Backup uses Removable Storage Manager (RSM) to control access to specific media within a library. *See also* library, media pool, Removable Storage Manager (RSM).

bandwidth   In communications, the difference between the highest and lowest frequencies in a given range. For example, a telephone line accommodates a bandwidth of 3000 Hz, the difference between the lowest (300 Hz) and the highest (3300 Hz) frequencies it can carry. In computer networks, greater bandwidth indicates faster data-transfer capability and is expressed in bits per second (bps).

Bandwidth Allocation Control Protocol (BACP)   Provides a method of transmitting Point-to-Point Protocol (PPP) information over multiple physical data links.

Bandwidth Allocation Protocol (BAP)   Dynamically controls the use of multilinked lines. BAP eliminates excess bandwidth by allocating lines only as they are required, representing a significant efficiency advantage to users. The conditions under which BAP dials extra lines when needed, and hangs up underused lines, are configured through Dial-Up Networking.

basic disk   A physical disk that contains primary partitions, extended partitions, or logical drives. Basic disks may also contain spanned, mirrored, striped, and RAID-5 volumes created using Windows NT 4.0 or earlier. Basic disks can be accessed by MS-DOS. *See also* basic volume, extended partition, logical drive, primary partition.

basic volume   A logical volume (spanned, mirrored, striped, or RAID-5) that was created using Windows NT 4.0 or earlier, or a primary extended partition or logical drive created with Disk Management. You can create basic volumes only on basic disks. *See also* basic disk, volume.

CCP   *See* Compression Control Protocol.

certificate   A file used for authentication and secure exchange of data on nonsecured networks such as the Internet. A certificate securely binds a public encryption key to the entity that holds the corresponding private encryption key. Certificates are digitally signed by the issuing certification authority and can be managed for a user, a computer, or a service.

Challenge Handshake Authentication Protocol (CHAP)   A protocol used by Remote Access Service (RAS) to negotiate the most secure form of encrypted authentication supported by both server and client.

CMYK color space   Multidimensional color space consisting of the cyan, magenta, yellow, and black intensities that make up a given color. Commercial color printing devices generally use this system of four-color process inks. *See also* color space.

codec   Hardware that can convert audio or video signals between analog and digital forms (coder/decoder); hardware or software that can compress and uncompress audio or video data (compressor/decompressor); or the combination of coder/decoder and compressor/decompressor. Generally, a codec compresses uncompressed digital data so that the data uses less memory.

code page   A means of providing support for character sets and keyboard layouts for different countries. A code page is a table that relates the binary character codes used by a program to keys on the keyboard or to characters on the display.

color gamut   Particular range of colors that a device is able to produce. Devices such as scanners, monitors, and printers can produce a unique range of colors, which is determined by the characteristics of the device itself. *See also* color profile, hue.

color management   Process of producing accurate, consistent color among a variety of input and output devices. A color management system (CMS) maps colors between devices such as scanners, monitors, and printers; transforms colors from one color space to another (for example, RGB to CMYK); and provides accurate on-screen or print previews. *See also* CMYK color space, RGB color space.

color profile   A profile that contains the data needed for translating the values of a color gamut. This data includes information about color, hue, graphics, and brightness. *See also* color gamut, hue.

color space   A set of three values that defines how a color can be represented on computer devices such as monitors, scanners, and printers. In the LAB color space, the terms luminance or whiteness (L), redness-greenness (A), and yellowness-blueness (B) are used; in the HVC system, the terms are hue (H), value (V), and chroma (C). Color space refers to the three-dimensional space that is defined by the respective values, such as L, A, and B.

Compression Control Protocol (CCP)   Used in the protocol negotiation process in a PPP connection. CCP is one type of network control protocol. Network control protocols are used to establish and configure different network protocol parameters for IP, IPX, and NetBEUI. *See also* Internet Protocol (IP), Internetwork Packet Exchange (IPX), NetBIOS Enhanced User Interface (NetBEUI).

computer account   Created by a domain administrator to uniquely identify a computer on the domain. The Windows 2000 computer account matches the computer name of the computer joining the domain.

console tree   The tree view pane in Microsoft Management Console (MMC) that displays the hierarchical namespace. By default, it's the left pane of a console window, but it can be hidden. The items in the console tree (for example, Web pages, folders, and controls) and their hierarchical organization determine the management capabilities of a console. *See also* Microsoft Management Console (MMC), namespace, tree view.

Data Communications Equipment (DCE) An elaborate worldwide network of packet-forwarding nodes that participate in delivering an X.25 packet to its designated address—for example, a modem. *See also* node, packet.

Data Terminal Equipment (DTE) In the RS-232-C hardware standard, any device, such as an RAS server or client, that has the ability to transmit information in digital form over a cable or a communications line. *See also* Remote Access Service (RAS).

defragmentation The process of rewriting parts of a file to contiguous sectors on a hard disk to increase the speed of access and retrieval. When files are updated, the computer tends to save these updates on the largest continuous space on the hard disk, which is often on a different sector than the other parts of the file. When files are thus "fragmented," the computer must search the hard disk each time the file is opened to find all of the file's parts, which slows down response time. *See also* fragmentation.

device driver A program that allows a specific device—such as a modem, a network card, or a printer—to communicate with Windows 2000. For example, without serial port drivers, network connections cannot use a modem to connect to a network. Although a device may be installed on your system, Windows 2000 cannot use the device until you have installed and configured the appropriate driver. If a device is listed in the hardware compatibility list (HCL), a driver is usually included with Windows 2000. Device drivers load automatically (for all enabled devices) when a computer is started, and thereafter they run invisibly. *See also* hardware compatibility list (HCL).

DHCP *See* Dynamic Host Configuration Protocol.

dial-up connection Connects you to your network if you are using a device that uses the telephone network. This includes modems with a standard phone line, ISDN cards with high-speed ISDN lines, or X.25 networks. If you are a typical user, you may have one or two dial-up connections, perhaps to the Internet and to your corporate network. In a more complex server situation, multiple network modem connections might be used to implement advanced routing. *See also* Integrated Services Digital Network (ISDN).

digital video disc (DVD) A type of optical disc storage technology. A DVD looks like a CD-ROM, but it can store greater amounts of data. DVDs are often used to store full-length movies and other multimedia content that requires large amounts of storage space. A DVD is also known as a digital versatile disk. *See also* DVD decoder, DVD drive.

direct cable connection A link between the I/O ports of two computers created with a single cable rather than with a modem or another interfacing device. In most cases, a direct cable connection is made with a null modem cable. *See also* input/output (I/O) port, null modem cable.

direct memory access (DMA) Memory access that does not involve the microprocessor. DMA is frequently used for data transfer directly between memory and a peripheral device such as a disk drive.

directory service Both the directory information source and the services making the information available and usable. A directory service enables you to find an object given any one of its attributes (such as finding all duplex printers in Building 26). *See also* Active Directory.

dismount To remove a removable tape or disc from a drive. *See also* library.

DNS server In the DNS client-server model, the server containing information about a portion of the DNS database that makes computer names available to client resolvers querying for name resolution across the Internet. *See also* Domain Name System (DNS).

domain In Windows 2000, a collection of computers (defined by the administrator of a Windows 2000 Server network) that share a common directory database. A domain provides access to the centralized user accounts and group accounts maintained by the domain administrator. Each domain has a unique name.

domain controller In a Windows 2000 Server domain, the computer running Windows 2000 Server that manages user access to the network, which includes logging on, authentication, and access to the directory and shared resources.

domain namespace The database structure used by the Domain Name System (DNS). *See also* Domain Name System (DNS).

Domain Name System (DNS)   A static, hierarchical name service for TCP/IP hosts. The network administrator configures the DNS with a list of host names and IP addresses, allowing users of workstations configured to query the DNS to specify remote systems by host names rather than by IP addresses. For example, a workstation configured to use DNS name resolution could use the command *ping remotehost* rather than ping 1.2.3.4 if the mapping for the system named remotehost was contained in the DNS database. DNS domains should not be confused with Windows 2000 networking domains. *See also* domain.

dual boot   A computer configuration that can start two different operating systems. *See also* multiple boot.

DVD decoder   A hardware or software component that allows a digital video disc (DVD) drive to display movies on your computer screen. *See also* digital video disc (DVD), DVD drive.

DVD drive   A disc storage device that uses digital video disc (DVD) technology. A DVD drive reads both CD-ROMs and DVDs; however, you must have a DVD decoder to display DVD movies on your computer screen. *See also* DVD decoder, digital video disc (DVD).

DWORD   A data type composed of hexadecimal data with a maximum allotted space of 4 bytes.

dynamic disk   A physical disk that is managed by Disk Management. Dynamic disks can contain only dynamic volumes (that is, volumes created with Disk Management). Dynamic disks cannot contain partitions or logical drives, nor can they be accessed by MS-DOS. *See also* dynamic volume, partition.

Dynamic Host Configuration Protocol (DHCP)   A TCP/IP service protocol that offers dynamic leased configuration of host IP addresses and distributes other configuration parameters to eligible network clients. DHCP provides safe, reliable, and simple TCP/IP network configuration; prevents address conflicts; and helps conserve the use of client IP addresses on the network. DHCP uses a client/server model where the DHCP server maintains centralized management of IP addresses that are used on the network. DHCP-supporting clients can then request and obtain lease of an IP address from a DHCP server as part of their network boot process.

dynamic-link library (DLL)   An operating system feature that allows executable routines (generally serving a specific function or set of functions) to be stored separately as files with DLL extensions and to be loaded only when needed by the program that calls them.

dynamic volume   A logical volume that is created using Disk Management. Dynamic volumes include simple, spanned, striped, mirrored, and RAID-5. You must create dynamic volumes on dynamic disks. *See also* dynamic disk, volume.

EAP   *See* Extensible Authentication Protocol.

EFS   *See* Encrypting File System.

embedded object   Information created in another application that has been pasted inside your document. When information is embedded, you can edit the information in the new document using toolbars and menus from the original program. To edit the embedded information, double-click it; the toolbars and menus from the program used to create the information appear. Embedded information is not linked to the original. If you change information in one place, it is not updated in the other. *See also* linked object.

emergency repair disk   A disk created by the Windows Backup utility that contains information about your current Windows system settings. You can use this disk to repair your computer if it will not start or if your system files are damaged or erased. *See also* Automated System Recovery (ASR).

Encrypting File System (EFS)   Windows 2000 file system that enables users to encrypt files and folders on an NTFS volume disk to keep them safe from access by intruders. *See also* NTFS (the NTFS file system).

Enhanced Small Device Interface (ESDI)   A standard that can be used with high-capacity hard disks, floppy disk drives, and tape drives to allow these devices to communicate with a computer at high speeds.

Event Log service   Records events in the system, security, and application logs. The Event Log service is located in Event Viewer.

event logging   The Windows 2000 process of recording an audit entry in the audit trail whenever certain events occur, such as services starting and stopping and users logging on and off and accessing resources. You can use Event Viewer to review services for Macintosh events as well as for Windows 2000 events.

extended partition   A portion of a basic disk that can contain logical drives. Use an extended partition if you want to have more than four volumes on your basic disk. Only one of the four partitions allowed per physical disk can be an extended partition, and no primary partition needs to be present to create an extended partition. Extended partitions can be created only on basic disks. *See also* basic disk, logical drive, partition, primary partition.

Extensible Authentication Protocol (EAP)   A protocol that supports authentication methods—including token card, dial-up, one-time password, and public key—for virtual private network (VPN) users. An extension to the Point-to-Point Protocol (PPP), it works with dial-up, PPTP, and L2TP clients. This technology is critical to the security of VPNs. It helps to protect against brute-force, dictionary, and password-guessing attacks. *See also* Layer 2 Tunneling Protocol (L2TP), Point-to-Point Protocol (PPP), Point-to-Point Tunneling Protocol (PPTP), virtual private network (VPN).

FAT (file allocation table)   A table or list maintained by some operating systems to keep track of the status of various segments of disk space used for file storage. The file allocation table is also called the FAT file system or the FAT16 file system. *See also* FAT32, NTFS (the NTFS file system).

FAT32   A derivative of the File Allocation Table file system. FAT32 supports smaller cluster sizes than FAT, which results in more efficient space allocation on FAT32 drives. *See also* FAT (file allocation table), NTFS (the NTFS file system).

fault tolerance   Ensures data integrity when hardware failures occur. In Disk Management, mirrored volumes and RAID-5 volumes are fault-tolerant.

file system   In an operating system, the overall structure in which files are named, stored, and organized. NTFS, FAT, and FAT32 are types of file systems.

font   A graphic design applied to a collection of numbers, symbols, and characters. A font describes a certain typeface along with other qualities such as size, spacing, and pitch.

fragmentation   The scattering of parts of the same disk file over different areas of the disk. Fragmentation occurs as files on a disk are deleted and new files are added. It slows disk access and degrades the overall performance of disk operations, although usually not severely. *See also* defragmentation.

free media pool   A logical collection of unused data-storage media that can be used by applications or other media pools. When media are no longer needed by an application, they are returned to a free media pool so that they can be used again. *See also* media pool, Removable Storage Manager (RSM).

global group   For Windows 2000 Server, a group that can be used in its own domain and in trusting domains. A global group can be granted rights and permissions and can become a member of local groups. However, a global group can contain user accounts only from its own domain. Global groups provide a way to create sets of users from inside the domain, available for use both in and out of the domain. Global groups cannot be created or maintained on computers running Windows 2000 Professional. However, for computers running Windows 2000 Professional that participate in a domain, domain global groups can be granted rights and permissions at those workstations and can become members of local groups at those workstations. *See also* group, local group.

group   A collection of users, computers, contacts, and other groups. Groups can be used as security or as e-mail distribution collections. Distribution groups are used only for e-mail. Security groups are used both to grant access to resources and as e-mail distribution lists. *See also* global group, local group.

group account   A collection of user accounts. By making a user account a member of a group, you give that user all the rights and permissions granted to the group. *See also* user account.

group memberships   The groups to which a user account belongs. Permissions and rights granted to a group are also provided to its members. In most cases, the actions a user can perform in Windows 2000 are determined by the group memberships of the user account the user is logged on to. *See also* group, local group, global group.

group name   A unique name identifying a local group or a global group to Windows 2000. A group's name cannot be identical to any other group name or user name in its own domain or computer. *See also* global group, local group.

guest   Services for Macintosh users who do not have a user account or who do not provide a password. When a Macintosh user assigns permissions to everyone, those permissions are given to the group's guests and users.

guest account   A built-in account used to log on to a computer running Windows 2000 when a user does not have an account on the computer or domain or in any of the domains trusted by the computer's domain.

hardware compatibility list (HCL)   A list of computers and peripheral devices that have been extensively tested with various versions of Windows for stability and compatibility. If you experience problems during your installation of a Windows operating system, your first step in troubleshooting should be to verify that all of your computer's hardware components appear in this list. The list can be found at *http://www.microsoft.com/hwtest/hcl*.

hardware profile   Data that describes the configuration and characteristics of specific computer equipment. This information can be used to configure computers for using peripheral devices.

hexadecimal   A base-16 number system whose numbers are represented by the digits 0 through 9 and the (uppercase or lowercase) letters A (equivalent to decimal 10) through F (equivalent to decimal 15).

hub   A common connection point for devices in a network. Typically used to connect segments of a local area network (LAN), a hub contains multiple ports. When a packet arrives at one port, it is copied to the other ports so that all segments of the LAN can see all packets.

hue   The position of a color along the color spectrum. For example, green is between yellow and blue. This attribute can be set using Display in Control Panel.

Hypertext Markup Language (HTML)   A simple markup language used to create hypertext documents that are portable from one platform to another. HTML files are simple ASCII text files with codes embedded (indicated by markup tags) to denote formatting and hypertext links.

ICMP   *See* Internet Control Message Protocol.

IDE   *See* Integrated Drive Electronics.

IEEE 1394   A standard for high-speed serial devices such as digital video and digital audio editing equipment.

import media pool   A logical collection of data-storage media that has not been cataloged by Removable Storage Manager (RSM). Media in an import media pool should be cataloged as soon as possible so that they can be used by an application. *See also* media pool, Removable Storage Manager (RSM).

infrared   Light that is beyond red in the color spectrum. While the light is not visible to the human eye, infrared transmitters and receivers can send and receive infrared signals. *See also* Infrared Data Association (IrDA), infrared device, infrared port.

Infrared Data Association (IrDA)   The industry organization of computer, component, and telecommunications vendors who establish the standards for infrared communication between computers and peripheral devices, such as printers. *See also* infrared, infrared device, infrared port.

infrared device   A computer, or a computer peripheral such as a printer, that can communicate using infrared light. *See also* infrared.

infrared port   An optical port on a computer that uses infrared light to communicate with other computers or devices. Communication is achieved without cables. Infrared ports can be found on some laptops, notebooks, printers, and cameras. An infrared port may also be added to a computer with an infrared dongle (or hardware key security device) connected to a PCI card, a serial port, a parallel port (for a printer), or a direct connection to the motherboard. *See also* infrared device, infrared port.

input locale   Specifies what language you want to type in. Some programs that are designed for Windows 2000 recognize this setting. When you add a new input locale, a keyboard layout for that language is also added.

input method editor   A program used to enter the thousands of different characters in Asian written languages with a standard 101-key keyboard. An input method editor consists of both an engine that converts keystrokes into phonetic and ideographic characters and a dictionary of commonly used ideographic words. As the user enters keystrokes, the input method editor engine attempts to identify which character or characters the keystrokes should be converted into.

input/output (I/O) port   A channel through which data is transferred between a device and the microprocessor. The port appears to the microprocessor as one or more memory addresses that it can use to send or receive data.

Integrated Drive Electronics (IDE)   A type of disk-drive interface in which the controller electronics reside on the drive itself, eliminating the need for a separate adapter card.

Integrated Services Digital Network (ISDN)   A type of phone line used to enhance WAN speeds. ISDN lines can transmit at speeds of 64 or 128 kilobits per second, as opposed to standard phone lines, which typically transmit at 28.8 kilobits per second. An ISDN line must be installed by the phone company at both the server site and the remote site. *See also* wide area network (WAN).

International Telecommunications Union (ITU)   Formerly known as CCITT (the Comité Consultatif International Télégraphique et Téléphonique); it changed its name to ITU in March 1993. The ITU is responsible for telecommunication standards. Its responsibilities include standardizing modem design and operations, and standardizing protocols for networks and facsimile transmission. The ITU is an international organization within which governments and the private sector coordinate global telecom networks and services.

Internet Control Message Protocol (ICMP)   A maintenance protocol in the TCP/IP suite, required in every TCP/IP implementation, that allows two nodes on an IP network to share IP status and error information. ICMP is used by the ping utility to determine the readability of a remote system.

Internet Protocol (IP)   The messenger protocol of TCP/IP, responsible for addressing and sending TCP packets over the network. IP provides a best-effort, connectionless delivery system that does not guarantee that packets arrive at their destination or that they are received in the sequence in which they were sent. *See also* packet, Transmission Control Protocol/Internet Protocol (TCP/IP).

Internet Protocol security (IPSec)   An operating system component that is responsible for encrypting TCP/IP communication over a network or over the Internet.

Internet service provider (ISP)   A company that provides individuals or companies access to the Internet and the World Wide Web. When you sign a contract with an ISP, you will be provided a telephone number, a user name, a password, and other connection information so you can connect your computer to the ISP's computers. An ISP typically charges a monthly fee and/or hourly connection fees.

Internetwork Packet Exchange (IPX)   A network protocol native to NetWare that controls addressing and routing of packets within and between LANs. IPX does not guarantee that a message will be complete (no lost packets). *See also* IPX/SPX.

interrupt request (IRQ) line   Hardware line over which devices can send signals to get the attention of the processor when the device is ready to accept or send information. IRQ lines are numbered from 0 to 15. Each device must have a unique IRQ line.

I/O port   *See* input/output (I/O) port.

IP   *See* Internet Protocol.

IP address   Used to identify a node on a network and to specify routing information. Each node on the network must be assigned a unique IP address, which is made up of the network ID plus a unique host ID assigned by the network administrator. This address is typically represented in dotted-decimal notation, with the decimal value of each octet separated by a period (for example, 138.57.7.27). In Windows 2000, the IP address can be configured statically on the client or configured dynamically through DHCP. *See also* Dynamic Host Configuration Protocol (DHCP), node.

IPX/SPX   Transport protocols used in Novell NetWare networks, which together correspond to the combination of TCP and IP in the TCP/IP protocol suite. Windows 2000 implements IPX through NWLink. *See also* Internetwork Packet Exchange (IPX).

IRQ   *See* interrupt request (IRQ) line.

ISDN   *See* Integrated Services Digital Network.

ISP   *See* Internet service provider.

keyboard layout   Accommodates the special characters and symbols used in different languages. Keyboard layouts affect which characters appear when you press the keys on your keyboard. After you change your keyboard layout, the characters that appear on your screen may no longer correspond to the characters that are printed on your keyboard keys.

LAN   *See* local area network.

Layer 2 Tunneling Protocol (L2TP)   An industry-standard Internet tunneling protocol. Unlike Point-to-Point Tunneling Protocol (PPTP), L2TP does not require IP connectivity between the client workstation and the server. L2TP requires only that the tunnel medium provide packet-oriented point-to-point connectivity. The protocol can be used over media such as Asynchronous Transfer Mode (ATM), Frame Relay, and X.25. L2TP provides the same functionality as PPTP. Based on Layer 2 Forwarding and PPTP specifications, L2TP allows clients to set up tunnels across intervening networks. *See also* Point-to-Point Tunneling Protocol (PPTP), tunnel.

library   A data-storage system, usually managed by Removable Storage Manager (RSM). A library consists of removable media (such as tapes or discs) and a hardware device that can read from or write to the media. There are two types of libraries in an RSM system: robotic libraries (automated multiple-media, multidrive devices) and standalone drives (manually operated, single-drive devices). A robotic library is also called a jukebox or changer.

linked object   An object that is inserted into a document but still exists in the source file. When information is linked, the new document is updated automatically if the information in the original document changes. If you want to edit the linked information, double-click it. The toolbars and menus from the original program will appear. If the original document is on your computer, changes that you make to the linked information will also appear in the original document. *See also* embedded object.

Lmhosts file   A local text file that maps IP addresses to the computer names of Windows 2000 networking computers outside the local subnet. In Windows 2000, this file is stored in the *systemroot*\System32\Drivers\Etc folder.

local area network (LAN)   A group of computers and other devices dispersed over a relatively limited area and connected by a communications link that allows any device to interact with any other on the network.

local computer   The computer that you are currently logged on to as a user. More specifically, a local computer is a computer that you can access directly without using a communications line or a communications device, such as a network card or a modem. Similarly, running a local program means running the program on your computer, as opposed to running it from a network server.

local group   For computers running Windows 2000 Professional and member servers, a group that can be granted permissions and rights on the local computer. If the computer participates in a domain, a local group can include user accounts and global groups from that domain as well as from trusted domains. *See also* global group.

local user profiles   User profiles that are created automatically on the computer the first time a user logs on to a computer running Windows 2000 Professional or Windows 2000 Server.

logical drive   A volume you create within an extended partition on a basic disk. A logical drive can be formatted and assigned a drive letter. Only basic disks can contain logical drives. A logical drive cannot span multiple disks. *See also* basic disk, basic volume, extended partition.

logical printer   The software interface between the operating system and the printer in Windows 2000. While a printer is the device that does the actual printing, a logical printer is its software interface on the print server. This software interface determines how a print job is processed and how it is routed to its destination (to a local or network port, to a file, or to a remote print share). When you print a document, it is spooled (or stored) on the logical printer before it is sent to the printer itself. *See also* spooling.

mandatory user profile   A user profile that is not updated when the user logs off. It is downloaded to the user's desktop each time the user logs on. It is created by an administrator and assigned to one or more users to ensure consistent or job-specific user profiles. Only members of the Administrators group can change profiles. *See also* roaming user profile, user profile.

media   Any fixed or removable object that stores computer data. For example, hard disks, floppy disks, tapes, and compact discs are all data-storage media.

media pool   A logical collection of removable media that have the same management policies. Media pools are used by applications to control access to specific tapes or discs within libraries managed by Removable Storage Manager (RSM). There are four media pools: unrecognized, import, free, and application-specific. A media pool can only hold media or other media pools. *See also* Removable Storage Manager (RSM).

Message Digest 5 (MD5)   An industry-standard one-way encryption scheme used by various Point-to-Point Protocol (PPP) vendors for encrypted authentication. *See also* Point-to-Point Protocol (PPP).

Message Queuing Services (formerly Microsoft Message Queue Server) (MSMQ) Allows applications running at different times to communicate across heterogeneous networks and systems that may be temporarily offline. Applications send messages to MSMQ, and MSMQ uses queues to ensure that the messages eventually reach their destination. MSMQ provides guaranteed message delivery, efficient routing, security, and priority-based messaging.

Microsoft Distributed Transaction Coordinator (MS DTC) A transaction manager that coordinates transactions that span multiple resource managers, such as Message Queuing Services (MSMQ) and SQL Server. *See also* Message Queuing Services (MSMQ), transaction.

Microsoft Management Console (MMC) A framework for hosting administrative tools called consoles. A console is defined by the items on its console tree, which may include folders or other containers, World Wide Web pages, and other administrative items. A console has one or more windows that can provide views of the console tree along with the administrative properties, services, and events that are acted on by the items in the console tree. The main MMC window provides commands and tools for authoring consoles. The authoring features of MMC and the console tree itself may be hidden when a console is in user mode. *See also* console tree, snap-in.

Microsoft Point-to-Point Encryption (MPPE) A 128/40-bit encryption algorithm using RSA RC4. MPPE provides for packet security between the client and the tunnel server and is useful where Internet Protocol security (IPSec) is not available. The 40-bit version addresses localization issues based on current export restrictions. MPPE is compatible with Network Address Translation. *See also* Internet Protocol security (IPSec).

mirror A copy of a volume. Each mirror of a volume resides on a different disk. If one mirror becomes unavailable (due to a disk failure, for example), you can use the other mirror to gain access to the volume's data. *See also* fault tolerance, mirrored volume.

mirror set *See* mirrored volume.

mirrored volume A fault-tolerant volume that duplicates data on two physical disks. It provides data redundancy by using a copy (mirror) of the volume to duplicate the information contained on the volume. The mirror is always located on a different disk. If one of the physical disks fails, the data on the failed disk becomes unavailable, but the system continues to operate using the unaffected disk. A mirrored volume is slower than a RAID-5 volume in read operations but faster in write operations. You can create mirrored volumes only on dynamic disks. In Windows NT 4.0, a mirrored volume was known as a mirror set. *See also* dynamic disk, dynamic volume, fault tolerance, redundant array of independent disks (RAID), volume.

MMC *See* Microsoft Management Console.

modem Short for modulator/demodulator, a device that allows computer information to be transmitted and received over a telephone line. The transmitting modem translates digital computer data into analog signals that can be carried on a phone line. The receiving modem translates the analog signals back to digital form.

modulation standards Protocols that determine how modems convert digital data into analog signals that can be transmitted over telephone lines. Initially, Bell created modulation standards used in the United States, and the CCITT created international standards. The ITU (formerly called the CCITT) now sets standards generally adopted by modem manufacturers both internationally and in the United States. The ITU series V standards (such as V.34 and V.90) define data communication over the telephone network. The suffixes "bis" and "ter" (for example, V.32bis) indicate later versions of a standard. *See also* V.34, V.90.

MPPE *See* Microsoft Point-to-Point Encryption.

MSMQ *See* Message Queuing Services.

multihomed computer A system that has multiple network cards or that has been configured with multiple IP addresses for a single network card.

multilink dialing Combines the bandwidth of two or more physical communications links to increase your remote access bandwidth and throughput using Remote Access Service Multilink. Based on the Internet Engineering Task Force (IETF) standard RFC 1717, RAS Multilink lets you combine analog modem paths, ISDN paths, and mixed analog and digital communications links on both your client and server computers. This increases your Internet and intranet access speed and decreases the amount of time you need to be connected to a remote computer. *See also* Remote Access Service (RAS), Request for Comments (RFC).

multiple boot A computer configuration that runs two or more operating systems. For example, Windows 98, MS-DOS, and Windows 2000 operating systems can be installed on the same computer. When the computer is started, any one of the operating systems can be selected. *See also* dual boot.

namespace   Resources or items that are available to a computer. In MMC, the namespace is represented by the console tree, which displays all of the snap-ins and resources that are accessible to a console. *See also* console tree, Microsoft Management Console (MMC), resource, snap-in.

NetBIOS   An application programming interface (API) that can be used by application programs on a local area network (LAN). NetBIOS provides application programs with a uniform set of commands for requesting the lower-level services required to conduct sessions between nodes on a network and to transmit information back and forth.

NetBIOS Enhanced User Interface (NetBEUI)   A network protocol native to Microsoft Networking. It is usually used in small, department-sized local area networks of 1 to 200 clients. It can use Token Ring source routing as its only method of routing. It is the Microsoft implementation of the NetBIOS standard. *See also* router.

network administrator   A person responsible for planning, configuring, and managing the day-to-day operation of a network. This person may also be referred to as a system administrator.

node   In a Microsoft Management Console snap-in, a selectable item in the console tree. In the Macintosh environment, a node is an addressable entity on a network. Each Macintosh client is a node. *See also* console tree, local area network (LAN), Microsoft Management Console (MMC), snap-in.

nonpaged memory   Memory that cannot be paged to disk. Paging is the moving of infrequently used parts of a program's working memory from RAM to another storage medium, usually the hard disk. *See also* paging file.

nonpaged pool   Operating system memory that is never paged to disk. Paging is the moving of infrequently used parts of a program's working memory from RAM to another storage medium, usually the hard disk. In Task Manager, the amount of memory used by a process, in kilobytes. *See also* paging file.

NTFS (NTFS file system)   An advanced file system designed for use specifically with Windows NT and Windows 2000 operating systems. It supports file system recovery, extremely large storage media, long file names, and various features for the POSIX subsystem. It also supports object-oriented applications by treating all files as objects with user-defined and system-defined attributes. *See also* FAT (file allocation table), FAT32, Portable Operating System Interface for UNIX (POSIX).

null modem cable Special cabling that allows computers to communicate over short distances without using modems. A null modem cable emulates modem communication. *See also* asynchronous communication, modem.

NWLink An implementation of the Internetwork Packet Exchange (IPX), Sequenced Packet Exchange (SPX), and NetBIOS protocols used in Novell networks. NWLink is a standard network protocol that supports routing and can support NetWare client-server applications, where NetWare-aware sockets-based applications communicate with IPX/SPX sockets-based applications. *See also* Internetwork Packet Exchange (IPX), NetBIOS.

object An entity such as a file, folder, shared folder, printer, or Active Directory object described by a distinct, named set of attributes. For example, the attributes of a File object include its name, location, and size; the attributes of an Active Directory User object might include the user's first name, last name, and e-mail address. For OLE and ActiveX objects, an object can also be any piece of information that can be linked to, or embedded into, another object.

object linking and embedding (OLE) A way to transfer and share information between applications by pasting information created in one application into a document created in another application, such as a spreadsheet or word processing file. *See also* embedded object, linked object.

on-disk catalog Information stored on a local disk drive. The on-disk catalog contains a list of files and folders that have been backed up in a backup set. *See also* on-media catalog.

on-media catalog Information stored on backup storage media. The on-media catalog contains a list of files and folders that have been backed up in a backup set. *See also* on-disk catalog.

OpenType fonts Outline fonts that are rendered from line and curve commands, and can be scaled and rotated. OpenType fonts look good in all sizes and on all output devices supported by Windows 2000. OpenType fonts are an extension of TrueType font technology. *See also* font, TrueType fonts.

owner   In Windows 2000, the person who controls how permissions are set on every file and folder on an NTFS volume and who can grant permissions to others. In the Macintosh environment, an owner is the user responsible for setting permissions for a folder on a server. A Macintosh user who creates a folder on the server automatically becomes the owner of the folder. The owner can transfer ownership to someone else. Each Macintosh-accessible volume on the server also has an owner.

package   An icon that represents embedded or linked information. That information may consist of a complete file, such as a Paint bitmap, or part of a file, such as a spreadsheet cell. When you choose the package, the application used to create the object either plays the object (for example, a sound file) or opens and displays the object. If you change the original information, linked information is automatically updated. However, you must manually update embedded information. *See also* embedded object, linked object, object linking and embedding (OLE).

packet   A transmission unit of fixed maximum size that consists of binary information representing both data and a header containing an identification number, source and destination addresses, and error-control data.

packet header   In network protocol communications, a specially reserved field of a defined bit length that is attached to the front of a packet for carry and transfer of control information. When the packet arrives at its destination, the field is then detached and discarded as the packet is processed and disassembled in a corresponding reverse order for each protocol layer. *See also* protocol.

page fault   The interrupt that occurs when software attempts to read from or write to a virtual memory location that is marked "not present." In Task Manager, page fault is the number of times data has to be retrieved from disk for a process because it was not found in memory. The page fault value accumulates from the time the process started.

paged pool   The system-allocated virtual memory that has been charged to a process and that can be paged. Paging is the moving of infrequently used parts of a program's working memory from RAM to another storage medium, usually the hard disk. In Task Manager, the amount of system allocated virtual memory, in kilobytes, used by a process.

paging file   A hidden file on the hard disk that Windows 2000 uses to hold parts of programs and data files that do not fit in memory. The paging file and physical memory, or RAM, comprise virtual memory. Windows 2000 moves data from the paging file to memory as needed, and moves data from memory to the paging file to make room for new data. Also called a swap file. *See also* random access memory (RAM), virtual memory.

parity   Redundant information that is associated with a block of information. In Windows 2000 Server, parity is a calculated value used to reconstruct data after a failure. RAID-5 volumes (also known as stripe sets with parity) stripe data and parity intermittently across a set of disks. Within each stripe, the data on one disk is parity data and the data on the other disks is normal data. RAID-5 volumes therefore require at least three disks to allow for this extra parity information. The parity portion of each stripe contains the XOR (the Boolean operation called exclusive OR) of the data in that stripe. When a disk fails, Windows 2000 Server uses the parity information in those stripes in conjunction with the data on the good disks to recreate the data on the failed disk. *See also* fault tolerance, RAID-5 volume, striped volume, XOR (exclusive OR).

parity bit   In asynchronous communication, an extra bit used in checking for errors in groups of data bits transferred within or between computer systems. In modem-to-modem communications, a parity bit is often used to check the accuracy with which each character is transmitted. *See also* asynchronous communication.

partition   A portion of a physical disk that functions as though it were a physically separate disk. Partitions can be created only on basic disks. *See also* basic disk, extended partition, primary partition.

partition boot sector   A portion of a hard disk partition that contains information about the disk's file system and a short machine language program that loads the Windows operating system. *See also* system volume.

password   A security measure used to restrict logons to user accounts and access to computer systems and resources. A password is a unique string of characters that must be provided before a logon or an access is authorized. For Windows 2000, a password for a user account can be up to 14 characters and is case-sensitive. With Services for Macintosh, each Macintosh user has a user password to access the Windows 2000 Server. You can also assign each Macintosh-accessible volume a volume password that all users must type to gain access to the volume.

PC Card   A removable device, approximately the size of a credit card, that can be plugged into a PCMCIA (Personal Computer Memory Card International Association) slot in a portable computer. PCMCIA devices can include modems, network cards, and hard disk drives. *See also* modem.

Plain Old Telephone Service (POTS)   Basic dial telephone connections to the public switched network, without any added features or functions. POTS is also known as point of termination station.

Plug and Play   A set of specifications developed by Intel that allow a computer to automatically detect and configure a device and install the appropriate device drivers.

Point-to-Point Protocol (PPP)   A set of industry-standard framing and authentication protocols that is part of Windows 2000 RAS to ensure interoperability with third-party remote access software. PPP negotiates configuration parameters for multiple layers of the OSI model. *See also* Remote Access Service (RAS).

Point-to-Point Tunneling Protocol (PPTP)   Networking technology that supports multiprotocol virtual private networks (VPNs), enabling remote users to access corporate networks securely across the Internet by dialing into an Internet service provider (ISP) or by connecting directly to the Internet. The Point-to-Point Tunneling Protocol "tunnels," or encapsulates, IP, IPX, or NetBEUI protocols inside of IP packets. This means that users can remotely run applications that are dependent upon particular network protocols. *See also* Internetwork Packet Exchange (IPX), Internet service provider (ISP), NetBIOS Enhanced User Interface (NetBEUI), packet, tunnel, virtual private network (VPN).

port   Generally, a connection point on your computer where you can connect devices that pass data in and out of a computer. For example, a printer is typically connected to a parallel port (also known as an LPT port), and a modem is typically connected to a serial port (also known as a COM port).

Portable Operating System Interface for UNIX (POSIX)   An IEEE (Institute of Electrical and Electronics Engineers) standard that defines a set of operating-system services. Programs that adhere to the POSIX standard can be easily ported from one system to another. POSIX was based on UNIX system services, but it was created in a way that allows it to be implemented by other operating systems.

PostScript   A page-description language (PDL), developed by Adobe Systems for printing on laser printers, that offers flexible font capability and high-quality graphics. PostScript is the standard for desktop publishing because it is supported by imagesetters, the high-resolution printers used by printing services for commercial typesetting.

POTS   *See* Plain Old Telephone Service.

PPP   *See* Point-to-Point Protocol.

PPTP   *See* Point-to-Point Tunneling Protocol.

primary partition   A volume you create using unallocated space on a basic disk. Windows 2000 and other operating systems can start from a primary partition. You can create up to four primary partitions on a basic disk, or three primary partitions and an extended partition. Primary partitions can be created only on basic disks and cannot be subpartitioned. *See also* basic disk, dynamic volume, extended partition, partition.

process identifier (PID)   A numerical ID that uniquely identifies a process while it runs. Use Task Manager to view PIDs.

program information file (PIF)   Provides information to Windows 2000 about how best to run MS-DOS programs. When you start an MS-DOS program, Windows 2000 looks for a PIF to use with it. PIFs contain such items as the name of the file, a start-up directory, and multitasking options.

protocol   A set of rules and conventions for sending information over a network. These rules govern the content, format, timing, sequencing, and error control of messages exchanged among network devices.

public key cryptography   A method of cryptography in which two different keys are used: a public key and a private key. Data encrypted with the public key can be decrypted with the private key, and data encrypted with the private key can be decrypted with the public key.. Public key cryptography is also called asymmetric cryptography.

public switched telephone network (PSTN)   Standard analog telephone lines, available worldwide.

RADIUS (Remote Authentication Dial-In User Service)   A software-based security authentication protocol widely used by Internet service providers on non-Microsoft remote servers. RADIUS is the most popular means of authorizing dial-up and tunneled network users today. *See also* tunnel.

RAID-5 volume   A fault-tolerant volume with data and parity striped intermittently across three or more physical disks. Parity is a calculated value that is used to reconstruct data after a failure. If a portion of a physical disk fails, you can recreate the data that was on the failed portion from the remaining data and parity. You can create RAID-5 volumes only on dynamic disks. You cannot mirror or extend RAID-5 volumes. In Windows NT 4.0, a RAID-5 volume was known as a stripe set with parity. *See also* dynamic disk, dynamic volume, fault tolerance, parity, redundant array of independent disks (RAID), volume.

random access memory (RAM)   Memory that can be read from or written to by a computer or other devices. Information stored in RAM is lost when you turn off the computer. *See also* virtual memory.

RAS server   Any Windows 2000–based server configured to run the Remote Access Service. *See also* Remote Access Service (RAS).

reduced instruction set computing (RISC)   A type of microprocessor design that focuses on rapid and efficient processing of a relatively small set of instructions. RISC architecture limits the number of instructions that are built into the microprocessor but optimizes each so it can be carried out very rapidly, usually within a single clock cycle. Compaq's Alpha computer is the only RISC-based product supported by Windows 2000.

redundant array of independent disks (RAID)   A method used to standardize and categorize fault-tolerant disk systems. Six levels gauge various mixes of performance, reliability, and cost. Windows 2000 supports three of the RAID levels: Level 0 (striping), Level 1 (mirroring), and Level 5 (RAID-5). *See also* fault tolerance, mirrored volume, RAID-5 volume, striped volume.

Remote Access Service (RAS)   A service that provides remote networking for telecommuters, mobile workers, and system administrators who monitor and manage servers at multiple branch offices. Users with RAS on a computer running Windows 2000 can dial in to remotely access their networks for services such as file and printer sharing, electronic mail, scheduling, and SQL database access.

remote administration   The management of one computer by an administrator working at another computer connected to the first computer across a network. *See also* administrator.

Remote Storage Service (RSS)   For Windows 2000 Server, an application used to automatically move infrequently accessed files from local storage to remote storage. Remote files are recalled automatically upon user request when the file is opened.

Removable Storage Manager (RSM)   A service used for managing removable media (such as tapes and discs) and storage devices (libraries). RSM allows applications to access and share the same media resources. A group of libraries and associated media that are managed by RSM is called an RSM system. *See also* library.

Request for Comments (RFC)   The official documents of the Internet Engineering Task Force (IETF) that specify the details for protocols included in the TCP/IP family. *See also* Transmission Control Protocol/Internet Protocol (TCP/IP).

resource   Generally, any part of a computer system or network—such as a disk drive, a printer, or memory—that can be allotted to a program or a process while it is running. Also, any of four system components that control how the devices on a computer work. These four system resources are: interrupt request (IRQ) lines, direct memory access (DMA) channels, input/output (I/O) ports, and memory addresses. *See also* direct memory access (DMA), input/output (I/O) port, interrupt request (IRQ) line.

RGB color space   Multidimensional color space consisting of the red, green, and blue intensities that make up a given color. This system is typically used in scanners, digital cameras, computer monitors, and computer printers. *See also* color space.

RISC   *See* reduced instruction set computing.

roaming user profile   A server-based user profile that is downloaded to the local computer when a user logs on and is updated both locally and on the server when the user logs off. A roaming profile is available from the server when logging on to any computer running Microsoft Windows 2000 Professional or Microsoft Windows 2000 Server. When logging on, the user can use the local user profile if it is more current than the copy on the server. *See also* mandatory user profile, user profile.

router In the Windows 2000 environment, routers help LANs and WANs achieve interoperability and connectivity and can link LANs that have different network topologies (such as Ethernet and Token Ring). Routers match packet headers to a LAN segment and choose the best path for the packet, optimizing network performance. In the Macintosh environment, routers are necessary for computers on different physical networks to communicate with each other. Routers maintain a map of the physical networks on a Macintosh internet (network) and forward data received from one physical network to other physical networks. Computers running Windows 2000 Server with Services for Macintosh can act as routers, and you can also use third-party routing hardware on a network with Services for Macintosh.

SCSI *See* Small Computer System Interface.

security identifier (SID) A unique number that identifies user and group accounts. Every account on your network is issued a unique SID when the account is first created. Internal processes in Windows 2000 refer to an account's SID rather than the account's user or group name. If you create an account, delete it, and then create an account with the same user name, the new account will not have the rights or permissions previously granted to the old account because the accounts will have different SIDs.

Serial Line Internet Protocol (SLIP) An older industry standard that is part of Windows 2000 RAS to ensure interoperability with third-party remote access software. *See also* Remote Access Service (RAS).

serial port A computer port that allows asynchronous transmission of data characters one bit at a time. Also called a communication or COM port.

server In general, refers to a computer that provides shared resources to network users.

service A program, routine, or process that performs a specific system function to support other programs, particularly at a low (close to the hardware) level. When services are provided over a network, they can be published in Active Directory, facilitating service-centric administration and usage. Some examples of Windows 2000 services are Security Accounts Manager Service, File Replication Service, and Routing and Remote Access Service.

SID *See* security identifier.

simple volume A volume made up of disk space from a single disk. It can consist of a single region on a disk or multiple regions of the same disk that are linked together. You can extend a simple volume within the same disk or onto additional disks. If you extend a simple volume across multiple disks, it becomes a spanned volume. You can create simple volumes only on dynamic disks. Simple volumes are not fault-tolerant, but they can be mirrored. *See also* dynamic disk, dynamic volume, fault tolerance, mirrored volume, spanned volume, volume.

SLIP *See* Serial Line Internet Protocol.

Small Computer System Interface (SCSI) A standard high-speed parallel interface defined by the American National Standards Institute (ANSI). A SCSI interface is used for connecting microcomputers to peripheral devices such as hard disks and printers and to other computers and local area networks.

Smart Card A credit card–sized device used to enable certificate-based authentication and single sign-ons (SSOs) to the enterprise. Smart Cards securely store certificates, public and private keys, passwords, and other types of personal information. To use a Smart Card, you need a Smart Card reader attached to the computer and a personal identification number (PIN) for the Smart Card. *See also* authentication.

snap-in A type of management tool you can add to the console tree in a console supported by Microsoft Management Console (MMC); for example, Microsoft Directory Service Manager or Device Manager. A snap-in can be either a standalone or an extension snap-in. A standalone snap-in can be added by itself; an extension snap-in can only be added to extend another snap-in. *See also* Microsoft Management Console (MMC).

spanned volume A volume made up of disk space on more than one physical disk. You can add more space to a spanned volume by extending it at any time. You can create spanned volumes only on dynamic disks. Spanned volumes are not fault-tolerant and cannot be mirrored. In Windows NT 4.0, a spanned volume was known as a volume set. *See also* dynamic disk, dynamic volume, fault tolerance, mirrored volume, volume.

spooling A process on a server in which print documents are stored on a disk until a printer is ready to process them. A spooler accepts each document from each client, stores it, then sends it to a printer when the printer is ready.

Stop error   An error (also known as a fatal system error) that causes Windows 2000 to stop responding.

striped volume   A volume that stores data in stripes on two or more physical disks. Data in a striped volume is allocated alternately and evenly (in stripes) to the disks of the striped volume. You can create striped volumes only on dynamic disks. Striped volumes are not fault-tolerant and cannot be mirrored or extended. In Windows NT 4.0, a striped volume was known as a stripe set. *See also* dynamic disk, dynamic volume, fault tolerance, volume.

systemroot   The path and folder name where the Windows 2000 system files are located. Typically, this is C:\Winnt, although you can designate a different drive or folder when you install Windows 2000. You can use the value %systemroot% to replace the actual location of the folder that contains the Windows NT system files. To identify your systemroot folder, click Start, click Run, and then type %systemroot%.

system volume   The volume that has the hardware-specific files needed to load Windows 2000. *See also* volume.

TCP/IP   *See* Transmission Control Protocol/Internet Protocol.

Telephony Application Programming Interface (TAPI)   An application programming interface (API) used by communications programs to communicate with telephony and network services. Communications programs like Hyperterminal and Phone Dialer use TAPI to dial, answer, and route telephone calls on conventional telephony devices, including PBXs, modems, and fax machines. TAPI 3.0 also provides Internet Protocol (IP) telephony support, which Phone Dialer and other programs use to transmit, route, and control real-time audio and video signals over IP-based networks such as the Internet. *See also* Internet Protocol (IP).

terminate-and-stay-resident (TSR) program   A program running under MS-DOS that remains loaded in memory even when it is not running, so that it can be quickly invoked for a specific task performed while any other application is operating.

transaction   In Message Queuing Services (MSMQ), a transaction involves the pairing of two or more actions that are performed together as a single action; that is, the action succeeds or fails as a whole. Microsoft Distributed Transaction Coordinator (MS DTC) ensures that either both actions succeed or neither is executed.

Transmission Control Protocol/Internet Protocol (TCP/IP)   A set of networking protocols that provides communications across interconnected networks made up of computers with diverse hardware architectures and various operating systems. TCP/IP includes standards for how computers communicate and conventions for connecting networks and routing traffic. *See also* protocol.

tree view   A hierarchical representation of the folders, files, disk drives, and other resources connected to a computer or network. For instance, Windows Explorer uses a tree view to display the resources that are attached to a computer or a network.

Trojan horse   A program that masquerades as another common program in an attempt to receive information. An example of a Trojan horse is a program that behaves like a system logon to retrieve user names and password information that the writers of the Trojan horse can later use to break into the system.

TrueType fonts   Fonts that are scalable and sometimes generated as bitmaps or soft fonts, depending on the capabilities of your printer. TrueType fonts are device-independent fonts that are stored as outlines. They can be sized to any height, and they can be printed exactly as they appear on the screen. *See also* font.

trust relationship   A link between domains that allows passthrough authentication, in which a trusting domain honors the logon authentications of a trusted domain. With trust relationships, a user who has only one user account in one domain can potentially gain access to the entire network. User accounts and global groups defined in a trusted domain can be given rights and resource permissions in a trusting domain, even though those accounts don't exist in the trusting domain's directory database. *See also* authentication, domain.

tunnel   A private, secure link between a remote user or host and a private network, over a dial-up connection. *See also* dial-up connection, tunnel server.

tunnel server   A server or router that establishes a presence on both the dial-in server and the target network. It terminates tunnels on the dial-in server and forwards data streams to the host on the target network. *See also* tunnel.

Type 1 fonts Scalable fonts designed to work with PostScript devices. *See also* font, PostScript.

Unicode A 16-bit character encoding standard developed by the Unicode Consortium between 1988 and 1991. By using two bytes to represent each character, Unicode enables almost all of the written languages of the world to be represented using a single character set. (By contrast, 8-bit ASCII is not capable of representing all of the combinations of letters and diacritical marks that are used just with the Roman alphabet.) Approximately 39,000 of the 65,536 possible Unicode character codes have been assigned to date, 21,000 of them being used for Chinese ideographs. The remaining combinations are open for expansion.

universal serial bus (USB) A special type of high-speed port that allows you to connect and disconnect devices without shutting down or restarting your computer. Many manufacturers have developed devices that can be connected to your computer through the USB port. This includes speakers, telephones, CD-ROM drives, joysticks, tape drives, keyboards, mice, scanners, and cameras. A USB port is usually on the back of your computer near the serial port or parallel port. *See also* port.

UPS Service Manages an uninterruptible power supply (UPS) connected to a computer.

user account A record that consists of all the information that defines a user to Windows 2000. This includes the user name and password required for the user to log on, the groups in which the user account has membership, and the rights and permissions the user has for using the system and accessing its resources. For Windows 2000 Professional and member servers, user accounts are managed with Local Users and Groups. For Windows 2000 Server domain controllers, user accounts are managed with Microsoft Active Directory Manager. *See also* domain controller, group, user name.

user name A unique name identifying a user account to Windows 2000. An account's user name must be unique among the other group names and user names within its own domain or workgroup. *See also* user account.

user password The password stored in each user's account. Each user generally has a unique user password and must type that password when logging on or accessing a server. *See also* password.

user profile A profile that defines the Windows 2000 environment that is loaded by the system when a user logs on. It includes all the user-specific settings of a user's Windows 2000 environment such as program items, screen colors, network connections, printer connections, mouse settings, and window size and position.

V.34 Data transmission standard that provides for up to 33,600 bits-per-second (bps) communications over telephone lines. It defines a full-duplex (two-way) modulation technique and includes error-correcting and negotiation. *See also* modulation standards.

V.90 Data transmission standard that provides for up to 56,000 bits-per-second (bps) communications over telephone lines. The transmission speed from the client-side modem is 33,600 bps. The transmission speed from the host-side modem—such as an Internet service provider or a corporate network—is up to 56,000 bps, with 40,000 to 50,000 bps being typical. When the host-side modem does not support this standard, the fallback is V.34. *See also* modulation standards, V.34.

virtual memory Temporary storage that lets a computer run programs that need more memory than it has. For example, programs could have access to 4 gigabytes of virtual memory on a computer's hard drive, even if the computer has only 32 megabytes of RAM. The program data that does not currently fit in the computer's memory is saved into paging files. *See also* paging file, random access memory (RAM).

virtual private network (VPN) A remote LAN that can be securely accessed through the Internet using the new PPTP. *See also* local area network (LAN), Point-to-Point Tunneling Protocol (PPTP).

volume A logical/virtual entity that is made up of portions of one or more physical disks. A volume may be formatted and may have a file system and/or drive letter. A volume has a type (basic or dynamic) and a layout (primary partition, extended partition, simple, spanned, mirrored, striped, or RAID-5). *See also* basic volume, dynamic volume, mirrored volume, RAID-5 volume, simple volume, spanned volume, striped volume.

wide area network (WAN) A communications network that connects geographically separated areas.

Windows Internet Naming Service (WINS)   A service that provides dynamic name to IP address registration and resolution.

Windows Sockets (Winsock)   An application programming interface standard for software that provides the TCP/IP interface under Windows. *See also* Transmission Control Protocol/Internet Protocol (TCP/IP).

WINS proxy   A computer that listens to name query broadcasts and responds for those names not on the local subnet. The proxy communicates with the name server to resolve names and then caches them for a specific time period. *See also* Windows Internet Naming Service (WINS).

workgroup   A group of users who work on a common project and share information on computers that are interconnected, often over a local area network (LAN).

XOR (exclusive OR)   A Boolean operation that is true if and only if one of its operands is true and the other is false. This operator is used to reconstruct missing data on a failed disk or sector from the remaining disks in a RAID-5 volume. *See also* fault tolerance, RAID-5 volume.

INDEX

Note: Italicized page references indicate figures or tables.

SPECIAL CHARACTERS AND NUMBERS

H

I

Jerry Honeycutt

Jerry Honeycutt empowers people to work and play better by helping them use technologies such as the Internet and the Windows product family.

As a bestselling author, Jerry has written more than 20 books. Most of his books are sold internationally and have been translated into a variety of languages. Jerry is also a columnist for *Frisco Style Magazine,* and he writes feature articles for various trade and consumer magazines. He is a regular speaker at assorted public events, focusing on the Internet and the Windows product family as well as other development issues.

Jerry has a long history of using his skills for practical purposes, providing technical leadership to businesses of all sizes. Companies such as Travelers, IBM, Nielsen North America, IRM, Howard Systems International, and NCR have leveraged his expertise. Jerry continues to serve the business community through consulting, speaking, and training.

Jerry graduated from the University of Texas at Dallas in 1992 with a BS degree in Computer Science. Prior to attending UTD, he spent three years at Texas Tech University in Lubbock, Texas. In his spare time, Jerry plays golf, dabbles with photography, and travels. He lives in the Dallas suburb of Frisco, Texas. Please feel free to contact Jerry at *jerry@honeycutt.com* or at *http://www.honeycutt.com.*

http://mspress.microsoft.com/reslink/

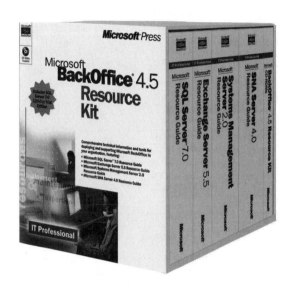

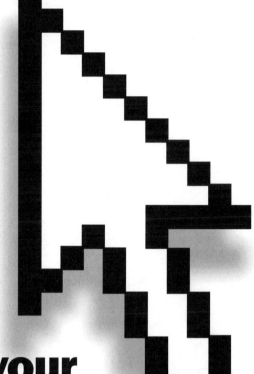

ResourceLink—your online IT library!

Access the full line of Microsoft Press® Resource Kits for the Windows® and BackOffice® families, along with MCSE Training Kits and other IT-specific resources at mspress.microsoft.com/reslink/. Microsoft Press ResourceLink is the essential online information service for IT professionals. Get Microsoft Press training resources, technical updates, support alerts, insider tips, and downloadable utilities—direct from Microsoft. If you evaluate, deploy, or support Microsoft® technologies and products, the information you need to optimize their performance—and your own—is on line and ready for work at ResourceLink.

For a complimentary 30-day trial CD packed with Microsoft Press
IT products, or for a no-cost, 15-day trial membership,
visit: mspress.microsoft.com/reslink/

Microsoft®

mspress.microsoft.com

Microsoft
official training for
the next generation of
Windows

U.S.A. **$79.99**
U.K. £74.99
Canada $119.99
ISBN 0-7356-0644-7

Get ready now for Microsoft® Windows® 2000 with this official Microsoft Training Kit. Through a system of modular, self-paced lessons and hands-on labs, you'll gain practical experience with the procedures needed to install, config-ure, and support this powerfully enhanced enterprise platform. Covering the technical beta editions of both Windows 2000 Server and Windows 2000 Professional, this prerelease systems support training can give you—and your organization—a running start with the next generation of Windows.

mspress.microsoft.com

Register Today!

Return this
Introducing Microsoft® Windows® 2000 Professional
registration card today

Microsoft®Press

mspress.microsoft.com

OWNER REGISTRATION CARD   0-7356-0662-5

Introducing Microsoft® Windows® 2000 Professional

_____ _____ _____
FIRST NAME   MIDDLE INITIAL   LAST NAME

_____
INSTITUTION OR COMPANY NAME

_____
ADDRESS

_____

_____

_____ _____ _____
CITY   STATE   ZIP

_____ ( )
E-MAIL ADDRESS   PHONE NUMBER

For information about Microsoft Press®

products, visit our Web site at

mspress.microsoft.com

Microsoft®*Press*